# STATE CAPITALISM AND INTERNATIONAL INVESTMENT LAW

This book explores how State capitalism affects and reshapes international investment law. It sheds new light on the various ways States actively influence business and commercial activity globally by using sovereign investors such as state-owned enterprises and sovereign wealth funds or pension funds. With a diverse group of contributors from a broad range of countries, the book offers a fresh and timely look into the fundamentals of State capitalism, focusing in particular on its actors and processes, the contextual elements that surround it, and the new political economy that comes with it.

The book is essential reading for researchers, regulators, policy makers and practitioners interested in the different ways State capitalism challenges and changes international investment law. As geopolitical considerations increasingly affect global economic activity, delving into the intricacies of State capitalism has never been more timely.

**Studies in International Trade and Investment Law: Volume 28**

**Studies in International Trade and Investment Law**

**Series Editors**
Gabrielle Marceau
Krista Nadakavukaren Schefer
Federico Ortino
Gregory Shaffer

This series offers a forum for publication of original and scholarly analyses of emerging and significant issues in international trade and investment law – broadly understood to include the whole of the law of the WTO, the public international law of foreign investment, the law of the EU common commercial policy and other regional trade regimes, and any legal or regulatory topic that interacts with global trade and foreign investment. The aim of the series is to produce works which will be readily accessible to trade and investment law scholars and practitioners alike.

**Recent titles in this series:**

*Balancing Human Rights, Environmental Protection and International Trade: Lessons from the EU Experience*
Emily Reid

*Public Procurement and Labour Rights: Towards Coherence in International Instruments of Procurement Regulation*
Maria Anna Corvaglia

*The China-Australia Free Trade Agreement: A 21st-Century Model*
Edited by Colin Picker, Heng Wang and Weihuan Zhou

*Regional Economic Integration and Dispute Settlement in East Asia: The Evolving Legal Framework*
Anna G Tevini

*The EU, World Trade Law and the Right to Food: Rethinking Free Trade Agreements with Developing Countries*
Giovanni Gruni

*Patent Games in the Global South: Pharmaceutical Patent Law Making in Brazil, India and Nigeria*
Amaka Vanni

*The Nationality of Corporate Investors under International Investment Law*
Anil Yilmaz Vastardis

*The Regulation of Product Standards in World Trade Law*
Ming Du

*Investors' International Law*
Edited by Jean Ho and Mavluda Sattorova

*Rethinking, Repackaging, and Rescuing World Trade Law in the Post-Pandemic Era*
Edited by Amrita Bahri, Weihan Zhou and Daria Boklan

*Flexible Regional Economic Integration in Africa: Lessons and Implications for the Multilateral Trading System*
Timothy Masiko

*International Investment Law: An Analysis of the Major Decisions*
Edited by Hélène Ruiz Fabri and Edoardo Stoppioni

# State Capitalism and International Investment Law

Edited by
Panagiotis Delimatsis
Georgios Dimitropoulos
and
Anastasios Gourgourinis

•HART•
OXFORD • LONDON • NEW YORK • NEW DELHI • SYDNEY

HART PUBLISHING
Bloomsbury Publishing Plc
Kemp House, Chawley Park, Cumnor Hill, Oxford, OX2 9PH, UK
1385 Broadway, New York, NY 10018, USA
29 Earlsfort Terrace, Dublin 2, Ireland

HART PUBLISHING, the Hart/Stag logo, BLOOMSBURY and the Diana logo are trademarks of Bloomsbury Publishing Plc

First published in Great Britain 2023



A catalogue record for this book is available from the British Library.

Library of Congress Cataloging-in-Publication data

Names: Delimatsis, Panagiotis, editor, contributor. | Dimitropoulos, Georgios, 1984- editor. | Gourgourinis, Anastasios, editor. | Al-Ahmadani, Mohammed, contributor.

Title: State capitalism and international investment law / edited by Panagiotis Delimatsis, Georgios Dimitropoulos, and Anastasios Gourgourinis ; contributors, Mohammed Al-Ahmadani [and others].

Description: Oxford ; New York : Hart Publishing, an imprint of Bloomsbury Publishing, 2023. | Series: Studies in international trade and investment law; 28 | Includes bibliographical references and index. | Summary: "This book explores how State capitalism affects and reshapes international investment law. It sheds new light on the various ways States actively influence business and commercial activity globally by using sovereign investors such as state-owned enterprises and sovereign wealth funds or pension funds. With a diverse group of contributors from a broad range of countries, the book offers a fresh and timely look into the fundamentals of State capitalism, focusing in particular on its actors and processes, the contextual elements that surround it, and the new political economy that comes with it. The book is essential reading for researchers, regulators, policy makers, and practitioners interested in the different ways State capitalism challenges and changes international investment law. As geopolitical considerations increasingly affect global economic activity, delving into the intricacies of State capitalism has never been more timely"—Provided by publisher.

Identifiers: LCCN 2022043225 | ISBN 9781509962976 (hardback) | ISBN 9781509963010 (paperback) | ISBN 9781509962990 (pdf) | ISBN 9781509962983 (Epub)

Subjects: LCSH: Investments, Foreign (International law) | Investments, Foreign—Law and legislation. | Investments—Law and legislation. | International commercial arbitration. | Capitalism.

Classification: LCC K3830 .S75 2023 | DDC 346/.092—dc23/eng/20221101

LC record available at https://lccn.loc.gov/2022043225

ISBN: HB: 978-1-50996-297-6
ePDF: 978-1-50996-299-0
ePub: 978-1-50996-298-3

Typeset by Compuscript Ltd, Shannon

# *Contents*

# *Contributors*

**Mohammed Al-Ahmadani** is an Associate at GBS Disputes, France.

**Leonardo Borlini** is an Associate Professor of International Law in the Legal Department/Centre for Applied Research on International Markets, Banking, Finance and Regulation at the University of Bocconi, Italy.

**Qingxiu Bu** is an Associate Professor at the University of Sussex, UK and Fellow at the Stellenbosch Institute for Advanced Study at Stellenbosch University, South Africa.

**Michail Dekastros** is an Associate at Sidley Austin LLP, Geneva, Switzerland.

**Panagiotis Delimatsis** is a Professor of Law and the Director of the Tilburg Law and Economics Center (TILEC) at Tilburg University, The Netherlands.

**Georgios Dimitropoulos** is an Associate Professor of Law and Associate Dean for Academic Affairs at Hamad Bin Khalifa University, Qatar.

**Ming Du** is a Professor of Law at Durham University, UK.

**Konstantina Georgaki** is a Policy Officer at the Directorate General for Financial Stability, Financial Services and Capital Markets Union (DG FISMA), European Commission, and a Lecturer in European Union Law and Constitutional Law at Mansfield College and St Catherine's College (University of Oxford), UK.

**Anastasios Gourgourinis** is an Assistant Professor in International Law at the National and Kapodistrian University of Athens, and a Research Fellow at the Academy of Athens, Greece.

**Rob Howse** is a Professor of Law at New York University, US.

**Olga Hrynkiv** is a PhD candidate at Tilburg University, The Netherlands.

**Sebastián Mantilla Blanco** is a Postdoctoral Researcher at the University of Bonn, Germany.

**Manu Misra** is a Postdoctoral Research Fellow at the Getúlio Vargas Foundation School of Law, Brazil.

**Bianca Nalbandian** is a Research Fellow at Max Planck Institute Luxembourg for International, European and Regulatory Procedural law and a PhD candidate at the Universities of Torino, Italy, and Luxembourg, Luxembourg.

**Josef Ostransky** is a Max Weber Fellow at the European University Institute, Italy.

**Stefano Silingardi** is an Assistant Professor of International Law in the Department of Italian and Supranational Public Law at the University of Milan, Italy.

**Jiangyu Wang** is a Professor of Law at the City University of Hong Kong, China.

# *List of Abbreviations*

| | |
|---|---|
| AB | Appellate Body |
| ACHR | American Convention on Human Rights |
| AD | Anti-dumping |
| ADGM | Abu Dhabi Global Markets |
| AIFC | Astana International Financial Centre |
| AIIB | Asian Infrastructure Investment Bank |
| ARSIWA | Articles on Responsibility of States for Internationally Wrongful Acts |
| ASCM | Agreement on Subsidies and Countervailing Measures |
| ASEAN | Association of Southeast Asian Nations |
| BIS | Bank for International Settlements |
| BIT | Bilateral Investment Treaty |
| BRI | Belt and Road Initiative |
| CAJAC | China-Africa Joint Arbitration Center |
| CAI | Comprehensive Agreement on Investment |
| CCCC | China Communications Construction Company International Holding Limited |
| CCP | Chinese Communist Party |
| CCP | Common Commercial Policy |
| CDB | China Development Bank |
| CPP | Canadian Pension Plan |
| CETA | Comprehensive Economic and Trade Agreement |
| CJEU | Court of Justice of the European Union |
| CFIUS | Committee on Foreign Investment in the United States |
| CICC | China International Commercial Court |

| | |
|---|---|
| CIETAC | China International Economic and Trade Arbitration Commission |
| CME | Coordinated Market Economy |
| CNI | Critical national infrastructure |
| CNOOK | China National Offshore Oil Corporation |
| CPTPP | Comprehensive and Progressive Agreement for Trans-Pacific Partnership |
| CSR | Corporate Social Responsibility |
| CVD | Countervailing Duties |
| DIFC | Dubai International Financial Centre |
| DRA | Dispute Resolution Authority |
| DSS | Dispute settlement system |
| DSU | Dispute Settlement Understanding |
| EC | European Community |
| EEC | European Economic Community |
| EPZ | Export Processing Zone |
| ESG | Environmental, Social and Governance |
| EU | European Union |
| FAB | First Abu Dhabi Bank |
| FINSA | Foreign Investment and National Security Act |
| FDI | Foreign Direct Investment |
| FET | Fair and Equitable Treatment |
| FIRRMA | Foreign Investment Risk Review Modernization Act |
| FPS | Full protection and security |
| FRB | Federal Reserve Board |
| FTA | Free Trade Agreement |
| GAAP | Generally accepted principles and practices |
| GATS | General Agreement on Trade in Services |
| GATT | General Agreement on Tariffs and Trade |

| | |
|---|---|
| GCC | Gulf Cooperation Council |
| GPFG | Government Pension Fund-Global |
| GPIF | Government Pension Investment Fund |
| ICSID | International Centre for Settlement of Investment Disputes |
| ICJ | International Court of Justice |
| ICommC | International Commercial Court |
| ICtHR | Inter-American Court of Human Rights |
| IEL | International Economic Law |
| IIA | International Investment Agreement |
| IIL | International Investment Law |
| IFSWF | International Forum of Sovereign Wealth Funds |
| ILA | International Law Association |
| ILC | International Law Commission |
| IMF | International Monetary Fund |
| IPR | Intellectual Property Right |
| IR | International relations |
| ISDS | Investor-State dispute settlement |
| ISM | Investment Screening Mechanism |
| IT | Information technology |
| IWG | International Working Group |
| KEXIM | Korean Export-Import Bank |
| LMEs | Liberal Market Economy |
| LPMO | Livestock Products Manufacturing Organization |
| M&A | Mergers and acquisitions |
| MFN | Most-Favoured Nation (principle) |
| MMC | Monopolies and Mergers Commission |
| MNC | Multi-national corporations |
| NAFTA | North American Free Trade Agreement |
| NBIM | Norges Bank Investment Management |

| | |
|---|---|
| NCP | National Contact Point |
| NDRC | National Development and Reform Commission |
| NGO | Non-Governmental Organization |
| NIEO | New International Economic Order |
| NZPT | New Zealand Permanent Trustees Ltd |
| OECD | Organization for Economic Cooperation and Development |
| OFDI | Outward foreign direct investment |
| PF | Pension fund |
| PTA | Preferential Trade Agreement |
| PRC | People's Republic of China |
| QFC | Qatar Financial Centre |
| QFCRA | Regulatory Authority of the Qatar Financial Centre |
| QICDRC | Qatar International Court and Dispute Resolution Centre |
| SASAC | State Assets Supervision and Administration Commission |
| SCA | Suez Canal Authority |
| SCE | State-Controlled Entity |
| SDGs | Sustainable Development Goals |
| SEZ | Special Economic Zone |
| SICC | Singapore International Commercial Court |
| SOCB | State-owned commercial bank |
| SOE | State-owned enterprise |
| SPC | Supreme People's Court |
| SRI | Socially responsible investment (principles) |
| SWF | Sovereign Wealth Fund |
| TFEU | Treaty on the Functioning of the European Union |
| TPA | Trade Promotion Agreement |
| TPR | Trade Policy Review |
| TRIMs | Trade-related Investment Measures Agreement |

| | |
|---|---|
| TRIPs | Agreement on Trade-Related Aspects of Intellectual Property Rights |
| UAE | United Arab Emirates |
| UKEF | United Kingdom Export Finance |
| UK | United Kingdom |
| UN | United Nations |
| UNCTAD | United Nations Conference on Trade and Development |
| UNEP | United Nations Environmental Programme |
| UNHRC | United Nations Human Rights Council |
| US | United States (of America) |
| USTR | United States Trade Representative |
| VCLT | Vienna Convention on the Law of Treaties |
| WTO | World Trade Organization |

# *State Capitalism and International Investment Law – An Introduction*

PANAGIOTIS DELIMATSIS, GEORGIOS DIMITROPOULOS AND ANASTASIOS GOURGOURINIS

## I. INTRODUCTION

INTERNATIONAL ECONOMIC LAW (IEL) and international investment law (IIL) were shaped as separate disciplines in the era of the dominance of the system of market capitalism. Both serve the freedom of movement of capital. The prevalence of the market and the retreat of the government in international economic law assume an ideology that may be described as capitalist or liberal. This is not of course an ideology that all states participating in the international economic system would necessarily subscribe to. But the implied ideological dominance of the system of market capitalism, as well as the trust in the system, has since been receding. The 'backlash' against international investment law is now commonplace and a symptom of the overall loss in faith in the institutions of global capitalism.[1] The backlash-related discussion in international investment law has been very productively transformed into a reform debate.[2] The backlash against, as well as the willingness to reform IIL has been expressed

[1] See M Waibel et al. (eds), *The Backlash Against Investment Arbitration. Perceptions and Reality* (Zuidpoolsingel, Kluwer Law International, 2010); M Langford, D Behn and OK Fauchald, 'Backlash and State Strategies in International Investment Law', in T Aalberts and T Gammeltoft-Hansen (eds), *The Changing Practices of International Law* (Cambridge, CUP, 2018) 70. This backlash derives from mounting tension in recent years due mostly to certain historical path-dependencies in the field; see generally G Dimitropoulos, 'The Conditions for Reform: A Typology of "Backlash" and Lessons for Reform in International Investment Law and Arbitration' (2019) 18 *The Law and Practice of International Courts and Tribunals* 413.

[2] The reform discussion process is prominently taking place within Working Group III (WGIII): Investor-State Dispute Settlement Reform of the United Nations Commission on International Trade Law (UNCITRAL), the workings of which are made available online at: www.uncitral.org/uncitral/en/commission/working_groups/3Investor_State.html (accessed 1 August 2019). On the academic side, the Academic Forum on ISDS has the purpose of providing a venue for academics to exchange views, explore issues and options, test ideas and solutions, and hopefully make a constructive contribution to the ongoing discussions on possible reform of ISDS, in particular to discussions in the context of UNCITRAL's WGIII; see Academic Forum on ISDS, *Statement of Purpose* (CIDS – Geneva Center for International Dispute Settlement, 12 March 2018), www.cids.ch/images/Documents/ISDS-AcademicForum/Academic_Forum_ISDS_Statement_of_Purpose.pdf.

by governments and other stakeholders in both the Southern and the Northern hemispheres.[3]

IIL has also been exposed to a different type of challenge by an ideologically opposing paradigm of 'state capitalism'.[4] State capitalism has been labelled as 'one of the most politicized and sensitive developments in the international investment regime'.[5] State capitalism is reshaping the foundations of IEL and the protection of Sovereign Investments, under International Investment Agreements (IIAs), and may potentially pose challenges to the system of investor-state dispute settlement (ISDS). State capitalism attempts to redefine the relationship between the state and the market suggesting a new political economy of IIL – and IEL, broadly speaking. Sovereigns increasingly operate in the international economic order via domestic institutions such as state-Owned Enterprises (SOEs)[6] and Sovereign Wealth Funds (SWFs),[7] hence reshaping IEL

[3] See WM Reisman, 'The Empire Strikes Back: The Struggle to Reshape ISDS', White and Case International Arbitration Lecture (The Lamm Lecture) (February 16, 2017), ssrn.com/abstract=2943514. Professor Reisman suggests that in large part the reaction against the 'Great Compact' of the contemporary international investment system has been spearheaded by the originally capital-exporting countries that have now found themselves also at the capital-importing end.

[4] I Bremmer, 'State Capitalism Comes of Age: The End of the Free Market' (2009) 88 *Foreign Affairs* 40; N Ferguson, 'We're All State Capitalists Now' (2012) 9 *Foreign Policy*; L-Wen Lin and CJ Milhaupt, 'We are the (National) Champions: Understanding the Mechanisms of State Capitalism in China' (2013) 65 *Stanford Law Review* 697; M Du, 'China's State Capitalism and World Trade Law' (2014) 63 *ICLQ* 409.

[5] LNS Poulsen, 'Investment treaties and the globalisation of state capitalism: opportunities and constraints for host states', in R Echandi and P Sauve (eds), *Prospects in International Investment Law and Policy* (Cambridge, CUP, 2013) 73, 90.

[6] On SOEs, see, among many, K Haywood, The Treatment of State Enterprises in the WTO and Plurilateral Trade Agreements, Commonwealth Secretariat Emerging Issues Briefing Note (March 2016), available at thecommonwealth.org/sites/default/files/inline/StateOwned%20EnterprisesTPP1008.pdf; M Feldman, 'State-Owned Enterprises as Claimants in International Investment Arbitration' (2016) 31 *ICSID Review* 24; Y Shima, 'The Policy Landscape for International Investment by Government-controlled Investors: A Fact Finding Survey', OECD Working Papers on International Investment, 2015/01 (2015), available at dx.doi.org/10.1787/5js7svp0jkns-en; I Willemyns, 'Disciplines on State-Owned Enterprises in International Economic Law: Are We Moving in the Right Direction?' (2016) 19 *Journal of International Economic Law* 657; J Ya Qin, 'WTO Regulation of Subsidies to State-Owned Enterprises (Soes) – a Critical Appraisal of the China Accession Protocol' [2004] *Journal of International Economic Law* 863; J Nakagawa, 'The Emerging Rules on State Capitalism and their Implications for China's Use of SOEs', in L Toohey, C Picker and J Greenacre (eds), *China in the International Economic Order: New Directions and Changing Paradigms* (Cambridge, CUP, 2015) 112; J Chaisse, 'Untangling the Triangle: Issues for State-Controlled Entities in Trade, Investment and Competition Law', in J Chaisse and T-y Lin (eds), *International Economic Law and Governance: Essays in Honour of Mitsuo Matsushita* (Oxford, OUP, 2016) 233.

[7] On SWFs, see the Generally Accepted Principles and Practices (Santiago Principles), International Working Group of Sovereign Wealth Funds (October 2008), available at www.ifswf.org/sites/default/files/santiagoprinciples_0_0.pdf; IMF, Sovereign Wealth Funds, available at www.imf.org/external/pubs/ft/gfsr/2007/02/pdf/annex12.pdf; M Burgstaller, 'Sovereign Wealth Funds and International Investment Law', in C Brown and K Miles (eds), *Evolution in Investment Treaty Law and Arbitration* (Cambridge, CUP, 2011) 163–186; J Wang, 'State Capitalism and Sovereign Wealth Funds: Finding a "Soft" Location in International Economic Law', in CL Lim (ed), *Alternative Visions of the International Law on Foreign Investment: Essays in Honour of Muthucumaraswamy Sornarajah* (Cambridge, CUP, 2016), 405; F Bassan (ed), *Research Handbook on Sovereign Wealth Funds and International Investment Law* (Cheltenham, Elgar, 2015); G Kratsas and J Truby,

in a bottom-up way. While the institutions of state capitalism are in the process of redefining the relationship between the state and the market, a different question persists: is the current system of international investment law positively, negatively or neutrally predisposed towards state capitalism and its institutions?

## II. PLURALISING THE INTERNATIONAL INVESTMENT REGIME

IIL has been developed in the second half of the twentieth century as colonial law was being replaced by the domestic laws of the newly emerging independent states. IIL was part of the new liberal world order that was in the process of being developed in the post-World War II era. The liberal world order assumed that capital would flow from private investors of the North and West into the developing countries of the South and East; it also assumed that the economies of the South and East would transition towards the market economy system and privatise government-owned assets and enterprises to private investors of the North and West. However, a paradigm shift is observed in recent times. This archetypical understanding underpinning the foundations of IIL is no longer in place. New actors, as well as different ways of mobilising capital emerged in the global economy.

### A. Actors

State capitalism is based on a relatively different economic paradigm in comparison to what is assumed by IEL. State capitalism appears in high-income economies and developing economies alike.[8] One may argue that IEL assumes the market as the driving force of liberalisation, whereby the state holds the backseat.[9] Nevertheless, this conception does not go unchallenged. According to Josef Ostřanský, state capitalism in IIL is a story of (re)organisations and transformations of the world economy, since modern IIL has always been state capitalist. In this vein, distinguishing between 'normal' or 'liberal' capitalism and the 'new' state capitalism may be misleading. IIL has developed in the twentieth century as a facet of the internationalisation, legalisation and judicialisation of economic relations. Indeed, the intellectual history of IIL, critical

'Regulating Sovereign Wealth Funds to Avoid Investment Protectionism' [2015] *Journal of Financial Regulation* 95; W Yin, 'Regulating the State Capitalism: Is There an Optimal Regulatory Model for Sovereign Wealth Fund Investment?' (2020) 54(1) *Journal of World Trade* 155.

[8] K Kim, 'Locating new 'state capitalism' in advanced economies: an international comparison of government ownership in economic entities' (2021) 28(3) *Contemporary Politics* 285.

[9] See generally D Rodrik, *Straight Talk on Trade: Ideas for a Sane World Economy* (New Jersey, Princeton University Press, 2018); G Shaffer, 'How Do We Get Along? International Economic Law and the Nation-State' (2019) 117 *Michigan Law Review* 1229. See also P Muchlinski, *Multinational Enterprises and the Law*, 3rd edn (Oxford, OUP, 2021) for the well-known comprehensive account of the instruments used to regulation MNEs at the national, regional and multilateral levels.

state theory, and global political economy, all reveal how and why the state has always been the main driving actor and factor for the growth of IIL as a neoliberal form of capitalism.[10]

China is the most striking example, but not the only one. The BRICS countries (Brazil, Russia, India, China, and South Africa), for example, have developed in very different ways from other developing nations, and sometimes are also closer when it comes to their foreign and international economic policy to northern and western countries. Moreover, the South and East of the world is currently in a direct competitive relationship to the West and North of the world when it comes to investment opportunities and the promotion of their own interests abroad,[11] be it in other countries in the South and East, or the West and North. Countries in the South, such as Brazil, are now on the outward side of investment, and interested in protecting their investors doing business abroad. States in the Gulf Region and other emerging markets such Vietnam are competing on both the inward and the outward side of investment. The world economic order of the twenty-first century is now being reshaped based on the new premises of polycentricity and pluralism: the emerging markets of the South and East are not only recipients, but also exporters of capital; global capital exportation is streamlined both towards the southern and the northern hemisphere; foreign investment is not solely based on private capital, but also on public money invested by institutional investors, such as pension funds, SWFs, national oil companies (NOCs) and various other types of SOEs or State-Controlled Entities (SCEs).

As argued by Leonardo Borlini and Stefano Silingardi in this volume, the regulation of SOEs in international investment law and international trade law appears to be inarticulate and unbalanced; ergo, no concrete answers are provided to key normative questions pertaining, for instance, to the coverage of SOEs under IIAs; national security carve-outs; Article XVII of the General Agreement on Tariffs and Trade (GATT 1994) and subsidies disciplines. As a result, the commercial and political challenges posed threaten the balance between liberal market and institutional innovation.[12]

The overall strategies of capital accumulation and mobilisation are different. National policies, such as the Belt and Road Initiative (BRI) and China's Go Global strategy, give rise to even more complex issues when it is state enterprises that are given incentives to invest overseas. Chinese state capitalism is indeed the par excellence case study of tensions to the liberal international economic order.[13] Qingxiu Bu traces the main rationale underlying the BRI

[10] See ch 2, in this volume. For a class analysis of state capitalism, see N Sperber, 'Servants of the state or masters of capital? Thinking through the class implications of state-owned capital' (2021) 28(3) *Contemporary Politics* 264.

[11] This is particularly the case in Asian countries; see Asian Development Bank, Asia 2050: Realizing the Asian Century (2011), www.adb.org/publications/asia-2050-realizing-asian-century, 1.

[12] See ch 1, in this volume.

[13] For a historical perspective regarding the emergence of state capitalism in China, see the contributions in B Naughton and K Tsai (eds), *State Capitalism, Institutional Adaptation and the*

in China's overcapacity and cautions that international standards of transparency and equal opportunity go hand-in-hand with effective global governance.[14] Ming Du explains how reforms in China since 1992 aimed at balancing between ensuring the market competitive capacity of SOEs and the maintenance of then Chinese Communist Party (CCP) control over them.[15] Jiangyu Wang analyses the actors, rules and processes of state capitalism in China and discusses whether Chinese state capitalism goes against the letter and spirit of IEL; whether effective rules for SOEs are in place under IEL; and whether the operation of Chinese state capitalism prevents the establishment of such rules. He emphasises the lack of international regulation of state capitalism and argues that the future development of China's state capitalism model will determine whether it undermines the liberal world order.[16] In this context, Ming Du also explains how Chinese SOEs have access as claimants in ISDS under both the so-called Broches test and customary international law on attribution for the purposes of international responsibility.[17]

State capitalism may also be about establishing higher standards of conduct for its actors. The chapter authored by Sebastián Mantilla Blanco in this volume addresses the due diligence standards of conduct pertinent for SCEs. It first distinguishes between due diligence of SCEs and due diligence duties of states in respect of activities of their – owned or controlled – SCEs. The analysis then turns to soft law and hard law corporate social responsibility (CSR) instruments and their impact on the adjudication of investment claims involving SCEs. Indeed, the assessment of SCE's due diligence may pose challenges (compared to private operators), substantive investment protection standards, as is evidenced by a discussion regarding illegality objections or claims for violation of substantive investment protections such as full protection and security (FPS) and fair and equitable treatment (FET).[18] In a similar vein, Bianca Nalbandian's chapter situates sovereign investors vis-à-vis the risks of occurrence of financially disruptive events caused by climate change ('green swan risks'). She concludes that fiduciary duty theories, in the context of trust law schemes and

*Chinese Miracle* (Cambridge, CUP, 2015), identifying the roots of a well-thought set of institutional design. For an institutional analysis, see BL Liebman and CJ Milhaup (eds), *Regulating the Visible Hand?: The Institutional Implications of Chinese State Capitalism* (Oxford, OUP, 2015). Furthermore, see the contributions taking stock of an integration process that allowed China to gradually integrate the international economic order, covering trade, financial and monetary aspects, competition and intellectual property, in L Toohey, CB Picker and J Greenacre (eds), *China in the International Economic Order* (Cambridge, CUP, 2015).

[14] See ch 12, in this volume.

[15] See ch 8, in this volume. See also J Kurlantzick, *State Capitalism – How the Return of Statism in Transforming the World* (Oxford, OUP, 2016) for a political economy perspective of the global shift towards state capitalism in several countries, including China.

[16] See ch 4, in this volume.

[17] See ch 8, in this volume. *cf* J Chaisse, 'State Capitalism on the Ascent: Stress, Shock, and Adaptation of the International Law on Foreign Investment' [2018] *Minnesota Journal of International Law* 342, 386; B Nalbandian, 'State Capitalists as Claimants in International Investor-State arbitration' (2021) 81 *QIL Zoom-out* 7.

[18] See ch 9, in this volume.

public pension funds which encompass a duty of care and a duty of loyalty, long-term investment mandates and self-regulatory frameworks, such as the Santiago Principles and the One Planet Summit Initiative, are only moderately effective in tackling sustainability issues.[19]

## B. Layers

Before being transferred onto the international realm, state capitalism was created domestically. State capitalism has a long history in domestic politics, but found an expression in actual practice with the opening up of China. State capitalism in the sphere of international investment law has taken shape through the active involvement of China in the international economic system. State capitalism became a domestic ideological-political-legal paradigm, and was then transferred onto the international plane. It has accordingly developed a domestic layer, an international layer, and middle layers with different mixes of domestic/international and capitalist/paternalistic features.

### *i. The International Layer*

Under the international investment law system that was developed in the twentieth century, there are no general international obligations for market access to foreign investors, and no general obligation to admit foreign investments into the economy of a state. The typical BIT does not grant a right of admission to the potential host state market to a foreign investor, or any other type of pre-entry protection for foreign investment. According to Article 2(1) of the Model BIT of Germany (2008), for example:[20]

> Each Contracting Party shall in its territory promote as far as possible investments by investors of the other Contracting State and admit such investments *in accordance with its legislation* (emphasis added)

Indeed, IIAs typically defer admission and establishment to the requirements of the host state's legislation on market access.[21] Accordingly, it is generally up to domestic law and institutions to decide whether a foreign investment and investor should be admitted to the domestic market in the first place, as well as the appropriate mechanisms for control of foreign investment. Nevertheless, there are some IIAs which grant market access to prospective investors. They generally grant a right of admission, which is limited in scope, and is usually based

[19] See ch 13, in this volume.
[20] See also UK Model BIT (2005, 2006) art 2(1).
[21] R Dolzer, U Kriebaum and C Schreuer, *Principles of International Investment Law,* 3rd edn (Oxford, OUP, 2022) 132–145.

on a national treatment clause.[22] In this vein, Michail Dekastros demonstrates why it is necessary to always distinguish between 'Limited Entry' BITs (where host states undertake best efforts obligations to promote investments, but do not guarantee admission) and 'Liberalisation' BITs (which do provide pre-establishment rights) when analysing market access for state capitalists.[23]

The rights for sovereign investors under IIAs are also combined with treaty-based exceptions designed to safeguard national security interests of host states of sovereign investments. At the same time, national security carveouts hold a noticeable place in the multilateral trade regime, governed primarily by Article XXI GATT, Article XIV$^{bis}$ of the General Agreement on Trade in Services (GATS), and Article 73 of the Agreement on Trade-Related Aspects of Intellectual Property Rights (TRIPs Agreement). In this context, and given the organic links between trade and investment, Panagiotis Delimatsis and Olga Hrynkiv in their chapter in this volume engage in a thorough analysis of trade and investment case law and argue that cross-fertilisation between trade and investment adjudicators could foster the coherent application of security exceptions under both regimes in cases involving sovereign investors.[24]

### *ii. The Domestic Layer*

IEL, and IIL more specifically, has entered a new era of unilateralism.[25] There are multiple types of economic unilateralism that stand in a continuum between unilateral liberalisation of trade and investment as in the classical trade era, and 'aggressive unilateralism' on the other.[26] National security unilateralism is on the rise. Under the foreign trade policy of the Trump administration, the world witnessed a new era of '*trade wars*',[27] discussed in terms of unilateralism as

[22] A good example is Art 3(1) of the US Model BIT of 2004: 'Each Party shall accord to investors of the other Party treatment no less favorable than that it accords, in like circumstances, to its own investors with respect to the establishment, expansion, management, conduct, operation, and sale or other disposition of investments in its territory'. Also, see C Annacker, 'Protection and Admission of Sovereign Investment under Investment Treaties' (2011) 10(3) *Chinese Journal of International Law* 531, 546–550.

[23] See ch 5, in this volume.

[24] See ch 10, in this volume.

[25] See J Chaisse and G Dimitropoulos, 'SEZs in International Economic Law: Towards Unilateral Economic Law' (2021) 24(2) *Journal of International Economic Law* 229, where the authors identify four types of unilateralism: Classical unilateralism; Embedded unilateralism; Environmental unilateralism; and National Security unilateralism.

[26] See also for this differentiation J Bhagwati, 'Introduction: The Unilateral Freeing of Trade versus Reciprocity', in J Bhagwati (ed), *Going Alone: The Case for Relaxed Reciprocity in Freeing Trade* (Cambridge, MA, MIT Press, 2002).

[27] See generally A van Aaken, CP Bown and A Lang, 'Special Issue: Trade Wars' (2019) 22 *Journal of International Economic Law* 4. According to one account, '[a] trade war is when a nation imposes tariffs or quotas on imports and foreign countries retaliate with similar forms of trade protectionism'; see K Amadeo, 'Trade Wars and Their Effect on the Economy and You: Why trade wars are bad and nobody wins', *The Balance*, www.thebalance.com/trade-wars-definition-how-it-affects-you-4159973.

well, and referred to as '*Trump unilateralism*'.[28] The justification for this type of unilateralism was the protection of national security interests of the US.[29] Similarly, a number of states have developed doctrines largely (and explicitly) shaped by national security unilateralism.[30] China's BRI is also fundamentally driven by national security motives since China is developing this strategy, in part, to address potential external threats.[31]

In the current phase of intense political and economic contestation of the BIT system and, more specifically, international investment arbitration, countries have started placing regulatory emphasis on the investment pre-entry stage. This has led to an explosion of domestic investment laws. Depending on the political preferences as well as the economic needs of countries, different types of domestic legislative frameworks have been developed. Certain frameworks are meant to attract state capital. Investment promotion laws are mostly to be found in the South and East. A great number of countries are now introducing restrictions on FDI. The most common FDI restrictive legislative and regulatory frameworks are: (a) foreign equity limitations; (b) investment screening mechanisms (ISMs); (c) restrictions on the employment of foreigners as key personnel; (d) operational restrictions, eg restrictions on branching, capital repatriation or land ownership.[32] ISMs, in particular, are on the rise.[33]

While screening mechanisms have existed since the 1970s, there has been a tendency to create new or tighten existing ones.[34] Screening is almost always based on national security grounds, either as the primary factor or as one among others, and invariably the most prominent one. Third-state control is one of the key factors of the 2019 European Union (EU) FDI Screening

[28] See generally HH Koh, 'Trump Change: Unilateralism and the "Disruption Myth" in International Trade: Epilogue to the Yale Symposium on Trade Law Under the Trump Administration' (2019) 44 *Yale Journal of International Law Online* 96; MJ Baltz, 'What lies beneath the 'tariff man'? The Trump administration's response to China's 'state capitalism' (2022) 28(3) *Contemporary Politics* 328.

[29] See generally A Roberts, HC Moraes and V Ferguson, 'Toward a Geoeconomic Order' (2019) 22(4) *Journal of International Economic Law* 655. See also for the view of a leading figure of the Trump administration, RE Lighthizer, 'Trump's Trade Policy Is Making America Stronger', (2020) 99(4) *Foreign Affairs*, www.foreignaffairs.com/articles/china/2020-07-20/trumps-trade-policy-making-america-stronger.

[30] See, eg, UK Department for Business, Energy and Industrial Strategy, 'National Security and Infrastructure Investment Review (Green Paper)' (2017), assets.publishing.service. gov.uk/government/uploads/system/uploads/attachment_data/file/652505/2017_10_16_NSII_Green_ Paper_final.pdf.

[31] See J Slawotsky, 'The National Security Exception in US-China FDI and Trade: Lessons from Delaware Corporate Law' (2018) 6(2) *The Chinese Journal of Comparative Law*.

[32] See OECD, FDI Regulatory Restrictiveness Index, www.oecd.org/investment/fdiindex.htm.

[33] According to UNCTAD, 24 countries have ISMs. These are Australia, Austria, Belgium, Canada, China, Finland, France, Germany, Hungary, Iceland, India, Italy, Japan, Latvia, Lithuania, Mexico, New Zealand, Norway, Poland, the Republic of Korea, the Russian Federation, South Africa, the UK and the US: UNCTAD, Investment Policy Monitor No 22: Special Issue – National security-related screening mechanisms for foreign investment an analysis of recent policy developments, unctad.org/system/files/official-document/diaepcbinf2019d7_en.pdf, 92–93.

[34] See generally G Dimitropoulos, 'National Security: The Role of Investment Screening Mechanisms', in J Chaisse, L Choukroune and S Jusoh (eds), *Handbook of International Investment Law and Policy – Volume I* (Singapore, Springer, 2020) 507.

Regulation analysed in this volume by Konstantina Georgaki. As the author explains, the FDI Screening Regulation covers extra-EU (foreign direct and portfolio) investment and intra-EU (direct and portfolio) investments, and while it is ownership-neutral, its adoption was rather the response to the proliferation of sovereign investments and the security concerns they may pose.[35]

According to UNCTAD there are three main types of ISMs: sector-specific, cross-sectoral, and entity-specific.[36] The first category of mechanisms focuses on sectors such as utilities, energy, telecommunication, transportation, media and financial industries that are viewed as important for national security purposes.[37] The second category of cross-sectoral legislation allows for screening in all sectors.[38] Legislation of the third category focuses on the destination of the investment, rather than the investor as the screening mechanisms of the previous two categories do. These legislative frameworks single out domestic companies, usually state-owned and operating in sectors that are perceived as sensitive from a national security point of view, and allow for the review of foreign acquisitions for these entities.

Manu Misra's chapter focuses on foreign investments in critical infrastructure and argues that the relevant ISMs may be conceptually understood as a reflection of the lack of trust in international relations theory. Contrary to conventional wisdom, Manu Misra explains why ISMs are expressive of legitimate concerns over technology-related security risks and have minimal impact on FDI flows. The function of ISMs is essentially an executive political one, since they are all about trust towards the SCE and its home state, especially in the case of critical infrastructure projects.[39]

ISMs could also prima facie be at odds with the pre-establishment commitments undertaken in 'Liberalisation BITs'. As Michail Dekastros argues, it is only the specific regulatory concerns regarding government ownership of SWFs and respective host states' national security issues that distinguish SWFs from non-sovereign investors. He analyses how and why host states have provided regulatory responses to the proliferation of SWFs' investments, mainly via the establishment of ISMs and posits that ISMs could violate admission rights under specific type BITs.[40]

[35] See ch 6, in this volume.

[36] UNCTAD, Investment Policy Monitor No 22: Special Issue – National security-related screening mechanisms for foreign investment an analysis of recent policy developments, unctad.org/system/files/official-document/diaepcbinf2019d7_en.pdf, 93.

[37] Under the new Investment Law No 1 of 2019 of Qatar, for example, which applies exclusively to foreign investors, foreign investors are prohibited from investing in banks and insurance companies unless the Council of Ministers allows such an investment. Article 4(a) Investment Law No 1 of 2019 'Regulating the Investment of Non-Qatari Capital in Economic Activity'.

[38] The Committee on Foreign Investment in the US process is a characteristic example of such a legislative framework.

[39] See ch 7, in this volume.

[40] See ch 5, in this volume.

### *iii. The New Intermediate Layer(s)*

A new layer that has been brought to the surface in the era of state capitalism is that of the use of domestic institutions for the purposes of promoting international investment. The most characteristic of these institutions are Special Economic Zones (SEZs) and International Commercial Courts (ICommCs).

SEZs represent a new compromise between the state and the market. While SEZs may be viewed as promoters of trade and investment liberalisation, they only allow this within the confines of a limited jurisdiction and under the strict supervision of powerful government agencies for a given period of time.[41] SEZs rely on proactive government intervention.[42] They are almost invariably governed by very powerful government entities, which are separate from ordinary domestic agencies. These may have different degrees of independence from the central and local government, and enjoy different degrees of powers reaching from construction and operation to regulation in the SEZ.

ICommCs, such as the Abu Dhabi Global Markets (ADGM) Courts and the Singapore International Commercial Court (SICC),[43] are intermediate institutions of state capitalism, closely intertwined with seminal projects of the latter, such as SEZs and the BRI. As explained by Georgios Dimitropoulos and Mohammed Al-Ahmadani, ICommCs can operate without *domestic* institutional complementarities, but have the potential of establishing international institutional complementarities; they can also eventually accommodate claims against SOEs themselves. ICommCs, as institutions of a new variety of state capitalism, appear thus bound to proliferate and interconnect.[44]

## III. IS STATE CAPITALISM AN OXYMORON?

Are the two worlds of state and capitalism compatible? Is state capitalism an oxymoron? The same question was raised some time ago when policymakers in the UK, US and elsewhere, influenced by the insights of cognitive psychology and behavioural economics, started developing regulatory responses that go

[41] See generally on SEZs, J Chaisse and X Ji, 'The Pervasive Problem of SEZs for International Economic Law: Tax, Investment, and Trade Issues' (2020) 19 (4) *World Trade Review* 567; DZ Zeng, 'The Past, Present, and Future of Special Economic Zones and Their Impact' (2021) 24 (2) *Journal of International Economic Law* 259.

[42] According to Ginsburg, 'Paradoxically, […] SEZs may be most effective in an environment in which a strong central government is seeking to gather information about the policy effects of liberalization'; T Ginsburg, 'Special Economic Zones: A Constitutional Political Economy Perspective', in J Basedow and T Kono (eds), *Special Economic Zones: Law and Policy Perspectives* (Tuebingen, Mohr Siebeck, 2015) 119, 127.

[43] Generally on ICommCs, see G Dimitropoulos, 'The Design of International Commercial Courts: From Organizational Hybridity to Functional Interoperability', in S Brekoulakis and G Dimitropoulos (eds), *International Commercial Courts: The Future of Transnational Adjudication* (Cambridge, CUP, 2022) 251.

[44] See ch 11, in this volume.

beyond traditional command-and-control interventions and incentives. Policy makers, instead, identify cognitive biases that humans are subject to in order to propose appropriate responses by the regulator.[45] The response is usually a 'nudge',[46] that is, a light form of regulatory control which purports to maintain people's freedom of choice; examples of nudges are disclosure of better, different, smart or more information, warnings, debiasing through procedural and substantive law and, above all, altering legal default rules.[47] Nudges are thus opposed to both command-and-control regulation and incentives: the desired behaviour is not induced with the use of financial prompts.

The combination of the need for regulation with the preservation of freedom of choice has been described as 'libertarian paternalism' as the political philosophy of nudging. Libertarian paternalism is 'an approach that preserves freedom of choice but that authorizes both private and public institutions to steer people in directions that will promote their welfare'.[48] Libertarian paternalism justifies legal interventions that both increase individuals' economic welfare by freeing them from the limitations of their cognitive biases, and second, change individuals' behaviour without limiting their choices. Libertarian paternalism is the result of the marriage of choice preservation and regulation.[49]

Whether state capitalism is viewed as an oxymoron depends on one's view of the relationship between the state and the market in the international economic regime. The interplay between market and the state may be seen as what has shaped the modern political economy more than any other concept. In the international plane, the power of the state is expressed in the concept of sovereignty. The balance between the state and the market has oscillated between the two poles post-WWII, and in the years leading up to the dominance of the market until the financial crisis. The two main post-war milestones in the shaping of this relationship have been the efforts to establish a New International Economic Order (NIEO) and the Washington Consensus.[50]

[45] CR Sunstein, C Jolls and RH Thaler, 'A Behavioral Approach to Law and Economics' (1998) 50 *Stanford Law Review* 1471; R Korobkin and TS Ulen, 'Law and Behavioral Science: Removing the Rationality Assumption from Law and Economics' (2000) 88 *California Law Review* 1051; A Alemanno and A-L Sibony (eds), *Nudge and the Law: a European Perspective* (Oxford, Hart Publishing, 2015).

[46] RH Thaler and CR Sunstein, *Nudge: Improving Decisions About Health, Wealth, and Happiness* (New Haven, Yale University press, 2008); CR Sunstein, *Why Nudge: The Politics of Libertarian Paternalism* (New Haven, Yale University Press, 2014).

[47] See, eg, C Jolls, and CR Sunstein, 'Debiasing through Law' (2006) 35 *Journal of Legal Studies* 199.

[48] CR Sunstein and RH Thaler, 'Libertarian Paternalism Is Not an Oxymoron' (2003) 70 *Chicago Law Review* 1159.

[49] G Mitchell, 'Libertarian Paternalism Is An Oxymoron' (2005) 99 *Northwestern University Law Review* 1245.

[50] UN General Assembly Resolution 3201(S-VI) Declaration on the Establishment of a New International Economic Order (1 May 1974). On the NIEO, see among many, RW Cox, 'Ideologies and the New International Economic Order: reflections on some recent literature' (1979) 33(2) *International Organization* 257; A Anghie, Imperialism, Sovereignty and the Making of International Law (Cambridge, CUP, 2012) 208–211.

In a similar vein, one may question whether the inclusion of provisions on competitive neutrality in international trade and investment agreements is necessary and/or advisable. Focusing on flawed attempts to incorporate competitive neutrality in regional trade agreements, such as the US – Mexico – Canada Agreement (USMCA) and the Comprehensive and Progressive Agreement for Trans-Pacific Partnership (CPTPP), Rob Howse traces ideological bias against state enterprises and cautions against such an approach; the author also emphasises the need to properly apply the principle of non-discrimination to tackle protectionist practices.[51]

## IV. CONCLUSION

The variety of actors and the multicentricity prompted in new international investment law because of state capitalism has led to the development of new layers in the international investment regime. Domestic law started being relevant again more recently with the rise of investment control mechanisms. Mostly countries in the West have developed ISMs to control inward investment flows from countries in the South and East, while countries from certain regions have already had a longstanding tradition of controlling foreign investment flows. At the same time, SOEs have drawn attention not only because of China's policy as a global actor, but also because of their role to boost financial recovery after the global Covid-19 pandemic.[52]

The relationship between the state and the market has not been constant in the years of the recent development of IIL. The rise of new powers and actors gave rise to a certain contestation of the old equilibrium. State capitalism tried to redefine this. This led to the development of new institutions at the international and the domestic level of governance. Hence, state capitalism is not an oxymoron. It does not radically change the foundations and structures of international investment law. It is an effort to redefine the relationship between the market and the state. Against this backdrop, the present edited volume offers a fresh and timely look into the fundamentals of state capitalism, focusing in particular on its actors and processes, the contextual elements that surround it and the new political economy that comes with it. Contributions in this volume engage with the conceptual analysis offered in this introduction to reflect on the status and evolution of the actors of state capitalism and reflect on the scope and adequacy of the existing international legal order to harness potential distortions and unfair practices at the political and market level.

It is in this spirit that focus should be had on state capitalism as a form of recalibration of IEL and IIL that takes into account the needs of a market

[51] See ch 3, in this volume.

[52] *cf* B van Apeldoorn and N de Graaff, 'The state in global capitalism before and after the Covid-19 crisis' (2022) 28(3) *Contemporary Politics* 306.

economy and the role that the state is bound to play to pursue non-economic objectives. Ergo, the new law and political economy framework of IIL is one that is pushed more towards the state without abandoning the market framework, in which economic activity takes place. The new political economy of IIL is more deferential to the state. In addition, the new political economy is more plural; it adds new actors and new layers into the overall structure of the international investment regime.

# Part I

# State Capitalism and International Economic Order

# 1

# *The Foundations of International Economic Order in the Age of State Capitalism*

**LEONARDO BORLINI AND STEFANO SILINGARDI***

## I. INTRODUCTION

ANDREAS LOWENFELD BEGAN his landmarking publication *International Economic Law* by asking 'whether there is such a thing as international economic law [IEL], a body of law that can be subjected to systematic treatment between the covers of a book'.[1] In fact, as he promptly observed,

> international conventions, collaborative arrangements, roughly uniform national laws, and customary laws apply to much of the international economy; while (…) the system of remedies does not reach as far as the system of rules, there are a surprising number of consequences of deviant behavior, and a growing number of *fora* for resolving disputes among states and between states and private participants in the international economy.[2]

Thus, rather than a lack of materials, the main problem in undertaking a systemic analysis of such a subject is 'how to make a selection, and – more ambitious – how to link the apparently diverse topics with some general concepts that serve to explain, guide, limit, and predict the development of an international economic law'.[3]

* The present article was conceived and written together. However, sections 1, 2, and 4 were written by Leonardo Borlini, and section 3 by Stefano Silingardi.

[1] AF Lowenfeld, *International Economic Law Oxford*, 2nd edn (Oxford, OUP, 2012) v.

[2] ibid. T Cottier, 'Linking the Traits of International Economic Law' (2022) 23 *Journal of World Investment and Trade (JWIT)* 1, has very recently revitalised the discussion on the opportunity of providing IEL's different segments with more systemic connections.

[3] Lowenfeld (n 1) v.

In the following decades, IEL has proved to be one of the fastest growing areas of international law. Different traits of international economic law have developed in isolation and fragmentation, at different speeds and different layers of governance.[4] Thousands of agreements, mostly in the form of regional, bilateral or other preferential trade agreements, investment contracts, and bilateral investment treaties have been signed. Furthermore, there has been an exponential growth in the number of disputes being resolved by investment arbitration tribunals and the WTO dispute settlement system.[5] Besides, the quest for international financial regulation has increasingly captivated economists and legal scholars,[6] and financial law (eg, rules on capital requirements for banks, rules for trading derivatives and securities or resolution mechanisms for institutions that fail) has moved to a more central place in international regulatory discussions alongside traditional topics such as trade, direct investment, and monetary exchange.[7] New (and predominantly non-binding) international norms and institutional mechanisms have contributed to structure and legitimate new forms of authority with the task of securing international financial stability.[8] As a result, IEL appears today as a complex regulatory framework 'flowing from different sources of law governing international economic relations and transboundary economic conduct by States, international organizations, and private actors'.[9]

[4] And this will be arguably the trend in the future. Along these lines, Cottier (n 2) 7 argues: 'International economic law will continue to grow incrementally, commensurate with transnational regulatory needs. It cannot develop the aspiration of a top down, comprehensive and fully consistent legal order.'

[5] Suffice it here to refer to the caselaw reported by sectoral advanced textbooks, such as, for example, M Matsushita, TJ Schoenbaum, PC Mavroidis and M Hahn, *The World Trade Organization: Law, Practice and Policy*, 3rd edn (Oxford, OUP, 2015); JHB Pauwelyn, A Guzman, and JA Hillman, *International Trade Law*, 3rd edn (Aspen Publishing, 2016); and P Van der Bossche and W Zdouc, *The Law and Policy of the World Trade Organization Text, Cases, and Materials,* 5th edn (Cambridge, CUP, 2021) for international trade disputes; and JW Salacuse, *The Law of Investment Treaties*, 3rd edn (Oxford, OUP, 2022) 53 ff.; and R Dolzer, U Kriebaum and C Schreuer, *Principles of International Investment Law*, 3rd edn (Oxford, OUP, 2022), for international investment law.

[6] JH Jackson, 'The Quest for International Law in Financial Regulation and Monetary Affairs: Introductory Note' (2010) 13(3) *Journal of International Economic Law (JIEL)* 525; C Brummer, 'Why Soft Law Dominates International Finance and Not Trade', (2010) 13(3) *JIEL* 623; JP Trachtman, 'The International Law of Financial Crisis: Spillovers, Subsidiarity, Fragmentation and Cooperation' (2010) 13(3) *JIEL* 719; D Rodrik, *The Globalization Paradox: Democracy and the Future of the World Economy* (New York, W.W. Norton, 2011); E Avgouleas, *Governance of Global Financial Markets: The Law, The Economics, The Politics* (Cambridge, CUP, 2012); D Schoenmaker, *Governance of International Banking: The Financial Trilemma* (Oxford, OUP, 2013); RM Lastra, 'Do We Need a World Financial Organization?' (2014) 17(4) *JIEL* 787.

[7] L Borlini, 'On Financial Nationalism and International Law: Sovereignty, Cooperation and Hard/Soft Governance in International Finance' (2020) 30(3) *European Journal of International Law (EJIL)* 1123, 1123–5. On this topic see, generally, F Lupo-Pasini, *The Logic of Financial Nationalism* (Cambridge, CUP, 2017).

[8] See further T Cottier, JH Jackson and RM Lastra (eds), *International Law in Financial Regulation and Monetary Affairs* (Oxford, OUP, 2012); RM Lastra, *International Financial and Monetary Law,* 2nd edn (Oxford, OUP, 2015); C Brummer, *Soft Law and the Global Financial System: Rule-Making in the 21st Century*, 2nd edn (Cambridge, CUP, 2015).

[9] M Herdegen, 'International Economic Law', MPEPIL (November 2020) para 1.

Despite its expansion and increasing sophistication, heterogeneity remains a distinctive aspect of this area of international law so that even the definition of its precise contours is controversial. In the interest of tangible demarcation, indeed, the notion of IEL is sometimes confined to a narrow concept that exclusively refers to the area of public international law 'directly governing – rather than merely affecting – economic relations between States or international organizations'.[10] By contrast, a broader understanding reflects also the role of private actors or hybrid entities administering public goods of major relevance to the international community.[11] This broader concept of IEL includes 'international conventions and codes of conduct addressing transboundary activities of private enterprises as well as problems of jurisdiction of States' and, what is more important for the purposes of the present study, '*conflicting interests of States concerning the regulation of economic activities in an international context*'.[12] Understood in this way, IEL includes the following core segments: the regulation of the exchange of goods and services across borders (international trade law), cross-border movement of capital and promotion and protection of foreign investments (international investment law), monetary relations (international monetary law); international cooperation on supervision, regulation and crisis management of financial institutions (international financial law); international protection of intellectual property (international property rights law); and the interplay of domestic competition rules concerning the issue of undertakings (international antitrust or competition law).

The quest for coherence and integration has led scholars to the identification of a few general concepts and principles (eg, reciprocity and non-discrimination;[13] proportionality and good governance); interests (eg, development); as well as shared challenges[14] that characterise IEL and its progressive developments. Along this line of thought, the imperative of liberalising trade and the objective of creating the conditions for internationally contestable markets;[15] the creation

[10] ibid, para 1.

[11] Two different, but equally important and known, cases are the Internet Corporation for Assigned Numbers and Names (ICANN), and the Financial Action Task Force (FATF).

[12] Herdegen (n 9) para 1, emphasis added. See also L Choukroune and JJ Nedumpara, *International Economic Law. Texts, Cases and Materials* (Cambridge, CUP, 2022) vii–viii.

[13] N DiMascio and J Pauwelyn, 'Nondiscrimination in Trade and Investment Treaties: Worlds Apart or Two Sides of the Same Coin?' (2008) 102(1) *American Journal of International Law* 48.

[14] These challenges may be contingent – for instance, nationalism lately on the rise with international institutions under stress – or more structural in nature – eg, relations of international economic legal rules to non-strictly economic but key concerns: the protection of the environment in the age of climate change, the respect and promotion of human rights and the rule of law within a decentralised system of governance, and the challenges of global labour and non-labour migration flows. For an introductory discussion of these latter kind of challenges see Cottier (n 2) 3–4.

[15] Explicitly, a market is 'internationally contestable' when the competitive conditions allow access without obstacles to goods, services, ideas, investments, and persons involved in commercial transactions, coming from other countries. In short, it is a market in which the competitive process is unimpeded by private or public anticompetitive conduct, including any advantage governments secure for enterprises under their control. See TJ Schoenbaum, 'The Concept of Market Contestability and New Agenda of the Multilateral Trading System' (1996) 1(2) *ASIL Insights*.

of a stable and predictable environment that favours foreign investments and the related establishment of rights for private (non-state) investors, which can be directly applicable against host countries;[16] the surveillance of currency arrangements and assistance to states in case of balance of payment deficits;[17] and the prevention of systemic financial failure,[18] if not unifying principles of IEL,[19] are conventionally considered as the organising, (and inter-related), functions of its main segments.

Still, it is the *common subtext* of these different segments that seems to characterise the body of law under discussion *as a whole*: this subtext being the promotion of liberal market values, the integration of international markets, and the retreat of the state in the allocation of resources unless otherwise necessary to correct market failures or achieve specific societal goals. Although seemingly reductive,[20] such a reading has the advantage of making it clear why the resurgence (or, as Rob Howse aptly puts it in chapter three of this volume, the 'resilience'[21]) of the state as a business actor, and, particularly, the increasing role of state enterprise[22] in both domestic markets and international transactions, is

[16] See U Kriebaum, 'The Nature of Investment Disciplines', in Z Douglas, J Pauwelyn and JE Vinuales (eds), *The Foundations of International Investment Law: Bringing Theory into Practice* (Oxford, OUP, 2014) 45–72; Salacuse (n 5) 53–55; Dolzer (n 5) 20.

[17] Lastra (n 8) 15. However, as 'monetary affairs amount to one of the last and most solid bastions of national sovereignty', E Baltensperger and T Cottier, 'The Role of International Law in Monetary Affairs' (2010) 13 *JIEL* 912, 927 correctly pointed out, as a matter of fact, 'there are hardly any substantive [international law] rules on the subject … [and] even the procedural and structural rules are weak'.

[18] The concept of financial stability is somehow elusive. Often, it is described negatively as the absence of crisis. The true value of financial stability is indeed best illustrated in its absence, in periods of financial instability. During these periods, banks are reluctant to finance profitable projects, asset prices deviate excessively from their intrinsic values and payments may not arrive on time. Major instability can lead to bank runs, hyperinflation or a stock market crash. It can severely shake confidence in the financial and economic system. *cf*, Reiser, 'Financial Stability', in T Cottier and KN Shefer (eds), *Elgar Encyclopaedia of International Economic Law* (Cheltenham, Edward Elgar, 2017) 251.

[19] RM Gadbaw, 'The Prevention of Systemic Failure as a Unifying Principle of International Economic Law' (2014) 17(4) *JIEL* 823.

[20] In-depth critical analyses are offered, among many by D Kennedy, *A World of Struggle. How Power, Law, and Expertise Shape Global Political Economy* (New Jersey, Princeton University Press, 2016), esp. Part III; A Carty, *Philosophy of International Law*, 2nd edn (Edinburgh, Edinburgh University Press, 2017) Ch 7; A Orford, 'Theorizing Free Trade', in A Orford and F Hoffmann (eds), *The Oxford Handbook of the Theory of International Law* (Oxford, OUP, 2016), 701.

[21] See ch 3, in this volume. See also R Howse, 'Official Business: International Trade Law and the Resurgence (or Resilience) of the State as an Economic Actor' [July 23, 2021] *University of Pennsylvania Journal of International Law*, forthcoming, NYU Law and Economics Research Paper No 15, NYU School of Law, Public Law Research Paper No 21-31, at: ssrn.com/abstract=3892415 (accessed 9 September 2021.) See also ch 2, in this volume.

[22] In this chapter we will use the term 'state enterprises' to designate in general a range of business entities over which the state has influence beyond the use of general policy tools like regulation. What level or kind of influence triggers the different concerns discussed in the book is itself a matter of debate and indeed some confusion, with the highest level of concern often being expressed over enterprises that are owned in whole or in part by the state and through which it exercises control through appointment of the board and/or managers. Yet these are hardly the only ways in which the state can influence the operational or business decisions of enterprises. Thus, in using the term 'state enterprises' I leave open the question of what level of state involvement or influence, and what kind,

attracting so much attention among states, international organisations, scholars and practitioners, who are increasingly confronted with different legal issues concerning such entities. To put it crudely, the increasingly free international movement of goods, services and capitals and the underlying implicit trust in competition and free markets have brought with them growing suspicion about the motives of state enterprises when they invest, allocate scarce resources, move goods and services across borders, procure goods and services.[23]

The present chapter is premised on the assumption that the promotion of liberal market values is an important objective of the international economic order, but that so too is (and will be) the preservation of institutional diversity and the capacity for institutional innovation, against which it has always to be balanced.[24] A number of different international rules may apply to state enterprises. After situating state enterprises in the contemporary international legal system looking particularly at economic relations among states, this chapter will focus on the main challenges to regulation that government influence on state enterprises' activities poses to the two areas of international trade law and international investment law in light of their foundational principles and common subtext.

## II. STATE ENTERPRISES AND THE INTERNATIONAL LEGAL SYSTEM IN THE TWENTY-FIRST CENTURY: SOME INTRODUCTORY REMARKS

Across the ages and geographically, states have always intervened in the economy through various forms of state enterprises. The last 30 years are featured by mixed trends, however. The end of the twentieth century was a time of privatisation; so far, the new millennium has presaged a resurgence of state capitalism.[25] State involvement in the economy is today less obvious but no less important than in the past. It is both pervasive and opaque, but in surveying the economic battlefield today, one can easily conclude that state capitalism still looms large in both developed and developing countries:[26] state-owned enterprises (SOEs),

should trigger international economic rules, new or proposed. Conversely, when a certain form and/or level of state influence triggers a specific legal issue or is considered in a given international rule, I will explicitly refer to that instance.

[23] See J Chaisse, 'Untangling the Triangle: Issues for State-controlled Entities in Trade, Investment, and Competition Law', in J Chaisse and T-Y Lin (eds), *International Economic Law and Governance* (Oxford, OUP, 2016) 233.

[24] See also A Lang, 'Heterodox Markets and "Market Distortions" in the Global Trading System' (2019) 22(4) *JIEL* 680, 687. *cf* also ch 2, in this volume.

[25] Howse (n 21) 2.

[26] Whereas their importance increased dramatically over the past two decades, state enterprises have been in existence for a long time. FAM Riad, 'L'entreprise publique et semi-publique en droit international privé' [1963] *Recueil des Cours* 565: 'Il est notoire que la participation de l'Etat à la vie économique est un phénomène fort ancien, et les auteurs ne manquent pas de rappeler que, dans l'ancienne Égypte, l'État exploitait les huileries, que les Empereurs romains exploitaient les arsenaux et les Rois de France des manufactures d'art.'

development banks, sovereign wealth funds (SWFs), among other vehicles of governmental capitalism, have taken centre stage in the global economy.[27] Both long-term and more immediate factors have made possible the exponential growth of state enterprises in market sectors that are traditionally occupied by purely commercial entities. One such long-term factor leading to the prominence of the state capitalism model has been the decades-long rise of China and its state enterprises.[28] Beyond this, the impact of the latest financial crisis has led to a reconsideration of the state role in the economy. Countries that had liberalised various parts of the economy – when, due to mounting costs of state-led development, privatisation was a financial no-brainer – reacted to the 2007–2009 Great Recession and its prolonged aftermath via increased state ownership interest in strategically important firms. While this phenomenon is not new, it is notable for its extent: companies that are both state-controlled and organised according to private priorities now participate in a much broader range of economic activities, including but not limited to the energy, mining, transportation, defence, and banking sectors.[29]

At the same time, an increasing number of countries have established SWFs that invest in both real and financial assets on a global scale.[30] Their rise has shown a new side to state capitalism; SWFs have been transforming themselves from passive or portfolio investors to active capitalists, involved in private equity and even venture capital.[31] It is estimated that today almost 100 SWFs with a total of more US$10 trillion in assets exist.[32] However, the regulatory instruments

[27] A Musacchio, SG Lazzarini, *Reinventing State Capitalism: Leviathan in Business, Brazil and Beyond* (Cambridge, MA, Harvard University Press 2014) 45–52.

[28] Chinese SOEs have played a key role in the enormous growth China has experienced over the past three decades and have become more powerful than ever. While, in 2005, there was no single SOE among the top 10 firms of the Fortune Global 500 list, in 2013 there were three SOEs: Sinopec Group, China National Petroleum (two of China's national oil companies) and State Grid (a Chinese utility), among the top 10: money.cnn.com/magazines/fortune/global500/2013/full_list/ (accessed 18 February 2022). In 2021, these three companies respectively rank fourth, fifth and second: fortune.com/global500/ (accessed 18 February 2022).

[29] See, among others, J Kurlantzick, *State Capitalism. How the Return of Statism is Transforming the World* (Oxford, OUP, 2016) especially ch 1.

[30] State enterprises are obviously not limited to China: they are an integral part of the economic structure of several countries both in the western and eastern hemispheres, across different economies. In some states, like Germany, India and Russia, they number in the thousands. Some are also multinationals, operating around the world. OECD, 'The Size and Sectoral Distribution of SOEs in OECD and Partner Countries' (OECD 2017).

[31] OECD, 'Measuring Distortions in International Markets: Below-Market Finance', OECD Trade Policy Paper # 247, May 2021, 10.

[32] See at: globalswf.com (accessed 18 February 2022). The most important SWF today is the Norges Bank Investment Management (NBIM), which was founded in 1997 and operates as the asset management unit of the Norwegian Central Bank, on behalf of the Government Pension Global Fund. Its assets under management amount to US$1.4 trillion. Overall, there are 4 Chinese SWFs in the top 10 SWFs ranking, amounting to a total of almost US$3 trillion assets under management; and four SWFs from the Gulf States, with a total of almost US$2.5 trillion assets under management. Overall, the first SWF not from the Far East or the Gulf States (apart from NBIM), is Future Fund from Australia which is in 15th place (which was seeded in 2006 with a number of transfers from Australia's Department of Finance, most of them, related to the partial privatisation of national telecom company Telstra).

concerning the operation of SWFs are not particularly satisfactory, both on the international and at the regional/domestic level. They have a (moreover) *soft* and (in particular at the domestic level) *hard* law character; but they are unable to provide effective and satisfactory answers to the many legal concerns that the activities of SWFs pose. This is mainly due to two reasons: first, the fact that there is a certain lack of transparency and clear communication concerning the SWF operations, on the part of the fund themselves; and second, because there are indeed many definitions of what a SWF is, ranging from a very broad to some which are more precise, but a precise and comprehensive definition of what exactly a SWF is.[33]

Besides, state enterprises have lately contributed to stimulus worldwide after the outburst of the Covid-19 global pandemic. Over the last two years, governments around the world have instructed their infrastructure state enterprises to deliver public goods and services more widely and equitably among the population – not only to minimise the pandemic's impact but also to address the economic downturn.[34] Moreover, as supply chains have been interrupted or export bans for key goods were in place, governments have engaged state enterprises to provide medical products or services.[35] And states, such as in Brazil, Canada, Germany, and India have instructed their public banks to help alleviate the impact of the current pandemic.[36] As a result, in today's closely-knit global society, state enterprises take up a significant proportion of markets, international trade and foreign direct investments (FDI).[37]

The conflation of such entities' economic governance with the political order of the state creates an assortment of legal issues. Despite the manifold forms state enterprises take – from SWFs, to state-owned energy companies or national development banks – they touch upon fundamental institutions of

[33] See C Tietje, 'Investment Law and Sovereign Wealth Funds', in M Bugenberg, J Griebel, S Hove and A Reinisch (eds), *International Investment Law* (CH Beck/Hart, 2015) 1802, 1803; and Chaisse (n 23) 237.

[34] See, among others, IMF, 'Fiscal Monitor. Policies to Support People During the Covid Pandemic', April 2020 (IMF 2020), chs 1–3; IMF, 'Fiscal Monitor. Policies for the Recovery', October 2020 (IMF 2020), esp. ch 1; J Brumby and N Gökgür, 'Time to Rethink State-Owned Enterprise Performance Trade-offs' (WorldBankBlogs, 11 March 2021) blogs.worldbank.org/governance/time-rethink-state-owned-enterprise-soe-performance-trade-offs (accessed 18 February 2022).

[35] For example, Indonesia asked its state-owned aircraft manufacturer to produce ventilator prototypes. China, provided corporate income tax and value-added tax incentives to companies engaged in producing medical supplies while also turning its SOEs to the manufacture of masks.

[36] V Gaspar, P Medas and J Ralyea, 'State-owned Enterprises in the Time of Covid 19' (IMFBlog, 7 May 2020) blogs.imf.org/2020/05/07/state-owned-enterprises-in-the-time-of-covid-19/ (accessed 14 July 2022).

[37] ibid 'The share of state-owned enterprises among the world's 2000 largest firms doubled to 20 percent over the last two decades, driven by state-owned enterprises in emerging markets-their assets are worth $45 trillion, equivalent to half of global GDP'. According to the International Finance Corporation (IFC), state enterprises account for 20% of investment, 5% of employment and up to 40% of domestic output in countries around the world, delivering critical services in key economic sectors, including utilities, finance, and natural resources.

international law in most complex terms, with special regard to the attribution of their conduct to the state, their legal standing in international and domestic litigation, and sovereign immunity form jurisdiction and execution. Their common features of being owned/controlled/influenced by the state gives rise to unique challenges in respect of their place and regulation in the international legal order. Thus, state ownership/control creates opportunities in terms of corporate governance, enhancing their contributions to development,[38] and the promotion of human rights.[39] Yet, it also comes with the risk that the creation of state enterprises serves as a mechanism to circumvent state responsibility and reduce access to justice for victims of human rights violations.[40] Likewise, the regulation of state control of multinational enterprises which have a tendency to export environmental risks is particularly complex.

Still, the resurgence of the state as an economic actor and the internationalisation of state enterprises pose challenges particularly in the different areas of IEL. One broad challenge is commercial, given concerns that state ownership, combined with their sheer size and the share of their output in some markets, may affect the terms of competition. Another is political, given concerns that trade and investment by state enterprises may be driven by public policy goals rather than, or in addition to, commercial considerations.[41] The murky world of state enterprises in countries where even the number of such firms is uncertain adds a further layer of complexity.[42] More specifically, concerns about unfair advantage that state enterprises may have over private firms because of government support have spilled across national borders and fuelled protectionist measures.[43] This is accentuated by the rise of China as a global power, as Chinese firms and state enterprises establish branches and participate in large projects abroad.[44] Apprehension is mounting that such firms undermine

[38] Asian Development Bank, 'Reforms, Opportunities and Challenges for State-Owned Enterprises' (ADB 2020).

[39] Human Rights Council, 'Report of the Working Group on the issue of human rights and transnational corporations and other business enterprises', 4 May 2016, UN Doc. A/HRC/32/45.

[40] LC Backer, 'The Human Rights Obligations of State-Owned Enterprises (SOEs): Emerging Conceptual Structures and Principles in National and International Law and Policy' (2017) 50 *Vanderbilt Journal of Transnational Law* 827.

[41] RJ Gilson and CJ Milhaupt, 'Economically Benevolent Dictators: Lesson s for Developing Democracies' (2011) 59 *American Journal Comparative of Law* 227.

[42] DM Shapiro and S Globerman, 'The International Activities and Impacts of State-owned Enterprises', in KP Sauvant, LE Sachs, and WPF Schmit Jongbloed (eds), *Sovereign Investment Concerns and Policy Reactions* (Oxford, OUP, 2012) 98, 115–125.

[43] State enterprises may indeed receive preferential treatment in the form of outright subsidisation, tax reduction, regulatory advantages, etc, creating an uneven playing field for privately owned competitors A further complexity is that, unlike regulation and taxation, intervention in state enterprises can be quite informal and non-transparent; devising legal norms to prohibit informal influence or require transparency is a complex regulatory exercise. For an overview of possible forms of preferential treatment, see, eg, M Du, 'China's State Capitalism and World Trade Law' (2014) 63 *ICLQ* 421.

[44] See the recent report by the European Court of Auditors documenting increasing Chinese investments in the EU. European Court of Auditors, Review No 03/2020: The EU's Response to China's State-Driven Investment Strategy (10 September 2020) www.eca.europa.eu/en/Pages/DocItem.aspx?did=54733 (accessed 18 February 2022).

competitors in the countries into which they expand due to the support of the Chinese Government.[45] Hence, the notion that state enterprises engage in unfair competition in international markets is now a common refrain.[46]

Furthermore, with the increased recourse to investor-state arbitration, challenges often arise in terms of ascertaining whether the conduct of a state enterprise – eg, a state-owned port company terminating a concession agreement – can be regarded as the conduct of the state for purposes of finding a violation of an international investment agreement. Also, state enterprises' governance, asserted lack of transparency and proximity with regulators have attracted considerable attention by inter-governmental institutions with the (explicit or implicit) mandate of furthering open markets and competition.[47]

Other issues surrounding state enterprises are less discussed but no less significant in terms of their impact on international economic relations and stability. To start with, in key economies like China, state enterprises are known to be highly indebted, which has recently led the International Monetary Fund (IMF) to intensify its scrutiny in the context of its surveillance functions. The state enterprises' share of corporate debt in China is indeed much higher than their share of economic output. Rising defaults in early 2021, including several large SOEs, among them Yongcheng Coal and Electricity and Tsinghua Unigroup, have alarmed investors worldwide.[48] Because of the mounting concerns about the overall impact of high levels of corporate debt, the IMF is increasingly attentive to them in the Article IV consultations process.[49] Related is the problem of establishing state liability under international law for the debts of the enterprises it owns,[50] or for their breach of a contract. Symmetrically, another underdeveloped question, which lies at the interface between domestic law and

[45] Note also that the West's state enterprises have long expanded abroad with the help of the state. See M Stothard 'France: The Politics of State Ownership' *Financial Times* (London, 13 November 2016); P Toral 'The Foreign Direct Investments of Spanish Multinational Enterprises in Latin America, 1989–2005' (2008) 40 *Journal of Latin American Studies* 513.

[46] The new OECD study, n 31 above at 10, refers with concern to 'the outsized role that SOEs continue to play in the global economy'. The latest Joint Communiqué issued by the G7 countries at the G7 Trade Track on 28 May 2021, calls, in the context of WTO reform, 'for the start of negotiations to develop stronger international rules on market-distorting industrial subsidies and trade-distorting actions by state enterprises'. See www.gov.uk/government/news/g7-trade-ministers-communique (accessed 18 February 2022). In the words of one commentator: 'The failure of [WTO] treaties and agreements to make a proper assessment of the problem of state-owned companies has caused major imbalances and a huge image problem for free trade and its advocates, as they are seen as defending the indefensible.' A Chafuen, 'Trade by State-Owned Companies; Global but Is It Fair?' *Forbes* (31 October 2019).

[47] See, eg, World Bank, 'Corporate Governance of State-Owned Enterprises. A Toolkit' (World Bank 2014), OECD, 'Recommendations of the Council on Competitive Neutrality', 31 May 2020: legalinstruments.oecd.org/en/instruments/OECD-LEGAL-0462 (accessed 18 February 2022).

[48] S Yu, 'China Rushes to Set up Bailout Funds for Indebted State-run Firms', *Financial Times* (London, 22 July 2021).

[49] IMF, 'The People's Republic of China 2020 Article IV Consultation – Press Release; Staff Report; and Statement by the Executive Director for the People's Republic of China', International Monetary Fund, IMF Country Report No 2021/006.

[50] See, eg, *Mykhaylenky and Others v Ukraine* App nos 35091/02, 35196/02, 35201/02, 35204/02, 35945/02, 35949/02, 35953/02, 36800/02, 38296/02, and 42814/02 (ECHR, 6 June 2005).

international law, is as follows: in dealing with a state corporation, when can the corporation be assimilated with the state, so as to allow the corporation to be held liable for the state's debts?[51] Finally, the reality of foreign investment and the prospect that foreigners may control strategic assets have led national and regional legislators to develop new mechanisms to control foreign investments, particularly in light of national security.[52]

## III. STATE CAPITALISM AND STATE ENTERPRISES IN INTERNATIONAL INVESTMENT LAW

The rapid rise, over the last decade, in the number and influence of state enterprises engaging in FDI has raised widespread concern among host countries. As one commentator has observed, state enterprises are a challenge to the international investment regime because 'they represent assets worth dramatically more than 'normal' investors and there is, at least potentially, the risk of direct political influence on their investment activities'.[53] Some argue that state enterprises – whether in the form of SOEs, SWFs or similar *parastatals* investment vehicles – might pursue political objectives rather than purely economic/ commercial objectives and that their ties with foreign governments may pose national security risks to the host countries. Other concerns are about competitive neutrality, transparency, and the risk that these entities commit military or industrial espionage.[54] For instance, one may consider the 2016 failed investment plans by State Grid, a Chinese SOE and the biggest electric utility corporation in the world, to acquire a 50.4 per cent stake in electricity distribution firm Ausgrid (the largest electricity distributor on Australia's east coast), and a 14 per cent stake (totalling €830 million) in the Belgian power and gas distribution system operator, Eandis. The plans were rejected because both the Australian Government and the Belgian State Security Agency were warned of the link between State Grid and the Chinese authorities, and the risk that the technology concerned could be used for military purpose.[55]

Another issue is that a large proportion (if not, *the majority*) of cross-border investments originating from state enterprises have emerging or developing

[51] C Miles, 'State Debts and State-owned Corporations: Trans-Atlantic Perspectives' (2021) 81 *QIL Zoom-Out* 31.

[52] See C Esplugues, *Foreign Investments, Strategic Assets and National Security* (Cambridge, Intersentia 2018).

[53] *cf* Tietje (n 33) 1815.

[54] See, recently, among others, M McLaughlin, 'Defining a State-Owned Enterprise in International Investment Agreements' (2019) 34 *ICSID Review* 596; B Nalbandian, 'State Capitalists as Claimants in International Investor-State arbitration' (2021) 81 *QIL Zoom-out* 7.

[55] See K Vaswani, 'Australia blocks Chinese firm from stake in electricity grid' (*BBC News*, 11 August 2016) www.bbc.com/news/business-37043119 (accessed 18 February 2022); Z Bantley, 'China State Grid's €830m Belgian grid deals falls through' (*Infrastructure Investor*, 7 October 2016) www.infrastructureinvestor.com/china-state-grids-e830m-belgian-grid-deal-falls-through/ (accessed 18 February 2022).

economies as their home state.[56] This raises two different kinds of problems. First, concerns have been advanced considering that the home countries of SOE and (especially) SWFs are states in which the rule of law is not yet fully developed or implemented.[57] Second, it is also evident that the influence of FDI from state enterprises (especially from China and the Gulf States) is likely to further grow in a world that is still in the wake of an economic and financial crisis. This would result in a shift in the global economic system and in the governments' conceptions of their role in the economy.[58] In essence, it is not naïve to think that the emergence of state capitalism in contemporary investment global policy would end up in a radical redistribution of political power, with countries using investments in infrastructure and public utilities to create political leverage in various regions of the world. However, whether this spells disaster or a desirable realignment of power is, of course, a matter of opinion.[59]

The constant tension between state sovereignty and control over economic decisions, on the one hand, and the inner goal of IIAs to favour cross-border investments on the other sets the frame for a number of questions of great legal intricacy. For instance, can sovereigns be both investors and regulators? Should sovereign entities be allowed a vote on company matters like any other shareholder? And above all, should we be alarmed if the investment activity of state enterprises is moved by motivations other than profit-maximisation?[60] This conundrum – the so-called public/private divide – lies at the very heart of modern international investment law, and has been the focus of much legal scholarship that seeks to identify the proper degree of involvement of state enterprises in the global economy.[61] This tension becomes particularly pronounced when taking into account that the need for international investments in developed economies (such as the US and EU) will likely continue to grow as the economic and financial crisis is still not ended.[62] This will inevitably increase the probability 'that

[56] But see UNCTAD, 'World Investment Report 2021' (UNCTAD 2021) 27, noting that some of the vast array of measures, that have been taken by many governments to support the business sector in response to the Covid-19 crisis, include (especially in developed economies, and in particular in Europe) the acquisition of equity stakes in companies in financial distress, potentially increasing the number and presence of SOEs in the economy.

[57] *cf* Tietje (n 33) 1803.

[58] As correctly observed, see G Shaffer, 'How Do We Get Along: International Economic Law and the Nation-State' (2019) 117 *Michigan Law Review* 1229, 1244, 'while economies globalize, politics remain local'. The consequences on international investment law of this new phase of reassertion of sovereignty by states have been recently addressed by G Dimitropoulos, 'National Sovereignty and International Investment Law: Sovereignty Reassertion and Prospects of Reform' (2020) 21 *Journal of World Investment and Trade* 71.

[59] See M Steinitz, 'Foreign Direct Investment by State-controlled entities at a crossroad of economic history: Conference Report of the Rapporteur', in Sauvant, Sachs and Schmidt Jongbloed (n 42) 538.

[60] ibid 536.

[61] On this, see the review of the contemporary academic and professional debate about the involvement of state enterprises in global economy, by PM Blyschak, 'State-Owned Enterprises in International Investment' (2016) 31 *ICSID Review* 5.

[62] We refer to the circumstance (and it is a matter of fact) that significant levels of FDI now flow from – and not just to – developing states, and that they flow to – and not just from – developed

state enterprises will face obstacles on foreign markets and hence will resort to international dispute settlement to resolve this kind of new issues'.[63] In the following pages we will address two of the most significant of these legal issues, leaving to other chapters of the present book the task to give them (and other issues) a more focused and in-depth analysis.

The first challenge, when one considers state enterprises from the viewpoint of the conceptual foundations of international investment law, is whether they should be considered qualified investors and whether their investments are subjected to treaty protections, including access to ISDS against a host state. To understand this, what exactly is a state enterprise is an essential question. If state enterprises are to be classed as private actors, they would be regarded as any other private entity/investor and be allowed access to ISDS; but if they are to be categorised as an extension of state sovereignty, they would not. This is because IIAs and ISDS were originally designed to provide legal protection to private corporations investing abroad, and not to address disputes between states. In other words, state enterprises should not be entitled *locus standi* in investment arbitral disputes, but to specific arbitral (state-to-state) arrangements or to other means of peaceful dispute settlement in the sense of Article 33 of the UN Charter.[64] Unfortunately, there is no unified definition of state enterprises in international investment law and, more significantly, IIAs often do not adequately address the unique characteristics of these entities. A starting point of the discussion about the nature of state enterprises in international investment law is, therefore, that IIAs do not provide clear answers to these issues.[65] Further, if it is true that the new generation of investment and trade agreements seem to growingly encompass sovereign entities within their coverage,[66] IIAs expressly including such *parastatals* investment vehicles within their definitions

states. Traditional capital exporters and importers countries are thus formulating bilateral and multilateral investment treaties that attempt to strike a balance between the opposing interests. See J Chaisse, 'The Regulation of Sovereign Wealth Funds in the European Union: Can the Supranational Level Limit the Rise of National Protectionism?', in Sauvant, Sachs and Schmidt Jongbloed (n 42) 464–466.

[63] Chaisse (n 23) 247.

[64] See *Ceskoslovenska Obchodni Banka, A.S. v Slovakia*, ICSID Case No ARB/97/4, Decision of the Tribunal on Objections to Jurisdiction, 24 May 1999, para 16 '[t]he Centre does not have jurisdiction over disputes between two or more Contracting States'.

[65] *cf* McLaughlin (n 54) 597. Moreover, with regard to SWFs, it has been noted that they 'usually lack transparent structures … [and] operate in an opaque way, publishing neither statistics on their composition nor on their investments and strategies'. See Chaisse (n 23) 237.

[66] See, for instance, the *Canada–China Foreign Investment Protection Agreement* (FIPA), signed 9 September 2012, entered into force 1 October 2014; the *Comprehensive and Progressive Agreement for Trans-Pacific Partnership* (CPTPP), signed 8 March 2018 and entered into force 30 December 2018, ch 17.1; the *United States-Mexico-Canada Agreement* (USMCA), entered into force 1 July 2020, Art 22.1; the *EU-China Comprehensive Agreement on Investment* (CAI), agreement in principle 30 December 2020. The latter does not refer explicitly to SOEs but uses a broader concept of 'covered entities' to define coverage. Art 3bis, s II, requires that covered entities act according to commercial considerations, a commitment that is enforceable through dispute settlement. For more on the EU

of 'investor' are still a minority proportion, to date. Otherwise put, it logically results that in the current legal framework a state enterprise should not benefit from ISDS clauses in a state-to-state BIT, unless that treaty explicitly provides the contrary.[67]

But the discussion does not stop here. Quite to the contrary, it goes much further to include new, inter-related, questions. To start with, should a state enterprise be prohibited from having access to ISDS in general, or should they be so prohibited only if they are discharging governmental functions? And when can we assess for sure that they are performing governmental functions? Should it be under an *ownership test*, or under a less-demanding *control test*? In the former case, is a significant minority ownership sufficient to satisfy the test, or it is required that the state has a significant control through full majority? And for the latter, which is the extent and form of control that a state must exercise over an entity in order that it may be considered a state enterprise, whether in the form of a SOE, a SWF, or other investment vehicle? And finally, would the power to appoint a majority of the board of directors similarly confer governmental control?

As international lawyers know very well, ownership and control can be extremely difficult to evaluate. The legal literature on the exact contours of the rules of attribution of conducts under the ILC 2001 *Draft Articles on the Responsibility of States for Internationally Wrongful Acts* is endless.[68] The practice of ISDS tribunals on the rules of attribution under international investment law is also extremely wide and complex. Suffice is to say that the normative operation by ISDS proceedings for the attribution of conduct to state enterprises consists in two steps: a *structural* test, which aims to identify a state instrumentality (SOE or SWF) as being such; and then a *functional* test, which looks to the attribution of the specific act (or omission) based on the exercise of sovereign authority.[69] This two-tier test, which largely mirrors the

approach, see ch 6, in this volume. For more references to IIAs and BITs that expressly include SOEs in their definition of 'investor', see also C Annacker, 'Protection and Admission of Sovereign Investment Under Investment Treaties' (2011) 10 *Chinese Journal of International Law* 531; and Salacuse (n 5) 250. For an overall assessment of Preferential Trade Agreements (PTA) containing provisions on SOEs, see in particular L Rubini, T Wang, 'State-Owned Enterprises', in A Mattoo, N Rocha and M Ruta (eds), *Handbook of Deep Trade Agreement* (World Bank Group, 2020) 463–504.

[67] L Trakman, 'Resolving the Tension Between State Sovereignty and Liberlizing Investor-State Disputes: China's Dilemma', in J Chaisse, L Choukroune and S Jusoh (eds), *Handbook of International Investment Law and Policy* (Singapore, Springer, 2021) 2417, 2429.

[68] The rules of attribution embodied in the ILC Draft Articles are generally recognised and applied by arbitrary tribunals as a codification of customary international law. However, IIAs – as agreements inter se – may codify different tests of attributability of acts and omissions to sovereigns and consequently bind arbitrators to their application. See C De Stefano, *Attribution in International Law and Arbitration* (Oxford, OUP, 2020) 105.

[69] *cf* De Stefano (n 68) 153; and M Du, 'The Status of Chinese State-owned Enterprises in International Investment Arbitration: Much Ado about Nothing?' (2021) 20 *Chinese Journal of International Law* 785. These two tests were most significantly applied by ISDS tribunal in *Emilio Agustín Maffezini v The Kingdom of Spain*, ICSID Case No ARB/97/7, Decision on Objections to Jurisdiction, 25 January 2000, para 76.

customary international law rules codified in the 2011 *Draft Articles* (in particular, Articles 5 and 8) was firstly proposed by Aron Broches, the first Secretary General of the ICSID, in 1972.[70] And it is on such basis that the two arbitral tribunals (one ICSID, one not-ICSID) which have addressed, to date, the question of whether Chinese SOEs should be considered qualified investors and allowed access to ISDS against a host state, have both rejected the respondent state's claim that Chinese SOEs are not qualified investors.[71] In the ICSID case, for instance, the fact that the Chinese Government was the ultimate decision-maker for the claimant – a publicly funded, wholly state-owned entity established by the Chinese Government, indeed 'one of the top 500 state-owned enterprises' in China – was not found to be decisive to define it as a state agent, as the tribunal maintained that no evidence could be found that the claimant 'was discharging a PRC governmental function rather than a commercial function'.[72]

However, much has changed since tests like Broches' were once formulated: to begin with, Chinese SOE's were not the behemoths they are today in the global market.[73] Further there were virtually no SWFs, while today SWFs (especially from the Gulf states) are carving a widening niche as pro-active cross-border investors.[74] Most importantly, one should also consider that the impact of these entities taken together exceeds their impact individually. We refer to the fact that the vast majority of the Chinese SOEs that are investing abroad does not count in the current framework only as singular commercial entities; indeed, they are, in conjunction, also furthering the Government of China's *Belt and Road Initiative* (BRI) and the *Made in China 2025* plan, both reinforcing the *Going out* policy adopted in 2000, that specifically entrusted Chinese SOEs with fostering cross-border activity to actualise China's economic and policy goals.[75] One could think, for instance, to the purchase, in 2016, of the Greek port of Piraeus by Chinese SOE COSCO (China Ocean Shipping Company).[76] Not only is Piraeus

[70] See A Broches, *Selected Essays: World Bank, ICSID, and Other Subjects of Public and Private International law* (Dordrecht, Kluwer Academic Publishers, 1995) 202: 'for purposes of the Convention a mixed economy company or government-owned corporation should not be disqualified as a "national of another Contracting State" unless it is acting as an agent for the government or is discharging an essentially governmental function'. *cf* the relevant analysis in ch 8, in this volume.

[71] The two cases are: *Beijing Urban Construction (BUCG) v Republic of Yemen*, ICSID Case No ARB/14/30, Decision on Jurisdiction, 31 May 2017; *China Heilongjiang International Economic & Technical Cooperative Corp., et al v Mongolia*, PCA Case No 2010-20 Award, 30 June 2017.

[72] *Beijing Urban Construction (BUCG) v Republic of Yemen* (n 71) 32.

[73] See S Miner and GC Hufbauer, 'State-owned Enterprises and Competition Policy: The US Perspective', in Peterson Institute for International Economics, *Toward a US-China Investment Treaty* (PIE Briefing 15-1, 2015) 17.

[74] *cf* Nalbandian (n 54) 6.

[75] For more on this, see ch 12, in this volume.

[76] COSCO acquired a 51% stake in operator Piraeus Port Authority in 2016. On 12 October 2021 COSCO acquired an additional 16% stake, lifting its stake to 67%. See D Glass 'Cosco completes increased stake in Piraeus Port Authority' (*Seatrade Maritime News*, 12 October 2021) www.seatrade-maritime.com/ports-logistics/cosco-completes-increased-stake-piraeus-port-authority (accessed 18 February 2022).

the biggest Greek port and one of the biggest ports in the Mediterranean, but it is also a very important link in the BRI and one of the many terminals in countries and regions related to the BRI where COSCO has invested.[77] In this context, the risk exists that the completion of investments by Chinese companies 'might be motivated by long-term national or even CCP priorities rather than private profit-making objectives',[78] and, as we have already discussed, that FDI can be used to create political leverage in numerous (peripheral) countries.

There is nothing inherently apologetic about the deployment by arbitrators of such legal techniques as the Broches test in order to tame one of the most explosive contradictions of global political economy. However, there is nothing inherently progressive about these efforts either, especially to the extent that they ignore issues like sovereign investors' geopolitical goals, which challenge the very core of international investment law. Otherwise put, one wonders if the conservative attitude by arbitrators is capable of delivering long-term investment sustainability – if one takes into account, for instance, that in privatising state enterprises China has retained some level of authority over them, including a direct financial interest[79] – or whether, to quote one commentator, they would end-up 'impinging on one of the very foundations of ISDS, that is adjudicating investor-states disputes, and so contributing to the undermining of its institutional legitimacy in the eye of policymakers and civil society'.[80]

One could point at the essence of that question even from a slightly different perspective. We refer to the increasing national security concerns raised by host states for the acquisition of critical assets by foreign state enterprises, because of a concern that these assets could be used to further foreign policy goals. Over the past few years, the national security exception has risen to preeminence globally as the primary justification to put barriers to trade flows. The US-China 'trade war', and the Ukraine-Russia dispute before the WTO are just some examples of this growing practice. Coupled with this, the trend has been reinforced to strengthen the 'self-judging' character ('which it considers') of the essential security provision both in international trade (WTO) law and investment law (see, in particular, the practice of US BITs).

[77] It has been reported that at the end of June 2021, COSCO had invested in 36 ports and terminals worldwide, of which 18 are linked to the BRI. See S Watanabe, 'China's COSCO raises stake in top Greek port Piraeus to 67%' (*Nikkei Asia*, 26 October 2021) asia.nikkei.com/Business/Transportation/China-s-COSCO-raises-stake-in-top-Greek-port-Piraeus-to-67 (accessed 18 February 2022).

[78] M Leonard, J Pisani-Ferry, E Ribakova, J Shapiro and GB Wolff, 'Redefining Europe's Economic Sovereignty' *European Council on Foreign Relations* (June 2019) www.ecfr.eu/publications/summary/redefining_europes_economic_sovereignty (accessed 18 February 2022)

[79] *cf* Trakman (67) 2430. On the process of SOEs' reform in China, see J Hoogmartens, 'Can China's Socialist Market Survive WTO Accession – Politics, Market Economy and Rule of Law' (2001) 7 *Law and Business Review of the Americas* 37–83; and European Parliamentary Research Service, 'State-owned enterprise (SOE) reforms in China: A decisive role for the market at last?' Briefing May 2016. See ch 8, in this volume.

[80] *cf* Nalbandian (n 54) 29. But see also, for a totally different understanding, Du (n 69).

Once again, academic literature on the issue is extensive,[81] and national security exceptions under IIAs are the focus of another chapter of this book.[82] Here, we would like to stress that if one considers the conceptual foundations of international investment law – that is, *promotion* and *protection* of investments – the potential paradigm shift for the global economic system from global capitalism to state capitalism has also significant second-order implications for national and international security. Both the US and its western allies are likely to experience domestic political backlash against foreigners owning key strategic industries, whether or not their domestic industries can survive without such foreign investment.[83] This would likely result in setting stricter screening procedures on foreign state enterprises and, more generally, in the attempt to bar certain deals due to national security considerations. The practice of western countries taking a very aggressive stance to restrict and block foreign state enterprises' investments (in particular, those involving China) on account of national security considerations has been very significant over the last few years.[84]

The fact that FDI are more than just a financial flow but can be used for leverage by third countries has been acknowledged, for instance, by the EU, when it adopted in March 2019 a Regulation establishing a framework for the screening of foreign direct investments into the Union in all strategic areas to maintain security and public order.[85] This is not the place to investigate the objectives,

[81] See Salacuse (n 5) 474; L Wang, 'Chinese SOE Investments and the National Security Protection under IIAs', in J Chaisse (ed), *China's International Investment Strategy: Bilateral, Regional, and Global law and Policy* (Oxford, OUP, 2019) 67, 72; and J Mendenhall, 'The Evolution of the Essential Security Exception in U.S: Trade and Investment', in Sauvant, Sachs and Schmidt Jongbloed (n 42) 310–402. See also for a very recent overview of the security exceptions as 'Self-Judging Obligations' in the case law of the ICJ, WTO panels and investment tribunals, M Milanov, 'A Lauterpachtian Affair: Security Exceptions as 'Self-Judging Obligations' in the Case Law of the International Court of Justice and Beyond' (2021) 22 *Journal of World Investment & Trade* 509.

[82] See ch 10, in this volume. See also MA Clodfelter and FMS Guerrero, 'National Security and Foreign Government Ownership Restrictions on Foreign Investment', in Sauvant, Sachs and Schmidt Jongbloed (n 42) 173–220; P DeSouza and WM Reisman, 'Sovereign Wealth Funds and National Security', in Sauvant, Sachs and Schmidt Jongbloed (n 42) 283–294.

[83] See on this, JE Alvarez, 'Sovereign Concerns and the International Investment Regime' in Sauvant, Sachs and Schmidt Jongbloed (n 42) 258–282.

[84] See Wang (n 81) 68–70; and C Bian, 'Foreign Direct Investment Screening and National Security: Reducing Regulatory Hurdles to Investors Through Induced Reciprocity' (2021) 22 *Journal of World Investment & Trade* 561. Most recently, on 27 November 2020, the Canadian Government, for instance, exercised its authority under the national security review mechanism to block the US$207 million M&A acquisition of a Canadian gold producer by a Chinese SOE. See UNCTAD, cit., at 120. On 8 April 2021, the Italian Prime Minister, and former European Central Bank President, Mario Draghi, barred a Chinese group from taking control of an Italian semiconductor company through the exercise of the 'golden power' veto on basis of national security concerns. See at: www.bloomberg.com/news/articles/2021-04-08/italy-s-draghi-seeks-broader-shield-from-chinese-corporate-bids (accessed 18 February 2022).

[85] European Parliament and the Council of the European Union Regulation (EU) 2019/452 of the European Parliament and of the Council of 19 March 2019 establishing a framework for the screening of foreign direct investments into the Union [2019] OJ L791. The mechanism entered into force on 10 April 2019, and became fully operation in October 2020.

content and shortcomings of this instrument in depth; suffice it here to remark that, mainly because of stricter screening by EU Member States, foreign M&A transactions in the EU undertaken by investors whose ultimate owner is based in China fell by 63 per cent in 2020, compared to a year earlier.[86] That being said, we should also consider that no country has provided an exhaustive and clear-cut definition of 'national security' in the context of foreign investments to date.[87] Thus, it is debatable whether such responses to foreign state enterprises are designed to protect 'genuine' national security interests or constitute protectionist measures that favour local companies.

Under that perspective, it is thus quite evident that the security national concerns raised by the investment's activism of state enterprises unveil one of the most salient conceptual foundations of international investment law. We refer to the regulatory relationship that it establishes between host states (as *governors*) and foreign investors (as *governed*),[88] and to the circumstance that states will indeed participate in that system only if the expected costs of constraining their sovereignty through IIAs and subjecting it to control through compulsory international adjudication mechanisms does not exceed the expected net benefits of such relationship.[89] But the emergence of an increasing number of super-rich, state-oriented/controlled/owned foreign investors destroy the relationship upon which the system is based. If international investment law (as an extension of international public law) constantly struggles to overcome and/or discipline national control over political economy and investment policies – especially when it comes to guarantees for trade, free investment and free enterprise – the appearance of state entities as governed subjects in that relationship set the scene for a clash of paradigms that is both descriptive and normative. It is descriptive, as the conceptual foundations of investment law need to reflect social practice in treaty-making and dispute settlement; but it is above all normative, because an inevitable variation needs to occur of how legal norms are interpreted and applied.

In conclusion, the tension between state sovereignty and its attributes on the one hand and the need to promote the free flows of investments, on the other, has been the focus of much legal scholarship that seeks to strike a balance between these two forms of authority (the *governor* v the *governed*). However, the debate seems to ignore two fundamental and intertwined threads.

[86] See Report from the Commission to the European Parliament and the Council, *First Annual Report on the screening of foreign direct investments into the Union*, COM(2021) 714 final, Brussels 23 November 2021, 5. The Covid-19 pandemic crisis is also a factor, but, as the EU Commission observed, 'Chinese outward investments into Europe have shown the sharpest reduction starting from November 2019, i.e. two months prior to the lock-down in Wuhan (China) at end-January 2020, and this regardless of the early re-opening of the Chinese economy in mid-2020.'

[87] See Wang (n 81) 69.

[88] For the use of these terms, see A Roberts, 'Clash of Paradigms: Actors and Analogies Shaping the Investment Treaty System' (2013) 107 *AJIL* 45.

[89] See A Van Aaken, 'Control Mechanisms in International Investment Law', in Douglas, Pauwelyn and Vinuales (n 16) 411.

First, the fact that this tension reflects the very real contradictions of global capitalism as a system that relies on state power while seeking to overcome each and every border. Second, that global capitalism is no longer the sole point of reference, but the place of free-market has been to some extent taken by 'state capitalism, a system in which the state functions as the leading economic actors and uses market primarily for political gain'.[90] To make things more complex, one should also add that within this new economic scenario, as some commentators has correctly observed, 'trade and investment policies are becoming essential tools of geopolitics', and the geo-politicisation of trade corresponds to a 'space where geo-economics is both a product and a tool of security policies'.[91]

## IV. STATE ENTERPRISES AND INTERNATIONAL TRADE LAW

WTO agreements do not contain any provisions differentiating between approaches to property rights at the domestic level. In other words, WTO law is neutral with regards to the regard to the model of ownership or control of companies.[92] A WTO member 'is free to establish and maintain state owned/controlled entities if it wishes to do so'.[93] Yet, to a limited extent, state capitalism is regulated. This is the case when the position of state enterprises overlaps with a different legal status (eg, 'state-trading enterprise', 'monopoly or exclusive service supplier', 'public body'), which may de facto coincide with state-ownership or control. That many provisions of the WTO are thus applicable to state enterprises is not in doubt,[94] but they leave gaps and ambiguities. Article XVII GATT, for instance, is of limited use in regulating the booming nature of today's state capitalism. Its application is restricted to very limited commercial transactions,[95] and it is also surrounded by uncertainty as to the

[90] I Bremmer, 'State Capitalism Comes of Age. The End of Free Market?' (*Foreign Affairs*, May/June 2009) 40.

[91] S Meunier and K Nicolaidis, 'The Geopoliticization of European Trade and Investment Policy' (2019) 57 *Journal of Common Market Studies* 103, 106.

[92] T Cottier and PC Mavroidis, 'State Trading in the Twenty- First Century: An Overview', in T Cottier and PC Mavroidis (eds), *State Trading in the Twenty-First Century: The World Trade Forum* (Ann Abor, University of Michigan Press, 1999) 3.

[93] Du (n 43) 427. This theory relies on the fundamental basic principle of public international law that each state has the sovereign right to choose freely its own political, social, and economic system, and that the multilateral trading system must accommodate the divergent views as to the proper roles of the government and the state-owned sector in the national economy, even if 'the right mix of public and private ownership remains a challenge for many countries'. See E-U Petersmann, 'GATT Law on State Trading Enterprises: Critical Evaluation of Article XVII and Proposals for Reform', in Cottier and Mavroidis (n 92) 72.

[94] Other GATT provisions that relate either directly or indirectly to STEs are Arts II (Schedule of Concessions) and XX (General Exceptions). Also, an Interpretative note to Arts XI, XII, XIII, XIV, and XVIII specifies that throughout these provisions, the term 'import restrictions' and 'export restrictions' include restrictions made effective through state trading operations.

[95] Under such provisions, each member undertakes that its state trading enterprises (STEs), SOEs or private enterprises operating under state-conferred monopolies or privileges shall, with respect to purchases or sales involving either imports or exports, act in a non-discriminatory manner and make

principle of national treatment. Furthermore, case law has been significantly weakened by the finding that it suffices for STEs to act in a non-discriminatory manner to comply with the provision.[96] While it is questionable whether in so doing, *ipso facto*, STEs act also in accordance to commercial considerations and afford competitors adequate opportunity to compete for participation – and economic logic would not support this view of the WTO Appellate Body (AB) – this interpretation is by now water under the bridge, as 'there is not one single deviation from this case law'.[97] Finally, Article XVII GATT does not apply to an STE's transactions when no foreign enterprises are directly involved.[98]

Things get decisively more complicated when considering the position of state enterprises in relation to subsidies. Existing WTO trade rules as interpreted by the AB have proved substantially inadequate to address the use (or abuse) of subsidies and countervailing measures by governments,[99] and of subsidies to and through state-controlled entities by China (a criticism that China obviously rejects).[100] As widely known, these practices have exacerbated tensions especially among the US, China and the EU. A particularly vexing question is the determination of public bodies and, relatedly, for the purposes of the Agreement on Subsidies and Countervailing Measures (ASCM), which was adopted by the AB in several reports.[101]

such purchases and sales solely in accordance with commercial considerations. For a more detailed reconstruction of the uncertainties surrounding the application of WTO rules, including the GATS, the Protocol of Accessions of Members such as China and the Russian Federation and transparency mechanisms, to state enterprises see L Borlini, 'When the Leviathan Goes to the Market: A Critical Evaluation of the Rules Governing State-Owned Enterprises in Trade Agreements' (2020) 33 *Leiden Journal of International Law* 313, 315–320 and the literature referred to therein,

[96] Appellate Body Report, *Canada–Measures Relating to Exports of Wheat and Treatment of Imported Grain*, adopted 30 August 2004, AB-2004-3, WT/DS276/R, paras 93–106.

[97] See PC Mavroidis and ME Janow, 'Free Markets, State Involvement and the WTO: Chinese State-Owned Enterprises in the Ring' (2017) 16(4) *World Trade Review* 571.

[98] Appellate Body Report, (n 96), para 157.

[99] Allegedly trade-distorting subsidies conferred on domestic industries by WTO members have been a long-standing issue of contention in trade policy circles. According to K Leitner and S Lester, 'WTO Dispute Settlement 1995–2016 – A Statistical Analysis', (2017) 20 *JIEL* 171, disputes regarding subsidies and countervailing duties accounted for 109 issues in dispute in formal trade proceedings between the creation of the WTO in 1995 and 2016 – more than any other GATT/WTO agreement aside from anti-dumping and the basic GATT itself.

[100] SOEs are obviously not limited to China. They are present in numerous countries across different economies. In some, like Germany, India and Russia, they number in the thousands. SOEs are major players in many economies and some are multinationals, operating around the world. According to a recent estimate by the IMF, SOEs undertake 55% of total infrastructure investment in emerging and developing economies. The share of SOEs among the world's 2,000 largest firms doubled to 20% over the last two decades, driven by state-owned enterprises in emerging markets – their assets are worth US$45 trillion, equivalent to half of global GDP. *cf* Gaspar, Medas and Ralyea (n 36).

[101] Appellate Report, *United States–Definitive Antidumping and Countervailing Duties (China)*, adopted 25 March 2011, WT/DS379/AB/R, para 317; Appellate Report, *United States–Countervailing Duty Measures on Certain Products from China*, adopted 18 December 2014, WT/DS437/AB/R, paras 317–22. See, among others, TJ Prusa and E Vermulst, 'United States-Definitive Anti-Dumping and Countervailing Duties on Certain Products from China: Passing the Buck on Pass-Through' (2013) 12 *World Trade Review* 197, 227–8; R Ding, 'Public Body or Not: Chinese State-Owned

Such a reading – ie 'public body' as an entity that, although not institutionally a part of a government, still functions like one – had an important corollary: the recognition that state enterprises can be run as genuine commercial enterprises and operate on a level playing field with private enterprises. The reasoning underlying this reading thus implies that state enterprises should not be treated differently simply because of majority-ownership by a government.[102] The AB's narrow interpretation seems also to adhere to the original intent of the drafters, which presumably was not to extend the influence of government too widely. Even if one assumes that the assessment is correct, however, this leaves unaddressed the issues raised by state enterprises as pass-through vehicles for subsidies. At the heart of the matter is the following question: what is the standard of proof that a commercial entity is part of the state? Having refuted the formal ownership test, the AB should have clarified what else matters.[103]

Case law shows that the AB insisted on drawing a malleable line, providing a multi-factor test to reply to the question above.[104] Still, the additional evidence that may be required was not made entirely clear.[105] This interpretation rendered by the Appellate Body is one of the main grounds of the US complaint against the AB jurisprudence, which contributed to the blockage of appointments of AB members and resulted in effectively paralysing the dispute settlement system (DSS) at the end of 2019.

As the WTO Agreements fail to provide an adequate avenue to address these concerns multilaterally,[106] states are left to their own devices in addressing the issue of foreign subsidies.[107] Moreover, with the internationalisation of SOEs, concerns about the unfair advantage they may have over private firms because

Enterprises' (2014) 48 *Journal of World Trade* 167, 170–1; M Wu, 'The "China Inc." Challenge to Global Trade Governance' (2016) 57 *Harvard International Law Journal* 261, 300–5; J Wang, 'State Capitalism and Sovereign Wealth Funds: Finding a "Soft" Location in International Economic Law', in CL Lim (ed), *Alternative Visions of the International Law of Foreign Investment* (Cambridge, CUP, 2016) 405, 411–14.

[102] For a recent application of the same test see *Panel Report United States – Countervailing Duty Measures on Certain Pipe and Tube Products from Turkey*, adopted on 18 December 2018, WT/DS523/R & WT/DS523/R/ Add.1, paras 7.34–7.50, a finding that, not surprisingly, was appealed by the US on 25 January 2019.

[103] Pauwelyn, Guzman and Hillman (n 5) 507–12.

[104] Wu, (n 101) 304. See, eg, *Appellate Report United States–Countervailing Measures on Certain Hot-Rolled Carbon Steel Flat Products from India*, adopted 8 December 2014, WT/DS436/AB/R, para 4.43.

[105] J Pauwelyn, 'Treaty Interpretation or Activism? Comment on the AB Report on United States – ADs and CVDs on Certain Products from China' (2013) 12 *World Trade Review* 235, 235–7.

[106] The European Commission claims that current WTO rules do not provide appropriate remedies against foreign subsidies as these rules do 'not apply to subsidies related to trade in services and in relation to the establishment and operation of undertakings in the EU which are backed by foreign subsidies and which do not entail any trade in goods'. European Commission, White Paper on Levelling the Playing Field as Regards Foreign Subsidies, COM(2020) 253 final (17 June 2020) 42.

[107] The EU recently published a proposal to tackle such foreign subsidisation in its own market. European Commission, Proposal for a Regulation of the European Parliament and of the Council on Foreign Subsidies Distorting the Internal Market, COM(2021) 223 final (5 May 2021).

of government support have recently spilled across national borders and fuelled protectionist measures.[108] This is accentuated by the rise of China as a global power, as Chinese firms and SOEs establish branches and participate in large projects abroad (see section II above, with regard to the BRI and the program 'China 2025'). Concerns are mounting that SOEs undermine competitors in the countries into which they expand due to the support of the Chinese Government. Hence, the notion that state enterprises engage in unfair competition in international markets is now a common refrain. Further, as the Covid-19 pandemic has accelerated and focused attention on these shifts, more adaptive interpretations of multilateral rules on subsidies along with the formulation of additional rules to limit market distortions of both subsidies and state enterprises are currently among the core issues addressed by the bulk of proposals on WTO reform.

From the WTO's ownership-neutral position, which embodies the basic principle of international law that each state has the sovereign right to freely choose its own political, social, and economic system, the seemingly new perspective of 'competitive neutrality' has emerged and inspired negotiators in making new legal rules on SOEs in PTAs. This notion was originally elaborated through soft law instruments under the aegis of the OECD, then entered the international trade and competition discourse through applied research published by the same institution, as well as policy documents of countries such as the US, Australia and within the EU.[109] It emphasises inefficiencies and allocative distortions arising out of public ownership and impairment of the competitive process.

As we observed elsewhere, that notion is a 'highly condensed form of rhetorical material' that 'through the practice of repetition among trade lawyers, it has come to seem real and part of legal routine in current trade negotiations'.[110] Like the SCM agreement in 1994, the formulation of rules on state enterprises

[108] A further complexity is that, unlike regulation and taxation, intervention in state enterprises can be quite informal and non-transparent; devising legal norms to prohibit informal influence or require transparency is a complex undertaking, and enforcing them in dispute settlement is even more daunting.

[109] For example, its recent policy paper on WTO reform, the European Commission asserts that: 'the importance of SOEs is not yet matched with sufficient disciplines to capture any market-distorting behaviour. New international state enterprises rules should focus on the behaviour of SOEs in their commercial activities, in line with the disciplines already agreed in several free trade and investment agreements. Apart from industrial subsidies and state enterprises disciplines, there is a need to reflect on what other elements could be part of new WTO rules aiming at ensuring the principle of "competitive neutrality" and promoting a level playing field.' European Commission, 'Trade Policy Review – An Open, Sustainable and Assertive Trade Policy', Annex to Communication from the Commission to the European Parliament, the Council, the European Economic and Social Committee and the Committee of the Regions, COM(2021) 66 final, 9–10 (18 February 2021).

[110] Borlini (95) 321. We argued that in raising the 'competitive neutrality' argument, most authors unfortunately fail to address two central issues. First, at the macro-level, they do not correlate the emerging trade rules on SOEs with the understanding of the world, values and priorities that underlie these rules. Nor do they seem to question or contextualise the policy design those rules entail. Second, and more specifically (although with some notable exceptions), they neglect to examine whether the new rules address the tensions arisen in WTO law. While the latter issue must be addressed by analysing the relevant treaties, the former lends itself to immediate reflections.

in modern PTAs shows a continuity with the recent history of free trade, traditionally framed as a struggle against protectionism and militant economic nationalism, while trade liberalisation itself is full of political implications about the relations between the state, market, and society. In essence, both sets of rules aim at ensuring the free trade of goods and, in case of rules on state enterprises, services under normal conditions of competition. Also, they both raise fundamental questions concerning the nature and degree of government involvement in commercial affairs and the right of other governments to inquire into such involvement. State enterprises trade regulation is, indeed, ultimately more than a legal issue: the causes of trade-and-competition problems produced by such entities have systemic roots; most importantly, a government's conception of its role in the economy. Therefore, the formulation of new international trade rules on state enterprises inevitably means addressing this underlying system of causes.

There are currently three main positions about such normative exercise. The first approach takes the SOE chapters in recent plurilateral and bilateral trade treaties as a model. According to this reading, a clarification of the WTO rules on state enterprise inspired by existing regulatory solutions at the plurilateral level would address the issues at stake.[111] Similarly, other scholars note that rules on state enterprises of the Comprehensive and Progressive Agreement for Trans-Pacific Partnership (CPTPP) were drafted with Chinese SOEs in mind, and could be useful to address the non-commercial activities of Chinese state enterprises.[112] The second (more nuanced) approach can be described as an improved-CPTPP approach and suggest that the future state enterprises rules should allow enough flexibility for state enterprises that deal with market failures situations and provide public goods.[113] Finally, the third approach challenges the solidness of amendments to WTO rules based on the CPTPP's chapter on SOEs on two different grounds. First, because much of these proposed changes would add incoherence to the existing WTO rules, making more difficult, inter alia, to address the economic consequences of the Covid-19 pandemic.[114] Second, because the extensive carveouts and exceptions in these treaties render the rules less effective to remedy trade and investment distorting behaviours of state enterprises, and, at the same time, the developing countries should not be deprived of using SOEs as a way of improving social welfare.[115] State enterprises are,

[111] PC Mavroidis and A Sapir, *China and the WTO: Why Multilateralism Still Matters* (New Jersey, Princeton University Press, 2021).

[112] Wu (n 101).

[113] M Matsushita and CL Lim 'Taming Leviathan as Merchant: Lingering Questions about the Practical Application of Trans-Pacific Partnership's State-Owned Enterprises Rules' (2020) 19 *World Trade Review* 402.

[114] R Howse, 'Making the WTO (Not So) Great Again: The Case Against Responding to the Trump Trade Agenda Through Reform of the WTO Rules on Subsidies and State Enterprises' (2020) 23 *JIEL* 371.

[115] Borlini (n 95) 327–334.

indeed, not limited to being potential agents of productive and technological development, or instruments for carrying out macroeconomic stimulus at home or advancing economic interests abroad; they also perform important socio-economic functions in both advanced economies and developing countries.

The formulation of international trade rules to control the negative spill-overs from subsidies and government influence on state enterprises, which affects firms from other countries is, in sum, a difficult normative exercise. Part of the reasons is exquisitely technical: the definition itself and measurement of subsidies turn out to be extraordinarily complex.[116] The same holds true with the definition of state enterprises and the assessment of government influence on their activities. Beyond that, the question is inherently *political:* with subsidies and state enterprises, what is ultimately involved is a confrontation between different ideological, political, and social conceptions of the role of state intervention in the economy. In essence, international trade rules on subsidies and state enterprises aim at ensuring the free trade of goods and services under normal conditions of competition. At the same time, both sets of rules raise *fundamental questions* concerning the nature and degree of government involvement in commercial affairs and the right of other governments to inquire into such involvement. Moreover, Covid-19 has created uncertainty about the future of free trade and, in particular, sparked a rethinking of global value chains.[117] Hence, the world largest economies' governments are considering using subsidies and regulation to ensure that jobs and production remain within their state territories, as well as to re-shore production and value chains post-Covid-19.[118] Finally, central to their reinvigorated policies on climate change is the shift to renewable energy, and key in sustainable energy transition are subsidy and incentive schemes.[119]

[116] Lowenfeld (n 1) 216: 'No question in international trade law is as contentious, and as complicated, as the question of subsidies.'

[117] BS Javorcik, 'Global Supply Chain Will Not Be the Same in the Post-Covid-19 World', in RE Baldwin and SJ Evenett (eds), *Covid-19 and Trade Policy: Why turning Inward Won't Work* (CEPR Press, 2020) 111.

[118] Japan has launched in both 2020 and 2021 a Program for Promoting Investment in Japan to Strengthen Supply Chains in the context of the METI's Support Measures for Companies Concerning the Impacts of the Novel Coronavirus Disease, www.meti.go.jp/english/press/2021/0702_003.html (accessed 18 February 2022). Among others, the US and EU too are developing plans to re-shore supply chains. See, respectively, M Heller, 'Biden's Administration Unveils Plans to Shore Up Supply Chains' (*American Manufacturing Blog*, 18 June 2021) www.americanmanufacturing.org/blog/biden-administration-unveils-plans-to-shore-up-supply-chains/ (accessed 18 February 2022); and European Parliament, Directorate-General for External Policies Policy Department, 'Post-Covid-19 Value Chains: Options for Reshoring Production Back to Europe in a Globalized Economy', EP/EXPO/INTA/FWC/2019-01/LOT5/R/07 EN, March 2021.

[119] See, eg, European Council, 'Conclusions on the MFF and Next Generation EU, COVID-19, Climate change, Security and External Relations Brussels', EUCO 22/20 CO EUR 17 CONCL 8 (11 December 2020); METI, 'Green Growth Strategy through Achieving Carbon Neutrality in 2050' (18 June 2021), www.meti.go.jp/english/press/2021/0618_002.html (accessed 18 February 2022). The US administration is finalising a tax plan to replace US fossil fuel subsidies with clean energy incentives. See 'The Biden Plan for a Clean Energy Revolution and Environmental Justice', / joebiden.com/climate-plan/ (accessed 18 February 2022). According to experts, China's Covid-19

By keeping investing in both renewables and fossil-fuel-based electricity generation, SOEs remain strategic too.[120]

Against the background of these new challenges, the configuration, interpretation and application of international trade rules will play a central role for three main reasons. The first and most obvious is that such rules constitute the main external constraint on the measures just described. Second, and related, the design and structure of global trade governance, to which international rules on subsidies and state enterprises contribute, attempts to shape the state itself in order to achieve desirable forms of governance (ie, regulation and administration of life) within states.[121] Particularly, despite the basic understanding of ownership neutrality of multilateral trade rules, the WTO subsidies regime is based on assumptions that are not shared by all members.[122] Third, the recent conflicts among major trade powers, intensified by the global pandemic, are not a temporary incident, but rather an outgrowth of a long-brewing tension within the multilateral trade system.[123] Another issue, noted here only briefly, is that the transparency provisions in the state enterprises chapters of the most advanced plurilateral trade agreement are quite burdensome. However, the institutional designs of such provisions do not offer a useful corrective to the scarce information we have about the extent to which state action – the only thing subject to international trade rules – alters the terms of competition in relation to the operation of state enterprises.[124] In a somewhat ironic isolation, Wolfe raised a valid point when he opined that, in the absence of reliable data, concerns with the potential for negative spill-overs on the trading system as a result of state enterprises operations may appear to be ideological rather than empirical.

To conclude, the regulation of state capitalism by international trade law is essentially a problem of interface between economic models, viz. a problem in

stimulus measures are more targeted at investing in carbon-heavy infrastructure for economic stability. However, the pandemic has not stopped Beijing's policy machinery for more sustainability and a greener economy. Beijing's strategic bet for its sustainable future is on achieving state-guided and funded technological breakthroughs. A Holzmann and N Grünberg, '"Greening" China: An analysis of Beijing's Sustainable Development Strategies' (*MERICS Mercator Institute for China Studies*, 7 January 2021), merics.org/en/report/greening-china-analysis-beijings-sustainable-development-strategies (accessed 18 February 2022).

[120] A Prag, D Röttgers and I Scherrer, 'State-Owned Enterprises and the Low-Carbon Transition', OECD Environment Working Papers No 129 (2018).

[121] As put by D Kennedy, *A World of Struggle. How Power, Law and Expertise Shape Global Political Economy* (New Jersey, Princeton University Press, 2016) 11 'law not only regulates things, it creates them. The history of political and economic life is therefore also a history of institutions and laws'.

[122] Mavroidis and Sapir (n 104) ch 5.

[123] VK Aggarwal and AW Reddie, 'Economic Statecraft in 21st Century: Implications for the Future of the Global Trade Regime' (2021) 20(2) *World Trade Review* See also E-U Petersmann, 'The Law of Political Economy: Transformation in the Function of Law; Ordo-Liberalism, Law and the Rule of Economics. The Law of Political Economy. Transformation in the Function of Law' (2021) 24 *JIEL* 221.

[124] R Wolfe, 'Sunshine over Shanghai: Can the WTO Illuminate the Murky World of Chinese SOEs?' (2017) 16(4) *World Trade Review* 713, 721–3.

international trade caused by differences in economic systems or differences in operations of enterprises among economic systems.[125] International economic legal institutions need interface mechanisms to 'allow different economic systems to trade together harmoniously'.[126] International trade rules regulating subsidies and state enterprises are designed as a central piece of an interface mechanism to ensure smooth trading relationships. The main problem is that the current legal framework is not suitable to ease, let alone to solve, conflicts caused by the resurgence of the state as an economic actor. There is a growing perception that WTO law is neither conceptually coherent nor practically effective in tackling heterodox institutional forms like China's state capitalism. Also, absent reforms, multilateral trade rules will not measure up to the challenges states have to address in the post-Covid-19 world. Suffice here to recall that WTO rules do not apply to subsidies related to trade in services, and, since the ASCM provisions on the so-called 'green light' (permitted) subsidies expired in 2000, there is no multilateral regime on the use of industrial subsidies for research and development, compliance with environmental regulations and assistance to disadvantaged regions.

## V. CONCLUDING REMARKS

The rise (or return) of state enterprises is a complex phenomenon, which reflects, among other things, the new role of developing countries, a shift in emphasis of the global economy, and, arguably, a reconsideration of the role of the state in the economy impelled by the Covid-19 pandemic also in western economies. Armed with the acknowledgement that the state may abuse their sovereign right to organise their economic activities by eluding specific international rules through state entities, and that, at the same time, unbalanced scale of regulation may disincentive institutional variety and experimentation, this chapter contributes to the ongoing discussion about the regulation of state enterprises in IEL by elucidating the problems faced by private companies and States when confronting the commercial and financial operations of such entities, particularly when such entities are involved in cross-border business and investment.

[125] The 'interface' notion in international economic law was first suggested by the late professor John H Jackson in 1978. The concept was originally mentioned in a conference held at the Airlie House on July 21st and 22nd, 1978 under the sponsorship of the Departments of State and the Treasury of the United States. See D Wallace, *Interface one: conference proceedings on the application of U.S. antidumping and countervailing duty laws to imports from state-controlled economies and state-owned enterprises* (Institute for International and Foreign Law 1980).

[126] JH Jackson, *The World Trading System: Law and Policy of International Economic Relations*, 2nd edn (Cambridge, MIT Press 1997) 248.

# 2

# *State Capitalism, 'Normal' Capitalism and Other Capitalisms? A Discreet Place of the State in Neoliberal International Investment Law*

JOSEF OSTŘANSKÝ

## I. INTRODUCTION

RECENT TRANSFORMATIONS IN the global economy that are manifested, among others, in the increased role of the state in administering, directing, and organising global capital accumulation have led to labelling our times as an era of new state capitalism.[1] More specifically, various forms of state-led development forms such as sovereign wealth funds (SWFs), state-owned enterprises (SOEs), investment screening, and renewal of industrial policies have mushroomed across the world, both in the Global South and North, on a historical scale. These new forms contributed to the growing integration of state-controlled capital into the global networks of production, finance, infrastructure, and corporate ownership.[2] The main narrative against which these complex developments have been portrayed is the geopolitical stand-off between the rising China and the West – the new Cold War.[3] In less loaded terms, the narrative has been that of an emergence of a new 'alternative' model indirectly challenging the Western model of liberal economy. Besides the purchase of this narrative at the level of public and policy discourse, the scholarly framing of new state capitalism especially in international law literature often

[1] I Alami and others, 'Geopolitics and the 'New' State Capitalism', (2021) Geopolitics, Forum Article, accessible at: doi.org/10.1080/14650045.2021.1924943 (last accessed 7 October 2021).

[2] ibid.

[3] Eg, I Bremmer, *The End of the Free Market: Who Wins the War between States and Corporations?* (New York, Penguin, 2010); CA McNally, 'The challenge of refurbished state capitalism: Implications for the global political economic order,' (2013) 6 *DMS – Der Moderne Staat* 33.

relies on problematic binaries such as liberal/illiberal, state/market, democratic/non-democratic, commercial/political etc.[4] Not only these binaries reflect unspoken normative hierarchies privileging idealised historic institutional forms prevailing in the North, they also hide from the view the ways in which the state and its institutions have been involved in the construction of global capitalism that had been prevalent before the advent of new 'state capitalist' forms in the twenty-first century; a form of global capitalism that reflected the tensions and contradictions accompanying the Western global economic expansion as well as tensions within social relations at the national level in the North during the twentieth century.

In this chapter, I want to take an issue with one aspect of the way international investment law (IIL) scholarship relates to the emergence of something it calls state capitalism: the relationship between the state and capitalism. Drawing on the intellectual history of IIL, critical state theory, and global political economy, this chapter problematises a common conception of 'state capitalism' in IIL discourses that insists on the view that particular parameters of the state-market interaction are normalcy whereas others are exceptional, anomalous, and pathological. By shedding light on how modern IIL relied on particular modes of state intervention, the chapter shows that contrasting 'normal' capitalism with 'new state capitalism' produces important epistemological, political, and analytical effects.[5] Specifically, the framing of 'normal' or 'liberal' versus 'state' capitalism is grounded in the view that 'normal' capitalism is depoliticised and the state, or political, as opposed to economic or commercial logic, plays little or no role in it.[6] This assumption, first, obscures the historical and existing alignments of the state and capital in the liberal epicentre of global capitalism as

[4] C Cutler, 'Artifice, ideology and paradox: the public/private distinction in international law' (1997) 4 *Review of International Political Economy* 261.

[5] One should note that the interest in the emergence of state capitalism in IIL scholarship has been so far largely oblivious to the immensely rich literature on the varieties of capitalism that have been burgeoning in comparative political economy since the 1990s. See, eg, GM Hodgson, 'Varieties of capitalism and varieties of economic theory' (1996) 3 *Review of International Political Economy* 3, 380; PA Hall and D Soskice, (eds), *Varieties of Capitalism: The Institutional Foundations of Comparative Advantage* (Oxford, OUP, 2001); Coates, *Models of Capitalism: Growth and Stagnation in the Modern Era* (Oxford, Polity Press, 2000); W Streeck and K Yamamura (eds), *The Origins of Nonliberal Capitalism: Germany and Japan in Comparison* (Ithaca, Cornell University Press, 2002); W Streeck and K Yamamura (eds), *The End of Diversity? Prospects for German and Japanese Capitalism* (Ithaca, Cornell University Press, 2003); A Nölke (ed), *Multinational Corporations from Emerging Markets: State Capitalism 3.0* (Basingstoke, Palgrave Macmillan, 2014); C Hay, 'Does capitalism (still) come in varieties?' (2020) 27 *Review of International Political Economy* 2, 302.

[6] The canonical texts in the varieties of capitalism scholarship, such as Hall and Soskice (n 5), have been also criticised for positing as a privileged type the 'liberal market economy' that they naively portray as institutionally-light, as if it came straight out of neo-classical economics textbooks, and in this sense appears as a one-dimensional caricature. This hides from the view that empirically and historically, state institutions played crucial role in the construction of the really existing liberal market economies. See Hay (n 5) 312; C Howell, 'Review: Varieties of Capitalism: And Then There Was One?' (2003) 36 *Comparative Politics* 103, 119.

well as elsewhere. This is to say that all historically existing capitalism relied on the state in one way or another. Second, it delegitimises the emergence of alternative conceptions of international investment governance in the mainstream discourses. Third, it contributes to the strengthening of institutional and political power of specific politico-economic actors that already have access to the knowledge-creating discourse, institutional avenues for policy-making, and economic resources, and more broadly delegitimises the entering of new and powerful actors into the competitive capitalist world order. Finally, if state capitalism describes various modes of state intervention that appear not only in the emerging large economies, such as China, but also in the Global North, especially after the global economic crisis, there may be an issue with the analytical value of the concept of state capitalism itself.[7]

In the first part of the chapter, I clarify some of the conceptual issues that often attend discussions about the state, market, and capitalism in conventional IIL scholarship. Next, analysing the intellectual history of modern IIL by focusing on the thought system of an influential group of thinkers that are often referred to as neo- or ordo-liberals, I flesh out how the state has been indispensable in actualising this distinctively neoliberal form of capitalism. Then, I briefly draw out the parameters of the state and state intervention sanctioned by the modern practice of IIL that is closely inspired by the neoliberal thought system. In the final part of the chapter, I put the institutional and discursive parameters of this neoliberal IIL against the transformations of global capitalism accompanying the emergence of 'state capitalism' in the early twenty-first century. By way of conclusion, I suggest reframing the debate about state capitalism in IIL that offers novel avenues for research that are more productive in explaining the role of investment law and the state in the (re)organisations of the world economy. Importantly, however, I will neither attempt to define the concept of state capitalism in this chapter, nor discuss its various conceptions that have emerged in scholarship.[8]

## II. THE STATE AND CAPITALISM IN THE INTELLECTUAL UNIVERSE OF INTERNATIONAL INVESTMENT LAW: THE STATE AND THE INVESTOR VERSUS THE STATE AND CAPITALISM

The relationship between the state and capital in IIL, although rarely problematised in conventional literature, is generally considered as a relationship of antagonism or, in more accommodating terms, as a relationship of juxtaposition.

[7] 'I.e. describes much, explains nothing.' I Alami and A Dixon, 'State Capitalism(s) Redux? Theories, Tensions, Controversies' (2020) 24 *Competition & Change* 70, 71.

[8] Although, as may be implicit already, I am in agreement with Alami and Dixon that 'state capitalism, as it is currently deployed in much of the literature, does not bring 'recognizability', even less 'clarity', to the seemingly more visible role of the state across the world capitalist economy. […] Consequently, […] at this stage, the analytical value of the concept is weak.' Alami, Dixon (n 7) 72.

Indeed, most of the modern accounts legitimating the existing IIL regime frame the relationship between the state and the investor in a mutually supporting manner. As one of the most used IIL textbooks states:

> Investment treaties do not cast the interests and benefits of the host state and of the investor in an antithetic mode; instead, the motivation underlying such treaties assumes that the parties share a joint purpose. In this sense, it would be alien to the nature of an investment treaty to contrast the interests of the host state and of the foreign investor as opposed to each other. The mode and spirit of investment treaties is to understand the two interests as mutually compatible and reinforcing, held together by the joint purpose of an implementation of the investment consistent with the business plan of the investor and the legal order of the host state.[9]

Judge Schwebel praises the emergence of investor-state arbitration[10] as an ultimate progress due to its capacity to restrain the state: 'entitlement to international arbitration is one of the most progressive developments in the procedure of international law of the past 50 years, indeed in the whole history of international law. *It is consistent with the development of international human rights, including the right to own property, and with the dethroning of the State from its status as the sole subject of international law*.'[11] Similarly, Jan Paulsson, one of the most prominent international investment lawyers of the past three decades, casts the relationship between the investor and the state in a mutual supportive manner, singling out instead 'bad investors', as a pathology, to blame for potential problems related to the regulation of foreign investment through IIL:

> It is a serious mistake to focus on the opposition between investor and host State. The true dividing line goes within the community of investors; there are good investors and bad investors. Good investors are there for the long haul, and want to make a decent return, as is understood by everyone from the beginning. In order to merit that reward, they expect that they will be held to making a real contribution, which they are happy for anyone to evaluate. Their enemy is not the host State, because they have shared interests, but the bad investor, a dubious operator who wants to make a quick buck, getting vast profits for shoddy goods, procuring signatures on all sorts of opaque documents, contracts, amendments and certificates designed as a legal cover for poor performance – or worse. The bad investor creates a climate of suspicion and despair which also harms good investors.[12]

[9] R Dolzer and C Schreuer, *The Principles of International Investment Law*, 2nd edn (Oxford, OUP, 2012) 24 (emphasis added).

[10] I recognise that the ISDS acronym possibly encapsulates other dispute settlement mechanisms but for the sake of brevity and due to its prevalence in public discourse, I use it throughout the chapter to denote investor-state treaty-based arbitration.

[11] S Schwebel, 'In Defence of Bilateral Investment Treaties' (2015) 31 *Arbitration International* 181, 186 (emphasis added).

[12] J Paulsson, 'The Power of States to Make Meaningful Promises to Foreigners' (2010) 1 *Journal of International Dispute Settlement* 341, 351.

However, the fact that interests of the state and the investor are portrayed in terms of mutual convergence does not tell us much about the relationship between the state and capitalism which the mainstream scholarship assumes and reproduces. Even if one takes the above propositions at their face value, it is evident that the interests of the state and capital (personified in the foreign investor) have not been historically always aligned. If this were so, serious questions about the function of investment treaties would arise. The assertion of the mutual compatibility of interests is better understood as a normative or ideological proposition. The reproduction of the mutual supportive interests between the states and investors can be viewed as an instance of 'ideology of mutuality' in the recent decades prevalent.[13] In line with her earlier work, Susan Marks uses the term ideology to denote the rhetorical and other symbolic processes that help to sustain prevailing privilege and making it seem justified and legitimate.[14] Writing at the end of the first decade of the twenty-first century, at the dawn of the global financial and economic crisis, she observes that in international law, as well as in international politics, and even in our daily lives:

> [T]he *Zeitgeist* is surely all about mutual advantage. Our talk is of 'win-win', 'good for the planet, good for you', and 'a rising tide lifts all boats'. We study techniques of 'principled negotiation', 'mutual gains bargaining', and 'creative collaboration'. Synergies, interdependence, and teamwork are our abiding preoccupations, and when someone claims to discern a 'zero-sum' game, we say: try harder, there is always some angle from which everyone can be shown to be better off.[15]

Marks reminds us that, while the ebb and flow of disarming critiques of capitalism by transformations and co-optations into new social forms and discourses always breeds the necessity and ground for a fresh critique, any claims about mutual supportiveness must be counterposed against 'the critique of a distribution of advantages which is systematically asymmetrical'.[16]

Fast forward a little more than a decade, various contestations of the mainstream narrative about win-win globalisation are seen everywhere one looks.[17] And while IIL practice and scholarship have become more receptive to these, as the current volume attests, our understanding of the type of state and capitalism

[13] S Marks, 'Exploitation as an International Legal Concept', in S Marks (ed), *International Law on the Left: Re-examining Marxist Legacies* (US, Cambridge University Press, 2008) 281, 302–5.

[14] ibid 303. This framework draws on the Marxist tradition of ideology critique. Note that ideology is not used here as a descriptor of a set of political preferences, which is the most common usage of the term. For a recent work that uses ideology in this iteration as a set of more or less cohesive ideas, see Voeten, *Ideology and International Institutions* (New Jersey, Princeton University Press, 2021). For a more detailed discussion on the use of ideology critique in international law, see typically S Marks, *The Riddle of All Constitutions* (Oxford, OUP, 2003).

[15] Marks (n 13) 303–4.

[16] Note that Marks emphasises that ideology does not involve falsehood, but rather it conceals and masks important aspects of reality. ibid 305.

[17] See recently, A Roberts and N Lamp, *Six Faces of Globalization* (Cambridge, MA, Harvard University press, 2021).

supported by IIL operates still as a more or less taken-for-granted idea than as an object of inquiry that requires unpacking and problematisation.

The fact that modern IIL scholarship portrays the state and the investor in a mutually supportive way, while at the same time supposing that the market is inherently a domain reserved for private (ie non-state) investment activities operating according to the supposedly 'commercial' logic may appear as running counter to my argument that linking the state and capitalism is a feature integral to modern IIL. However, it is precisely this discursive, or ideological, position which conceals the myriad of ways in which the state has been indispensable to IIL and the twentieth century global capitalism. And as I explain below, these ways go much beyond the obvious understanding of the state as the subject of international law that concluded investment treaties, that is endowed with regulatory powers, and is a respondent in ISDS.

To unpack the ways in which the state is crucial for this 'normal' capitalism, we must start by noting that capitalism is not the same thing as the economy or the market, although these terms are often used somewhat interchangeably in common parlance and liberal theorising. In fact, it is close to impossible to productively discuss capitalism without engaging with the Marxist tradition of political economy. It was Marx who first sought to understand why commodity production and exchange proliferated in Western societies during the nineteenth century, and why social relations of production, exchange, and distribution appear to us as relations between things.[18] In this sense, the very concept of the 'economy' or 'market' as a separate sphere of social interaction is a distinctively capitalist feature. As opposed to the economy and market, capitalism is a historically specific type of social organisation characterised by a generalised mode of production, which is commodity production.[19] In this sense, the state and capitalism are appraised as social relations.[20]

Empirically, the capitalist mode of production comes in various social formations, is expressed in diverse institutional arrangements, social and legal norms, and discursive and ideational frameworks.[21] The state under capitalism may assume various roles vis-à-vis the economy at different historical periods and geographical locations, but generally it will provide institutions, discourses, and practices that allow for reproduction of capitalist social relations and create conditions for capital accumulation. In other words, the portrait of the state and

[18] The very first phrase in Capital, Volume I is the following: 'The wealth of those societies in which the capitalist mode of production prevails, presents itself as an immense accumulation of commodities […].' 1.

[19] See, eg, EM Wood, 'Historical Materialism and the Specificity of Capitalism', in EM Wood (ed), *Democracy against Capitalism: Renewing Historical Materialism* (Cambridge, CUP, 1995) 17; R Albritton, M Itoh, R Westra and A Zuege (eds), *Phases of Capitalist Development: Booms, Crises and Globalizations* (Basingstoke, Palgrave Macmillan, 2001); traditionally K Marx, *Capital: A Critique of Political Economy* (1977, originally published 1867).

[20] B Jessop, *The Future of the Capitalist State* (Oxford, Polity Press, 2002).

[21] The literature mentioned in note 4 throws some of these differences into relief.

investor in terms of mutuality, first, does not tell us much about the relationship between the state and capitalism that IIL assumes, and, second, it can be considered as discursive intervention in an ideological mode legitimating the extant social and legal arrangements.

If the interests of the state and capital do not always align, which is an empirical fact, and investment treaties are meant to make them compatible, this suggests that only a state with certain parameters is sanctioned by IIL. Furthermore, it hints at the necessity of the state for the realisation of investment projects, ie for capital accumulation. Thus, for our further assessment of the relationship between IIL, the state, and capitalism(s), we must note, with Gonzalez-Vicente, that 'a proper assessment of state capitalism needs to start from the recognition that all capitalism is statist'.[22] Additionally, 'it is not sufficient to look at state capitalism in isolation, but instead how it is entangled with wider-held beliefs and knowledge systems'.[23] The question that then arises is: what type of the state is characteristic for the material and ideational universe of modern IIL? The answer to that question in most cases will be that it is a characteristically neoliberal state.[24]

The emergence of this version of the state, however, has been neither an historical accident nor natural progress. This vision of the state, society, and the market can be traced back to a specific historic period and specific group of thinkers who deployed their ideas as a reaction to what they perceived as urgent problems to be addressed. And, as I will discuss in the final part of the chapter, the emergence of new forms of state capitalism that do not comport to the neoliberal model can be viewed as different ways of creating conditions for capital accumulation; just not those that necessarily favour the same fractions of global capital but rather those that strengthen new entrants in the competitive world order.

[22] R Gonzalez-Vicente, 'The Visible Hand of the Market: Emerging Economies, State Capitalism and the Global Realignment of Capitalist Political Power', in Alami and others (n 1) 6.

[23] IA Medby, 'Performing the State, Performing Capitalism', in Alami, Dixon (n 7) 21.

[24] The term neoliberalism is often considered as analytically vague. In this chapter, however, I do not refer to it as an analytical category, but instead as a particular thought system, political project, and governance practices associated with a varied group of intellectuals coalescing around the cities of Freiburg, Geneva, and Chicago, all members of the Mont Pelerin Society, whose intellectual production and political campaigning from the mid-twentieth century onwards have been documented as leaving a significant impact on public policies and discourses. Approaching neoliberalism as a political project, we can draw out its characteristic features that distinguish it from the previous and upcoming governance approaches. While in terms of economic policies there are differences between the Chicago-style neoliberals (eg Friedman, Buchanan) and German and Austrian ordoliberals (eg Hayek, Röpke, Rüstow, Müller-Armack, Heilperin, Erhardt), for the purposes of this chapter, which is their thoughts about the state and law, I band them together under an admittedly somewhat arbitrary banner of neoliberalism. For a more detailed discussion see P Mirowski and D Plehwe (eds), *The Road to Mont Pelerin: The Making of the Neoliberal Thought Collective* (Cambridge, MA, Harvard University Press, 2009); W Bonefeld, *The Strong State and The Free Economy* (London, Rowman & Littlefield International, 2017); Q Slobodian, *The Globalists: The End of Empire and the Birth of Neoliberalism* (Cambridge, MA, Harvard University Press, 2018); P Dardot and C Laval, *The New Way of the World: On Neoliberal Society* (London, Verso Books, 2014).

## III. THE INTELLECTUAL ORIGINS OF MODERN INTERNATIONAL INVESTMENT LAW

Intellectual resources on which modern IIL draws are varied, but a diverse group of neoliberal thinkers stands out the most in the comprehensiveness of their politico-economic thought as well as in the impact of their ideas. Intellectuals like Friedrich Hayek, Wilhelm Röpke, Alexander Rüstow, Alfred Müller-Armack, Michael Heilperin and others, often associated with the Mont Pelerin Society and the so-called Freiburg school of ordoliberalism, and to a lesser extent their American counterparts of Chicago, played a pivotal role in shaping the state and international organisations' policies which eventually led to what we now consider modern IIL. These intellectuals directly and indirectly shaped influential legal documents such as the Abs-Shawcross Draft, the OECD Draft Convention on the Protection of Investment Abroad, the ICSID Convention, as well as foreign investment policy in Germany and Switzerland, two states that pioneered the form and content of modern bilateral investment treaties.

Scholars who recently devoted significant efforts to document the neoliberals' impact on the IIL project and cognate fields of international economic governance, like Tzouvala, Slobodian, Bonefeld, Perrone, and Whyte, note that the main difference between the classical liberals of the nineteenth century and the twentieth century neoliberals is that the former believed in the natural balance created through free exchange in the market for which a non-interfering state in the spirit of laissez-faire is required.[25] The latter, on the other hand, replaced the emphasis on free exchange by the centrality of generalised competition which must be, in contradistinction to classical liberalism, imposed and maintained by the state.[26]

> Just as a free economic system needs a market police, with strong state authority for its protection and maintenance – in complete contradiction to the views of *laissez-faire* liberalism – so is the same state intervention necessary in other spheres of economic life – for economic as well as for non-economic reasons. A strong and independent state is the prime condition in every case.[27]

[25] Bonefeld (n 24); Slobodian (n 24); N Tzouvala, 'The Ordo-Liberal Origins of Modern International Investment Law: Constructing Competition on a Global Scale', in J Haskell and A Rasulov (eds), *New Voices and New Perspectives in International Economic Law: European Yearbook International Economic Law* (Cham, Springer nature, 2020) 37; N Tzouvala, 'Neoliberalism as Legalism', in B Golder and D McLoughlin (eds), *The Politics of Legality in a Neoliberal Age* (London, Taylor and Francis, 2017) 116; J Whyte, *The Morals of the Market: Human Rights and the Rise of Neoliberalism* (London, Verso Books, 2019); NM Perrone, *Investment Treaties and Legal Imagination: How Investors Play by Their Own Rules* (Oxford, OUP, 2021).

[26] Perrone's account, however, downplays the political purchase of neoliberals' ideas for the advent of modern IIL. I take issue with his position both at the level of historiography as well as analytically in Ostřanský, 'Beyond Legal Imagination: Nicolas M Perrone, *Investment Treaties and the Legal Imagination: How Investors Play by their Own Rules* (Oxford, OUP, 2021) – Review Essay' (forthcoming) in LE Sachs, L Johnson and J Coleman (eds), *Yearbook of International Investment Law & Practice 2020* (Oxford, OUP, 2020).

[27] Rüstow, 'General Sociological Causes of Economic Disintegration and Possibilities of Reconstruction', Appendix to W Röpke, *International Economic Disintegration* (1942) 281. It was Rüstow who apparently coined the term neoliberalism in 1938 in opposition to von Mises, whom he

As Whyte puts it, neoliberals promoted 'a strong security state [...] so as to protect the market and enforce the morals of the market across the globe'.[28]

The strong state, however, must be limited in its intervention precisely to 'a market facilitating, enabling and embedding policy, which, in the face of the destructive sociological and moral effects of the free economy [contra classical *laissez-faire* liberals], has to be pursued relentlessly to sustain and maintain the free economy'.[29] This means avoiding the state be 'weakened' by the demands of particular interests, especially in terms of wealth distribution policies,[30] the welfare state, and other social equality demands.[31]

A corollary to the requirement of the strong state enforcing the competitive market relations was the neoliberals' general apprehension of democracy and mass politics.[32] The vivid memory of the failures of the Weimar Republic, advent of the National Socialism in Germany, horrors of the World War II, and the attending economic depression (or disintegration), were all to the ordo-liberal thinkers such as Walter Eucken, Alexander Rüstow, Wilhelm Röpke, Gottfried Haberler, Peter Bauer and Alfred Müller Armack, linked causally to the rise of mass democracy *and* the welfare state, such that they called for a strong state to curtail democracy as a precondition for the liberal economy.[33] Their convictions only grew stronger with the dawn of decolonisation and the newly independent states' demands for a more equitable and just global economic governance, such as the NIEO movement and various efforts to regulate MNCs at the international level.[34] This also suggests that the ideas which framed the neoliberal

'called a paleo-liberal because of his seemingly unerring belief in the natural capacity of the market to self-regulate itself [sic]. Rüstow and other ordoliberals rejected laissez-faire as a theological idea.' Bonefeld (n 24) 11.

[28] Whyte (n 25) 32.

[29] Bonefeld (n 24) 7. *cf* on the balance between liberal market and institutional innovation, ch 1, in this volume.

[30] I prefer to use the term wealth distribution, instead of the more common term redistribution, for the latter suggests that the state is redistributing an already naturally existing and ready-made wealth, which is first being maximised through essentially private initiative and industry. Yet, due to the role of state in the creation and maintenance of wealth through law, monetary policy etc, the suggestion of property, money, economy or wealth beyond the law and state is difficult to conceive, yet it is habitually taken for granted by both classical and neoliberals. See, eg, McCluskey, 'Against the Economic Pie: How 'Redistribution' Limits Political Economic Analysis', LPE Blog (29 March 2019), at lpeblog.org/2019/03/27/against-the-economic-pie-how-redistribution-limits-political-economic-analysis/.

[31] Note that the concerns to which the neoliberals reacted were of a very different kind that the current advent of state direction and control of hybrid forms such as SOEs and SWFs.

[32] W Brown, *Undoing The Demos: Neoliberalism's Stealth Revolution* (New York, Zone Books, 2015); J Bair, 'Taking Aim at the New International Economic Order', in P Mirowski and D Plehwe (eds), *The Road to Mont Pelerin: The Making of the Neoliberal Thought Collective* (Cambridge, MA, Harvard University press) 347; Tzouvala (n 25) 9.

[33] Bonefeld (n 24) 9. Particularly Haberler and Bauer were later active in the discussions related to and campaigns against the NIEO, and argued vehemently against the economic policies the NIEO had represented, especially foreign aid. See Bair (n 32).

[34] While in conventional IIL literature of the last 20-30 years, the NIEO has been portrayed as a radical economic programme, its economic pillars represented more of continuity with at the time prevailing Keynesian paradigm, although the fact that the Keynesian agenda was then being transposed to the international level could be considered as a rupture with the existing international economic governance at the time. See Bair (n 32) 351.

'counter-revolution in development economics' that have dominated the development discourse from the 1980s onwards had their origins in a much earlier period than is usually thought.[35]

Generally speaking, the idea of the state that neoliberal thinkers propounded is the 'framing of competition [as] a political task [that] defines the liberal state as a strong state. The purpose of the strong state is the "policing of the market order." [...] It means also, and importantly so, the policing of the *social* order, including the ethical, moral and normative frameworks of individual behaviour.'[36]

For the purposes of IIL, the neoliberal state must, therefore, retain *political* power to *depoliticise* market relations and instil and maintain the freedom to compete. The state's capacity to police the market 'depends on its independence from society, and thus on its strength to neutralise mass democracy'.[37] For this, the right institutions, rules, practices, and discourses are necessary. International law and adjudication appeared as the ideal contenders to do the heavy lifting.[38] International law due to its power to disenfranchise potential democratic developments that may disrupt the competitive order within a particular state; adjudication for its potential to mask an essentially political project of neoliberalism as depoliticised and disinterested application of legal rules, and thus legitimise it.

### A. The Prominence of Judicialisation, Appeal of Depoliticisation, and Disappearance of Labour

From the 1970s onwards, especially in the North, the state has been gradually reoriented in a manner in which issues traditionally perceived as questions of political contestation moved to the area where they are to be solved according to legal rules enforced through judicialised dispute settlement mechanisms.[39] Modern discourses on IIL are generally fixated on the role of dispute settlement and the virtue of the rule of law.[40] The dispute settlement preoccupation

[35] Bair (n 32) 357.

[36] Bonefeld (n 24) 14 (emphasis original).

[37] ibid 47.

[38] Tzouvala (n 25) 116.

[39] See Slobodian (n 24); T John, *The Rise of Investor-State Arbitration* (Oxford, OUP, 2018); Tzouvala (n 25); D Kennedy, 'Law in Global Economy: Now You See It, Now You Don't', in F Kjaer (ed), *The Law of Political Economy* (Cambridge, CUP, 2020) 127.

[40] See, eg, S Schill, 'In Defense of International Investment Law', (2017) Amsterdam Law School Legal Studies Research Paper No 2017-10; R Dolzer, 'The Impact of International Investment Treaties on Domestic Administrative Law' (2005) 37 *NYU Journal of International Law and Politics* 953; S Schill, 'International Investment Law and Comparative Public Law – An introduction', in S Schill (ed), *International Investment Law and Comparative Public Law* (Oxford, OUP, 2010); V Zivkovic, 'Pursuing and Reimagining the International Rule of Law Through International Investment Law' [2019] *Hague JRoL;* R Echandi, 'What Do Developing Countries Expect from the International Investment Regime?' in JE Alvarez et al. (eds), *The Evolving International Investment Regime: Expectations, Realities, Options* (US, Oxford University Press, 2011) 3, 13.

in IIL discourses conceals the fact that this reorientation to the detriment of mass politics has been occurring at all. It also obscures the transformation of the state's roles in this process.[41] If the resolution of investment disputes is posited as the major issue to be addressed by IIL, a discourse thus framed screens off the ways in which the emphasis on dispute settlement rearranges social relations and impacts traditional political channels, mass politics, and democracy. At the same time, this professional and disciplinary preoccupation removes from the view the transformations which the state has undergone in relation to the historically developed social antagonisms between capital and labour, and their forms against the backdrop of the drive to capitalist accumulation.[42]

In international economic law generally, and IIL specifically, it is the idea of depoliticisation and the rule of law, which have then gained a nigh universal acclaim and an undeniable normative priority in the milieu of professional and academic international lawyers.[43] However, the idea of governing global economic and investment relations through a vehicle of international legal rules enforced via judicialised dispute settlement procedures has not come from nowhere. As mentioned above, it emerged as a reaction to complex interconnected trends and events, such as decolonisation, the ascendance of the welfare state in the North, increased salience and importance of mass politics, demands of the states in Asia, Africa, and Latin America for more equitable structures, institutions, and processes of international economic governance to replace the inherited unjust and oppressive colonial vestiges in the second half of the twentieth century.

The countervailing forces with an interest in protecting capital either from the governments in the South with their calls for control over their natural resources and wealth, or from the governments in the North with their democratic accountability to their constituencies' demands for full employment, just wage, and social security frameworks, viewed these events as economic disintegration and a threat to the global economic order, freedom, or, worse yet, the 'Western civilisation.'[44] It is in reaction to these events that the judicialised

[41] For a discussion on an analogous process within international trade law, drawing on similar strands of critical state theory see Tzouvala (n 25).

[42] See Tzouvala's discussion on the state and law transformations towards and then away from the Keynesian welfare state and their impact on the developments in international economic law, ibid 126–33.

[43] For early interventions see mostly A Broches, 'Conciliation and Arbitration of Investment Disputes', Address to World Conference on World Peace through Law, June 30-July 6, 1963, Athens, Greece, 5, at pubdocs.worldbank.org/en/162881399487976375/wbg-archives-1651418.pdf; I Shihata, 'Towards a Greater Depoliticisation of Investment Disputes: The Role of ICSID and MIGA' (1986) 1 *ICSID Rev-FILJ* 1.

[44] Tzouvala notes that neoliberal thinkers of the 1950s and 1960s treated often the concepts or economic order, freedom, and the 'Western civilization' as synonymous, Tzouvala (n 25) 43. The neoliberal thinkers were fairly aligned in viewing the welfare state in the North and the economic policies of the new states in the South as a same kind of threat to the economic order. Mises ironically wrote in 1952: 'If it is right for the British to nationalize the British coal mines, it cannot be wrong for the Iranians to nationalize the Iranian oil industry. If Mr. Attlee were consistent, he would have congratulated the Iranians on their great socialist achievement.' Röpke similarly quipped

version of IIL with its emphasis on depoliticisation of the investment relations as a virtue arose as a viable institutional strategy that was actively pursued and campaigned for.[45]

While in the area of international trade, the trend towards greater legalisation and judicialisation occurred formally in 1994 with the establishment of the WTO, and the boom of ISDS did not happen until the late 1990s, the political inception of the two disciplinarily and institutionally separate branches of international economic law can be traced to the events and processes taking hold from the end of 1970s and early 1980s. Indeed, the bilateral investment treaty programmes of the major capital exporting countries started taking shape during the decade of the 1980s.[46] The various regional projects of economic integration, most notably the EU, also gained speed during the same period.[47] This suggests that changes in the prevailing thinking and practices regarding economic and social policies and institutions went beyond regulation of foreign investment.

The notion of depoliticisation in IIL literature features two distinct understandings of the concept. Generally, we find a narrow understanding of depoliticisation, as an absence of the home state, an absence of diplomatic rows, interventions, and conflicts.[48] This depoliticisation argument is usually framed as a progress from the so-called gunboat diplomacy, by which colonial and imperial states used their military might to protect their economic interests abroad.[49] This conception has animated the vision of modern IIL held by many of the regime's founding fathers (indeed, the formative period of modern IIL is marked by a conspicuous absence of women) and finds its legal expression in Article 27 of the ICSID Convention.

As ISDS is presented as a progress from and juxtaposed against the unruly days of diplomatic interventions in favour of foreign capital,[50] this framing operates in an ideological mode too. The options of institutions regulating foreign

'the Mossadeqs appeal to the Atlees and the Bevans, who have inspired them with the idea of nationalization.' Quoted in Slobodian (n 24) 139. Coates's study shows that it was purposeful actions of employers in coordination with the state under Thatcher's government that turned Britain away from a traditionally mixed economy into a distinctively (neo)liberal political economy; Coates (n 5).

[45] See specifically Perrone (n 26).

[46] As is well-known the first BIT arbitration was initiated in 1987, *Asian Agricultural Products Ltd. v Republic of Sri Lanka*, ICSID Case No ARB/87/3. And the technique of advance consent was envisioned already by the drafters of the ICSID Convention, John (n 39).

[47] See, eg, European Commission, 'Completing the Internal Market', White Paper from the Commission to the European Council, COM(85) 310 (1985).

[48] For a classic text see Shihata (n 43); CH Schreur et al., *ICSID Convention: A Commentary*, 2nd edn (Cambridge, CUP, 2011) 416; more recently U Kriebaum, 'Evaluating Social Benefits and Costs of Investment Treaties: Depoliticization of Investment Disputes' (2018) 33 *ICSID Rev-FILJ* 14.

[49] See K Miles, *The Origins of International Investment Law: Empire, the Environment, and the Safeguarding of Capital* (Cambridge, CUP, 2014); K Miles, 'History and international law: Method and mechanism – empire and 'usual' rupture', in SW Schill, CJ Tams and R Hofmann (eds), *International Investment Law and History* (Cheltenham, Edward Elgar, 2018) 136.

[50] See typically Dolzer, Schreuer (n 9) 11–24.

investment disputes are dichotomously 'presented in terms of stark oppositions, in which actuality and its polar opposite appear as the only option.'[51] However, this account flattens the historical events leading to the advent of BITs. St John has documented that despite the later prevalence of the depoliticisation language in the conventional accounts of ISDS, most if not all of the government and international organisations officials involved in the drafting of ICSID actually did not understand ISDS as a replacement of other means of governance of investment relations, but rather as their complement.[52] In fact, as opposed to the international organisation officials who spearheaded the ICSID and later the BITs, capital-exporting governments as well as businesses were, in the early 1960s, equally if not more interested in the idea of investment insurance than in arbitration.[53] Most of the conventional IIL scholarship produced during the last 20 years thus ignores that, first, the judicialised dispute settlement was viewed by the architects of the modern IIAs system as one among many options to govern foreign investment relations,[54] and, second, the language of depoliticisation was much less prominent than the later literature suggests. More importantly, though, empirical research has shown that this is kind of depoliticisation simply did not happen anyways. Powerful states have often intervened in developing countries regardless investment treaties and arbitration.[55]

However, there is more to the idea of depoliticisation than simply an absence of diplomatic intervention.[56] Depoliticisation in a broader sense is understood as removing the matters of foreign investment from the reach of ordinary political channels.[57] The matters are moved from 'lowly politics' to a 'higher law'.[58] This understanding of depoliticisation can be broadly associated with the views

[51] Marks (n 14) 22.

[52] John (n 39) 68–109, 199. Puig argues that Ibrahim Shihata (ICSID Secretary General 1983–2000) stressed the depoliticisation role of the ICSID with particular vehemence, at times 'perhaps opportunistically.' 'Emergence and Dynamism in International Organizations: ICSID, Investor-State Arbitration, and International Investment Law' (2012) 44 *'Georgetown Journal of International Law* 531, 550.

[53] John (n 39) 99–108.

[54] By architects, here, I mean the state representatives and international organisations officials that concluded and promoted the traditional BITs. In the text, I often refer to intellectual forefathers or neoliberal thinkers, such as the Freiburg ordoliberals or Chicago neoliberals, whose ideas about international regulation of the global economy have served as an intellectual backdrop or inspiration for the actual architects. Yet, only some of these thinkers, such as Heilperin, dealt with international investment regulation directly, whereas others, such as Hayek and Röpke only more tangentially; Slobodian (n 24) 136–43

[55] G Gertz, S Jandhyala and LS Poulsen, 'Legalization, diplomacy, and development: Do investment treaties de-politicize investment disputes?' (2018) 107 *World Development* 239.

[56] See, eg, D Schneiderman, 'Revisiting the Depoliticisation of Investment Disputes', in KP Sauvant (ed), *Yearbook on International Investment Law and Policy, 2010–11* (New York, Oxford University Press, 2012) 693; M Paparinskis, 'The Limits of Depoliticisation in Contemporary Investor-State Arbitration' (2010) 3 *Select Proceedings of the European Society of International Law.*

[57] Schneiderman (n 56); more generally see P Fawcett at al. (eds), *Anti-Politics, Depoliticisation & Governance* (Oxford, OUP, 2017).

[58] Schneiderman (n 56) 694.

of Hayek, Röpke and other ordoliberals, who considered it necessity to protect the market economy by legal means.[59] Depoliticisation, hence, may be understood not merely as a concept, but as an institution-building project, whereby 'political and economic power should [...] be strictly circumscribed through an 'economic constitution' policed by strong independent institutions, such as constitutional court, an anti-trust commission and a legally independent central bank'.[60] And one may add, investment treaty tribunals and other international courts and tribunals.

The depoliticisation narrative in IIL, either in its narrow or broader understanding, is generally reserved to the debates about dispute settlement.[61] More recently, however, authors have pointed to other areas on which the depoliticisation rationale may bear. Perrone's discourse analysis of the UNCTAD's World Investment Reports, an important policy document used widely by national governments as a state-of-the-art reference, puts into sharp relief that this approach to governance dividing the rational and efficient markets from irrational and inefficient politics has permeated the UNCTAD reports throughout their history.[62] As the 2008 report puts it: 'Clear, transparent and well-enforced rules of conduct, grounded in law, are important for reducing the risk of political or popular backlashes [...].'[63]

Finally, an important corollary to the judicialisation and depoliticisation of investment relations is the reframing of capital-labour relations at the national level.[64] At the level of political discourse, the advent of neoliberal governance has been associated with recasting the concept of labour into a form of capital itself.[65] Labour has been transformed into an individualised entrepreneurial subject. The neoliberal intellectual framework *postulates* theoretical equality, or conflation, between capital and labour, treating the latter as capital itself, while it recognises the danger labour in reality poses to the laws of private property.[66]

[59] Whyte (n 25); Slobodian (n 24); D Schneiderman, 'Hayek's Dream: International Investment Law and the Denigration of Politics', at papers.ssrn.com/sol3/papers.cfm?abstract_id=3397624.

[60] M Wilkinson and H Lokdam, 'Law and Political Economy', LSE Law, Society and Economy Working Papers 7/2018.

[61] A typical example is CH Schreuer et al., *The ICSID Convention: A Commentary*, 2nd edn (Cambridge, CUP, 2010), para 416; also Shihata (n 43), Paparinskis (n 56).

[62] NM Perrone, 'UNCTAD's World Investment Reports 1991–2015: 25 Years of Narratives Justifying and Balancing Foreign Investor Rights', (2017) 19 *Journal of World Trade & Investment* 7.

[63] UNCTAD, World Investment Report (2008) 150.

[64] I expand the discussion on a class nature of IIL in a companion paper J Ostřanský, 'International Investment Law, the State, and the Making of Transnational Capitalist Class' (on file).

[65] I thank Ntina Tzouvala for highlighting this to me. Howell also notes that there is an assumption behind much of the variety of capitalism scholarship that the social relations that undergird capitalist political economies are fundamentally nonconflictual. He asks 'what is gained by redefining the ubiquitous workplace conflict between employers and workers as a coordination problem'. (n 6), 110–2. Critical political economy demonstrates that this assumption does not fit the reality of capitalist economic development. See, eg, Coates (n 5).

[66] It is interesting that Röpke, Rüstow, and Müller-Armack recognised the material plight of the proletariat of the inter-war period and denounced the capitalism of that period as a 'degenerate form of the market economy', which they considered, together with socialism, as a result of

To pacify this latent social conflict, it requires an *authoritarian* state as an independent power over society which depoliticises the socio-economic relations by violence if necessary. Authoritarian liberalism, a term used by Bonefeld to denote the neoliberal state theory, thus demands the strong state which polices capitalist economy as a political project, instead of a natural order.[67] The material security and freedom from want, which, for neoliberals, represents the false freedom, cannot be the preoccupation of the state. Instead, the strong state must instil the entrepreneurial spirit which is competitive, risk-taking, self-reliant, and self-responsible in all spheres of life as liberal social and moral policy.[68]

Bonefeld's analysis of the ordoliberal thought system shows that its conception of class (ie the ordoliberal 'problem of 'proletarianisation') is not material in character, let alone a manifestation of social relations. It is instead a psychological attitude. It is a problem of 'vitality, i.e., a non-economic, spiritual problem'.[69] The class conflict is thus recast as a conflict of psychological attitudes which must be tackled through social and moral policy that promotes enterprise as a character trait, and an alternative means of securing material subsistence through the promotion of property and self-reliance within family, community, and, in cases of thinkers like Müller-Armack, also Christian values.[70] Therefore, the class conflict for ordoliberals is not a function of material conditions grounded in the capital-labour relation characteristic of the capitalist mode of production. It is a psychological issue.

This understanding of capital-labour relations directly underpins the broader concept of depoliticisation in IIL, which relies on the force of the typical liberal distinction between the private and public sphere.[71] Whereby the economic is

laissez-faire liberalism. However, as they considered 'proletarianisation' as a problem of personality caused by classical liberalism (see above n 78), the ordoliberal strong state must supply the requisite moral foundation to instil the civilisation of individual responsibility. Bonefeld (n 24) 95–8. For an account of how this moral and social aspect of neoliberalism transformed the policies related to social reproduction in the recent decades see M Cooper, *Family Values: Between Neoliberalism and the New Social Conservatism* (New York, Zone Books, 2017); also Whyte (n 25); Dardot, Laval (n 24).

[67] Bonefeld (n 24) 50–1. Harvey also echoes Karl Polanyi's fear that the liberal, as well as neoliberal, utopian project could ultimately be sustained only by resort to authoritarianism, D Harvey, *A Brief History of Neoliberalism* (Oxford, OUP, 2005) 70. This view can be contrasted with the conventional varieties of capitalism literature – eg Hall, Soskice (n 5) – that, at the epistemological and normative levels, privileges a 'liberal market economy' model derived from broad-brush observations of institutional arrangements present at a given historical period in the US and UK through a lens of neo-classical economic theory.

[68] Bonefeld (n 24) 99.

[69] Röpke and Rüstow quoted in Bonefeld (n 24) 94. We can observe parallels with nowadays common public political discourses which treat poverty as a consequence of 'bad decisions' or 'lack of morale'. Although not grounded in the analysis of the neo(ordo)liberal thoughts, for an analysis of how the ideology of productivity, enterprise, and 'business' has materially transformed modern societies see D Markovits, *The Meritocracy Trap: How America's Foundational Myth Feeds Inequality, Dismantles the Middle Class, and Devours the Elite* (London, Penguin Books, 2019).

[70] Bonefeld (n 24) 103–10.

[71] C Cutler, *Private Power and Global Authority: Transnational Merchant Law in the global Political Economy* (Cambridge, CUP, 2012) speaks of 'the liberal art of separation', 57–8.

gradually assigned to the private sphere, thereby hollowing up the public sphere, the latter being traditionally considered as the place for democracy, politics, and deliberation on collective matters.[72] Additionally, the scaling up of political power to international institutions further helped to consolidate this neoliberal version of the state.[73] However, just as there is no clear boundary between commercial and political logics as an empirical matter, these conceptual binaries have symbolic, material, and legal consequences. I now turn to the brief discussion how the above discussed neoliberal intellectual framework finds expression in the institutional arrangements and legal practice of IIL.

## IV. A SNAPSHOT OF THE NEOLIBERAL STATE IN MODERN INTERNATIONAL INVESTMENT LAW

Consolidation of the world market during the twentieth century created states devoted to crafting of 'enabling environments' that lure mobile capital flows in.[74] The prevailing rationale for the conclusion of investment treaties by developing countries in the 1990s was, indeed, the belief they will bring in foreign investment, the latter understood as a recipe for economic development.[75] Historically, the state has played a central role in the quest for new markets according to two different logics: first, by a military and imperial quest; second, by creating global regulatory institutions that facilitate business mobility.[76]

Since the emergence of the neoliberal governance model in the 1980s, the state logic at the national level have become gradually associated with its market counterpart, through flexible regulations for capital, market competition in the provision of basic public goods, and extensive legal protections for owners of various assets.[77] And while the massive privatisations did reduce state direction of and control over market vehicles, the state and political power has been scaled up away from national political deliberations through international and transnational institutions, such as the WTO, World Bank, and investment arbitration.[78]

[72] UN Special Rapporteur on Extreme Poverty and Human Rights singled out the phenomenon of depoliticisation as one of the causes of poverty: '[T]he inability of pared-down Governments to exercise meaningful supervision, the difficulty of monitoring disparate private providers, *the removal of much economic decision-making from the purview of democratic contestation*, and the wide-ranging consequences of empowering profit-seeking corporate actors in what used to be the public sphere.' (26 Sep 2018, A/73/396), para 85 (emphasis added).

[73] See on the scaling up, eg S Pahuja, *Delocolizing International Law: Development, Growth, and the Politics of Universality* (Cambridge, CUP, 2011).

[74] T Carroll, R Gonzalez-Vicente and DSL Jarvis, 'Capital, Conflict and Convergence: A political understanding of neoliberalism and its relationship to capitalist transformation' (2019) 16 *Globalizations* 6, 778.

[75] See LNS Poulsen, *Bounded Rationality and Economic Diplomacy* (Cambridge, CUP, 2015).

[76] Gonzalez-Vicente (n 22) 7. See also Gindin and L Panitch, *Global Capitalism and American Empire* (Basingstoke, Palgrave Macmillan, 2003); T Ruskola, *Legal Orientalism: China, the United States, and Modern Law* (Cambridge, MA, Harvard University press, 2013).

[77] See K Pistor, *The Code of Capital* (New Jersey, Princeton University Press, 2019).

[78] See, eg, Slobodian (n 24); R Howse, 'From Politics to Technocracy – and Back Again: The Fate of the Multilateral Trading Regime' (2002) 96 *AJIL* 94; Perrone (n 26).

In line with the neoliberal project, the discursive rendering of modern IIL and its institutions presents the latter as rational and a-political, in juxtaposition to the state as political and irrational. This framing contributes to naturalising of the existing economic arrangements and portrays the state intervention in the market as exceptional and inherently suspicious. Due to its insistence on the liberal separation of the market and politics,[79] it removes from the view the fact that the private market interaction is premised on the state involvement at every turn, since the state and market power are always already deeply intertwined and co-constitutive.[80]

Space limitations do not allow me to provide a detailed analysis of legal materials underpinned by and reproducing this particular conception of a neoliberal state but the general contours of the state sanctioned by IIL can be gauged fairly accurately.[81] Arbitral decision-making, scholarship, and other legal materials point in the direction of the state that gives primacy to the individual and corporate economic actors in the questions of national economic ordering – most of IIL is based on the liberal state/individual dichotomy.[82] This state also presumes that private capital and individual enterprise is creative of public wealth and economic development, the latter being abstract and semantically vague concepts,[83] while state is generally 'interfering' in the private equilibrium. The political economy which underlies most of the current IIL practice thus projects a knee-jerk suspicion towards the state intervention that goes beyond market-inducement and correction of market failures.[84] It gives preference and protection to the property's purpose of wealth maximisation over other societal purposes of property.[85] It supports the state's maintenance of generalised competition.[86] It projects an idea of one-directional regulatory stability, i.e. it condones or is indifferent to regulatory changes that create possibilities for

[79] See EM Wood, 'The Separation of the 'economic' and the 'political' in capitalism', in EM Wood, *Democracy against Capitalism: Renewing Historical Materialism* (Cambridge, CUP, 1995) 19.

[80] I thank Umut Özsu for highlighting this for me. More generally, see Bonefeld (n 24).

[81] For reference to such an analysis see Ostřanský, 'The State's Regulatory Powers in International Investment Law', (PhD thesis, Graduate Institute of International and Development Studies 2017), Conclusion; J Ostřanský, 'From a Fortuitous Transplant to a Fundamental Principle of Law? The Doctrine of Legitimate Expectations and the Possibilities of a Different Law', in I Venzke and K Heller (eds), *Contingency and the Course of International Law* (Oxford, OUP, 2021) 426; Perrone (n 26).

[82] Slobodian speaks of the 'doubled world' of *imperium* and *dominium*, harking back to the intellectual forefathers of the current global economic governance, such as Hayek and Röpke; see Slobodian (n 24) ch 1.

[83] See A Leiter, 'The Silent Impact of the 1917 Revolutions on International Investment Law' (2017) 6 *ESIL Reflections* 10.

[84] Perrone documents how UNCTAD's narratives post-2008 crisis are more sensitive to the public regulation of investment for certain goals, but they still do not abandon the commodity conception of investment, let alone move towards the conception of investment which would reflect local preferences, Perrone (n 62).

[85] Perrone, 'The Emerging Global Right to Investment: Understanding the Reasoning Behind Foreign Investor Rights' (2017) 8 *JIDS* 673.

[86] Tzouvala (n 25).

investors' capital accumulation ('regulatory givings'), while it rejects regulatory changes that limit capital accumulation for the protection of other societal goals ('regulatory takings').[87] Concomitant to this view is an understanding of the state-investor relations as essentially transactional.[88] Finally, broader legalisation and formal adjudication are ideal institutional vehicles for enforcing this economic constitution; more specifically, a type of adjudication that is transnational in its practice and spirit, abstracting from local contexts, and is operated by people with a globalised outlook.[89]

We can see that the role of the state is certainly not passive or minimal, as the conventional wisdom often assumes, for it requires active measures on the state's part in order to put in place and safeguard legal infrastructure to facilitate market exchange, competition, and liberalisation of the market, both at the national as well as international levels.[90] The establishment of ISDS and institutional framework for its enforcement are thus important elements in the building of a neoliberal state.

If this is the conception of state undergirding the modern ISDS regime, the discourse of mutuality of state and capital interests suggests that anytime when the state deviates from the political economy sanctioned by IIL practice, the state is going rogue. From the perspective of capitalism as social relations, we should understand this situation as a temporal and spatial misalignment of the state and capital interests which requires intervention in order to re-establish specific conditions for capital accumulation. The final question this chapter turns to is how new state capitalist forms fit within this neoliberal IIL framework? Does it represent a threat to the neoliberal depoliticised economy leading to economic disintegration, as the prevailing discourse on state capitalism suggests? Can it be considered a realignment in favour of labour and the Global South more generally? Or does it rather represent new avenues for capital accumulation and reconfigurations within the global capitalist class?

## V. NEW STATE CAPITALISM IN NEOLIBERAL INTERNATIONAL INVESTMENT LAW?

Whereas the development of modern IIL can be understood and explained as an institutional reaction to the brewing capital-labour antagonisms in the North (mass democracy and the welfare state) as well as in relation to the

[87] Perrone (n 26), also A Rasulov, 'The empty circularity of regulatory takings: the legacy of a legal-realist critique for a 21st century context', in U Mattei and JD Haskell (eds), *Research Handbook on Political Economy and Law* (Cheltenham, Edward Elgar, 2016) 371; Ostřanský (n 81); Ostřanský (n 26); J Ostřanský 'An Exercise in Equivocation: A Critique of Legitimate Expectations as a General Principle of Law under the Fair and Equitable Treatment', in A Gattini, A Tanzi and F Fontanelli (eds), *General Principles of Law and International Investment Arbitration* (Brill, Leiden, 2018) 344.

[88] Perrone (n 26).

[89] C Cutler, 'Transformations in Statehood, the Investor- State Regime, and the New Constitutionalism' (2016) 23 *Indiana Journal of Global Legal Studies* 95; Perrone (n 26).

[90] See Perrone (n 62); Tzouvala (n 25).

South (decolonisation and the NIEO), the current anxiety about state capitalism is more likely driven by the emergence of new powerful fractions of capital supported by state institutions that are not easily at the disposal of the established fractions of global capital. It is evident that the challenge to the consolidated neoliberal transnational legal complexes such as IIL posed by the rise of market actors hailing from countries like China, with their considerable state backing, direction, and ownership are a different challenge than mass democracy movements and decolonisation. While the former developments threatened to disrupt the then existing inter-class dynamics at home and abroad by politically and institutionally empowering labour and the South, the present challenge to the traditional global capital is different in that it rather brings in new capitalist actors threatening the global capitalist incumbents. New state capitalism formalises economic power into new institutional complexes away from control of 'established fractions of transnational capital and are not entirely 'legible' in the globalist ideology espoused by neoliberal orthodoxy'.[91] The main point of friction between Western liberal capitalism and Chinese state capitalism may thus be intra-class frictions that represents transformation of the competitive world order.

A few examples may elucidate the point. Past US interventions used various means to secure and maintain the position of American capital abroad, ranging from military interventions, to conditionality, and the creation of multilateral institutions. The Chinese state focuses on subsidising and protecting Chinese capital with so far limited attempts at creating multilateral rules.[92] Chinese state capitalism is hence not viewed as threatening when China participates in the existing multilateral institutions or when it is active in functions that are habitually considered as non-market functions, such as welfare provision. It is perceived as threatening when it creates new institutional complexes that are at the disposal of Chinese domestic fractions of capital that are increasingly transnationalised. And it is precisely this market-oriented support that threatens the hegemony of traditional actors within the world market that is viewed as problematic.[93]

Thus, while Chinese SOEs may eschew short-term profit maximisation strategies in their approaches to capital accumulation, they undoubtedly act as capital in relation to labour and the environment.[94] Similarly, the goals of multilateral development banks sponsored by China are commercial,[95] even if they promote public-private partnerships and enter into co-financing deals

[91] Gonzalez-Vicente (n 22) 8.

[92] ibid 8. Think, for instance, of the vaunted flexibility of law and regulation along the Belt & Road Initiative, which eschews formal adjudication in favour of bilateral political negotiations and dispute prevention. See, eg, G Shaffer and H Gao, 'A New Chinese Economic Order?' (2020) 23 *JIEL* 3, 607.

[93] Gonzalez-Vicente (n 22) 8.

[94] ibid. Also B Apeldoorn, N De Graaff and H Overbeek, 'The reconfiguration of the global state–capital nexus' (2012) 9 *Globalizations* 4, 471.

[95] K Gallagher and A Irwin, 'China's Economic Statecraft in Latin America: Evidence from China's Policy Banks' (2015) 88 *Pacific Affairs* 1, 99.

with the established multilateral development banks, such as the case with the Asian Infrastructure Investment Bank.[96] If we compare these examples with the past alignments between Western capital and Western states, this suggests that Chinese state capitalism is at best a difference in format. It also suggests that what is 'new' about these forms of state control and direction is their orientation on capital accumulation and increased transnational outlook.[97]

Rather than viewing the prevailing neoliberal model as an opposite or distinct model from that of state capitalism, the latter is better viewed as a heuristic which sheds some light on recent transformations of the state reflective of rearrangements in the global market associated with the rise of China and other emerging economies.[98] 'The political hand of the market only *appears* more visible in the developing world because it challenges pre-established hierarchies and introduces new powerful actors into the competitive world order.'[99] No historically existing capitalism could reproduce without the state. As Harvey notes, this goes much beyond the capitalism's 'original sin' of accumulation by dispossession.[100] It is continuously present with different intensity in different spaces and at different times, through the creation of new rights to exploit nature, through recurrent privatisations, through the creation and protection of new financial assets and intellectual property rights, etc.[101]

What the above points make clear is that any comparison or analysis of different capitalist forms requires foregrounding of the temporal element in an analysis of any historic 'models' of capitalism. Various scholars in critical political economy stress that comparing various institutional arrangements outside of their historical contexts makes analyses of viability of any model of capitalism deeply unsatisfactory. Because they fail to account for the fact that capitalism as a system of social ordering based around generalised commodity production functions with episodic effectiveness, and its internal contradictions as well as exogenous shocks continuously transform the capitalist institutional forms.[102]

Changes over time in the effectiveness of different sets of political-economic arrangements are themselves products of changes in the underlying nature of

[96] G Gabusi, 'Global Standards in the Asian Infrastructure Investment Bank: The Contribution of the European Members' (2019) 10 *Global Policy* 4, 631.

[97] A Grosman, I Okhmatovskiy and M Wright, 'State control and corporate governance in transition economies: 25 Years on from 1989' (2016) 24 *Corporate Governance: An International Review* 3, 200, 202.

[98] Some of the literature on varieties of capitalism stresses the importance of state at key moments, for instance, by highlighting the regulatory role of the state in fuelling bank-based finance. See, eg, S Vitols, 'The Origins of Bank-Based and Market-Based Financial Systems: Germany, Japan, and the United States', in Streeck, Yamamura (n 5) 171. Importantly, Coates demonstrates that many of the institutional differences between national political economies in the West are due to distinct historically contingent developments within national capitalist fractions, such as the difference between the strength of industrial and financial capital in Germany and the UK respectively; (n 5) 177.

[99] Gonzalez-Vicente (n 22) 6.

[100] D Harvey, *The New Imperialism* (Oxford, OUP, 2005).

[101] See also Pistor (n 77).

[102] Coates (n 5) 233.

capitalist economic growth. Models based upon a major industrial policy role for the state eroded as the space for autonomous state action shrank, while corporatist models fell victim to the mobility of capital and the weakening of national labour movements. Thus, charting the rise and fall of each model of capitalism requires recognising the manner in which capitalism periodically transforms itself.[103]

The core of the discipline of IIL has been captured in the intellectual universe that appears universal while in fact it emerged as a particular vision of regulation of investment relations in a particular period of development of global capitalism. This intellectual universe casts the state into the role of a threat to the depoliticised competitive market order, while it conceals the necessity of a strong state in order to put in place the machinery that will oversee and enforce this particular vision of a capitalist economic order. A view that a neoliberal form of capitalism should be still viewed as necessarily statist helps explain, for instance, the typical retort by the proponents of ISDS responding to the critics of the investment treaty regime that if states were so dissatisfied with the regime, they would have changed it. If we see capitalist states as historically specific condensations of class relations that reflect past social struggles, instead of as willing monolithic subjects, we can understand why this has not happened.

Additionally, the conceptual tools that IIL utilises to deal with new state capitalist forms rely on the problematic binaries such as state/market, commercial/political, democratic/non-democratic. These concepts are treated as self-evident. But if one digs deeper, one realises that there is no clear-cut boundary between these logics. Although not speaking to legal scholarship, Alami and Dixon helpfully show the limitations of analysing the emergent state capitalist formations through these dichotomies:[104]

> Much scholarship tends to view the [(geo)politics/commercial binary] as a clear-cut dichotomy that traps the debate in the following question: is the emergence of the 'new' state capitalism driven by commercial or (geo)political logics? This forecloses the possibility that state capitalist transformations may be the result of the contradictory fusion of these imperatives. Another example is the national/international binary, where the 'new' state capitalism is conceived as a national and relatively coherent model of capitalism which is then globally exported (under the form of SWFs or internationalised SOEs), and as a unitary actor in world politics. Both assumptions downplay the multi-scalar character of state capitalism, and the numerous forms of conflict and cooperation between state agencies and capital at play in processes of state capitalist transnationalisation.

Placing new state capitalism in the context of transformations of global capitalism in the late twentieth and early twenty-first century, we will find that state capitalism is much more variegated in forms than the common discourse that presents it as monolithic, linear, and essentially nationally created (just as any

[103] Howell (n 6) 121.
[104] Alami, Dixon (n 7). 4 (citations omitted).

'non-state' liberal capitalism is). Authors such as De Graaf, have demonstrated that transnationalising Chinese state capital is increasingly entangled with and partly supported by Western elite networks, through corporate ownership and control.[105] Only a small part of the Chinese firms in the sectors such as finance, infrastructure, technology, and energy, are SOEs proper; the majority are a hybrid mixture of private, listed and listed SOE-subsidiaries.[106] Whereas the discourse of a threat to the Western dominated international economic law delegitimises the new entrants, these findings also show a potential domain of cooperation, consensus and integration among the transnational networks of Chinese and Western capital. Again, none of these emerging 'fault lines of cooperation and conflict [...] can be capture by a simple geo-political framing'.[107]

The reader should be reminded that by stressing the role of the state in the construction of modern IIL, I am not in any way suggesting that because the state mattered for modern IIL and it is also deployed in different forms by the emerging 'state capitalist' economies, we can rest and stop analysing different institutional and legal parameters of various national, international, and transnational forms of global capitalism. To the contrary, we should continue our search for explanations for the more visible role of state globally and why it has been so diverse across the globe. Equally, our scholarship must account for the pervasive and permanent roles of the state in capitalism, ie be based on a robust theory of the state.[108]

Modern IIL is a creature of specific historic period and is underpinned by an intellectual framework that is still reflective of those historic concerns. Despite the great resilience the regime has shown to various threats to its survival, absence of the acknowledgement of a greater role of the state in its intellectual and institutional framework makes legal scholarship ill-equipped to deal with new institutional forms that do not comport to the disciplinary ideational core.

What does this mean practically for IIL and ISDS is hard to predict at the present juncture. It may be that the fundamental assumptions about the 'normal' state-market interaction underpinning IIL practice may no longer reflect the parameters of the real-world capitalism (if they ever have). But practice as well as scholarship may need to rethink some of their core assumptions, such as the questions of legal and political authority in and through capitalist markets and the legitimate scope of state intervention, if they want to accommodate the new state capitalist forms in the market. This will equally impact many doctrinal questions which IIL practice have to grapple with, as many contributions in this volume show. Such accommodations may gain the support of the new entrants,

[105] N De Graaf, 'Unpacking the Geopolitics of Chinese State Capitalism: the Transnationalisation of Chinese State-capital Nexus', in Alami and Dixon (n 5) 22; N De Graaf, 'China Inc. goes global. Transnational and national networks of China's globalizing business elite' (2020) 27 *Review of International Political Economy* 2, 208.

[106] De Graaf (n 105) 24.

[107] ibid 25.

[108] Alami and Dixon (n 5) 85.

allowing IIL to reproduce. And as modern IIL essentially functions to protect foreign capital against various political risks and state interventions, an important empirical question arises as to whether new entrants will find IIL useful in consolidating and strengthening their position within the global capitalist order. And inversely, whether the incumbents of global capital will continue their support of IIL in the face of transfer of the global centre of economic and political power Eastwards. These 'fault lines of cooperation and conflict' among the elites of global capital will be crucial for the fate of IIL as we know it. Either way, global labour and nature is unlikely to gain from the reproduction of IIL.

## VI. CONCLUSION

IIL has had a role in reconfiguring the relationships between the state and the economy, the economy and politics, the state and capitalism, and between and within various classes. This contribution aimed to highlight that the state, in a particular incarnation, has been an indispensable part of neoliberalism considered as an institutional and normative project. By parsing through neoliberal political theory which in large part inspired modern IIL, I have brought out to light the roles and functions the state ought to fulfil in this universe. The material reality (which in this instance includes also the real-world impacts of ideological and symbolic discourses) of the practices engendered by modern IIL reveals that IIL reconfigures the state, and consequently also the class relations, to the benefit of specific fractions of global capital. This is despite the ideational and normative backdrop of modern IIL being couched in the language of class-free enterprise society.

Drawing on critical strands of state theory, the contribution highlighted the contentious, ambiguous and instrumental nature of the state and its relations to class and capital. Conceptualising the state as a historical condensation of various class relations which are simultaneously fragmented through the operation of the state apparatus and various modes of consolidation and resistance makes visible the insufficiencies of both the orthodox Marxist views of the state as an instrument of class rule as well as the traditional liberal view of the state as a neutral and a-historical institution tasked with solving coordination problems in a fundamentally non-conflictual society. Applied to IIL, insights from critical state theory help to understand how capitalism from the mid-twentieth century onwards was occasioned by internationalisation, legalisation and judicialisation of economic relations – all three phenomena well manifested in the IIL regime.

Ultimately, I aimed to challenge the contention that we are witnessing a qualitative transition from capitalism without the state towards 'state capitalism'. In other words, the capitalism which modern IIL is part of has always been state capitalism. Granted, the degree, nature, and form of state involvement have differed in various times and places, as this volume bears witness to, but the contention that we are witnessing a turn to a different kind of capitalism, which can be characterised by a new (re)appearance of the state juxtaposed against capitalism without the state, is argued as being theoretically and empirically untenable. It fails to explain the historic and actual role of IIL in its interaction with the state and economy. Moreover, contrasting 'normal' or 'liberal' capitalism to new state capitalism contributes to normalising a particularly narrow conception of politico-economic arrangements as normalcy, while perceiving others as anomalies.

At the same time, I warn against downplaying the extent of transformations of global capitalism that are commonly grouped under the banner of state capitalism. Instead, I use this chapter as an invitation to reinvigorate analyses drawing on critical state theory and political economy to contribute to our better understanding of the role of the IIL in the current state transformations. I pointed to various avenues in which such an analysis of IIL can be taken further.

3

# *Disciplining State Capitalism under International Economic Law: Non-Discrimination vs. Competitive Neutrality*

**ROB HOWSE**

## I. INTRODUCTION

THE INCREASING PRESENCE of state enterprises in global markets has given rise to an extensive debate about the appropriate approach to state capitalism under international economic law. One aspect of the discussion is the application of subsidies rules in the World Trade Organization (WTO) to the state sector; a concern largely triggered by a controversial decision of the then WTO Appellate Body that state-owned Chinese banks do not necessarily qualify as public actors to whom subsidies disciplines apply. This ruling has been greatly criticised and was qualified by the Appellate Body itself in later case law. In related scholarship, I have addressed its defects in some depth and proposed that state ownership and/or control should create a strong presumption that an enterprise is a 'public body' to which the subsidies rules ought to apply. Beyond the question of state enterprises[1] there is also the broader issue of

[1] In this chapter, I have used the term 'state enterprises' to designate a range of business entities over which the state has influence beyond the use of general policy tools like regulation. What level or kind of influence triggers the concerns discussed here is itself a matter of debate and indeed some confusion, with the highest level of concern often being expressed over enterprises that are owned in whole or in part by the state and through which it exercises control through appointment of the board and/or managers. Yet these are hardly the only ways in which the state can influence the operational or business decisions of enterprises. Thus, in using the term 'state enterprises' I have left open the question of what level of state involvement or influence, and what kind, should trigger WTO disciplines new or proposed. This chapter draws in certain respects on other work, 'Official Business: International Trade Law and the Resurgence (or Resilience) of the State as an Economic Actor' (23 July 2021). *University of Pennsylvania Journal of International Law*, Forthcoming, NYU Law and Economics Research Paper No 15, NYU School of Law, Public Law Research Paper No 21-31, Available at SSRN: ssrn.com/abstract=3892415.

the adequacy of subsidies rules to address appropriately contemporary industrial policy (especially in the case of China), which also involves government influence on the (ostensibly) private sector.

Setting the specialised WTO rules on subsidies aside, there is a more foundational divide between the traditional approach of international economic law to state enterprises, which focuses on the application of non-discrimination and related anti-protectionist norms to such entities, and an increasingly heard demand that IEL regimes incorporate a concept of 'competitive neutrality', which would in some way require states to establish a level playing field between state and private capitalism. In a recent paper on WTO reform the European Commission asserts the importance of SOEs is not yet matched with sufficient disciplines to capture any market-distorting behaviour. New international SOE rules should focus on the behaviour of SOEs in their commercial activities, in line with the disciplines already agreed in several free trade and investment agreements. Apart from industrial subsidies and SOE disciplines, there is a need to reflect on what other elements could be part of new WTO rules aiming at ensuring the principle of 'competitive neutrality' and 'promoting a level playing field'.[2]

The present chapter aims to defend the traditional approach and to raise a number of problems with both the concept of competitive neutrality and its possible application in legal rules and norms in trade and investment.

## II. NON-DISCRIMINATION AND STATE ENTERPRISES: THE GATT ACQUIS

Two principles have governed the approach of the multilateral trading system to state capitalism from its inception in the post-World War II GATT. First: 'the General Agreement [does not] sanction discrimination against State-trading enterprises which are, in this regard, placed on the same basis as any other enterprise'.[3] Thus, the trading order should not impose any *particular* burden or constraint on a state (GATT Contracting Party) that chooses state ownership as a tool of public policy. Second, states are internationally responsible for the conduct of enterprises they own and/or control, and such conduct is thus subject to basic anti-protectionist norms, above all that of non-discrimination between domestic and imported products (National Treatment) as well as between the products of different GATT Contracting Parties (MFN).

It is hardly surprising that, coming into existence at the end of the War, the GATT would be accommodating of state capitalism. It was part of the strategy

[2] Annex To The Communication From The Commission To The European Parliament, The Council, The European Economic And Social Committee And The Committee Of The Regions Trade Policy Review – An Open, Sustainable And Assertive Trade Policy, Brussels, 18.2.2021 COM(2021) 66 final, 9–10.

[3] Report of the Committee on the Legal and Institutional Framework of the GATT in Relation to Less-Developed Countries, L/2281, paras 9–10, March 1964.

for economic reconstruction in every European country where the economy had been devastated, whether West or East. In many cases, including in France for example, it was a large part. More fundamentally, as has been widely noted, the interface of the GATT with domestic policymaking was understood in terms of 'embedded liberalism': a commitment to avoid beggar-thy-neighbour external commercial policies while accepting wide differences in approaches to domestic social and economic governance.

Governments may have a range of legitimate rationales for choosing state ownership as a policy tool:

> Advocates [of state capitalism] claim that government involvement in the economy expedites the resolution of market failure. Some say that SOEs may be better placed to tackle the externalities associated with the provision of public goods. The social view underscores the achievement of societal objectives, which depart from purely profit-maximizing goals. Others favor SOE involvement in the production of basic commodities such as water, health care, and education while not necessarily providing them for profit. Governments also provide basic services on equity considerations, such as universal access to essential services, and create jobs in backward areas. …[4]

As for the second principle, it could be considered as the corollary or mirror image of the first. Just as IEL should not impose any particular burden on a state that seeks to use state enterprise as a governance tool, it should not be more permissive of protectionist conduct where it is channelled through a state enterprise rather than a law or regulation, even if the enterprise has some sort of formal legal autonomy from government organs. Even if every decision of a state enterprise cannot be traced to explicit government influence or direction, as Sappington and Stiglitz note, state ownership makes government intervention less costly in terms of transaction costs relative to regulation and taxation; this creates a strong temptation to pursue policy, or political, objectives through influencing the decisions of state-owned enterprises.[5] To ensure that the decision-making of 'state trading enterprises' would be subject to non-discrimination norms, the drafters of the GATT including a provision, Article XVII, which contains a conception of non-discrimination in terms of such enterprises basing their purchase and sales decisions on 'commercial considerations'. Whatever the exact meaning of 'commercial' here, Article XVII has been interpreted by the WTO Appellate Body as establishing non-discrimination as an obligation of result in respect of 'state trading enterprises'.

In addition to Article XVII, as one GATT panel observed, 'the note to Articles XI, XII, XIII, XIV and XVIII provided that throughout these Articles the terms "import restrictions" and "export restrictions" include restrictions made

[4] Preface, in E Ginting and K Naqvi (eds), 'Reforms, Opportunities, and Challenges for State-owned Enterprises' (Asian Development Bank, 2020), xii–xiii.

[5] D Sappington and J Stiglitz, 'Privatization, Information and Incentives', Working Paper No 2196, National Bureau of Economic Research Washington DC, March 1987.

effective through state-trading operations'.[6] Thus, in addition to National Treatment and MFN, GATT disciplines on discriminatory border measures such as import quotas also apply to the conduct of state enterprises, where they are responsible for administering such restrictions. Further, Article II:4 of the GATT provides that state monopolies may not circumvent tariff bindings under the GATT by imposing substitute measures that have price impacts on imports that are comparable to tariffs in excess of MFN bound rates. Article II:4 provides:

> If any contracting party establishes, maintains or authorizes, formally or in effect, a monopoly of the importation of any product described in the appropriate Schedule annexed to this Agreement, such monopoly shall not, except as provided for in that Schedule or as otherwise agreed between the parties which initially negotiated the concession, operate so as to afford protection on the average in excess of the amount provided for in that Schedule.

Jurisprudence of the GATT and the WTO has evolved to include de facto or disparate impact discrimination as disciplined by both the National Treatment and MFN provisions. Thus, a crucial test is whether a given measure disrupts the 'equality of competitive opportunities' between like domestic and imported products to the disadvantage of the latter. At the same time, a measure that is found to be inconsistent with National Treatment or MFN, may be justified in certain cases under Article XX of the GATT, as serving certain legitimate objectives, such as the protection of public morals, or of human or animal life or health, for example. Such justification is subject to an overriding condition that the measure should not be applied in such a manner as to create *unjustifiable* or *arbitrary* discrimination.

It has become fashionable to maintain that the application of these principles to disputes involving state capitalism has been ineffective in addressing protectionism channelled through state companies. Along the lines of the European Commission (cited in the introduction), Michael Sturmo, for the Coalition for a Prosperous America, has recently claimed:

> The GATT's Article III National Treatment obligation is the core fairness principle underlying the multilateral trading system. And while it disciplines the laws, taxes, and regulations of governments belonging to the WTO, it does not adequately address the challenge of state capitalism, where policy is advanced through market actions by state-controlled entities, not laws or regulations.[7]

Critiques of this kind typically avoid any serious engagement with the case law of the GATT and WTO addressing disputes over the (allegedly) protectionist conduct of state enterprises. Generally speaking, claimants have been successful in the cases, which raises serious questions about the validity of the critiques.

[6] GATT Panel Report, *Canada – Import, Distribution and Sale of Alcoholic Drinks by Canadian Provincial Marketing Agencies*, L/6304, adopted 22 March 1988, BISD 35S/37, para 4.24.

[7] M Sturmo/Coalition for a Prosperous America, Written Testimony before the Senate Finance Committee, *WTO Reform: Making Global Rules Work for a Global Economy*, 12 August 2020, available at prosperousamerica.org/written-testimony-before-the-senate-finance-committee/.

In one set of GATT cases, the claimants challenged various business practices and policies of provincial liquor monopolies in Canada.

In 1985, the EC filed a formal GATT complaint with respect to both the markup and the listing practices. The EC argued that the Canadian provincial liquor boards in question systematically used higher price mark ups with respect to imported drinks relative to competing domestic alcoholic beverages. The EC further claimed that practices of these state enterprises in determining when products were listed or unlisted for retail sale discriminated against imports. The resultant panel decision held that Canada was, in both respects, in violation of its GATT obligations.[8]

> The Panel … concluded that the mark-ups which were higher on imported than on like domestic alcoholic beverages (differential mark-ups) could only be justified under Article II:4, to the extent that they represented additional costs necessarily associated with marketing of the imported products, and that calculations could be made on the basis of average costs over recent periods. The Panel also concluded that the burden of proof would be on Canada if it wished to claim that additional costs were necessarily associated with marketing of the imported products.[9]

Further, 'The Panel … concluded that the practices concerning listing/delisting requirements and the availability of points of sale which discriminate against imported alcoholic beverages were restrictions made effective through state-trading operations contrary to Article XI:1.'

In a second case, a wider range of measures was claimed, this time by the US, to have violated various provisions of the GATT, including Article XVII. At the same time, the US asserted that almost all provinces in Canada were cheating on their commitment to implement the earlier EC panel ruling by using methodologies for calculating differentials in markups based on marketing costs in such a way as to reintroduce protectionism, ie, a greater differential than justified on the basis of real additional costs of sale. This last claim particularly would seem to have been likely to drive the panel to consider Article XVII because in effect it invited the panel to penetrate the internal business decisions of an STE and determine whether particular decisions, as opposed to general policies, were being made in accord with commercial considerations (in this case, the actual additional cost of bringing to market imported products).

Also, the US complained about at least two kinds of measures or practices that seemed on their face to be non-discriminatory. One such measure was a minimum price requirement for retail sales. While applicable both to domestic and imported products equally, this was said to disadvantage foreign producers in as much as it prevented them from competing on the basis of a cost advantage they possessed over Canadian producers with respect to beer, the minimum price being set in relation to the wholesale price of domestic product.

[8] Canada – Import, Distribution and Sale of Alcoholic Drinks by Canadian Provincial Marketing Agencies, BISD 35S/37 (1987–88).

[9] ibid, para 4.19.

Another measure related to a purported environmental tax on all beer containers not part of a deposit/return system; American brewers did not have access to the existing system, run by a consortium of domestic brewers in the case of Ontario, and setting up their own parallel system would be, it was claimed, prohibitively expensive. In the case of the methodologies for calculating the cost-of-service charges, the Panel simply found that the charges, or differential markups, included costs not 'necessarily associated with imported beer' and thus conferred additional protection in violation of Article II.4. In order for Canada to prove the contrary, it would have to adopt some kind of independent audit, or reference to an independent expert, who – familiarised with the applicable law of the GATT – that would examine in detail the accounts of provincial liquor monopolies. With respect to minimum price requirements, the Panel found that there was a de facto violation of Article III.4, with equal competitive opportunities not being provided to imported beer, given that the minimum price was based on the wholesale price of the domestic product.

In a related case where the US this time was the claimant against Canada, the parties reversed as it were, the Panel found that various listing/delisting practices of state liquor boards (even in those instances where they did not operate a complete monopoly) violated the National Treatment obligation of the GATT. The panel held:

> 'in the states of **Mississippi** and **Pennsylvania**, imported wine can be sold at the wholesale and at the retail level, respectively, only by the liquor control boards, whereas domestically-produced wine can be sold directly to retailers. The Panel further noted that in the state of **Idaho**, the liquor control board has the monopoly on the importation of wine, although not on its sale at retail. The Panel considered that the result of these measures is that imported wine is necessarily subject to the listing/delisting procedures of the liquor control board whereas domestic like product can be sold without regard to such requirements. The listing criteria are designed to place certain restrictions on the products which can be sold within the state, including perceived need, quantitative restrictions and expected profitability. The Panel considered that the listing/delisting requirements of these states deny Canadian wine competitive opportunities accorded to United States like products, inconsistent with Article III:4. ... With respect to **Vermont** and **Virginia**, the Panel noted that certain imported wines cannot be sold in state-operated liquor stores whereas the like domestic wine can. The Panel recalled States argument that the number of state-operated sales outlets was relatively small compared to the number of private outlets. The Panel considered that although Canadian wine has access to most of the available sales outlets in these states, it is still denied competitive opportunities accorded to domestic like products with respect to sales in state-operated outlets. Therefore, the Panel considered that the Vermont and Virginia measures are inconsistent with Article III:4.'[10]

[10] GATT Panel Report, *United States – Measures Affecting Alcoholic and Malt Beverages*, DS23/R, adopted 19 June 1992, BISD 39S/206.

In the *Korea-Beef* dispute the US challenged the import restrictive practices of the Korea Livestock Products Manufacturing Organization (LPMO), a state enterprise. The US claimed that the LPMO engaged in a variety of protectionist policies that disfavoured imports, amounting to quantitative restrictions under Article XI of the GATT or in the case of import surcharges Article II:4. The Panel found:

> The mere existence of producer-controlled import monopolies could not be considered as a separate import restriction inconsistent with the General Agreement. The Panel noted, however, that the activities of such enterprises had to conform to a number of rules contained in the General Agreement, including those of Article XVII and Article XI:1. The Panel had already found that the import restrictions presently administered by the LPMO violated the provisions of Article XI:1.[11]

The Panel further held that import surcharges were merely ancillary to the administration of quantitative restrictions it had already found to violate Article XI, but it also warned that

> in the absence of quantitative restrictions, an import monopoly was not to afford protection, on the average, in excess of the amount of protection provided for in the relevant schedule, as set out in Article II:4 of the General Agreement. Furthermore, in the absence of quantitative restrictions, an import monopoly was not to charge on the average a profit margin which was higher than that 'which would be obtained under normal conditions of competition (in the absence of the monopoly).[12]

Early in the WTO era, in *Canada-Periodicals*, the WTO Panel examined, inter alia, certain pricing policies of the Canada Post Corporation, a state enterprise that nevertheless had an independent corporate status under Canadian law. The Panel found:

> the design, architecture and structure of Canada Post's different pricing policy on domestic and imported periodicals all point to the effect that the measure is applied so as to afford protection to the domestic production of periodicals. In the case of 'funded' rates, the scheme is clearly designed to promote domestic production of periodicals with Canadian content under the supervision of Canadian Heritage. In the case of 'commercial Canadian' rates, the very fact that they are lower than 'international' rates which are applied to imported products strongly suggests that the scheme is operated so as to afford protection to domestic production.[13]

In the *Canada-Wheat Board* case, admittedly, the US was unsuccessful in its claim in respect of the market activities of the state enterprise in question. But this was because, on the facts, the Panel was not persuaded that the US had

[11] GATT Panel Report, *Republic of Korea – Restrictions on Imports of Beef – Complaint by the United States*, L/6503, adopted 7 November 1989, BISD 36S/268, para 115.

[12] ibid, para 128.

[13] Panel Report, *Canada – Certain Measures Concerning Periodicals*, WT/DS31/R and Corr.1, adopted 30 July 1997, as modified by Appellate Body Report WT/DS31/AB/R, DSR 1997:I, 481, para 5.38.

established that the Canada Wheat Board engaged in discrimination between markets; the Appellate Body further rejected the US argument that Article XVII of the GATT applies to impose competitive disciplines on the decision-making of state enterprises, even where there is no practice of discrimination in product markets.[14]

More recently, Australia challenged (among other Canadian measures) markups, fees, and taxes of the Nova Scotia and Quebec liquor boards as discriminatory against imported wine, under both National Treatment and the non-discrimination provisions of GATT Article XVII.[15] Canada settled the case with Australia before the Panel made public its Interim Report. The settlement involved Canada removing discriminatory measures and satisfied the Australian wine industry's concerns about market access.[16]

Even more recently a panel has been established in a case brought by the EU against Russia, alleging that through various government policies state enterprises are compelled to discriminate against foreign goods and services in their purchasing decisions (the procurement exception to National Treatment applies only in the case of products and services for the government's own use, not the case here, according to the EU).[17]

In sum, under existing GATT rules on non-subsidies measures, claimants have often been successful in obtaining rulings against protectionist discrimination in the policies or practices of state enterprises or government treatment of them. Indeed, as we have just seen WTO Members continue to bring such disputes. It is from this perspective that we must consider whether and why the introduction of a conception of 'competitive neutrality' into the legal order of international trade would be advantageous in addressing ways in which state enterprises or government measures concerning them create barriers to international trade of a protectionist nature and not justified by legitimate non-protectionist public policy objectives.

## III. CONCEPTUALISING COMPETITIVE NEUTRALITY

While proposals for new rules on state enterprises rarely define 'competitive neutrality', they may presuppose a version of this concept that is alien to WTO law as it currently stands. An OECD study on the subject states: 'Competitive neutrality implies that no business entity is advantaged (or disadvantaged) solely because of its ownership.' The GATT contains neither a code on anti-trust

[14] Appellate Body Report, *Canada – Measures Relating to Exports of Wheat and Treatment of Imported Grain*, WT/DS276/AB/R, adopted 27 September 2004, DSR 2004:VI, 2739.

[15] *Canada-Measures Governing the Sale of Wine: Request for Consultations of Australia*, WT/DS537/1, 16 January 2018.

[16] 'Australia-Canada Wine Dispute Settlement Proves Value of WTO', Wine Titles Media, 23 April 2021, available at winetitles.com.au/australia-canada-wine-dispute-settlement-proves-value-of-the-wto/.

[17] *Russian Federation – Certain Measures Concerning Domestic and Foreign Products and Services: Request for Consultations by the European Union*, WT/DS604/1, 26 July 2021. Currently, the panel proceedings have been suspended at the request of the complainant, the EU.

nor any obligation of non-discriminatory treatment as between *like or similar enterprises or investments.* The WTO Trade-related Investment Measures Agreement (TRIMs) addresses non-discrimination but only through affirming that treatment of foreign investment must not result in discrimination between like imported and domestic *products* contrary to GATT Article III.

By contrast, IIAs, or newer PTAs that cover both trade and investment, typically impose a National Treatment obligation with respect to investors and investments. This requires non-discriminatory treatment of investors or investments from other treaty parties, where the latter are in like circumstances with domestic investors or investments. The absence of a competition code in the WTO was among the reasons that the Appellate Body rejected the US claim in the *Canada Wheat Board* dispute that Article XVII of the GATT covers forms of anti-competitive practices that are not evidenced by discriminatory treatment, as disciplined in other GATT provisions: 'We see no basis for interpreting that provision as imposing comprehensive competition-law-type obligations on STEs, as the United States would have us do.'

One must question at the outset the notion that anti-trust norms should be introduced into the WTO selectively, applying to state enterprises but without corresponding disciplines on private anti-competitive behaviour. In this sense introducing the idea of competitive neutrality into WTO law would be decidedly non-neutral-as WTO Members' state enterprises would be constrained by competition norms while rival private firms are not subjected to WTO-level disciplines on anti-competitive practices. As Joseph Stiglitz observes, 'the distinction between competitive and non-competitive (including bureaucratic) forms of economic organization may be more important than the distinction between private and public ownership …'.[18]

A conceptually rigorous approach to competitive neutrality would entail a consistent attempt to ensure that (except where the government is attempting to achieve some specific legitimate policy goal) government regulation is neutral in relation to all forms of ownership and related aspects of firm structure. This is at least the aspiration in the way in which the OECD currently articulates the concept of competitive neutrality: 'competing enterprises should be subject to equivalent rules irrespective of their ownership, location or legal form'.[19] But, as we know, tax, corporate and securities laws treat different forms of private ownership in different ways-publicly held companies, family offices, private equity, etc.

Apart from that, the availability of these different forms of capital to private enterprises is itself in many ways determined or shaped by the state-through securities and corporate governance regulation (for example disclosure requirements), tax rules (the tax advantage that private equity partnerships may enjoy for instance), and other norms such as fiduciary duties. In sum, the kinds of

[18] J Stiglitz, *Selected Works of Joseph Stiglitz Vol II Information and Economic Analysis* (Oxford, Oxford University Press, 2013) 33.

[19] OECD Competitive Neutrality Recommendation, OECD/LEGAL/0462, 2021, Recommendation (II)1(b).

business strategies or (anti-) competitive practices that *private* firms engage in are also in many ways constrained or enabled by state policies. How then does one set this all out to determine that state-owned firms *overall* have more state-created advantages than comparable private firms or investors?

While ownership neutrality of this kind is arguably a matter of good economic governance (preventing the organisation of assets in ownership structures that undermine policy objectives and circumvent regulatory obligations), it is not this kind of neutrality that the trade policy community is concerned about when they seek to introduce 'competitive neutrality' into the trade legal order. Rather, what is supposed is that state enterprises are often not subject to the same anti-trust norms under domestic law than private enterprises, and this allows them to compete unfairly in international trade. This seems simply a reformulation of the critique that WTO law is hobbled in its capacity to ensure competitive global markets for lack of an anti-trust code.

But, in the absence of a consensus among WTO Members to develop such a code, why focus on the situation of state enterprises as opposed to anti-competitive practices more generally? The prejudice here seems to be that domestic anti-trust laws may be adequate in disciplining the anti-competitive practices of *private* firms, or a greater tolerance for private monopoly capitalism than the state sector. As Leonardo Borlini puts it, 'competitive neutrality … reveals a clear ideological connotation (of the free market variety)'.[20]

As Wolfe suggests (focusing on China), the question of good domestic economic governance, which is how competitive neutrality arises in the OECD context, is different in the context for concerns about state enterprises in the trading order:

> Are SOEs a problem? And are they a trade policy problem? If one is asking about national welfare – that is, the *economic efficiency* of SOEs as a vehicle for achieving policy objectives in the many countries where they exist …. The Chinese government itself sees an efficiency problem, and has been reforming the sector for years – the objectives and process if not the results are well-described in successive WTO Trade Policy Review (TPR) reports on China. On the other hand, if one is asking about the trading system – that is, the potential for *negative spillovers* affecting other firms – then that would be a trade policy problem in the domain of the WTO. And either way, are Chinese SOEs a special case? These questions can appear to be ideological rather than empirical in the absence of data, …'.[21]

Such data as have been presented in reports by the US and the EU more recently tend to give credence to the ideological dimension of the trade policy communities'

[20] L Borlini, 'When the Leviathan goes to the market: A critical evaluation of the rules governing state-owned enterprises in trade agreements' (2020) 35 *Leiden Journal of International Law* 313–334, 321. *cf* also ch 2, in this volume.

[21] R Wolfe, 'Sunshine over Shanghai: Can the WTO Illuminate the Murky World of Chinese SOEs?', Robert Schuman Centre for Advanced Studies Research Paper No RSCAS 2017/12 (March 2017), Available at SSRN: ssrn.com/abstract=2928159 or dx.doi.org/10.2139/ssrn.2928159.

concern with imposing a notion of 'competitive neutrality' on state enterprises (in fact some kind of anti-trust type constraints not necessarily also applied in trade law to private firms). There is a sparsity of examples of state enterprises practices or governmental policies toward them that distort international trade but that could not be addressed through the existing disciplines discussed in the first part of this chapter.

The USTR publishes an annual National Trade Estimate Report on Foreign Trade Barriers. The latest Report, published in March 2021, elaborates on many thousands of foreign government practices that are viewed by the USTR as trade barriers. Given the economic significance of state enterprises, and their dominant role in a range of sectors and countries, it is notable that they are mentioned, directly or indirectly, only a hundred times at most. There is an analogous annual report of the European Commission to the Parliament; the latest version, which covers 2019, hardly mentions state enterprises as a trade barrier, except implicitly as part and parcel of the discussion of China's 'state-led' economic model.[22] The absence of state enterprises as a theme beyond the case of China is especially noticeable, since the Report covers not only trade but also investment barriers.

## IV. FLAWED ATTEMPTS TO INCORPORATE COMPETITIVE NEUTRALITY IN REGIONAL TRADE AGREEMENTS

A careful reading of the CPTPP chapter on State-Owned Enterprises and Designated Monopolies (chapter 17) suggests that the CPTPP does not, overall, address the potential trade barriers associated with state enterprises in a more coherent or satisfactory manner than existing WTO rules and case law. First, the chapter applies only to state-*owned* enterprises, defined by state ownership of more than 50 per cent of share capital or majority of voting rights or the power to appoint a majority of the board (Article 17.1). But even where these formal criteria are absent, there may be structures that allow the government to exert considerable influence. As Borlini notes:

> … the quantitative thresholds in the CPTPP fail to consider the many other, lower levels of ownership or board appointment that can actually be structured so as to retain governmental control, as … situations of indirect control. Furthermore, there is no provision on interlocking directorates [footnote omitted]. More generally rigid rules provide actors with incentives to reframe a control/ownership pattern in order to dodge their application-not an implausible hypothesis given contemporary corporate practices.[23]

[22] European Commission-Directorate General For Trade, Report Of The Commission To The Parliament And The Council On Trade And Investment Barriers, January To December 2019, Brussels, June 2020.

[23] Borlini (n 20).

On non-discriminatory treatment and 'commercial considerations' (Article 17.4) the CPTPP largely repeats the content of Article XVII of the GATT, albeit including services as well as goods. There are two main differences. The first is that the obligation to act 'in accordance with commercial considerations' (except to 'fulfil any terms' of a public service mandate) is separated from the obligations on non-discrimination. This goes back to the discussion of the *Canada Wheat Board* case above. Why *should* trade law be concerned with whether state enterprises act commercially as a general matter, apart from situations where the non-commercial behaviour reflects an alteration in the conditions of competition that disadvantages imports? The general definition of 'commercial considerations' includes any 'factors that would normally be taken into account in the commercial decisions of a privately-owned enterprise in the relevant business or industry'.

Again, one notices what appears to be an ideological bias against state enterprises. Why would the decision-making considerations of private firms be the baseline against which state enterprises should conform themselves? As Stiglitz points out, both public and private enterprises rely on managers/agents to attain the objectives of their principals, the owners. Different kinds of private and public enterprises exhibit different incentive structures for managers, some of these addressing agency costs better than others but, in any case, there is no systematic evidence of distortion of global competition from the way in which agency costs are managed in the incentive and monitoring structures of public firms as opposed to private ones. Managers in privately owned firms that are regularly traded on stock markets may have incentives to make decisions that maximise short term share prices for the firm; managers of different kinds of private as well as public enterprises may well be rewarded based on longer-term revenue growth in the enterprise.

Does the CPTPP imply that the benchmark for 'commercial' decision-making is short-term maximisation of share value? Motivated by the pursuit of super-competitive rents, a private monopolist or private firm with dominant market power may charge what the non- or imperfectly competitive market will bear. A state enterprise may be motivated by the goal of normal profits, but not necessarily seek rents that gouge consumers who are also citizens. Again, here is the behaviour of the private monopolist to be taken as the benchmark for 'commercial' decision-making? Certainly the 'commercial' rent-seeking activity of the private firm would hardly produce superior social welfare. These issues become more acute when one brings into the picture ESG investing, where managers are supposed to take into account environmental and social goals in firm decision-making or Corporate Social Responsibility, which entails that firms' decisions meet certain non-commercial standards of conduct, concerning matters such as human rights, labour practices, and sustainability.

Article 18.5 of the Canada-EU Trade Agreement (CETA) also contains a 'commercial considerations' obligation on state enterprises that is separate and autonomous from the non-discrimination norm. The CETA contains what might be described as a question-begging definition of 'commercial considerations': 'consistent with customary business practices of a privately held enterprise in the relevant business or industry'. This presupposes that a norm can be discerned from the conduct of private firms in a given sector, that there is a customary standard for commercial behaviour abstracting from government and inequalities of market power/imperfect competition-equal contracting parties bargaining over price and quality and related considerations in a state of nature, as it were. This reflects an ideological fantasy of the 'private market'. In the real world of private capitalism, firm strategies on issues such as pricing and sources of supply are diverse, reflecting considerations such as the firm's market power, and also the background framework of governmental regulation and taxation in the jurisdictions that matter for the firm. As Borlini suggests: 'Actions such as selling at very low prices to hook customers can be practiced by commercially-motivated firms and those with further motives alike.'[24]

The problem of a concept such as 'customary business practices' is illustrated by the practice of transfer pricing. Where a particular sector is characterised by multinational firm activity, it may be customary to price transactions between affiliated entities within the multinational for purposes of tax minimisation. This could result in much higher prices in some jurisdictions and lower ones in others than if prices did not reflect tax avoidance considerations. Is the manipulation of taxation rules or 'arbitration' between tax jurisdictions 'commercial' behaviour? It is, if 'commercial' means maximising the firm's net revenues or profits. It is not, if one understands 'commercial' as the behaviour that firms engage in in an unregulated perfectly competitive world where supply and demand determine prices. But in any case, why would one constrain the pricing practices of a state enterprise by a norm generated through customary practices that are motivated by regulatory arbitrage of private firms?

Similar questions arise from the 'commercial considerations' requirement for state enterprises in the USMCA, the successor Agreement to the North American Free Trade Agreement (NAFTA). There, in chapter 22, 'commercial considerations' are defined as 'factors normally … taken into account in the commercial decisions of a privately owned enterprise in the relevant business or industry …'. The fantasy is that of a 'normal' private firm in a particular business or industry, begging the question of what goes into the understanding of 'normal'? As with the notion of 'custom' in the case of the CETA, one might well ask whether practices that reflect regulatory arbitrage or anti-competitive behaviour in imperfect markets are 'normal'? Practices such as kickbacks are 'normal', even pervasive, in certain industries (construction and pharmaceuticals are often cited examples), even if in some jurisdictions they constitute criminal forms of corruption (while being tolerated or less comprehensively legally sanctioned in others).

[24] Borlini (n 20) 330.

## V. CONCLUSION

The evidence does not bear out the now-conventional wisdom in mainstream trade policy circles that existing WTO norms are inadequate to counter protectionism (other than subsidies) that emanates from the behaviour of state enterprises or the use by states of such enterprises. Right from the GATT onward, a range of disciplines constraining protectionist and discriminatory behaviour has been applied to state enterprises, and indeed the text of the GATT was designed for such application. This includes National Treatment, the Article XI prohibition on quantitative measures, and the ban on imposition of fiscal levies on imports in excess of bound tariffs rates that is set out in Article II. As is illustrated by the jurisprudence discussed in this chapter, taken together these norms have been successfully invoked by claimants against state enterprise protectionism over many decades. There are few data that indicate a range of non-subsidy practices in the state sector that are not caught by existing norms and would require new WTO rules.

Those who advocate for such rules often invoke the concept of 'competitive neutrality', a notion developed in particular in the OECD to support the practice of neutrality toward ownership structure as good domestic economic governance. As the discussion in this chapter suggests, attempts to translate this concept into international economic law norms (in particular, illustrated by the CETA, CPTPP, and USMCA), are largely incoherent and have an ideological (if incoherent) free market flavour, suggesting there is some 'norm' or 'custom' of how a private firm behaves under some set of ideal or idealised circumstances (unarticulated) to which the conduct of state enterprises should be held as a matter of international economic law. This is a dangerous as well as unnecessary path for the WTO to take, given the commitment to respecting regulatory diversity and the well-established principle of not favouring or prioritising private over public enterprise.

# Part II

# Actors and Processes of State Capitalism

# 4

# *Chinese State Capitalism in the World Order: An International Law and International Relations Perspective*

JIANGYU WANG

## I. INTRODUCTION

THE RETURN TO state capitalism, in an arguably capitalist world economy embedded in the 'liberal world order' of ours today, is no longer a marginal phenomenon. Joshua Kurlantzick noted that, though the rise of state capitalism is most conspicuous in China, 'state capitalism is not just about China':[1]

> Although China's SOEs have received the most coverage of any state companies around the world, they are hardly alone. China is just but one example of a new era of state capitalism born over the past decade …… Throughout the developing world, many states are increasing their intervention in their economies. State capitalism today is hardly monolithic; instead, it is better understood as a continuum, just as free market capitalism runs along a continuum from extreme laissez faire economics to a French or Scandinavian model of a highly regulated market economy.

State capitalism, narrowly defined in this context as an economic system in which the state controls a large number of business companies' corporate governance and business operation through owning a controlling percent of the companies' ownership and, on this basis, to advance the state's political agenda in case of need, though not always being so as often the state realises that it is in its best interest to allow these companies, namely the state-owned enterprises (SOEs), to operate on a commercial basis. State capitalism can monopolise a

[1] J Kurlantzick, *State Capitalism: How the Return of Statism is Transforming the World* (Oxford, OUP, 2016) 7.

country's economy but can also co-exist with other forms of ownership and economic systems, such as the private economy, in a market or mixed economy. In this sense, state capitalism exists in many countries/economies around the world, which include not only the non-western states – and thus many of them authoritarian polities – such as China, Russia, India, Brazil, Egypt, Kazakhstan, Malaysia, Singapore, Saudi Arabia, United Arab Emirates, Venezuela, inter alia, but also western economies such as Norway, Finland, and some other European states.[2] In short, state capitalism is on the rise and here to stay, and China is the leading driver behind this wave.

An important question to ask is what does the rise of state capitalism in general, and Chinese state capitalism in particular, do to the world order of our age? The Bretton Woods System established in the aftermath of the World War II has aimed to promote the free flow of factors of economic production, a spirit deeply embedded in the rules of international economic law which fosters free trade and investment, such as those on most-favoured-nation treatment, national treatment, market access, reciprocity, prohibition on quantitative restrictions, tariff reductions, rules against subsidies, removal of non-trade barriers, investor protection (fair and equitable treatment, protection of legitimate expectations, prompt, adequate, and effective compensation, etc), capital movement (current and capital accounts liberalisation), and many others. If state capitalism goes against the fundamental rules of international economic law, it may very much sabotage the foundation of the liberal international economic system constructed in the past seven plus decades, and in turn, threatens the liberal world order.

G John Ikenberry argued that the current, US-led, world order is liberal internationalism-based, or a 'liberal world order'.[3] In his definition,[4]

> Today's international order is the product of a two-order building projects that began centuries ago. One is the creation and expansion of the modern state system, a project dating back to the Peace of Westphalia in 1648. In the years since then, the project has promulgated rules and principles associated with state sovereignty and norms of great power conduct. The other project is the construction of the liberal order, which over the last two centuries was led by the United Kingdom and the United States and which in the twentieth century was aided by the rise of liberal democratic states.

Such an order, according to Ikenberry, is not just one for liberal democracies, even though it was originally American or western for historical reasons. The order is organised around multilateral institutions, alliances, special relationships, and client states, so it is 'a hierarchical order with liberal characteristics'.[5]

[2] See, eg, Z Cheung, E Aalto and P Nevalainen, 'Institutional Logic and the Internationalization of a State-owned Enterprises: Evaluation of International Venture of Opportunities by Telecom Finland 1987–1998' 55 (2020) 101140 *Journal of World Business*.

[3] GJ Ikenberry, 'The Future of the Liberal World Order: Internationalism After America' (2011) 90 *Foreign Affairs* 56.

[4] ibid 58–59. *cf* on IIL as a neoliberal form of capitalism, ch 2, in this volume.

[5] ibid 61.

The order is easy to join, as long as a state accepts the rules. China has already joined the order and benefited tremendously from it.[6] In our contemporary world, 'the hierarchical aspects are fading while the liberal aspects persist'.[7] That is, the biggest advantage of the liberal international system, as an open and rules-based order, can accommodate rising powers who have no choice but place reliance on the liberal order.[8] In other words, '[S]tate power today is ultimately based on sustained economic growth, and China is well aware that no major state can modernize without integrating into the globalized capitalist system.'[9] As such, the 'road to global power, in effect, runs through the Western order and its multilateral economic institutions'.[10]

So far so good, as it may sound. However, the rise of state capitalism, as a potent alternative to the liberal capitalism, may pose a different story.[11] True, state capitalism has come out quickly as a formidable force in the international economy. However, size alone is not a problem per se, just like being big in size should not be treated as an original sin, as long as the same rules are followed. After all, capitalism itself comes in varieties. David Hundt and Uttam (2017) pointed out that, in Asia alone, there exists Japan's collective capitalism, Confucian capitalism in Korea and Taiwan, entrepôt capitalism in Hong Kong and Singapore, Malaysia's state capitalism, Thailand's alliance capitalism, India's democratic capitalism, and China's market socialism.[12] As the world's economic power is shifting to the East and national economic systems are becoming increasingly diversified, state capitalism as a 'grand' institutional design that combines political power with market strengths has been generating tensions with the US-led, West-dominated international economic system which is a key component of the liberal world order. In this chapter, I will use Chinese state capitalism as a case study to illustrate the tensions and examine whether systemic challenges have been made to the current liberal international economic order.

Briefly, three tensions between state capitalism and the liberal international economic order will be critically discussed. The first is whether Chinese state capitalism, in its own nature, contradicts the spirit and principles of the international economic system. This concerns the corporate objectives of the SOEs, corporate governance of SOEs, as well as whether the state – or the party-state in China's political context – respect the commercial autonomy of SOEs. The second tension concerns whether international economic law has proper and

[6] ibid, 62.

[7] ibid 61.

[8] GJ Ikenberry, 'The Rise of China and the Future of the West: Can the Liberal System survive?' 87 (2008) *Foreign Affairs* 23, 31.

[9] ibid 32.

[10] ibid.

[11] 'Special Report: State Capitalism', *The Economist* (21 January 2012) 1.

[12] See D Hundt and J Uttam, *Varieties of Capitalism in Asia: Beyond the Developmental State* (Basingstoke, Palgrave Macmillan, 2017) 17–21.

adequate rules to regulate state capitalism. Third, it is about whether Chinese state capitalism stands in the way for forming new rules and regulations governing itself.

## II. THE NATURE OF CHINESE STATE CAPITALISM

If SOEs function and operate like private firms, there should not be much to worry about state capitalism. In theory, an SOE operating on a commercial basis is not different from a private enterprise, except that, in the case of an SOE, the state is a controlling shareholder. Are Chinese SOEs such firms? The law on paper would say 'yes' to this question. Chinese SOEs are generally governed by the PRC Company Law,[13] while a very small number of SOEs which have not gone through the corporatisation process are still subject to the PRC Law on Industrial Enterprises Owned by All the People which provides rules for traditional SOEs.[14]

### A. The Purpose of Companies (including SOEs) under Chinese Law

According to the Company Law, all business companies,[15] including incorporated SOEs, are independent enterprises with 'legal person property rights', which entails that a company, as a legal person, is the owner of its own property and has the right to possess, use, benefit from and dispose of its assets.[16] In theory, this provides a legal basis for all Chinese companies, SOEs included, to be the decision-maker of their own business operations merely in the capacity of property owners, paving the way for them to operate, again theoretically, on a commercial basis, with mainly profitmaking-oriented objectives. The following clause of China Telecom represents the style of most Chinese companies in terms of stating their objectives in the Articles of Association:[17]

> The Company's objectives are: comply with State laws and regulations, be market-driven, actively adopt advanced communications technologies, and develop telecommunications and information business; strengthen management and increase service quality; provide fast, convenient and accurate communications services to society and satisfy the needs of society; improve enterprise efficiency, increase enterprise competitiveness and create profits for shareholders.

[13] Company Law of the People's Republic of China, originally adopted on 29 December 1993, revised on 28 August 2004, 27 October 2005, 28 December 2013 and 26 October 2018, respectively.

[14] Law of the People's Republic of China on Industrial Enterprises Owned by All the People, adopted on 13 April 1988 and revised on 27 August 2009) (hereinafter the SOE Law).

[15] All companies registered under the PRC Company Law must be 'business companies' because their activities are all considered 'for profit' business and all incomes are taxable. Non-profit organisations, including charities, cannot take the corporate form.

[16] PRC Company Law, Art 3.

[17] Articles of Association of China Telecom Corporation Limited (inclusive of alterations approved by the shareholders' general meeting up to 30 November 2021), Art 13.

As can be seen, China Telecom, one of China's largest SOEs and doubtlessly a key part of Chinese state capitalism, at least rhetorically places maximising shareholders' value through quality business operation and technological innovation as its main objective.

### B. Corporate Governance

Again, the PRC Company Law alone does not give the impression that China's state-owned companies shall not operate on commercial basis with the requisite enterprise autonomy. Under the Company Law, corporate governance structure in a business firm consists of four institutions: the shareholders' General Meeting, a Board of Directors, a Supervisory Board, and the Management.[18] The General Meeting is the company's 'power organ', namely the highest authority, in which the shareholders exercise their rights through voting.[19] Below the General Meeting is a two-tier board system.[20] The Board of Directors makes important business decisions, sets up the company's management system, and appoints the Manager (popularly known as General Manager or CEO) and other senior executives on the recommendation of the Manager.[21] The Supervisory Board provides disciplinary oversight of the performance of the directors and senior executives.[22] Finally, the Manager runs the company's business on a daily basis.[23]

It is important to note that, compared to the rights of shareholders in many other jurisdictions, Chinese shareholders are remarkably more powerful according to the rights conferred upon them by Company Law. In general, the shareholders are not only entitled to profit distribution and election of the directors, but also 'to participate in important decision-making' of the company.[24] More specifically, the shareholders, in the form of shareholders' resolutions in the General Meeting, decide on issues concerning the company's business strategy, investment plans, financial budgets, profit distribution, increase or decrease of capital, amending the articles of association, as well as fundamental corporate changes such as mergers and acquisitions.[25]

The shareholder primacy approach in the Company Law has profound implications for the state's control of SOEs. The Chinese state is typically – though not always – the majority shareholder in an SOE. Since shareholders can partake in making decisions for the company only through voting for or against resolutions at the General Meetings in which the majority rules, the state

[18] See generally, J Wang, *Company Law in China* (Cheltenham, Edward Elgar, 2014) ch 6.
[19] PRC Company Law, Art 37. See also Wang (n 18) 153.
[20] Wang (n 18) 161.
[21] PRC Company Law, Art 46.
[22] ibid, Art 53.
[23] ibid, Art 49.
[24] ibid, Art 4.
[25] ibid, Art 37.

shareholder can easily control a company simply by exercising its rights as a majority shareholder. On the other hand, legal protection of minority shareholders is relatively weak, though, in the 2004 revision of the Company Law, the doctrine of fiduciary duties was introduced together with the derivative action mechanism to enable the minority shareholder to enforce those duties.[26] This gap already gives the state, merely by being a majority shareholder, tremendously power in controlling the company.

The Party-state's grip on SOE corporate governance does not stop here. As this author observed in a different paper, there exist a twin governance structure in Chinese SOEs: legal governance and political governance.[27] The legal governance structure has already been depicted in the preceding paragraph, through which the state merely needs to act in the capacity of the majority shareholder in order to control it, but it must do so through the firm's legalised corporate governance structure as provided in the Company Law and Articles of Association.

This formal governance structure lives in tandem with the 'political governance structure' embodied in the organisational system of the CCP in the SOE. In short, the CCP holds the power to appoint personnel and play a role – often determinative – in the company's major decision-making, through the following mechanisms:

First, the CCP is a Leninist party with strict discipline. The CCP Constitution requires, without exception, that all CCP members must comply with the Party's political line and instructions, whether they are policy-based directions or concrete requests. There are specifically four principles: (i) individual Party members must obey the Party organisation (in which they are a member); (ii) in a Party organisation, the minority must obey the majority after voting; (iii) the lower Party organisation must obey the higher Party organisations; and (iv) all Party members and organisations must obey the Party Central, which officially means the CCP National Congress and the Central Committee elected by the former, but in practice means the Standing Committee (currently comprising seven members led by General Secretary Xi Jinping) that is the highest power organ within the CCP.[28] The significance of this line of discipline is that Party organisations at all levels must faithfully implement the CCP's Party line, policy, and instructions, and all individual CCP members in the relevant Party organisation are required to work together to ensure the success of the aforesaid implementation.[29] That is, their highest loyalty is supposed to belong to the

[26] ibid, Arts 147–151. See also generally, Wang (n 18) ch 8.

[27] J Wang, 'The Political Logic of Corporate Governance in China's State-owned Enterprises' (2014) 47:3 *Cornell International Law Journal* 631, 647.

[28] Constitution of the Communist Party of China, initially adopted in July 1921 and most recently amended on 24 October 2017, Art 10(1), at www.12371.cn/special/zggcdzc/zggcdzcqw/. See also Wang (n 27) 654.

[29] Wang (n 27) 654.

CCP in accordance with the Party Constitution, wherever they are and which institution employs them.

Second, the CCP controls the appointment of personnel in SOEs in accordance with the political principle of *Dang Guan Gan Bu* (the Principle of Party Control of Cadres) under which the CCP dominates the appointment of all Party-state officials in China. Although, as discusses before, legally incorporated SOEs are treated as independent legal persons by the law on paper, the *Dang Guan Gan Bu* rule applies to all SOEs. As such,

> [p]ersonnel in SOEs, especially top leaders such as the chairperson and deputy chairperson of the board of directors or the senior corporate executives, are managed and openly appointed by the CCP's organizational departments. Each SOE is placed in the political system of the Party-state and given a bureaucratic ranking; the personnel management of SOE leaders is managed by the organizational department of that bureaucratic level.[30]

Third, the Party organisation in the SOE may – though it does not do so in exceptional cases of some SOEs – directly participate in the firm's major decision-making, although not in the capacity of a shareholder since the state shareholder is in abstract 'the whole people' (*quanmin*) and in concrete the government who authorises the central or local State Assets Supervision and Administration Commission (SASAC) to exercise shareholders' rights on behalf of the state.[31] A salient feature of the PRC Company Law which may sound strange to outsiders is that it has a provision about the establishment of CCP organisations in companies, be it an SOE or private firm, and requires the company to 'provide necessary conditions for the activities' of the Party organisation.[32] It is not clear whether it is compulsory for all private and foreign-owned firms to establish such organisations: implicitly, when the CCP members in a private firm or foreign invested company decide to do so, this must be allowed and facilitated by the company. It is, however, clear that Party cells must be present in all SOEs. The Party organisation has a hand in the SOE's corporate governance through the following means.

Traditionally, Party participation in SOE decision-making was mainly done through the 'cross-holding of positions' mechanism, in which Party members in the SOE are appointed directors or senior executives, and vice versa, the latter serving as standing members of the Party committee. The CCP policy on Party-building in SOEs encourages the Secretary of the Party committee and the Chairman of the Board of Directors to be assumed by the same person, provided that the separation of Chairman and General Manager/CEO is maintained.[33] In this approach, the CCP's participation in firm decision-making is informal,

[30] ibid 658.

[31] ibid 652–654. For such reason the SASAC is conveniently regarded as the state shareholder in companies with state-owned stakes.

[32] PRC Company Law, Art 19.

[33] Wang (n 27) 657.

without clear procedures and rules as to what the Party organisation should specifically do in the firm's corporate governance process.[34]

The Party's involvement in SOE corporate governance has been brought to an unprecedented level in the Xi Jinping era. In October 2016, President Xi convened a two-day 'National Conference on Party-building in SOEs', the first of its kind, through which he emphasised that Party leadership of SOEs was a 'glorious tradition' of Chinese SOEs and a 'significant political principle' in Chinese society, and explicitly asked that the Party's role in SOEs to be 'organizationalised, institutionalised and concretized'.[35] Following the speech, a number of regulatory and policy guidelines have been issued by various Party-state authorities to lay out specific rules for Party participation in SOE governance. The new rules aim to integrate Party leadership into the corporate decision-making process while struggling still to draw a line between the political governance structure and legal governance structure so as to pay minimum respect for the 'face' of the Company Law. As such, the rules, on one hand, require that an SOE's 'major decisions concerning management and business operation' must be discussed and deliberated by the Party Committee. On the other hand, they also provide that the final decisions must be made by the Board of Directors or the Management team in accordance with the relevant rules of the Company Law or the company's Articles of Association.[36]

One however may not be so naïve as to believe that the Board or Management will go against the opinions of the Party organisation in an SOE. The 'major decisions' refer to the following matters: (i) significant measures to implement the decisions and arrangements of the CCP Central and the state's national development strategy; (ii) the SOE's development strategy, medium and long-term development plan and important reform plans; (iii) fundamental issues concerning the SOE's asset reorganisation, ownership transfer, capital operation and large investment; (iv) establishment and adjustment of the SOE's corporate organisational structure, as well as the formulation and modification of important rules and by-laws; and (v) important issues concerning work safety, stability within the enterprise, employee rights and benefits, corporate social responsibility, etc.[37] This wide range of 'major decisions' comprehensively cover all important aspects of an SOE's business operation and governance, making the CCP a less mysterious but even more omnipresent existence in the SOEs.

Institutionalisation of Party leadership in SOE governance is conspicuously reflected by the incorporation of the role of the CCP in companies' Articles of Association. The requirement for writing the Party into the corporate charter was

[34] ibid.

[35] X Jinping, 'Speech at the National Conference on Party-building in SOEs', 10-11 October 2016, www.12371.cn/special/xjpgqdjjh/.

[36] Trial Regulations of the Chinese Communist Party on Grassroot Party Organizations in State-owned Enterprises, adopted by the CCP Politburo on 29 November 2019, www.gov.cn/zhengce/2020-01/05/content_5466687.htm (hereinafter CCP Regulations on Party Organizations in SOEs), Art 15.

[37] ibid.

announced for the first time in 2015,[38] marking a significant break from the CCP's traditional approach of 'controlling cadres to control behaviour' to requesting SOEs to explicate the role, powers, and functions of the Party organisation about Party leadership. As observed by John Zhuang Liu and Angela Huyue Zhang,

> [i]n the past, the Party and the government has [*sic*] issued policies calling for the strengthening of the Party's leadership over SOEs. What is unusual this time, however, is that the Party is no longer satisfied with mere slogans as commitments. Rather, the SOEs need to credibly commit themselves by amending their corporate charters to formerly institutionalize the Party's leadership role in the firms.[39]

Companies acted quickly to respond to this call. As Lauren Yu-hsin Lin has noted,[40]

> By October 2017, all group-level central SOEs had completed the revisions of their articles of association. As for the second- and third-level affiliated companies of central SOEs, more than 3,900 of them had completed revisions of their articles of association, more than 2,800 had single individuals fulfilling the jobs of party committee secretary and chairman of the board, more than 2,600 had appointed full-time deputy party secretaries, and more than 12,000 had added the prescribed procedural requirements into their articles.

## C. The State Retreats and the Party Advances

It is fair to say now that the political governance structure has totally triumphed over the legal governance structure, with only a legal formality remained. Jiangyu Wang and Cheng-han Tan observed a phenomenon in the Chinese Party-state's recent approach to SOEs, which is that 'the state retreats' and 'the Party advances'.[41] The umbrella mandate that the role of the CCP is institutionalised in the formal corporate governance regime of an SOE is contrasted with another regulatory change: the state/government has been asked to retreat from SOE governance and not interfere with the day-to-day management at the firm level.[42] The mixed-ownership reform (MOR), which is now the main theme of China's SOE reform, aspires to switch the operational philosophy of state ownership from 'asset management' to 'capital management', which entails that the state should act generally as an owner of the shares or equity interest translated from the capital invested by the state in the SOE, rather than an owner of

[38] L Yu-Hsin Lin, 'Institutionalizing Political Influence in Business: Party-building and Insider Control in Chinese State-owned Enterprises' (2021) 45 *Vermont Law Review* 437, 447. See also JZ Liu and AH Zhang, 'Ownership and Political Control: Evidence from Charter Amendments' (2019) 60 105853 *International Review of Law and Economics* 3–4.

[39] Liu and Zhang (n 38) 4.

[40] Lin (n 38) 449.

[41] J Wang and CH Tan, 'Mixed ownership Reform and Corporate Governance in China's State-owned Enterprises' (2020) 53:3 *Vanderbilt Journal of Transnational Law* 1055, 1090–1097.

[42] ibid 1089.

the assets in SOEs. From a regulatory perspective, this move entails 'separation of government functions and enterprises' (*zhengqi fenkai*)' and 'separation of government functions and capital'.[43] For this purpose, the MOR programme has adopted a 'negative-list' approach to transfer autonomy to SOEs from the hands of the state. The essence of the approach is, based on an order from the State Council, China's Central Government, the SASAC, which was both the owner and the almighty regulator of SOEs, is now required to produce a list of powers and responsibilities in which it must specify which powers are to be returned to SOEs. Moreover, the SOEs now command the residual powers (ie any power which not included in the negative list will be regarded as, by default, belonging to the SOEs though they were previously held by the SASAC). As Wang and Tan have observed,[44]

> The guiding principle for the list is that the SOEs will eventually regain, through the list, the autonomy legally conferred upon them by the PRC Company Law and other laws. Under the list, the state shareholders' reach does not go beyond the board of directors and is explicitly not allowed to touch on the management of the companies. The first negative list, the SASAC Power Authorization List (2019), gave twenty-one powers back to central SOEs. Significantly, the SOEs have been allowed to decide on issues concerning MOR of subsidiaries, asset restructuring of subsidiaries, shareholding change in nonlisted subsidiaries, bond issuances, hiring of managerial personnel on market-based principles, approving the dividend distribution plans of subsidiaries involved in high-tech industries, extension of business to other areas, etc.

## III. THE COMPATIBILITY OF CHINESE STATE CAPITALISM WITH THE LIBERAL ORDER: AN ANALYSIS

### A. State Capitalism and the Nature of the Liberal Global Economic Order

It is now clear to us that there is a tension – or a mismatch between the legal nature and political nature of China's SOE system. China's civil and corporate laws dictate that SOEs are defined as legally independent legal persons with enterprise autonomy to make business decisions in line with the rules and procedures of their own corporate governance structure, at least according to China's corporate law on paper. In reality, the CCP Party organisation dominates the decision-making in individual SOEs.

It has been taken for granted that Chinese state capitalism, featuring a body of SOEs which dwarf state enterprises in any other part of the world by both the number of firms and size of assets, naturally and always run against the liberal internationalism as its nature is inconsistent with the liberal international economic order. This understanding is not necessarily wrong, but it requires

[43] Wang and Tan (n 41) 1090.
[44] ibid 1094.

more nuanced analysis in light of the nature of the liberal order itself. I would make three observations here.

First, the liberal order, in its original design and current form, does not prohibit state capitalism, and can probably accommodate it. Regarding the economic nature of the liberal order, G John Ikenberry argued that, 'unlike the imperial system of the past, the Western order is built around rules and norms of non-discrimination and market openness, creating conditions for rising states to advance their expanding economic and political goals within it'.[45] In other words, one of the main features – or logics – of the post-war order built by the US is the 'open markets',[46] which provide non-discriminatory access to resources and markets, peaceful economic competition based on countries' comparative advantages, and progressive reduction of tariffs and non-tariff barriers. One may argue that, in general, state capitalism does not contradict the nature of this order, provided that the following conditions are met:

(1) The SOEs operate on commercial basis, and function no different from privately owned firms whose objective is to maximise profits;
(2) The state provides non-discriminatory treatments to foreign goods, services, traders, and investors, and continues to liberalise trade and investment through multilateral and bilateral agreements.

China's external economic liberalisation, in terms of reducing tariffs and providing increasingly larger market access for foreign service providers and investors adopted especially since its accession to the WTO, has made China the largest trading nation in the world and the second largest destination for FDI. In recent years, with a consensus formed in the US to treat China as a strategic – and doubtlessly hostile – competitor, there has been a rising wave criticising China's failure to comply with its WTO obligations and resistance to join the liberal international order. As Yeling Tan has argued, this consensus was overblown in this regard as one may not ignore China's sweeping trade and investment liberalisation as a result of its joining of the WTO when evaluating whether China has abandoned the liberal order.[47]

A more critical question is whether Chinese SOEs can really operate on a commercial basis to behave as a fair competitor in domestic and global markets. This would require two specific conditions to be fulfilled before determining whether Chinese state capitalism is disapproved of by the liberal order. The first is whether, given the tight Party control, the SOEs can make decisions as an independent participant in the market. The second is whether the Chinese state can cut the financial ties, including subsidies, to SOEs, in order to make it on an equal footing with privately and foreign owned enterprises. On the two

[45] Ikenberry (n 8) 29.
[46] GJ Ikenberry, *Liberal Leviathan: The Origins, Crisis, and Transformation of the American World Order* (Cambridge, MA, Princeton University Press, 2011),
[47] Y Tan, 'How the WTO Changed China?' (2021) 100:2 *Foreign Affairs* 90, 91.

conditions, all we can say at this stage is that the current rather confusing signals of Chinese SOE reform hold several possible scenarios for the future. That is, it is far too early to conclude that, because of the growth of state capitalism in China, Chinese economy has been driven into – or some would even argue that China itself is creating – an alternative, authoritarian, non-market based global economic order.

An optimistic view, based on an unconventional argument if one is to play the role of the devil's advocate, may lead to a scenario, though possibly a slim one, that Party-controlled SOEs may also be market participants and operate on a commercial basis with profit-making as their main objective. Indeed, this is true for most Chinese SOEs, as they are expected by the Party-state to make money in the markets. 'In other words, SOEs provide the economic foundation for the CCP's reign as they not only enable the Party-state to pay for the requisite human and political expenses, but also cause the citizens of China to depend on the Party-state for a living.'[48] As such, the Party-state's preference for these enterprises would be efficiency-led and profits-driven, presumably hoping for those SOEs to operate on commercial basis.

## B. The Lack of International Regulation of State Capitalism

A major difficulty in evaluating the compatibility of Chinese state capitalism, or any other form of state capitalism comprising state-owned companies, is that there is no effective legal framework at the international level to set the criteria for assessing the legality of state capitalism from the perspective of the WTO-led world trading system, which is possibly the only body of multilateral rules which has a limited number of 'hard law' rules for state enterprises. As this author observed in another publication,[49]

> It is important to emphasize that the world trading system (under the auspice of the WTO and the General Agreement on Tariffs and Trade (GATT) that is now part of the WTO regime) has adopted an ownership-neutral philosophy since its inception following the Second World War (WWII). Although the world trading system is conventionally understood as one based on market economies, this understanding has not prevented it from granting nonmarket economies, ranging from Eastern Europe to Latin America, GATT/WTO membership. As a matter of fact, the whole system is premised on the assumption that governments are impartial regulators that should treat all economic actors equally. In other words, the GATT/WTO does not have compulsory rules regarding property ownership for members to comply with. Accordingly, a 'WTO member is free to establish and maintain SOEs if it wishes to do so.'

[48] Wang (n 27) 639.

[49] J Wang, 'State Capitalism and Sovereignty Wealth Funds: Finding a 'Soft' Location in International Economic Law', in CL Lim (ed), *Alternative Versions of the International Law on Foreign Investment: Essays in Honour of Muthucumaraswamy Sornarajah* (Cambridge, CUP, 2016) 405, 410.

Currently, the only provision dealing with state-backed economic entities is Article XVII of the GATT 1994, which is merely about 'state trading enterprises' (STEs) and their trade activities and requires STEs, in their purchases or sales in foreign trade transactions, to act in accordance with the principles of non-discrimination and guided by commercial considerations their decisions concerning imports or exports. 'In other words, the original parties to the GATT only wanted to ensure that SOEs, or private enterprises with special privileges granted by their government, were not given a safe haven as a result of the privileged situation, so that they may escape the GATT rules of non-discrimination.'[50] This provision is of little, or at least limited use for regulating SOE-based state capitalism. After all, Article XVII is essentially about those firms which trade on behalf of the state, often based on a monopoly. However, an SOE is not necessarily an STE, if it can prove that it does not engage in state trading or are not granted special rights or privileges.

On the issue of subsidies, the WTO has a fairly adequate body of rules governing state aids to business companies in the form of subsidies, most of them are provided by the Agreement on Subsidies and Countervailing Measures (ASCM), together with GATT Articles VI and XVI.

In the GATT/WTO legal framework, an actionable subsidy, which may entitle other members to sue the government that has been alleged to provide the subsidy, contains three constituting elements: (i) there is a financial contribution; (ii) provided by a government or a public body within the territory of a WTO Member; and (iii) which confers a benefit.[51] It will not be a surprise if one assumes, on the basis that the givers of subsidies include 'public bodies', that the subsidies law's reach extends beyond the actions of governments to bodies such as SOEs.[52] Consequentially the WTO may treat SOEs as providers of subsidies, which can potentially make the transactions of SOEs with other enterprises illegal under the WTO law. Doubtlessly, this can generate a nightmare for countries with lots of SOEs, especially China.

Somewhat fortunately for China, the Appellate Body in the WTO case, *United States – Definitive Anti-Dumping and Countervailing Duties on Certain Products from China*, or *US – AD & CVD* (China), rendered a decision in China's favour,[53] though the panel report initially put the Chinese in a rather risky situation.[54] The case involves China's complaint concerning definitive anti-dumping and countervailing duties imposed by the US on the importation of certain Chinese products. One of the key issues concerns how to define subsidies in the unique economic, political and legal structure of the Chinese polity.

[50] ibid 411.

[51] ASCM, Art 1.1.

[52] World Trade Organization Secretariat (1998), 98.

[53] WTO Appellate Body Report, *United States – Definitive Anti-Dumping and Countervailing Duties on Certain Products from China*, WT/DS379/AB/R, adopted 25 March 2011.

[54] WTO Panel Report, *United States – Definitive Anti-Dumping and Countervailing Duties on Certain Products from China*, WT/DS379/R, issued 23 July 2010.

Specifically, it was about whether China's SOEs and state-owned commercial banks (SOCBs) are public bodies under the ASCM.

The panel report generated fear in China as it ruled that the US had not violated or acted inconsistently with any WTO rules by treating Chinese SOEs and SOCBs as public bodies. The panel concluded that a 'public body' under the ASCM 'is any entity controlled by a government'.[55] Specifically, the panel noted[56]

> [W]e consider that interpreting 'any public body' to mean any entity that is controlled by the government best serves the object and purpose of the SCM Agreement. This reading ensures that whatever form of a public entity takes (whether agency, Ministry, Board, corporation, etc.) the government that controls it is directly responsible for those of its actions that are relevant under the Agreement …… To read 'any public body' in Article 1.1(a)(1) as excusing form a Member government's direct responsibility a wide swathe of government controlled entities engaging in exactly the sorts of transactions listed in Article 1.1(a)(1)(i)-(iii) of the SCM Agreement would fundamentally undermine the Agreement's logic, coherence and effectiveness, and thus would be at odds with its object and purpose.

In other words, the panel concluded that all of China's SOEs and SOCBs are public bodies. Were the panel report adopted, the hundreds of thousands SOEs, which form the most important pillar of China's economy, would become public bodies in the WTO law with respect to the determination of subsidies (and possibly for many other purposes under the WTO's covered agreements), and the transactions involving them would most likely be regarded as activities providing actionable subsidies.

The Appellate Body, however, reversed most of the crucial elements in the panel's ruling, especially the one concerning the definition of a public body. It rejected the panel's interpretation of a 'public body' as lacking a proper legal basis.[57] As noted, the panel's interpretation follows a 'government control approach' on the basis of the belief that majority state ownership in an enterprise renders that firm a 'public body'.[58] The Appellate Body found this a troublesome approach which misunderstood the meaning of the relevant rules as well as the object and purpose of the ASCM. In the Appellate Body's view, 'the performance of government functions, or the fact of being vested with, and exercising, the authority to perform such functions are core commonalities between government and public body'.[59] It finally concluded,[60]

> We see the concept of 'public body' as sharing certain attributes with the concept of 'government'. A public body within the meaning of Article 1.1.(a)(1) of the SCM

[55] Panel Report, *U.S. – AD & CVD (China)*, para 8.94.
[56] ibid, para 8.79.
[57] ibid, para 322.
[58] See also R Ding, '"Public Body" or Not? Chinese State-owned Enterprises' (2014) 48:1 *Journal of World Trade* 273–274.
[59] Appellate Body Report, *U.S. – AD & CVD (China)*, para 290.
[60] ibid, para 317.

> Agreement must be an entity that possesses, exercises or is vested with government authority. Yet, just as no two governments are exactly alike, the precise contours and characteristics of a public body are bound to differ from entity to entity, State to State, and case to case. Panels or investigating authorities confronted with the question of whether conduct falling within the scope of Article 1.1.(a)(1) is that of a public body will be in a position to answer that question only by conducting a proper evaluation of the core features of the entity concerned, as its relationship with government in the narrow sense.

In short, the Appellate Body substantially limited the scope of SOEs that may be subject to the WTO's discipline on subsidies. According to the panel report, all the SOEs in which the government has a majority control would automatically be treated as public bodies, thus making it impossible – or at least extremely risky – for those SOEs to do business at the international level as ordinary commercial entities. The ruling of the Appellate Body cleared an immediate threat to China (and other countries with SOEs), but has actually created more uncertainties insofar as how to determine the nature of SOEs under international economic law.

## IV. CONCLUDING REMARKS

Chinese state capitalism, mainly based on the economic power of its SOEs, has become a formidable force in international economic relations. Joshua Kurlantzick contended that 'China's state capitalism has been successful enough – indeed, quite successful, by the standards of developing countries at any time in history and certainly in the period of the past thirty years – to allow for growth, that it can be maintained for a long time, even decades.'[61] Further, 'it has created a degree of legitimacy and stability for the government'.[62] That is, state capitalism in China is here to stay. The question then is whether it poses threats to the current liberal world order, one that remains most difficult to answer as it concerns the direction of China's development model. This is indeed an open question which points to several scenarios about China's future.

The CCP's firm control of Chinese SOEs is no longer a political gesture or general policy declaration without operative rules. For a short period in the early Reform and Opening Up era, the CCP policy on SOEs emphasised on 'separation of the Party from enterprises' (*zhengqi fenkai*). This has long become history. Now Party leadership has been institutionalised in SOEs' corporate governance and written into their Articles of Association. Whether such a tight grip on SOEs will negatively impact on enterprise autonomy is an interesting question. The conventional wisdom on corporate governance says that no doubt it does. However, an unconventional argument holds that the problem is more

[61] Kurlantzick (n 1) 98.
[62] ibid.

with the Chinese state, not the Party. There is at least a possibility that Party leadership, integrated into an SOE's corporate governance, might be regarded as part of the firm's decision-making system. This is certainly less 'evil' than allowing the government to directly interfere with an SOE's management with administrative and regulatory measures. Further, as economic development is still the CCP's *the* 'central task', meaning it is the single most important objective of the CCP in its rule of China, it is not unreasonable to expect that the CCP wants the commercial success of those SOEs which are tasked to make profits for the Party-state's rein.

In any event, China's SOE reform has not shown us a clear direction. Many mixed signals have been sent out from the Party-state, some of which were market-oriented initiatives, while others are loaded with political control. From an optimistic lens, this could mean the future direction of Chinese state capitalism can still be shaped by internal and external factors. For the latter, regional free trade agreements such as the CPTPP and numerous BITs have made novel rules for regulating SOEs, for which China does not seem to oppose, as evidenced in its application on 16 September 2021 to join the CPTPP, which would require China to embrace all the free trade rules in the agreement including the chapter on SOE.[63]

[63] 'China applies to join Pacific trade pact to boost economic clout', *Reuters* 18 September 2021.

# 5

# *Sovereign Wealth Funds and Foreign Investment Screening under International Investment Law*

MICHAIL DEKASTROS

## I. INTRODUCTION

SOVEREIGN WEALTH FUNDS (SWFs) are one of the new rising stars of International Economic Law. They have displayed a vast expansion over recent years both in number[1] and in value of total assets managed by them; according to some estimates, their total assets today amount to US$1.5–2.5 trillion and roughly equal to the combined assets of all hedge funds and private equity firms.[2] Indicatively, the Abu Dhabi Investment Authority – the largest SWF in the group – had assets with a combined value of US$625–875 billion in early 2009.[3] Furthermore, it is estimated that they will continue to grow due to the same factors that sparked their growth, such as the unrestricted international flows of capital, predicted trends in commodity prices and foreign exchange reserves, high growth in transition economies, demands on the public pension systems of aging societies, and high internal rates of return on the funds themselves.[4]

[1] Twenty new Sovereign Wealth Funds have been established since 2000 with 12 of them after 2005; for more on this point see M Audit, 'Is the Erecting of Barriers Against Foreign Sovereign Wealth Funds Compatible with International Investment Law?' (2009) 10 *Journal of World Investment and Trade* 617; G Lyons, 'State Capitalism: The Rise of Sovereign Wealth Funds' (2008) 14 *Law and Business Review of the Americas* 179.

[2] H Schweitzer, 'Sovereign Wealth Funds: Market Investors or 'Imperialist Capitalists'? The European Response to Direct Investment by Non-EU State-controlled Entities' [2011] *European Yearbook of International Economic Law* 79, 85; J Kozack, D Laxton and K Srinivasan, 'Sovereign Wealth Funds and Global Capital Flows: A Macroeconomic Perspective', in R Fry, W McKibbin and J O'Brien (eds), *Sovereign Wealth: The Role of State Capital in the New Financial Order* (London, Imperial College Press, 2011) 21.

[3] X Yi-chong, 'The Political Economy of Sovereign Wealth Funds', in X Yi-chong and G Bahgat (eds), *The Political Economy of Sovereign Wealth Funds* (Basingstoke, Palgrave Macmillan, 2010) 5.

[4] RJ Gilson and CJ Milhaupt, 'Sovereign Wealth Funds and Corporate Governance: A Minimalist Response to the New Mercantilism' (2007–2008) 60 *Stanford Law Review* 1345, 1360.

Indeed, it was presumed that by 2014 they had grown up to US$4–6 trillion[5] and some analysts had predicted that, by the end of the decade, total assets under their management would reach US$13.4 trillion.[6] Nonetheless, their combined assets are minute compared to the 'global value of traded securities [which] is about US$165 trillion'[7] whilst SWFs are also small compared with the US$62 trillion funds managed by private institutional investors.[8] However, they are increasingly investing abroad and moving into alternative assets.[9]

Such a move from portfolio to Foreign Direct Investment (FDI) can be perceived as quite positive from an economics perspective. Indeed, equity investments facilitate the recycling of trade surpluses and increase the supply of funds to the equity market, thus reducing the cost of capital.[10] Furthermore, equity investment, as compared to investment in debt, is also more stable as its withdrawal is less disruptive than a withdrawal from a debt market.[11]

In light of their sudden rise, it comes as no surprise that their investment strategies have invited an increasing amount of scrutiny from the recipient states. Indeed, relatively recently their operations have become much more visible[12] and western countries have appeared uncomfortable and somewhat unprepared for this development. Despite their economies' need for capital they have strived to maintain a supervisory role over its flow, and their regulatory approaches often reflect a protectionist agenda that is at odds with this new reality. In fact, SWFs have been called the 'new bogeymen of global finance'.[13]

In early 2007, government-controlled Chinese entities took the external stake (albeit non-voting) in Blackstone, a big private equity group that, indirectly through its holdings, is one of the largest employers in the US. The Government of Qatar is seeking to gain control of J Sainsbury, one of Britain's largest supermarket chains. Gazprom, a Russian conglomerate, in effect controlled by the Kremlin, has strategic interests in the energy sectors of a number of countries

[5] Kozack, Laxton and Srinivasan (n 2) 31.

[6] Lyons (n 1) 5.

[7] S Johnson, 'The Rise of Sovereign Wealth Funds' (2007) 44 *Finance and Development* 56, 56.

[8] Yi-chong (n 3) 11.

[9] See A Blundell-Wignall, Y Wei Hu and J Yermo, *Sovereign Wealth and Pension Fund Issues* (OECD Working Papers on Insurance and Private Pensions No 14, 2008).

[10] Gilson and Milhaupt (n 4) 18.

[11] This is due to the fact that, unlike government debt, SWFs cannot hold equity investments until they mature and then decline to reinvest; see CK Elwell, M Labonte and WM Morrison, *Is China a Threat to the US Economy?* (Congressional Research Service, Report for Congress, 2007) 45.

[12] For instance, in 2008, the investment and real estate arms of Dubai World acquired a 20% stake in Cirque du Soleil – the world's largest live entertainment business – whilst in 2007 Borse Dubai purchased a 19.9% stake in the NASDAQ Stock Market (whilst simultaneously acquiring NASDAQ's 28% interest in the London Stock Exchange); see, respectively, P Blyschak, 'State-Owned Enterprises and International Investment Treaties: When are State-Owned Entities and Their Investment Protected?' (2010–2011) 6 *Journal of International Law and International Relations* 1, 4 and K Badian and G Harrington, 'The Politics of Sovereign Wealth: Global Financial Markets Enter a New Era' [2008] *The International Economy* 52, 55.

[13] See J Plender, 'An Unseen Risk in Sovereign Funds' *Financial Times* (21 June 2007).

and even a stake in Airbus. Entities controlled by the Government of China and Singapore are offering to take a substantial stake in Barclay's, giving it more heft in its effort to pull off the world's largest banking merger, with ABN Amro.[14]

Furthermore, two highly controversial incidents in the US illustrate the political sensitivity that ensued after 9/11, especially in relation to SWFs' investments. In 2005, China National Offshore Oil Corporation (CNOOK), 70 per cent of which is owned by the Chinese government, withdrew a US$18.2 billion takeover bid for Californian energy firm Unocal Corporation due to political opposition.[15] Similarly, a Dubai company, Dubai Ports World, withdrew its bid to acquire London-based Peninsular and Oriental Steam Navigation Company, which had operations at six major ports, including New York and Baltimore.[16] Although it was initially allowed to proceed, subsequent congressional and media attention ultimately caused the company to sell the US portion of the business to a US company.[17]

For some time, such controversies became less common mainly as a result of the 2008–2010 crisis, which caused many previously sceptical states to re-evaluate their attitude towards incoming SWFs' investments.[18] Indeed, leading western-based corporations and governments are aggressively pursuing sovereign direct investment and public calls for opening financial markets to SWFs are now abundant.[19]

Nonetheless, it was not too long until these concerns returned, especially in relation to investments made directly or indirectly by Chinese state-owned companies and funds. Further, a transparent and coherent regulatory architecture has yet to be devised whilst political controversies continue to play a critical role in SWFs' investment strategies.[20] Indeed, there are signs that international disputes between SWFs and host states are already surfacing.[21]

[14] L Summers, 'Sovereign Funds Shake the Logic of Capitalism' *Financial Times* (30 July 2007).

[15] See B White, 'Chinese Drop Bid to Buy US Oil Firm' *Washington Post* (2 August 2005); For more information on this case from a legal perspective see DM Mostaghel, 'Dubai Ports World Under Exon-Florio: A Threat to National Security or a Tempest in a Seaport' (2006–2007) 70 *Albany Law Review* 583.

[16] See J Weisman and B Graham, 'Dubai Firm to Sell US Port Operations' *Washington Post* (9 March 2006).

[17] ibid; see also JW Casselman, 'China's Latest Threat to the United States: The Failed CNOOC-UNOCAL Merger and Its Implications for Exon-Florio and CFIUS' (2007) 17 *Indiana International & Comparative Law Review* 155.

[18] V Fotak and W Megginson, 'Are SWFs Welcome Now?' (21 July 2009) 9 *Columbia FDI Perpectives*.

[19] See Lyons (n 1).

[20] Blyschak (n 12) 9–10.

[21] See, eg, LE Peterson, 'Oman's Sovereign Wealth Fund is the Latest Claimant to Try to Hold a Sovereign State – this Time, Bulgaria – Liable for Losses Tied to a Bank Failure' Investment Arbitration Reporter, 23 October 2015; for a number of disputes that have involved State-Owned Enterprises but not SWFs stricto sensu, see C Annacker, 'Protection and Admission of Sovereign Investment under Investment Treaties' (2011) 10 *Chinese Journal of International Law* 531, 552–553 and accompanying footnotes.

## II. SWFS AND REGULATORY RESPONSES OF HOST STATES

### A. Regulatory Concerns

In 2007 and 2008, as a result of the aforementioned investment attempts by SWFs, a scare campaign was rampant in the US and some EU states: SWFs' investment, it was argued, 'might be used for overt or tacit political purposes'[22] that would even go as far as threatening countries' national interest by 'hollowing out economies and national flag companies, by taking over national resources and by controlling national infrastructures'.[23] In a similar vein, others emphasised that SWFs might, in reality, prove to be instruments of a 'New Mercantilism' and that, without proper global regulation of SWFs, they may gain access to national security interests, influence politics, create chaos in foreign economies, or destabilise international financial markets.[24] Soon thereafter, a political discussion commenced about how to properly address this new threat but misconceptions once popularised meant that a meaningful debate was stymied. The emerging consensus at the time was clear: SWFs were to be kept out.

Irrespective of the existence of this 'double standard', there have been some more serious debates in academia and policy circles about the regulatory challenges that the operation of SWFs might pose.[25] Some of the most commonly mentioned regulatory challenges are the risk of transmission of financial market shocks or the exercise of soft political power.[26] Furthermore, issues of corporate governance have arisen since there is little knowledge of SWFs' investment strategies or how investment decisions are made within SWFs.[27] Most importantly, however – given that more than two-thirds of SWFs are located in countries that are both politically and financially less open than OECD countries, while more than 90 per cent of their overseas investment has gone to OECD countries – there is a fear that SWFs might threaten the national economy and national security of recipient countries.[28]

[22] BJ Cohen, 'Sovereign Wealth Funds and National Security: The Great Tradeoff' (2009) 85 *International Affairs* 713, 713.

[23] X Yi-chong, 'Global Disequilibria', in X Yi-chong and G Bahgat (eds), *The Political Economy of Sovereign Wealth Funds* (Basingstoke, Palgrave Macmillan, 2010) 245.

[24] See EM Truman, *Sovereign Wealth Funds: the Need for Greater Transparency and Accountability* (Peterson Institute for International Economics, 2007) 6–7; see Summers (n 14); see also G Luft, *Sovereign Wealth Funds, Oil, and the New World Economic Order* (Speech delivered before the House Committee in Foreign Affairs, 21 May 2008) 3, 8.

[25] For a summary of the evolution of such debates over time see A Sandor, 'Leveraging International Law to Incentivize Value-Added Shareholding: Why Foreign Sovereign Wealth Funds Still Matter and How They Can Improve Shareholder Governance' (2015) 46 *Georgetown Journal of International Law* 947, 949 and accompanying footnotes.

[26] R Fry, W McKibbin and J O'Brien, 'Introduction: Sovereign Wealth Funds in an Evolving Global Financial System', in R Fry, W McKibbin and J O'Brien (eds), *Sovereign Wealth: The Role of State Capital and the New Financial Order* (London, Imperial College Press, 2011) 6.

[27] Yi-chong (n 3) 1–2.

[28] ibid 2; Fry, McKibbin and O'Brien (n 26) 6.

Nevertheless, there is often a tendency in policy analysis to lump all regulatory challenges in connection to SWFs' investments and present them as different facets of a single national security threat. However, there are distinct regulatory challenges that are not exclusively related to SWFs, which can be addressed through domestic regulation within the host states' markets. Such concerns include: (a) economic efficiency; (b) financial stability; (c) competition policy; (d) transparency; (e) national security stricto sensu.

## III. SWFS AND FOREIGN INVESTMENT SCREENING MECHANISMS

Despite some discussions and policy proposals for a 'light' or 'soft law' regulatory approach and/or a co-ordinated global response, host states were either not appeased or they fell prey to political pressure from domestic constituents. Either way, a series of states amended their domestic laws in order to enhance their control over SWF investment flows.

Consequently, most OECD governments introduced domestic regulation to monitor and/or control the flow of foreign investment. On most occasions, they have used already existing mechanisms, such as investment 'screening committees',[29] in order to establish control over the flow of SWF investment, often by increasingly expanding their mandate and powers. These mechanisms have the capacity to either block the entry of a foreign investment into the territory of the host state or to limit that entry when it comes to strategic economic sectors.[30] They usually involve a case-by-case review of proposed foreign investments in accordance with the economic or social policies of the host states.[31] Often, they ascertain whether purely commercial interests drive a specific investment,[32] a criterion obviously relevant for SWFs. In a nutshell, as will be demonstrated, host states have reserved and enhanced for themselves the right to block or restrict SWF investment *before* their entry into their markets.

[29] For a detailed overview accompanied by empirical data of a number of countries implementing some sort of investment 'screening' legislation see United States Government Accountability Office, *Foreign Investment: Laws and Policies Regulating Foreign Investment in 10 Countries* (Highlights of GAO-08-320, a report to the Honorable Richard Shelby, Ranking Member, Committee on Banking, Housing, and Urban Affairs, US Senate, 2008).

[30] M Burgstaller, 'Sovereign Wealth Funds and International Investment Law', in C Brown and K Miles (eds), *Evolution in Investment Treaty Law and Arbitration* (Cambridge, Cambridge University Press, 2011) 169; Yi-chong (n 3) 16.

[31] I Gomez-Palacio and P Muchlinski, 'Admission and Establishment', in P Muchlinski, F Ortino and C Schreuer (eds), *Oxford Handbook of International Investment Law* (Oxford, Oxford University Press, 2008) 238.

[32] Burgstaller (n 30) 170.

## A. European Union and its Member States

### *i. The Balance of Competences between the EU and its Member States*

The increasing presence of SWF investments in the EU has also given rise to significant concerns at the EU level. As a preliminary issue, however, the balance of competences between the EU and its Member States as regards the regulation of incoming SWFs' investments needs to be examined. Article 63 TFEU explicitly provides that:

> Within the framework of the provisions set out in this chapter, all restrictions on the movement of capital between Member States and between Member States and third countries shall be prohibited.[33]

Further, it is well established under the case-law of the CJEU that direct investment constitutes a sub-category of capital under the Treaty.[34] Therefore, the EU, in terms of both regulation and policy declares that, in principle, all restrictions on the movement of capital between Member States and third countries are prohibited.

Further, and as a consequence, the EU enjoys an exclusive competence over the regulation of capital movements – including FDI – from third countries at least at the pre-establishment stage. As pointed out by the Commission, with

[33] Art 63(1), Treaty on the Functioning of the European Union (Consolidated, as amended by the Treaty of Lisbon) OJ C326, 26 October 2012.

[34] See Council Directive 88/361 of 24 June 1988, which – for the purposes of the internal market – defined 'direct investment' in Annex I under Heading I as '1) Establishment and extension of branches or new undertakings belonging solely to the person providing the capital, and the acquisition in full of existing undertakings; 2) Participation in new or existing undertaking with a view to establishing or maintaining lasting economic links; 3) Long-term loans with a view to establishing or maintaining lasting economic links; 4) Reinvestment of profits with a view to maintaining lasting economic links.' In the Explanatory Notes of Annex I, it was further explained that for the purposes of the Directive and Nomenclature annexed thereto, direct investments mean: 'Investments of all kinds by natural persons or commercial, industrial or financial undertakings, and which serve to establish or to maintain lasting and direct links between the person providing the capital and the entrepreneur to whom or the undertaking to which the capital is made available in order to carry on an economic activity. This concept must therefore be understood in its widest sense.' The EC Treaty as amended by the Amsterdam Treaty substantially reproduced the contents of Article 1 of Directive 88/361 and extended the freedom to capital movements between Member States and third countries. In any case, under the ECJ's case-law, it is well established that the nomenclature annexed to Directive 88/361 'still has the indicative value, for the purposes of defining the notion of capital movements' under the Treaty: see Case C-222/97 *Trummer and Mayer* [1999] ECR I–1661 [20], [21] and, inter alia, Case C-483/ *The Commission v France* [2002] ECR I–4781 [36]. As to direct investments, as included in the material scope of application of the freedom of capital movement, see, inter alia, Case C-54/99 *Association Eglise de scientologie de Paris and Scientology International Reserves Trust v The Prime Minister* [2000] ECR I–1335 [14]; Case C-483/99 *The Commission v France* [37]. Also, for a pronouncement that Points I and III in the nomenclature set out in Annex I to Directive 88/361, and the explanatory notes appearing in that annex, indicate that direct investment in the form of participation in an undertaking by means of a shareholding or the acquisition of securities on the capital market constitute capital movements within the meaning of Article 73b of the Treaty see Joined Cases C-463/04 and C-464/04 *Federconsumatori and Others v Comune di Milano* [2007] ECR I–10419 [20].

regards to market access, 'the Union has exclusive competence to autonomously legislate on FDI, as in the other areas of the common commercial policy, such as the import and export regulation'.[35] Indeed, EU law provides a comprehensive regime to regulate both the establishment and the actions of foreign investors, which ultimately 'covers SWFs in exactly the same way as any other foreign investor'.[36]

Furthermore, after the Lisbon Treaty, the EU acquired an exclusive external competence over investment policy.[37] The difference is that now the EU has the exclusive competence to conclude agreements covering not only pre-establishment access, but also post-establishment protection of foreign investment.[38] In this context, the gradual unfolding of a common EU investment policy – through the conclusion of EU-wide BITs[39] – has the potential to raise again the question of whether an EU Committee on Foreign Investment should be established.

### *ii. EU Policy Towards SWFs*

Taking into account the exclusive EU competence over foreign investment, in 2008, the main European Institutions – the Commission, the Council and the European Parliament – decided to address the issue of SWFs and come up with an EU approach to the issue. An initial suggestion for the institution of an EU-wide 'screening mechanism' – similar to the one in the US – that would have the capacity to block inwards SWFs investments was considered but ultimately rejected.[40]

[35] Communication from the Commission to the European Parliament, the Council, the European Economic and Social Committee and the Committee of the Regions: 'Towards a Comprehensive European International Investment Policy' COM(2010) 343 fn 14; note, however, that Commission Communications to other EU institutions are not legally binding.

[36] Communication from the Commission to the European Parliament, the Council, the European Economic and Social Committee and the Committee of the Regions: 'A common European approach to Sovereign Wealth Funds', COM(2008) 115 provisional, 5.

[37] For a detailed account see A Dimopoulos, *EU Foreign Investment Law* (Oxford, Oxford University Press, 2011).

[38] It is, however, disputed whether the EU possesses all the necessary internal competences to be able to exercise its exclusive external competence vis-à-vis the post establishment protection of investments. As a matter of EU Law, the EU cannot have an external competence that is not also 'mirrored' internally. For instance, the EU does not have an internal competence over property protection and, as such, it would not be in a position to assume an international obligation to protect the property rights of investors from expropriation post-establishment. For a detailed analysis of these issues see M Dekastros, 'The Impact of the Lisbon Treaty on Investment Treaties Concluded by the EU and its Member-States' (LLM Thesis, University of Cambridge, 2011) esp. 13–24.

[39] See, eg, the recently signed – but not yet ratified – Comprehensive Economic and Trade Agreement, draft available at Foreign Affairs, Trade and Development Canada, 'Consolidated CETA Text'.

[40] J Chaisse, 'The Regulation of Sovereign Wealth Funds in the European Union', in KP Sauvant, LE Sachs and WPF Schmit Jongbloed (eds), *Sovereign Investment: Concerns and Policy Reactions* (Oxford, Oxford University Press, 2012) 469; for a similar proposal and its technical aspects that preceded these discussions see N Veron and L Hendrik-Roller, *Safe and Sound: An EU approach to Sovereign Investment* (Bruegel Policy Brief 2008/08, 2008) 7.

Despite that, in February 2008, the Commission presented a communication, titled '*A Common European Approach to Sovereign Wealth Funds*'.[41] Through the 2008 Communication, the Commission sought to avoid legislative actions and it opted instead for soft measures, such as guidelines, accompanied by efforts to increase transparency at the international level.[42] The Commission recommended a common approach premised on five key principles: 1) commitment to an open investment environment; 2) support of multilateral work; 3) use of existing instruments; 4) respect of EC Treaty and other international commitments; and 5) proportionality and transparency. Further, the Commission set out some of the options vis-à-vis regulating SWF operations within the EU Common Market.[43] Eventually, the European Council supported the objective of forming a consensus at the international level on a voluntary Code of Conduct for SWFs and defining principles for recipient countries – in line with the EU Communication. In this respect, the Council reiterated the EU's 'support for the ongoing work in the International Monetary Fund (IMF) and the OECD'.[44]

Nonetheless, it insisted that governments should be allowed to 'make use of national and EU instruments if necessary' to counter investment not justified for commercial reasons[45] – a possibility also envisaged in the EU Communication.[46] This consensus was – unsurprisingly – partly the result of the inability of Member States to produce a new comprehensive framework at the supranational level.[47] Therefore, it was decided that the EU Member States would be left to rely on the existing rules that allow derogation from the principle of movement of capital in some limited instances.

More recently, in March 2019, the European Council approved the regulation on the screening of FDI into the EU.[48] The new rules came into force in October 2020, following a transition period of 18 months after the regulation was enacted on 10 April 2019. The Regulation sets out a cooperation framework in relation to FDI into the EU. While the Regulation does not introduce an FDI screening process at the EU level, it establishes a cooperation mechanism between the European Commission and Member States which included the following operational requirements:

(a) the notification by EU Member States of their existing national investment screening mechanisms to the Commission;

[41] EU Communication on SWFs (n 36).

[42] Chaisse (n 41) 474.

[43] EU Communication on SWFs (n 36) 8–11.

[44] Presidency Conclusions, Brussels European Council, 13-14 March 2008, 7652/1/08 REV 1 [36].

[45] ibid [36].

[46] See EU Communication on SWFs (n 36) 7.

[47] Chaisse (n 41) 470; see also Case C-503/99 *The Commission v Belgium* [2002] ECR I–4809 [48]–[52].

[48] See EU Regulation 2019/452 of The European Parliament and ff The Council of 19 March 2019 establishing a framework for the screening of foreign direct investments into the Union.

(b) the establishment of formal contact points and secure channels in each Member State and within the Commission for the exchange of information and analysis;
(c) developing procedures for Member States and the Commission to quickly react to FDI concerns and to issue opinions; and
(d) updating the list of projects and programmes of Union interest annexed to the Regulation.

Further to the Regulation, the ultimate decision whether or not a Member States will permit the FDI in its territory remains exclusively with each Member State.

### a. Residual Member States' Competences Over SWFs' Investments

The aforementioned EU competence over investment flows and the free movement of capital declared in the Treaties are, however, not absolute. Though a fundamental principle of the TFEU, the movement of capital can be regulated in two ways at the European level.[49]

As per Article 64 TFEU, the EU may: 1) 'adopt, by qualified majority, measures on the movement of capital from third countries involving direct investment'; and (2) 'it is not excluded that the Commission can introduce (by a unanimous decision) measures that restrict foreign investments'.[50] The more narrowly these limits are construed, the easier it will be for SWFs to enter the EU market.[51] Thus, Article 64 of the TFEU gives the EU the competence to adopt measures with regards to the establishment of foreign investors in the EU.

Article 65, however, is arguably the most crucial with regards to SWFs' investments. It provides that:

> The provisions of Article 63 shall be without prejudice to the right of Member States: [...] (b): to take all requisite measures to prevent infringements of national law and regulations, in particular in the field of taxation and the prudential supervision of financial institutions, or to lay down procedures for the declaration of capital movements for purposes of administrative or statistical information, *or to take measures which are justified on grounds of public policy or public security*.[52]

Thus, this provision enables Member States to restrict the movement of capital to or from other Member States *or third countries* – as upheld by the ECJ in *Sanz de Lera* and others[53] – when given grounds as a matter of ensuring public order or public security.[54] Notably, the CJEU has held that whenever a Member

[49] Safeguard clauses, however, are also contained in Arts 66 and 75 of the TFEU. These concern third countries and are of a temporary nature, only to be applied in exceptional circumstances such as terrorism or threats to the operation of EMU.
[50] Art 64 TFEU.
[51] Chaisse (n 41) 484.
[52] Art 65(1)(b) TFEU (emphasis added).
[53] See Joined Cases C-163/94, C-165/94 & C-250/94 Criminal proceedings against Lucas Emilio Sanz de Lera, Raimundo Díaz Jiménez and Figen Kapanoglu [1995] ECR I–4821.
[54] Art 65(1)(b) TFEU.

State is invoking the justification measures of Article 65 TFEU, the country must demonstrate that the means that it used do not go beyond what is necessary to attain the stated end – in essence introducing a proportionality test.[55] Also, the Treaty provides that any such measures shall also 'not constitute a means of arbitrary discrimination or a disguised restriction on the free movement of capital and payments as defined in Article 63'.[56]

Indeed, even before investment explicitly came under the purview of Article 63 TFEU – ie, before the Treaty of Amsterdam – many European states had traditionally been much more apprehensive towards FDI in general in order to protect their 'national champions' or in the name of their (often ill-defined) security interests either by maintaining a preventive 'veto' power over investment flows or an ex post facto monitoring of the relevant investment.[57] In that context, even before the advent of SWF investments, they had already set up 'screening mechanisms' that could restrict FDI flows at will.

The EU had not been very content with these developments and, as it gradually solidified its competence over investment flows, some of these measures were challenged in the context of the 'golden share' case law.[58] In these cases, the legality of 'golden shares' was considered under Article 65(1)(a) TFEU on the free circulation of capital that, as mentioned, only allows derogations from this freedom on grounds of public order and public security. The scope of these exceptions was interpreted as including real and serious threats to an essential interest of the community,[59] imperative reasons of public interest[60] and energy services security.[61] It was also decided that these measures can only apply to the extent that they are proportionate and, thus, not all preventive authorisations

[55] Chaisse (n 41) 486.

[56] Art 65(3) TFEU.

[57] F Bassan, *The Law of Sovereign Wealth Funds* (Cheltenham, Edward Elgar Publishing, 2011) 64.

[58] Golden shares emerged in the beginning of 1980s in Great Britain – and later introduced by several EU states – and their main objective was the protection of a state's strategic interests by maintaining special rights in privatised companies. The idea behind their introduction was that some privatised companies have a special importance with regards to issues of public policy and national security. Thus, golden shares were a mechanism to safeguard these interests and protect companies against 'undesirable' influence or takeovers. To attain that goal, golden shares confer various special rights such as rights to appoint company directors or members of the Board, rights to veto and decision rights in the general meetings, rights to influence fundamental company decisions (eg, dissolution, mergers, takeovers etc), rights to influence and restrict acquisition of shareholding of the company in questions and others. For more see FS Benyon, *Direct Investment, National Champions and EU Treaty Freedoms: From Maastricht to Lisbon* (Hart Publishing, Oxford and Portland, Modern Studies in European Law 2010).

[59] See Case C-463/00 *The Commission v Spain* [2003] ECR I–4581, item 72.

[60] See Case C-174/04 *The Commission v Italy* [2005] ECR I–4933 [35]; See also Case C-367/98 *The Commission v Portugal* [2002] ECR I–4731 [49]; Case C-483/99 *The Commission v France* [2002] ECR I–4781 [45]; Case C-503/99 *The Commission v Belgium* (n 48) [45]; Joined cases C-282/04 and C-283/04 *The Commission v The Netherlands* [2006] ECR I–9141 [32].

[61] Case C-503/99 *The Commission v Belgium* (n 48) [48]; Case C-483/99 *The Commission v France* (n 34) [47]; Case C-463/00 *The Commission v Spain* (n 60) [71].

to the purchase of shares in a company would be allowed;[62] conversely an ex post intervention would be more tolerated.[63] As a result, some variations of the domestic laws introducing 'golden shares' were found to be unlawful under EU law.

It seems, thus, that the EU has adopted a more liberal approach to foreign investment – including SWFs – especially when it comes to preventive monitoring mechanisms.[64] These measures have to be strictly defined and be proportionate in nature, although, it has to be noted that in the case of SWFs, several legitimate interests like security, plurality of mass media and prudence will have to be taken into account.[65]

The EU Member States have supposedly modified their legislation to take into account the aforementioned case-law which only allows for the restrictions on the movement of capital when the 'state's vital interest' is threatened. However, they have tended to expand the meaning of the term in order to bypass these limitations – especially after the advent of SWFs. In the following subsections, the relevant screening mechanisms that have been instituted in different Member States to deal with foreign investment flows in general, and SWF investments in particular, will be presented.

### b. France

In France (despite having been condemned by the CJEU), the Ministry of Economy must provide a prior authorisation to a transaction falling within 20 'sensitive' sectors of the economy provided it is satisfied that there are no concerns over the effect of the investment on public order, public safety or national defence.[66] Notably, the latest decree on the screening of foreign investment that was enacted in July 2020 lowered the FDI screening threshold to 10 per cent participation interest (in terms of voting rights) in French listed companies for non-EU/EEA foreign investors acting alone, or in concert. This is deemed to be only a temporary protection up to 31 December 2020, to prevent hostile

[62] See Case *C-483/99 The Commission v France* (n 61) where an ex ante authorisation scheme to purchases of securities corresponding to only 10% of the total capitalisation was rejected; see also Case C-463/00 *The Commission v Spain* (n 60) [84]; see also Joined cases C-515/99, C-519/99 to C-524/99 and C-526/99 to C-540/99 *Hans Reisch and Others v Bürgermeister der Landeshauptstadt Salzburg and Grundverkehrsbeauftragter des Landes Salzburg and Anton Lassacher and Others v Grundverkehrsbeauftragter des Landes Salzburg and Grundverkehrslandeskommission des Landes Salzburg* ECR [2002] ECR I–2157.

[63] Case C-503/99 *The Commission v Belgium* (n 48) [48]–[52] where the measure was considered to be consistent with the Treaty partly because it was 'subsequent and not preventive' to the resolution.

[64] See EU Communication on SWFs (n 36) 7.

[65] ibid 7.

[66] See Law 2004–1343 and Enforcement Decree No 1739 of 2005; Décret n° 2019–1590 du 31 décembre 2019 relatif aux investissements étrangers en France; Décret et Arrêté du 22 Juillet 2020 relatif à l'abaissement temporaire du seuil de contrôle des investissements étrangers dans les sociétés françaises dont les actions sont admises aux négociations sur un marché réglementé.

or opportunistic acquisition in the context of the financial crises caused by the COVID-19 pandemic situation.

Additionally, in one of the most unusual regulatory responses to SWF investments yet, France enacted domestic legislation in November 2008 setting up a special purpose SWF called FSI (*Fond Stratégique d' Investissement*) that will act as a 'white knight' and block foreign government-controlled entities from acquiring stakes in French corporations.[67]

### c. Germany

In Germany, the rise of SWFs initiated a public debate that started in the summer of 2007. The acquisition of a three per cent stake in the European aircraft producer EADS by Dubai International Capital in July 2007 and rumours that the German companies Siemens AG and Deutsche Bahn AG could be targets of SWFs further fuelled an already negative public sentiment against SWFs.[68] The debate was also stimulated by Josef Ackermann, the CEO of Deutsche Bank, who claimed in June 2007 that Germany needs protection against SWFs from Russia, China, Kuwait, and Dubai.[69] Several other public officials – including Chancellor Merkel – espoused these fears, namely that SWFs could be used for politically motivated investments in sensitive sectors.[70]

In that context, the relevant legislation was revised in 2009,[71] and again in 2018, June 2020, and May 2021. It now provides that all foreign investors wishing to purchase more than 25 per cent of a German company (or 10 per cent of voting rights in a company which operates 'critical infrastructure') have to provide notice in that regard on a voluntary basis; if they do not, a committee composed of the Ministers of the Economy,[72] Finance, Foreign Affairs and Interior will start an inquiry which can result in the approval, cancellation or conditional approval of the investment.[73] The review is based on considerations of public order and security, as have been allegedly defined by the CJEU.[74]

[67] E Chalamish, 'Protectionism and Sovereign Investment Post Global Recession' (OECD Global Forum on International Investment, Geneva, 6–8 November 2002) 5.

[68] T Jost, 'Sovereign Wealth Funds and the German Policy Reaction', in KP Sauvant, LE Sachs and WPF Schmit Jongbloed (eds), *Sovereign Investment: Concerns and Policy Reactions* (Oxford, Oxford University Press, 2012) 453.

[69] ibid 453.

[70] ibid 453.

[71] ibid 457–458.

[72] See, eg, Simmons & Simmons, '*Germany extends FDI review mechanism to the healthcare sector*', available at www.simmons-simmons.com/en/publications/ckbqkf41gaf730979q77dwm4n/germany-extends-fdi-review-mechanism-to-the-healthcare-sector; and Simmons & Simmons, '*Germany expands its Foreign Direct Investment screening*', available at www.simmons-simmons.com/en/publications/ckocreu801fao0967t72ar9vb/germany-expands-its-foreign-direct-investment-screening.

[73] See Art 2.2 (1), Thirteenth Act amending the Foreign Trade and Payments Act and the Foreign Trade and Payments Regulation.

[74] See Federal Ministry of Economics and Technology, 'Frequently Asked Questions About the Government's Draft Legislation of August 29, 2008 Concerning the Acquisition of German Enterprises by Foreign Investors' 1.

However, in practice the scope of its meaning is likely to be widened to include considerations of energy supplies, telecommunication networks and strategic public services.[75] Also, over the years, the categories of companies that are considered to operate critical infrastructure has expanded considerably. Finally, the review of public order and security has been broadened since 2020 to cover also the potential impact on other EU Member States or projects and programmes of union interest

### d. United Kingdom

The UK traditionally maintained a liberal investment regime but also perceives SWF investment as an issue of economic governance and not security.[76] Indeed, many previous Labour and Conservative Governments rejected new legal controls based on overseas state ownership.[77] On the contrary, legal controls over mergers and takeovers were reduced under the 2002 Enterprise Act. Previously, ministers could refer a merger or takeover to an independent regulatory agency, the Monopolies and Mergers Commission (MMC, now called the Competition and Markets Authority); if the Commission was of the opinion that the transaction under investigation was 'against the public interest', then ministers could block it.[78] However, the 2002 Act reduced this power to much narrower grounds – notably only to potential threats to national security, media pluralism or financial stability.[79] Since 2013, 17 transactions have been reviewed or notified for review on national security grounds under these rules. Five of those 17 reviews have been during 2021, indicating the increased sensitivity in this area which appears to have led to the introduction of the new regime, despite historically low levels of reviews.

The UK recently introduced a new more extensive national security regime. The National Security and Investment Bill, published on 11 November 2020, became the National Security and Investment Act on 29 April 2021 after receiving Royal Assent and entered into force on 4 January 2022.[80] Under the new regime, certain acquisitions of entities active in 17 'sensitive' sectors will require mandatory notification and clearance before being implemented.[81]

[75] Bassan (n 58) 70.

[76] M Thatcher, *Western Policies towards Sovereign Wealth Funds Equity Investments: A Comparison of the UK, the EU and the US* (Policy Briefs, The London School of Economics and Political Science, London, UK, 2012) 3.

[77] ibid 3.

[78] ibid 3.

[79] ibid 3.

[80] See National Security and Investment Act, available at www.legislation.gov.uk/ukpga/2021/25/contents/enacted.

[81] The 17 sensitive sectors are as follows: civil nuclear; communications; data infrastructure; defence; energy; transport; artificial intelligence; autonomous robotics; computing hardware; cryptographic authentication; advanced materials; quantum technologies; engineering biology; critical suppliers to government; critical suppliers to the emergency services; military or dual-use technologies; and satellite and space technologies.

Other types of transactions (including acquisitions of assets and IP) will also be subject to voluntary notification and could be called in for review if not notified.

Mandatory notification will be required for certain 'trigger events' – the acquisition of more than 25 per cent, more than 50 per cent, or 75 per cent or more of votes or shares in a qualifying entity active in one of 17 specified sectors, or the acquisition of voting rights enabling or preventing the passage of any class of resolution governing the affairs of such an entity. Problematic transactions may be subject to conditions, or blocked as a last resort. There will also be significant sanctions for non-compliance with the new regime, including turnover-based fines, criminal liability and the risk of transactions subject to mandatory notification being void.

While the National Security and Investment Act does not define the concept of national security risk, the Secretary of State for Business, Energy and Industrial Strategy issued a draft Statement of Policy Intent on 2 March 2021, making it clear that national security risks are most likely to arise when the acquirers are hostile to the UK's national security, or when they owe alliance to hostile states or organisations, although it clarifies that the regime does not regard state-owned entities, sovereign wealth funds, or other entities affiliated with foreign states, as being inherently more likely to pose a national security risk.[82] Nonetheless, the new powers are deliberately flexible to address concerns in any sector and evolving national security risks.

### e. Interim Conclusion

It seems therefore that, despite the EU's best efforts, Member States seem to be willing to maintain a significant degree of regulatory control over incoming investment flows. In that context, it would only be natural to assume that the application of these measures in the light of SWF investment will be even more stringent. In fact, there are already hints that the governmental ownership of SWFs will be a determining factor in deciding whether to allow them to invest – at least for some EU countries.

For instance, the UK, while noting that the ownership of the bidder makes no difference in the way the bid is considered, has stated that government ownership might affect the UK's assessment of whether or not a bid raises public interest concerns. In particular, it could trigger concerns about whether the investor is influenced to behave in a non-commercial manner in pursuit of political objectives.[83] Similarly, Germany has declared that the ownership of the

[82] See Department for Business, Energy Industrial Strategy, Draft statement of policy intent, dated 2 March 2021, available at www.gov.uk/government/publications/national-security-and-investment-bill-2020/statement-of-policy-intent.

[83] K Gordon and A Tash, *Foreign Government-Controlled Investors and Recipient Country Investment Policies: A Scoping Paper* (OECD Investment Division, 10 January, 2009) 19.

foreign investment company (state or private) and its strategic interests will be taken into consideration.[84]

This expansion of the mandate of preventative 'screening mechanisms' as a response to the rise of SWFs' investments seems to be at odds with the expressed will of the EU about how to address the issue. Nonetheless, the EU has not yet shown any signs of asserting its competences on the matter or of challenging these developments at the CJEU.

### *iii. United States of America*

The US has traditionally maintained a certain degree of control over any type of foreign investment.[85] For instance, the International Banking Act of 1978 stipulates that, with some exceptions, no foreign bank may establish a branch or an agency or acquire ownership or control of a commercial lending company without the prior approval of the Federal Reserve Board (FRB). The FRB will only approve such a request if it determines that the foreign bank is subject to comprehensive supervision of regulation on a consolidated basis by the appropriate authorities in its home country.[86] Further, there are federal laws with provisions that specifically limit foreign ownership (including from SWFs) in a number of sectors, such as transportation, communications, natural resources, energy, banking and agriculture.[87] Generally federal laws do not restrict foreign investment but place some reporting requirements on foreign investments, including the regulation of FDI in certain sectors, the requirement of prior approval of foreign investment or the restriction of foreign activities of the foreign-owned firm once an investment has been made.[88] Moreover, there are state-level restrictions on foreign investment, most of them being in the insurance and real estate sectors. Many state laws ban a foreign insurer that is owned or controlled in any manner or degree by any government or governmental agency from transacting insurance.[89] Other state laws specifically prohibit foreign ownership of certain types of land, such as agricultural land.[90]

More importantly, however, in 1975, President Ford issued Executive Order 11858 establishing the Committee on Foreign Investment in the United States (CFIUS) in order to monitor and evaluate the impact of foreign investment

[84] ibid 19.

[85] Note, however, that the US – like other Members of the WTO – have subsequently agreed to some liberalisation of investment through the GATS and BITs, an issue to which we come to later.

[86] Federal Deposit Insurance Corporation, International Banking Act of 1978.

[87] G Bahgat, 'The USA's Policy on Sovereign Wealth Funds' Investments', in X Yi-chong and G Bahgat (eds), *The Political Economy of Sovereign Wealth Funds* (Basingstoke, Palgrave Macmillan 2010) 237–240.

[88] ibid 240.

[89] ibid 240.

[90] ibid 240.

in the US and make sure that the promotion of foreign investment is consistent with the goal of protecting national security.[91] The Order authorises CFIUS to undertake an investigation of any transaction that might threaten or impair the national security of the US and send a report to the President. If CFIUS finds that a covered transaction presents national security risks, then CFIUS may enter into an agreement with it, impose conditions on the parties in order to mitigate such risks, or may refer the case to the President for action. When CFIUS has completed all action with respect to a covered transaction or the President has announced a decision not to exercise their authority then the parties receive a 'safe harbour' with respect to that transaction.[92]

This already restrictive framework was further strengthened, partly as a response to the phenomenon on SWFs. Indeed, the legislation had been criticised as not being restrictive enough with respect to SWFs because it allegedly did not take into account risks related to economic security.[93] As a response to that criticism, in September 2007, the House of Representatives adopted a resolution that suggested the imposition of further restrictive measures in respect to SWFs.[94]

Congress, on 24 October 2007, enacted the Foreign Investment and National Security Act (FINSA) to supplement already existing regulation on the screening of foreign investment.[95] Under the Act, foreign investors are now prohibited from acquiring any stakes in defence companies or companies that handle sensitive technology.[96] Furthermore, the amendment extended the monitoring mandate of CFIUS to include transactions below the threshold of 10 per cent of capital stock – now also bringing portfolio investment into its ambit.

The Act defined covered transactions as any merger, acquisition or takeover that is proposed or pending by or with any foreign person that could result in foreign control of any person engaged in interstate commerce in the US. The definition of 'control' however, is quite broad since it looks at the 'functional abilities' of an acquirer to exercise control.[97] The regulations provided that there

[91] Executive Order 11858 – Foreing Investment in the United States.

[92] United States Department of Treasury, 'CFIUS Process Overview': www.treasury.gov/resource-center/international/Pages/Committee-on-Foreign-Investment-in-US.aspx (accessed 15 October 2015).

[93] See Truman, 'Sovereign Wealth Fund Acquisitions and Other Foreign Government Investments in the United States: Assessing the Economic and National Security Implications'.

[94] See MF Martin, *China's Sovereign Wealth Funds* (CRS Report for Congress, Order Code RL34337, 2008 who suggests the imposition of: '1) requirements that any SWF interested in investing in the United States publicly release audited financial statements, that follow international accounting standards on a regular basis; 2) restrictions on the percentage of a US company a SWF may own; and 3) restrictions on the type of investment a SWF may make in US companies – alternatives include restricting SWFs from negotiating a seat on the company's board of directors or representation on company's senior management'.

[95] Foreign Investment and National Security Act of 2007, PL 110-49, 121 Stat 246 which amends the 'Omnibus Trade and Competitiveness Act', already an amendment to the 'Exxon Florio' amendment which established the Committee on Foreign Investment in the United States (CFIUS).

[96] See ibid.

[97] Money and Finance, 31 Code of Federal Regulations, Appendix to Part 800 – Preamble on Mergers Acquisitions, and Takeovers by Foreign Persons [800.702].

is no control when voting securities are held 'solely for the purpose of investment', which is albeit defined in a circular fashion to mean that the acquirer 'has no intention of directing the basic business decisions of the issuer'.[98] Obviously, this is something that can hardly be assessed ahead of an investment rendering the scheme quite opaque and offering CFIUS a very wide margin of discretion.

Moreover, two more evaluation criteria were added to the already existing ones: an evaluation of whether: 1) the transaction concerns strategic infrastructure; 2) the transaction is made by parties controlled, even if only indirectly, by foreign states.[99] This is important, since for the first time in a piece of legislation of this kind a direct reference to state-controlled entities such as SWFs is made.

Moreover, the President of the US has the competence to bar any foreign investment on national security grounds, a condition that is left purposefully ill-defined in the Act.[100] In determining the effects of a foreign acquisition on national security, the President may consider the following factors: i) domestic production needed for projected national defence requirements; ii) the capacity of domestic industries to meet national defence requirements, including the availability of human resources, products, technology, materials and other supplies; iii) the control of domestic industries and commercial activity by foreign citizens as it affects the capability and capacity of the US to meet the requirements of national security; iv) the potential effects of the transaction on the sales of military goods, equipment or technology to a country that supports terrorism or proliferates missile technology or chemical or biological weapons; and v) the potential effects if the transaction on US technological leadership in areas affecting US National Security.[101]

After the enactment of FINSA, the focus of the national security discourse gradually shifted to China and, specifically, the question of 'technology transfer'. Further, the intensity of the CFIUS process during this period began to shift, with the Committee seemingly subjecting deals involving Chinese investors to increased scrutiny. This increased scrutiny was evidenced by CFIUS reviews resulting in the President blocking transactions involving Chinese investors in 2012,[102] 2016[103] and 2017[104] (with the latter transactions involving the semiconductor industry), all of which received significant media attention.

[98] ibid [800.219].

[99] Namely, the existence of credible evidence that the transaction might threaten the national security and lack of rules that allows coping with that threat adequately and appropriately. *cf* on investment screening mechanisms regarding critical infrastructure, ch 7, in this volume.

[100] An indicative list of factors to be considered includes domestic production needs for projected national defence requirements, capability and capacity of domestic industries to meet national defence requirements, control of domestic industries and commercial activity by foreign citizens as long as it affects the capability and capacity of the US to meet national security requirements.

[101] Section 721 of the Defence Production Act of 1050, 50 USC App 2170.

[102] Statement on the President's Decision Regarding the US Business of Aixtron SE (2 December 2016), available at www.treasury.gov/press-center/press-releases/Pages/jl0679.aspx.

[103] Statement on the President's Decision Regarding Lattice Semiconductor Corporation (13 September 2017), available at www.treasury.gov/press-center/press-releases/Pages/sm0157.aspx.

[104] Federal Register, Vol 83 No 197 (11 October 2018) 51322.

These trends culminated in the passage of the Foreign Investment Risk Review Modernization Act of 2018 (FIRRMA), which brought yet another expansion in CFIUS's authority, as well significant changes to the regulatory process itself. From an investor perspective, FIRRMA's biggest impact is found in the new 'mandatory declaration' provision. For the first time, investors affiliated with non-US governments (including sovereign wealth funds) and investors targeting certain types of US businesses designated by CFIUS will be required to file a short (about five pages) notification of certain proposed investments. After receiving a declaration, CFIUS will have 30 days either to approve the transaction or to require a full CFIUS review.

The FINSA and FIRRMA Acts are probably the most restrictive pieces of screening legislation in existence since they not only maintain a preventive screening and control mechanism over any investment in the US, but also de jure impose more stringent conditions on sovereign investors. Furthermore, the Acts purposefully choose a very widely constructed conceptualisation of 'national security' in order not to curtail the President's broad authority to protect the national security'.[105] Thus, such a definition could encompass commercial considerations or used to protect domestic industries.

## IV. THE COMPATIBILITY OF FOREIGN INVESTMENT SCREENING UNDER INTERNATIONAL INVESTMENT LAW

### A. SWFs' Investment and Pre-Establishment Rights

Admittedly – at least prima facie –there is no generally recognised right of individuals to invest in foreign markets or an international standard requiring states to admit inwards FDI without any qualification.[106] However, over the years, there has been a consistent push to allow the free flow of capital across borders. This has resulted in a limited, yet fragmented, international regulatory framework that provides certain pre-establishment rights to some classes of investors.

Accordingly, the use of 'investment screening mechanisms' to restrict SWFs' investments may be at odds with certain FTAs and BITs that extend their protection to the pre-establishment stage of investments.

As a preliminary issue, it should be noted that the protections of International Investment Law extend *ratione personae* to state-owned enterprises – including SWFs.

The overwhelming majority of BITs and FTAs, with only a few isolated exceptions, do contain definitions of 'investor' that cover SWFs. Indeed,

[105] See 31 CFR (n 98); FIRRMA Act, H.R. 5515–536, Sec. 1703, Definitions. *cf* on the EU's FDI Screening Regulation, see ch 6, in this volume.

[106] J-P Laviec, *Protection et Promotion des Investissements: Etude de Droit International Économique* (Presses, Universitaires de France, 1985) 77.

some treaties expressly include 'government-owned' or 'state' enterprises,[107] some even including governments themselves,[108] while most of them simply refer to 'legal persons' as protected investors without distinguishing on the basis of the type of ownership. In fact, most investment treaties and domestic investment statutes do not exclude state-owned companies or SWFs from their broad definitions of investors and,[109] whilst some Middle Eastern BITs expressly mention them as a class of protected investors.[110] In a 2012 survey of 851 investment agreements, the author identified only two agreements – both with Panama – that contained any provisions that would exclude a claim by a state-owned enterprise.[111]

Since SWFs would enjoy access to investment tribunals, the next issue that needs to be addressed is whether the relevant investment agreements provide for any pre-establishment rights to prospective SWF investors.

On this issue, we can broadly identify two different sets of state practice. On the one hand, we have BITs promoted mostly by European as well as developing countries. These BITs, whose origins we can trace back to the Abs-Shawcross Draft Convention – a Model BIT recommended by the OECD Council of Ministers in 1962 – lack binding provisions on the entry and establishment of foreign investors in the relevant domestic market.[112] Usually, these BITs contain a phrase that typically reads:

> Each Contracting Party shall in its territory promote as far as possible investments by investors of the other Contracting State and admit such investments in accordance with its legislation.[113]

[107] See, eg, Art 11.28, Free Trade Agreement between the United States of America and the Republic of Korea (2007); Art 1, Agreement between the Government of the United Mexican States and the Government of the People's Republic of China on the Promotion and Reciprocal Protection of Investments (2008); Arts 1(k) and 1(l), Asean Comprehensive Investment Agreement (2009); Arts 1(2) and (4), Agreement between the Government of the Republic of Korea and the Government of Japan for the Liberalization, Promotion, and Protection of Investment (2012).

[108] See, eg, Art 11.28, KORUS FTA; Art X.3, Comprehensive Economic and Trade Agreement, draft available at Foreign Affairs, Trade and Development Canada, 'Consolidated CETA Text'.

[109] Examples include US, Canadian or Australian BITs; for a detailed overview see C Annacker, 'Protection and Admission of Sovereign Investment under Investment Treaties' (2011) 10 *Chinese Journal of International Law* 531, 537–539.

[110] See, eg, BITs concluded by several Arab States such as Saudi Arabia, Qatar, Egypt, Kuwait and the United Arab Emirates; for a full account and examples of such Treaties see ibid 538–539.

[111] See J En Low, 'State-controlled Entities as 'Investors' under International Investment Agreements' (2012) 80 *Columbia FDI Perspectives*: Perspectives on Topical Foreign Direct Investment Issues by the Vale Columbia Center on Sustainable International Investment who is citing Panama BITs with Germany and Switzerland.

[112] See OECD, *Relationships between International Investment Agreements* (OECD Working Paper on International Investment, 2004); JM Kline and RD Ludema, 'Building a Multilateral Framework for Investment: Comparing the Development of Trade and Investment Accords' (1997) 6 *Transnational Corporations* 1, 10.

[113] For examples of this kind of clause see Art 2(1) Germany Model BIT (2008); Art 2(1) United Kingdom Model BIT (2006), Art 2(1) China Model BIT, all available in Z Douglas, *The International Law of Investment Claims*, vol 1 (Cambridge, CUP, 2009) 559 and 525 respectively.

This clause allows recipient states to escape any scrutiny of investment tribunals by enacting legislation that has the competence to block specific investments.

We can group all these investment treaties under the name 'Limited Entry BITs'. Under these agreements, states have only assumed an obligation to promote investments as far as possible, but not to automatically admit them. The vast majority of BITs now in force have followed this approach and there seems to be a broad acceptance of their underlying rationale.[114]

These BITs seem to reflect the idea – shared by many states – that FDI is generally welcome but remains subject to host state regulation at the point of entry.[115] The underlying rationale for such an approach is that sovereignty over economic decisions has to be affirmed and that government and private monopolies sometimes have to be protected.[116]

It is safe to assume that under these Treaties, which at the moment represent the majority of BITs in force,[117] the investment screening committees which have been set up by several states would escape the scrutiny of International Investment Law. Host states are free to block any investment they see fit or apply differential and even discriminatory treatment towards foreign investors.[118] Therefore, SWF investors that are covered by any of these Treaties would not have the opportunity to bring any claim in case their investments are blocked by the relevant states.

## B. Foreign Investment Screening Mechanisms under 'Liberalisation BITs'

There is, however, another family of BITs that has mostly been promoted by the US[119] and Canada and more recently by Japan, Finland and Norway. These BITs, which we can group under the title 'Liberalisation BITs', extend the national treatment obligation also to the pre-establishment stage of investments thus giving prospective investors the right to be admitted and to maintain a permanent establishment in the territory of the recipient state.[120] For instance the 2012 US Model BIT provides that:

> 1. Each Party shall accord to investors of the other Party treatment no less favorable than that it accords, in like circumstances, to its own investors with respect

[114] UNCTAD, *Admission and Establishment* (United Nations, New York and Geneva, 1999) 16, 20.
[115] ibid.
[116] I Gomez-Palacio and P Muchlinski, 'Admission and Establishment', in P Muchlinski, F Ortino and C Schreuer (eds), *Oxford Handbook of International Investment Law* (Oxford, Oxford University Press, 2008) 240.
[117] ibid 240.
[118] UNCTAD, Bilateral Investment Treaties 1995–2006: Trends in Investment Rulemaking (United Nations, New York and Geneva, 2007) 21–22.
[119] For the US Bilateral Investment Treaty Program and its instrumental role in that approach see KJ Vandevelde, 'The Bilateral Investment Treaty Program of the United States' (1988) 21 *Cornell International Law Journal* 201.
[120] See R Dolzer and CH Schreuer, *Principles of International Investment Law* (New York, OUP, 2008) 81; Gomez-Palacio and Muchlinski (n 117) 242–245; C Annacker, 'Protection and Admission

to the establishment, acquisition, expansion, management, conduct, operation, and sale or other disposition of investments in its territory.

2. Each Party shall accord to covered investments treatment no less favorable than that it accords, in like circumstances, to investments in its territory of its own investors with respect to the establishment, acquisition, expansion, management, conduct, operation, and sale or other disposition of investments.[121]

These BITs represented only a small fraction of the totality of BITs that had entered into force, perhaps about 4 per cent in 2005 – but their number has been steadily increasing.[122] Interestingly, however, this extension of protection to the pre-establishment stage is much more common in most modern FTAs.[123] The first such Treaty that introduced that approach was the US–Canada Free Trade Agreement in 1988[124] that was later copied in the North American Free Trade Agreement and its infamous Chapter 11,[125] and repeated in Article 14.4 of the recently concluded Agreement between the United States of America, the United Mexican States, and Canada (USMCA). Other similar agreements include the FTAs concluded by Taiwan with Guatemala, Panama and Nicaragua; Korea with Chile and Singapore; Canada with Chile; Mexico with Uruguay, El Salvador, Guatemala and Honduras; Japan with Chile, Brunei, Indonesia, Malaysia, Mexico, the Philippines and Singapore and all the FTAs or Trade Promotion Agreements (TPAs) of the US, except those with Israel and Jordan.[126] What is even more striking is that despite the fact that European countries have been reluctant to adopt a 'pre-establishment' protection type BIT in their bilateral relations, when it comes to the EU, the latter has been consistently pursuing agreements that incorporate this type of provision.[127] Indeed, the Association Agreements promoted by the EU focus a lot on securing entry and establishment rights for foreign investors. After the Lisbon Treaty, the EU also acquired an exclusive competence over Foreign Direct Investment and there are signs that it has been pursuing the incorporation of such clauses in the new FTAs (with investment chapters), as it seems to be adopting a model BIT that will largely resemble NAFTA.[128]

Furthermore, other types of agreements that have departed from the old NAFTA paradigm also include pre-establishment protection. The recently ratified ASEAN Investment Protection Agreement,[129] despite the fact that it

of Sovereign Investment under Investment Treaties' (2011) 10(3) *Chinese Journal of International Law* 531.

[121] United States 2012 Model Bilateral Investment Treaty.

[122] UNCTAD, Investor-State Disputes Arising from Investment Treaties: A Review (2005) 31.

[123] ibid 31.

[124] Art 105, Canada – United States Free Trade Agreement (1988) 27 ILM 281.

[125] Art 1102, North American Free Trade Agreement, 32 ILM 289, 605 (1993).

[126] M Molinuevo, *Protecting Investment in Services* (The Netherlands, Kluwer Law International, 2012) 88.

[127] ibid 87.

[128] See N Lavranos, 'The New EU Investment Treaties: Convergence towards the NAFTA Model as the New Plurilateral Model BIT Text?' (2013), available at ssrn.com/abstract=2241455.

[129] The Association for Southeast Asian Nations (ASEAN) is comprised of: Brunei Darussalam, the Kingdom of Cambodia, the Republic of Indonesia, the Lao People's Democratic Republic,

generally seeks to balance the liberalisation of investment with respect to the regulatory autonomy of the states, also provides for pre-establishment national treatment – subject to some sectoral limitations.[130] The same holds true for the MERCOSUR Colonia Protocol for the Promotion of Reciprocal Investments[131] and the Australia–Thailand FTA.[132]

The underlying economic rationale of these BITs is that optimum investment decisions are made when the state does not interfere and the economic actors make their decisions on purely economic grounds; under these, the competitive opportunities of investors, both domestic and foreign, are equalised.[133]

Typically, however, these Treaties are accompanied by a country-specific sectoral reservation list that is similar in its function to the GATS' schedules of commitments and determines the sectors to which national treatment is offered.[134]

Overall, recent developments seem to indicate that a paradigm shift is in progress in the field of BITs; the old NAFTA paradigm seems to be gaining ground. This is especially true for the most recent FTAs containing investment chapters.[135] If this trend continues, it is highly likely that a significant number, perhaps the majority, of investment flows will be covered by 'Liberalisation' BITs which grant pre-establishment rights to investors.[136] More importantly, however, the US already has and the EU soon will adopt this specific type of BIT. Given that SWFs at the moment seem to be investing more and more into mature developed markets, it is highly likely that in the future their investments will be covered by this type of BIT.

The cardinal issue is whether 'investment screening mechanisms' set up by many SWF host states are actually in conformity with the 'Liberalisation' BITs. The question is straightforward for 'Limited Entry BITs'. The renvoi to national law precludes any possibility of unlawfulness. Nonetheless, it is submitted that 'investment screening mechanisms' are not in conformity with 'Liberalisation'

Malaysia, the Union of Myanmar, the Republic of the Philippines, the Republic of Singapore, the Kingdom of Thailand, and the Socialist Republic of Vietnam.

130 See Arts 5 and 6, Asean Comprehensive Investment Agreement (2009).

131 See Protocol of Colonia for the Protection of Investments in Mercosur (1994).

132 See Art 904, Thailand – Australia Free Trade Agreement (2005).

133 Gomez-Palacio and Muchlinski (n 117) 243.

134 Molinuevo (n 127) 86.

135 Gomez-Palacio and Muchlinski (n 117) 251.

136 Such a development could potentially have far-reaching consequences for trade policy as well; see, eg, EJ Blanchard, 'Reevaluating the Role of Trade Agreements: Does Investment Globalization make the WTO Obsolete?' (2010) 82 *Journal of International Economics* 63; EJ Blanchard, 'Foreign Direct Investment, Endogenous Tariffs, and Preferential Trade Agreements' (2007) 7 *The BE Journal of Economic Analysis & Policy* who is arguing that 'as foreigners hold a greater stake in the local economy – either through direct investment or portfolio holdings – the host-government may recognize the opportunity to shift rents away from foreign owners in favor of local constituents through domestic policy changes' and that, partly as a consequence, 'preferential trade agreements may be a particularly effective means for harnessing the tariff liberalizing potential of foreign direct investment'.

BITs. These committees prime facie constitute preferential treatment to domestic investors since they do not have to go through the same process in order to proceed with their investments. Sornarajah – a scholar who has in general been very sceptical towards the liberalisation of investment – also concedes that whenever the relevant BIT extends its protection to the pre-establishment stage of an investment, screening legislation will in principle not be consistent with the national treatment treaty obligations.[137] But further, any possible refusal to admit an investment would also undoubtedly violate the Treaty.

Interestingly, so far there have been no published disputes involving the pre-establishment stage under any of these BITs.[138] This is, however, likely to change when the potential investor is actually a very big institutional investor having the financial and political resources of a state behind it.

## V. CONCLUSION

The aforementioned analysis indicates that recipient states of SWFs' investments enjoy a much more limited discretion to restrict or block these investment flows than previously thought. Indeed, several 'Liberalisation' BITs provide potential investors in the field of services with the right to move capital in relation to an investment and to set up a permanent commercial presence in the territory of the signatories.

The foreign investment screening mechanisms that have been set up to screen and potentially block SWFs' investments have generally been given a very wide mandate which prima facie violates the commitments undertaken under these instruments. Indeed, the current trend suggests that the power of the foreign investment screening mechanisms has expanded over the years. Admittedly, it could be argued that these committees would escape scrutiny under the 'exception' clauses contained in some of these Treaties. The wording of these clauses, however, only allows exemption in a few, narrowly constructed circumstances related to 'national security' stricto sensu.

Nonetheless, this does not mean that host states should be prevented from addressing the legitimate regulatory concerns that surround the operation of SWFs within their markets. On the contrary, IEL Agreements accord host states with significant regulatory space when it comes to regulating economic entities *after* their entry into their markets. The fact that SWFs possess some unique characteristics connected to their government ownership could, as a matter of law, justify this differential treatment and enable host states to regulate the operation of SWFs *differently* to other economic entities.

[137] M Sornarajah, *The International Law on Foreign Investment* (Cambridge, Cambridge University Press 2010) 137.

[138] Douglas (n 114) 141.

# 6

# *The Screening of Cross-Border Investments by State-Owned Enterprises under EU Law*

KONSTANTINA GEORGAKI*

## I. INTRODUCTION

THE PROMOTION OF cross-border investment, both foreign and among EU Member States, is one of the EU's top priorities.[1] Cross-border investment is a key driver to achieving and enhancing the EU's economic and social development, being an invaluable source of jobs and growth. It boosts productivity and enhances the competitiveness of the EU's internal market, in particular by bringing in capital, technologies and expertise, increasing competition and, in the case of foreign investment, by opening up new markets for the EU's exports.[2]

The EU has one of the most open investment regimes in the world,[3] an openness enshrined in its constitutive documents. Under Article 63 of the Treaty on the Functioning of the European Union (TFEU), all restrictions on the movement of capital and payments between Member States, as well as between Member States and third countries are, in principle, prohibited. The free movement of capital, which covers both EU and non-EU nationals, combined with the EU's increased external action in the field of trade and investment through the conclusion of Free Trade Agreements (FTAs) and International Investment

* The opinions expressed in this chapter are the author's own and do not reflect the views of the European Commission. The European Commission is not responsible for any use that may be made of the information included herein.

[1] See Commission Priorities 2019–2024, as part of the priority on 'A Stronger Europe in the World' and 'An Economy that Works for the People' respectively, available at ec.europa.eu/info/strategy/priorities-2019–2024_en (accessed 5 January 2021).

[2] Commission, 'Welcoming Foreign Direct Investment while Protecting Essential Interests' (Communication) COM(2017) 494 final, 4.

[3] ibid 3.

Agreements (IIAs) with third countries have classified the EU among the world's leading investment destinations.[4]

Although the EU's single market constitutes a 'unique area of investment opportunities',[5] third countries do not always reciprocate this openness to EU investors, maintaining significant barriers to market entry. Meanwhile, over the past decade, the EU has increasingly attracted investment from many third-country investors.[6] In fact, recent investment trends in the EU have shown an increase in foreign investment in critical technologies, infrastructure, inputs and sensitive information,[7] in particular by foreign SOEs, which may not always play by market rules. The risk that foreign investors, especially (but not exclusively) SOEs, may obtain ownership or control of EU undertakings in sectors of strategic importance, together with the lack of reciprocal openness of foreign markets to EU investors, have generated widespread concerns among the Member States, which called on the EU to take appropriate action.

The EU has adopted a number of so-called 'trade defence instruments' in an effort to protect critical assets against investment potentially detrimental to its own or to the Member States' legitimate interests, as well as to level the playing field with its trading partners and warrant third-country market access to EU investors.[8] In this context, Regulation 2019/452 establishing a framework for the screening of foreign direct investments into the Union on grounds of security and public order (the FDI Screening Regulation) was recently enacted. Without removing the ultimate responsibility on investment screening from the Member States, which remain free to choose whether they introduce or maintain a screening mechanism at national level, the Regulation aims at ensuring that such screening mechanisms adhere to certain basic requirements. In addition, it establishes a cooperation mechanism between the Member States and the Commission for the exchange of information on planned or completed FDI that may threaten security or public order.[9]

The adoption of the FDI Screening Regulation gave rise to two interrelated, yet distinct questions, which this chapter seeks to tackle in turn: first, under which legal framework does one assess the compatibility of national screening mechanisms of other types of cross-border investment with EU law? Second, does this legal framework also cover cases, where the investor planning or having made the investment is an SOE? Against this background, section II first distinguishes between the different investment types that may be observed in the EU,

[4] ibid.

[5] Commission, 'Protection of Intra-EU Investment' (Communication) COM(2018) 547 final, 1.

[6] With the most prominent players being the US, Switzerland, Canada, Brazil and China, ibid.

[7] Commission, 'Welcoming Foreign Direct Investment' (n 2) 5.

[8] Commission, 'A Balanced and Progressive Trade Policy to Harness Globalisation' (Communication) COM(2017) 492 final, 5–6.

[9] Commission, 'Proposal for a Regulation of the European Parliament and of the Council establishing a framework for screening of foreign direct investments into the European Union' COM(2017) 487 final, 2, 3.

namely third country (foreign direct and portfolio) investment and intra-EU (direct and portfolio) investment, analysing the legal framework for assessing the compatibility of national mechanisms on their screening with EU law. Section III then goes on to examine how – if at all – the EU legal framework for assessing national mechanisms screening cross-border investments would differ in case the investor is an SOE.

## II. THE EU LEGAL FRAMEWORK FOR ASSESSING NATIONAL CROSS-BORDER INVESTMENT SCREENING MECHANISMS

This section examines the EU regulatory framework, pursuant to which the compatibility of national investment screening mechanisms with EU law is to be assessed. Before tackling this question, a preliminary matter is to distinguish between the different types of investment that may be conducted in the EU. Against this background, a twofold distinction can be made between: first, direct and non-direct (portfolio) investment, depending on whether the investor aims at controlling the undertaking, to which capital is made available, or solely to make profit, without controlling or influencing its decisions respectively; and, second, extra-EU and intra-EU investment, based on the capacity of the investor as a third-country or EU national. This distinction is crucial as the different types of (envisaged) investments trigger the application of different EU rules.

### A. The Different Types of Cross-Border Investment in the EU

The EU Treaties do not define the concept of an 'investment'. While Articles 64 TFEU governing exceptions to the free movement of capital and payments from third countries, and 207(1) TFEU on the Common Commercial Policy (CCP) use the terms 'direct investment' and 'foreign direct investment' respectively, they do not elaborate on what these notions encompass.[10]

Despite the lack of a definition in the Treaties, the concepts of 'direct investment' and 'foreign direct investment' have been delineated by both secondary EU legislation and the case law of the Court of Justice of the European Union (CJEU). In interpreting 'direct investment' in the sense of Article 64 TFEU, the CJEU has relied on the definition of the term in Council Directive 88/361 implementing Article 67 of the EEC Treaty,[11] Article 1(1) of which provides that

[10] Opinion 2/15 *Free Trade Agreement with Singapore* [2016] ECLI:EU:C:2016:992, Opinion of AG Sharpston, para 310; Case C-446/04 *Test Claimants in the FII Group Litigation* [2006] ECLI:EU:C:2006:774, para 177; F Erlbacher and TM Rusche, 'Article 207 TFEU', in M Kellerbauer, M Klamert and J Tomkin (eds), *The EU Treaties and the Charter of Fundamental Rights. A Commentary* (Oxford, OUP, 2019) 1586, 1595.

[11] Council Directive of 24 June 1988 for the implementation of Article 67 of the Treaty (88/361/EEC) [1988] OJ L178/5.

capital movements are to be classified in accordance with the Nomenclature in Annex I.[12] The latter sets out an indicative[13] list of activities of capital movements qualifying as 'direct investment',[14] whereas it explicitly refers to the explanatory notes, which further define certain terms for the purposes of the Nomenclature and the Directive. According to the explanatory notes, the concept of 'direct investments' means[15]

> investments of all kinds by natural persons or commercial, industrial or financial undertakings, and which serve to establish or to maintain lasting and direct links between the person providing the capital and the entrepreneur to whom or the undertaking to which the capital is made available in order to carry on an economic activity. This concept must be understood in its widest sense.

Against that background, the CJEU has also consistently found the concept of 'direct investment' to cover[16]

> investments by natural or legal persons which serve to establish or maintain lasting and direct links between the person providing the capital and the company to which that capital is made available in order to carry out an economic activity.

While 'direct investment' is a broadly construed notion, encapsulating both intra-EU and extra-EU direct investment,[17] the EU Treaties include in Article 207(1) TFEU a specific term to connote 'foreign direct investment', namely direct investment with a non-EU component. By contrast to Article 64 TFEU, Article 207(1) TFEU only covers FDI and does not extend to intra-EU direct investment.[18] This has been confirmed by the CJEU's early case law[19] and has recently been

[12] *Ex multis*, see Joined Cases C-52/16 and C-113/16 *SEGRO and Horváth* [2018] ECLI:EU:C:2018:157, para 56 and further case law cited; S Schill, 'The European Union's Foreign Direct Investment Screening Paradox: Tightening Inward Investment Control to Further External Investment Liberalization' (2019) 46 *Legal Issues of Economic Integration* 105, 116.

[13] *Test Claimants* (n 10) para 179; Case C-222/97 *Trummer and Mayer* [1999] ECLI:EU:C:1999:143, para 21.

[14] Under 'direct investment', the Nomenclature lists the following activities: 1) establishment and extension of branches or new undertakings belonging solely to the person providing the capital, and the acquisition in full of existing undertakings; (2) participation in new or existing undertakings with a view to establishing or maintaining lasting economic links; (3) long-term loans with a view to establishing or maintaining lasting economic links; and (4) reinvestment of profits with a view to maintaining lasting economic links'.

[15] Directive 88/361 (n 11), explanatory notes to the Nomenclature.

[16] Case C-181/12 *Welte* [2013] ECLI:EU:C:2013:662, para 32; Case C-35/11 *Test Claimants in the FH Group Litigation* [2012] ECLI:EU:C:2012:707, para 102 and further case law cited there; see also A Steiblytė and J Tomkin, 'Article 63 TFEU', in M Kellerbauer, M Klamert and J Tomkin (eds), *The EU Treaties and the Charter of Fundamental Rights. A Commentary* (Oxford, OUP, 2019) 746, 754.

[17] See also S Hindelang, The Free Movement of Capital and Foreign Direct Investment: The Scope of Protection in EU Law (Oxford, OUP, 2009) 76 seq.

[18] Art 205 TFEU seq; see also R Yotova, 'The New EU Competence in Foreign Direct Investment and Intra-EU Investment Treaties: Does the Emperor Have New Clothes?', in F Baetens (ed), *Investment Law within International Law: Integrationist Perspectives* (Cambridge, CUP, 2013) 387, 389; P Craig and G de Búrca, *EU Law: Texts, Cases and Materials,* 7th edn (Oxford, OUP, 2020) 385.

[19] In *Opinion 1/75*, the CJEU held that permitting the Member States to exercise concurrent powers in the area of the CCP 'would amount to recognising that, in relations with *third countries* [emphasis added], Member States may adopt positions which differ from those which the [EU]

reaffirmed in its opinion on the allocation of powers between the EU and its Member States for the conclusion of the then envisaged Free Trade Agreement with Singapore (EUSFTA).[20] Following Advocate General (AG) Sharpston's comprehensive opinion in the case, the CJEU examined what constitutes an 'investment' that is both 'foreign' and 'direct'. In framing 'direct' investment, the CJEU drew a parallel with the notion of direct investment in the sense of Articles 63 and 64 TFEU on the free movement of capital and payments.[21] Against this background, the CJEU found the notion of direct investment to encompass[22]

> investments of any kind made by natural or legal persons, which serve to establish or maintain lasting and direct links between the persons providing the capital and the undertakings to which that capital is made available in order to carry out an economic activity.

Turning to 'foreign direct investment', the CJEU characterised as such any direct investment made by an EU natural or legal person in a third state or by a natural or legal person of a third state in the EU.[23] This definition is now reflected in the FDI Screening Regulation, under Article 2(1) of which

> 'foreign direct investment' means an investment of any kind by a foreign investor aiming to establish or to maintain lasting and direct links between the foreign investor and the entrepreneur to whom or the undertaking to which the capital is made available in order to carry on an economic activity in a Member State, including investments which enable effective participation in the management or control of a company carrying out an economic activity.

In framing 'direct investment' and 'foreign direct investment', the CJEU's case law has also distinguished these notions from another cross-border investment type, namely non-direct (portfolio) investment, which may equally be intra-EU or extra-EU, depending on the presence of a non-EU element.[24] As such, the CJEU characterised[25]

> the acquisition of securities on the capital market solely with the intention of making a financial investment without any intention to influence the management and control of the undertaking.

intends to adopt […]', see Opinion 1/75 *OECD Understanding on a Local Cost Standard* [1975] ECLI:EU:C:1975:145, 1364.

[20] Opinion 2/15 *Free Trade Agreement with Singapore* [2017] ECLI:EU:C:2017:376, para 35 and further case law cited there; see also *Opinion 2/15* (AG Sharpston) (n 10) paras 96, 313.

[21] K Georgaki, 'The EU's Competence over Cross-Border Investment in the Post-Lisbon Era' (2018) 1 *European Politeia* 125, 135.

[22] *Opinion 2/15* (n 20) para 80.

[23] *Opinion 2/15* (n 20) para 82; see also *Opinion 2/15* (AG Sharpston) (n 10) para 313.

[24] Erlbacher and Maxian Rusche (n 10) 1596.

[25] Opinion 2/15 (AG Sharpston) (n 10) para 321; Case C-81/09 *Idryma Typou* [2010] ECLI:EU:C:2010:622, para 48; Case C-182/08 *Glaxo Wellcome* [2009] ECLI:EU:C:2009:559, para 40 and further case law cited there; also Commission, 'Protection of Intra-EU Investment' (n 5) 5, fn 17.

The feature differentiating direct from portfolio investment is the element of control; when the investor invests solely with a view to making profit, without aiming at controlling or influencing the decisions of the undertaking, to which the capital is made available, the investment is not direct, but portfolio.[26] In that vein, the CJEU has indicated that an investor would not be considered as exercising 'control' over a company, if they hold less than 10 per cent of the share capital.[27]

## B. The EU Rules Applicable to National Investment Screening Mechanisms

Within the EU, the screening of cross-border investments, their control and possible restrictions are subject to EU law. However, the adoption of investment screening mechanisms remains to a great extent decentralised; it is up to the Member States to introduce within their national legal orders mechanisms to allow for the screening of investments with a cross-border element,[28] as long as said mechanisms are in line with EU law. Screening mechanisms may take various forms, ranging from ex ante mechanisms, in the form of systems of prior authorisation stricto sensu,[29] and restrictions on business operations, including authorisation requirements for certain management decisions of a company, such as mergers; to ex post restrictions on investments, in the form of special rights relating to the investment reserved in favour of the state (eg a veto power of the state for certain decisions in privatised companies, golden shares etc).[30]

Over the years, the CJEU has consistently affirmed that investment screening mechanisms constitute a restriction on the free movement of capital within the meaning of Article 63 TFEU.[31] According to Article 63 TFEU,

> 1. Within the framework of the provisions set out in this Chapter, all restrictions on the movement of capital between Member States and between Member States and third countries shall be prohibited.

[26] Commission, 'Protection of Intra-EU Investment' (n 5) 5.

[27] Joined Cases C-436/08 and C-437/08 *Haribo Lakritzen Hans Riegel* [2011] ECLI:EU:C:2011:61, para 137.

[28] Commission, 'Guidance to the Member States Concerning Foreign Direct Investment and Free Movement of Capital from Third Countries, and the Protection of Europe's Strategic Assets, Ahead of the Application of Regulation (EU) 2019/452 (FDI Screening Regulation' (Communication) COM(2020) 1981, final, 1; see also Art 1(3) FDI Screening Regulation.

[29] See Case C-302/97 *Konle* [1999] ECLI:EU:C:1999:271, para 39; Joined Cases C-515/99 and C-527-540/99 *Reisch and Others* [2002] ECLI:EU:C:2002:135, para 32; Case C-531/06 *Commission v Italy* [2009] ECLI:EU:C:2009:315, para 44.

[30] Case C-326/07 *Commission v Italy* [2009] ECLI:EU:C:2009:193, para 40; Case C-98/01 *Commission v United Kingdom* [2003] ECLI:EU:C:2003:273, para 50; Case C-367/98 *Commission v Portugal* [2002] ECLI:EU:C:2002:326, para 53; Case C-112/05 *Commission v Germany* [2007] ECLI:EU:C:2007:623, paras 56 and 68.

[31] *Ex multis* Joined Cases C-163/94, C-165/94 and C-250/94 *Sanz de Lera and Others* [1995] ECLI:EU:C:1995:451, paras 24 and 25; Case C-54/99 *Église de Scientologie* [2000] ECLI:EU:C:2000:124, para 14; *Commission v Italy* (n 30) para 40.

> 2. Within the framework of the provisions set out in this Chapter, all restrictions on payments between Member States and between Member States and third countries shall be prohibited.

Article 63 TFEU prohibits, in principle, all restrictions on the free movement of capital and payments between Member States, as well as between Member States and third countries.[32] Restrictions on the free movement of capital can, however, be accepted under the conditions and within the limits of the Treaty and, in particular, when they serve a legitimate public interest. More specifically, the EU Treaties allow the Member States to adopt restrictions on the free movement of capital to prevent infringements of national law and regulations, in particular in the field of taxation and prudential supervision (Article 65(1) TFEU); on grounds of public policy or public security (Article 65(1) TFEU); or to protect essential interests of national security (Article 346 TFEU). The CJEU's case law has further recognised that restrictions on the free movement of capital may equally be justified on a number of overriding reasons in the public interest,[33] including environmental protection,[34] consumer protection,[35] public health[36] and the protection of creditors and minority shareholders.[37] Furthermore, a restriction must directly contribute to the attainment of the objective pursued,[38] whereas it also needs to serve the latter in a proportionate manner.[39] In the context of cross-border investment screening, the most commonly invoked legitimate interests are public security and public policy. The CJEU has confirmed that the Member States are, in principle, free to determine the requirements of public policy and public security considering their national needs; nevertheless, that these grounds[40]

> must, in the Community context and, in particular, as derogations from the fundamental principle of free movement of capital, be interpreted strictly, so that their scope cannot be determined unilaterally by each Member State without any control by the Community institutions. […] Thus, public policy and public security may be relied on only if there is a genuine and sufficiently serious threat to a fundamental interest of society.

[32] C Barnard, *The Substantive Law of the EU: The Four Freedoms*, 6th edn (Oxford, OUP, 2019) 525; Schill (n 12) 116.

[33] A non-exhaustive list of 'overriding reasons relating to the public interest' based on the case law of the CJEU is included in Art 4, point 8 of Directive 2006/123/EC of the Parliament and of the Council of 12 December 2006 on services in the internal market [2006] OJ L376/36.

[34] Case C-400/08 *Commission v Spain* [2011] ECLI:EU:C:2011:172, para 74 and further case law cited.

[35] Case C-260/04 *Commission v Italy* [2007] ECLI:EU:C:2007:508, para 27 and further case law cited.

[36] Case C-531/06 *Commission v Italy* [2009] ECLI:EU:C:2009:315, para 51.

[37] Case C-106/16 *Polbud Wyconawstwo* [2017] ECLI:EU:C:2017:804, para 53.

[38] Case C-242/03 *Weidert and Paulus* [2004] ECLI:EU:C:2004:465, paras 10, 20-22; *Reisch* (n 29) para 34; Joined Cases C-105/12 to C-107/12 *Essent and Others* [2013] ECLI:EU:C:2013:677, para 59.

[39] *Commission v Italy* (n 30) para 42; *Commission v Germany* (n 30) para 73 and further case law cited.

[40] *Église de Scientologie* (n 31) para 17 and further case law cited; Case C-503/99 *Commission v Belgium* [2002] ECLI:EU:C:2002:328, para 47; Case C-463/00 *Commission v Spain* [2003]

Since the free movement of capital enshrined in Article 63 TFEU applies to all investment types, intra-EU and extra-EU direct and portfolio investment screening mechanisms equally fall within its scope. However, the characterisation of an investment as extra-EU (direct or portfolio) has implications on the application of Article 63 TFEU. As already explained, the free movement of capital is the only fundamental freedom extending to third-country nationals, thus granting the right to non-discriminatory market access to both EU and foreign investors. As a result, the general rule remains that the EU Treaties prohibit restrictions on the free movement of capital between Member States and third countries, including in the form of extra-EU investment screening mechanisms, unless duly justified.[41] Yet, the CJEU has enunciated two caveats on the possibility of foreign nationals to benefit from the free movement of capital under Article 63 TFEU. First, market access restrictions on third-country nationals that prohibit establishment in a Member State and are not merely consequences of the capital movement regulations cannot be assessed under the free movement of capital;[42] to the Court,[43]

> since the Treaty does not extend freedom of establishment to third countries, it is important to ensure that the interpretation of Article 63(1) TFEU as regards relations with third countries does not enable economic operators who do not fall within the limits of the territorial scope of freedom of establishment to profit from that freedom.

Second, even though the wording of Article 63 TFEU does not distinguish between intra-EU and extra-EU capital movements, this does not mean that the prohibition of restrictions has the same effects in both cases.[44] In analysing whether restrictions on capital movements to and from third countries are justified under Article 63 TFEU, the CJEU has recognised that different considerations may apply compared to purely intra-EU restrictions.[45] In the CJEU's words[46]

> […] it may be that a Member State will be able to demonstrate that a restriction on capital movements to or from non-member countries is justified for a particular reason in circumstances where that reason would not constitute a valid justification for a restriction on capital movements between Member States.

ECLI:EU:C:2003:272, para 72. Against this background, the CJEU has recognised, for example, energy security as a legitimate public security interest that may justify restrictions, as long as there is in fact a 'genuine and sufficiently serious threat to a fundamental interest of society', Case C-244/11 *Commission v Greece* [2012] ECLI:EU:C:2012:694, para 67; Case C-207/07 *Commission v Spain* [2008] ECLI:EU:C:2008:428, para 47.

[41] Case C-446/04 *Test Claimants in the FII Group Litigation* [2006] ECLI:EU:C:2006:240, Opinion of AG Geelhoed, para 121.

[42] *SEGRO and Horváth* (n 12) paras 54–55; Schill (n 12) 117.

[43] *Test Claimants in the FH Group* (n 16) para 100.

[44] Case C-452/01 *Ospelt and Schlössle Weissenberg* [2003] ECLI:EU:C:2003:232, Opinion of AG Geelhoed, para 40.

[45] *Test Claimants FII* (AG Geelhoed) (n 40) para 121.

[46] *Test Claimants FII* (n 10) para 171; also Case C-101/05 *A* [2007] ECLI:EU:C:2007:804, para 60.

Consequently, under the Treaty, additional grounds of justification may be acceptable in the case of restrictions involving third countries, whereas the permissible grounds of justification may also be interpreted more broadly.

The characterisation of an investment as FDI also impinges on the EU legal framework for assessing investment screening mechanisms, as the screening of FDI falls within the scope of the FDI Screening Regulation. During the past five years, the openness of the EU legal framework as regards inward investment, combined with an increasing number of strategic EU assets being taken over by foreign investors[47] and the lack of reciprocal openness of foreign markets to EU investors,[48] generated concerns among the Member States and the European Parliament.[49] Inter alia, in February 2017, Germany, France and Italy sent a joint letter to then Trade Commissioner Malmström, asking the Commission to address the issue of FDI in strategic sectors, as well as the (lack of) reciprocity of investment conditions in third countries.[50]

In an effort to mitigate these concerns, in 2017 the Commission put forward a proposal for a Regulation establishing a framework to screen FDI in the EU, aiming at protecting EU assets against takeovers that could be detrimental to the essential interests of the EU and its Member States, as well as to ensuring a level playing field for EU investments in third countries.[51] The FDI Screening Regulation, which entered into force in May 2019 and started to apply on 11 October 2020,[52] establishes a specialised framework for the screening by the Member States of FDI into the Union on grounds of security or public order. Without requiring the Member States to adopt or maintain a national screening mechanism,[53] the Regulation imposes on the Member States an obligation to notify to the Commission national investment screening mechanisms (existing and future) and sets a number of procedural standards such mechanisms must adhere to.[54]

The Regulation includes a non-exhaustive list of factors that the Member States and the Commission may consider in determining whether an (envisaged) FDI is in fact likely to affect security or public order, including the potential

[47] Commission, 'A Balanced and Progressive Trade Policy' (n 8) 6.

[48] ibid; see also recital 5 of the FDI Screening Regulation.

[49] European Parliament Resolution of 5 July 2017 on building an ambitious EU industrial strategy as a strategic priority for growth, employment and innovation in the EU, n 20, available at www.europarl.europa.eu/doceo/document/TA-8-2017–0305_EN.html (accessed 5 January 2021).

[50] Joint Letter to Commissioner Cecilia Malmström of the German, French and Italian Governments, www.bmwi.de/Redaktion/DE/Downloads/S-T/schreiben-de-fr-it- an-malmstroem.pdf?__blob=publicationFile&v=5 (accessed 5 January 2021).

[51] Commission, 'Welcoming Foreign Direct Investment' (n 2) 5.

[52] Art 17 FDI Screening Regulation.

[53] Schill (n 12) 106; Hindelang and Moberg argue that the FDI Screening Regulation constitutes essentially a 'light-touch' harmonisation of the Member States' screening mechanisms, see S Hindelang and A Moberg, 'The Art of Casting Political Dissent in Law: The EU's Framework for the Screening of Foreign Direct Investment' [2020] *Common Market Law Review* 1427, 1446.

[54] Art 3 FDI Screening Regulation.

effects of the investment on critical infrastructure, critical technologies and supply of critical inputs.[55] The Regulation further sets up a mechanism for cooperation between Member States and the Commission, including the possibility of the Commission to issue opinions.[56] As the Regulation only addresses the screening of FDI, intra-EU direct investment and (intra-EU and extra-EU) portfolio investment fall outside its regulatory scope and continue to be assessed under the general framework of Article 63 TFEU.

## III. THE EU LEGAL FRAMEWORK FOR ASSESSING NATIONAL MECHANISMS SCREENING CROSS-BORDER INVESTMENT BY SOES

Having examined how the compatibility with EU law of national screening mechanisms for (intra-EU and extra-EU) investment is to be assessed, this section goes on to analyse how – if at all – the applicable EU legal framework would differ if the cross-border investment at issue is (to be) conducted by an SOE. EU law does not provide a general definition as to what may be perceived as an SOE.[57]

[55] Art 4(1)(a), (b) and (c) of the FDI Screening Regulation respectively. *cf* on critical infrastructure in particular, ch 7, in this volume.

[56] Arts 6 and 7 FDI Screening Regulation.

[57] Although the EU Treaties do not use the actual term 'SOE', Art 106(1) TFEU refers to 'public undertakings'. This term is deployed to connote undertakings, for which the Member States must take special responsibility by reason of the particular influence they may exert over their actions and operation on the market, M Kellerbauer and TM Rusche, 'Article 106 TFEU' in M Kellerbauer, M Klamert and J Tomkin (eds), *The EU Treaties and the Charter of Fundamental Rights: A Commentary* (Oxford, OUP, 2019) 1088, 1090. The Treaties may not elaborate on the notion, yet further guidance on its content can be found in secondary EU legislation. In that vein, Art 2(b) of the Transparency Directive defines a 'public undertaking' as 'an undertaking over which the public authorities may exercise directly or indirectly a dominant influence by virtue of their ownership of it, their financial participation therein, or the rules which govern it', Commission Directive 2006/111/EC of 16 November 2006 on the Transparency of Financial Relations between Member States and Public Undertakings as well as on Financial Transparency within Certain Undertakings [2006] OJ L318/17. The Transparency Directive further provides for certain cases, where the dominant influence of the public authorities over an undertaking may be (rebuttably) presumed: 'A dominant influence on the part of the public authorities shall be presumed when these authorities, directly or indirectly in relation to an undertaking: (i) hold the major part of the undertaking's subscribed capital; or ii) control the majority of the votes attaching to shares issued by the undertaking; or iii) can appoint more than half of the members of the undertaking's administrative, managerial or supervisory body.' This definition of a 'public undertaking' is also used – with some wording tweaks to reflect the different context – in Art 7(4) of the Concessions Directive, see Directive 2014/23/EU of the European Parliament and of the Council of 26 February 2014 on the Award of Concession Contracts [2014] OJ L94/1, Art 7(4). Although this definition of a 'public undertaking' only applies for the purposes and in the context of the respective Directives, it can provide guidance on how also to delineate the concept in the sense of Art 106 TFEU. This is particularly so, given that the criteria set out to characterise a 'public undertaking' for the purposes of the Transparency Directive and the Concessions Directive are in line with the *rationale* underlying Art 106 TFEU, which is to ensure the widest possible opening of the internal market, Kellerbauer and Maxian Rusche (n 57) 1094.

As a general rule, EU law is to remain neutral in matters of company ownership.[58] Under the principle of neutrality, reflected in Article 345 TFEU,[59] '[t]he Treaties shall in no way prejudice the rules in the Member States governing the system of property ownership'. The Member States are, in principle, free to own undertakings and establish and maintain national rules relating to the public ownership and management thereof, subject to the fundamental rules of the EU Treaties.[60]

As explained above, restrictions on the free movement of capital, including national mechanisms for the screening of cross-border investments, are, in principle, prohibited unless they are non-discriminatory and proportionate to serving a legitimate public interest. Given that EU law is based on the principle of neutrality, Article 63 TFEU applies regardless of the ownership status of the investor undertaking an investment within the EU. The free movement of capital covers both private investments and investments by SOEs, which may equally invoke protection under Article 63 TFEU against unjustified national screening regimes.

As regards, in particular, the screening of FDI, the application of the FDI Screening Regulation does not depend on the ownership status of the foreign investor planning to make or having made the direct investment either. Yet, albeit ownership neutral, the FDI Screening Regulation introduces the element of (direct or indirect) control of the investor by a third state as one of the factors to be taken into consideration in determining whether the (envisaged) investment may affect security or public order.[61] In that vein, Article 4(2)(a) of the FDI Screening Regulation provides that Member States and the Commission may also take into account, in particular

> whether the foreign investor is directly or indirectly controlled by the government, including state bodies or armed forces, of a third country, including through ownership structure or significant funding.

The notion of (direct or indirect) third state control is further elaborated upon in Recital 13 of the FDI Screening Regulation. According to the latter,

> [...] it should also be possible for Member States and the Commission to take into account the context and circumstances of the foreign direct investment, in particular whether a foreign investor is controlled directly or indirectly, for example through

[58] *Ex multis*, see Opinion 2/15 (n 20) para 107; Case C-163/99 *Portugal v Commission* [2001] ECLI:EU:C:2001:189, para 58; G Lallemand-Kirche, C Tixier and H Piffaut, 'The Treatment of State-Owned Enterprises in EU Competition Law: New Developments and Future Challenges' (2017) 8 *Journal of European Competition Law & Practice* 295.

[59] M Klamert, 'Article 345 TFEU', in M Kellerbauer, M Klamert and J Tomkin (eds), *The EU Treaties and the Charter of Fundamental Rights: A Commentary* (Oxford, OUP, 2019) 2047; PJ Slot, 'The Application of the EU Merger Control Rules to State Owned Enterprises' (2015) 36 *European Competition Law Review* 484, 487.

[60] *Essent* (n 38) para 36.

[61] Art 4(1) and recital 13 of the FDI Screening Regulation; see also the analysis in the previous section.

significant funding, including subsidies, by the government of a third country or is pursuing State-led outward projects or programmes.

The inclusion of third state control among the factors to be considered in the assessment of the likely effects of an (envisaged) investment on security or public order was prompted by the increasing presence and prominence of foreign SOEs in the EU investment environment, especially in sectors of strategic importance, such as critical technologies, infrastructure, inputs or sensitive information.[62] Over the past few years, the Commission and the Member States have consistently expressed concerns related to 'strategic EU assets being taken over by foreign investors – in particular by subsidised and/or state-owned enterprises'.[63] The Commission viewed foreign acquisitions of control or influence in EU undertakings in strategic sectors, 'especially but not only when foreign investors are state owned or controlled, including through financing or other means of direction', as a possible threat to the EU's security and public order, as well as to the attainment of a fair, market-based competitive environment.[64] In his State of the Union address in 2017, then Commission President Jean-Claude Juncker intertwined the proposal of the EU framework on investment screening with investment in critical assets by foreign SOEs, viewing the former as a means of enhancing transparency, scrutiny and debate in cases where, for example, 'a foreign, state-owned, company wants to purchase a European harbour, part of our energy infrastructure or a defence technology firm'.[65] Meanwhile, Germany, France and Italy also explicitly referred to foreign state-led investment in their proposals to the Commission set out in the key issues paper accompanying their letter to Commissioner Malmström. In that vein, they suggested that the screening of FDI is particularly justified where[66]

(a) the decision for the envisaged direct investment by the third country does not comply with market rules (e.g. through investment instructions; through state-funded takeovers based on political programmes; through the requirement for state approval of investments) or
(b) the envisaged direct investment is made possible or is facilitated by state subsidies and this results in a market disturbance (e.g. through government loans which do not reflect market conditions).

Even though the FDI Screening Regulation does not delve deeper into what direct or indirect third state 'control' entails and how broadly it is to be construed, it

[62] Commission, 'Proposal for a Regulation' (n 9) 10; Commission, 'Welcoming Foreign Direct Investment' (n 2) 5.

[63] Commission, 'A Balanced and Progressive Trade Policy' (n 8) 6.

[64] Commission, 'Welcoming Foreign Direct Investment' (n 2) 5.

[65] President Jean-Claude Juncker's State of the Union Address 2017, available at ec.europa.eu/commission/presscorner/detail/en/SPEECH_17_3165 (accessed 5 January 2021).

[66] Proposals for Ensuring an Improved Level Playing Field in Trade and Investment, available at www.bmwi.de/Redaktion/DE/Downloads/E/eckpunktepapier-proposals-for-ensuring-an-improved-level-playing-field-in-trade-and-investment.pdf?__blob=publicationFile&v=4 (accessed 5 January 2021); see also M Bungenberg and F Blandfort, 'Investment Screening – a New Era of European Protectionism',

provides some pointers as to how the concept of 'control' is to be understood for its purposes.

First, Article 4(2) of the FDI Screening Regulation indicates that a third state may be perceived to exercise (direct) 'control' over a foreign investor through its ownership structure. However, the Regulation does not delineate which types of state control would qualify as 'ownership' in its sense. In the absence of more specific indications to that end, the concept of third state 'ownership' in the sense of the FDI Screening Regulation could be approached by reference to international agreements concluded by the EU, alone (EU international agreements) or alongside the Member States (mixed agreements).[67] Under Article 216(2) TFEU, EU international agreements (including the part of mixed agreements falling within EU competence)[68] form an integral part of EU law and are binding on the EU institutions and the Member States.[69] According to the CJEU, this is based on the fact that EU international agreements constitute acts of the EU institutions;[70] and that, in ensuring respect for these agreements, the Member States fulfil an obligation towards the EU, the latter having assumed responsibility on the international plane for the due performance of the agreement at issue.[71]

in M Hahn and G Van der Loo (eds), *Law and Practice of the Common Commercial Policy* (Leiden, Brill, 2021) 161, 164.

[67] Under Art 47 TEU 'the Union shall have legal personality'. Despite the recent insertion of this provision through the Treaty of Lisbon and its terse wording, the CJEU had early on upheld the EU's capacity to establish contractual links with third countries in the exercise of its external relations, see Case C-22/70 *Commission of the European Communities v Council of the European Communities* [1971] ECLI:EU:C:1971:32, para 14; Opinion 1/76 *Inland Waterways* [1977] ECLI:EU:C:1977:63, para 3; C Eckes and RA Wessel, 'An International Perspective', in R Schütze and T Tridimas (eds), *Oxford Principles of European Union Law*, Vol 1 (Oxford, OUP, 2018) 74, 76; T Hartley, *The Foundations of European Union Law*, 8th edn (Oxford, OUP, 2014) 180–191. The modalities relating to the exercise of the EU's international legal personality are elaborated in Arts 3(1)–(2) and 216(1) TFEU, which complement the EU's competence to take internal action for the regulation of a specific area with a parallel (exclusive or shared respectively) external competence also to conclude international agreements in that area, M Klamert, 'Article 3 TFEU', in M Kellerbauer, M Klamert and J Tomkin (eds), *The EU Treaties and the Charter of Fundamental Rights. A Commentary* (Oxford, OUP, 2019) 359; F Erlbacher, 'Article 216', in M Kellerbauer, M Klamert and J Tomkin (eds), *The EU Treaties and the Charter of Fundamental Rights. A Commentary* (Oxford, OUP, 2019) 1643, 1647; Georgaki (n 21) 128–129.

[68] See Case C-459/03 *Commission v Ireland* [2006] ECLI:EU:C:2006:345, para 84; Case C-239/03 *Commission v France* [2004] ECLI:EU:C:2004:598, para 25; Case C-13/00 *Commission v Ireland* [2002] ECLI:EU:C:2002:184, para 14.

[69] Consolidated Version of the Treaty on the Functioning of the European Union [2012] OJ C326, Art 216(2); Case C-87/75 *Bresciani v Amministrazione delle Finanze dello Stato* [1976] ECLI:EU:C:1976:18, para 18; M Cremona, 'Member States Agreements as Union Law', in E Cannizzaro, P Palchetti and RA Wessel (eds), *International Law as Law of the European Union* (Leiden, Brill, 2011) 291.

[70] Opinion 1/17 *Accord ECG UE – Canada* [2019] ECLI:EU:C2019:72, Opinion of Advocate General Bot, para 60; Case C-266/16 *Western Sahara Campaign UK* [2018] ECLI:EU:C:2018:118, para 45; Case C-386/08 *Brita GmbH v Hauptzollamt Hamburg-Hafen* [2010] ECLI:EU:C:2010:91, para 39; Case C-11/05 *Friesland Cobero Dairy Foods* [2006] ECLI:EU:C:2006:312, para 36; Case C-162/96 *Racke v Hauptzollapt Mainz* [1998] ECLI:EU:C:1998:293, para 41; Case C-322/88 *Grimaldi v Fonds des Maladies Professionnelles* [1989] ECLI:EU:C:1989:646, para 8; Case C-181/73 *R & V Haegeman v Belgium* [1974] ECLI:EU:C:1974:41, paras 4–5.

[71] Case C-104/81 *Hauptzollamt Mainz v Kupferberg & Cie* [1982] ECLI:EU:C:1982:362, para 13; M Mendez, *The Legal Effects of EU Agreements* (Oxford, OUP, 2013) xvii; P Eeckhout, *EU External*

According to settled case law of the CJEU, EU international agreements enjoy primacy over secondary EU law;[72] given that EU international agreements are binding on the EU institutions, they constitute the framework setting limits on the power of the institutions to legislate.[73] Since EU international agreements prevail over secondary EU legislation to the extent of a conflict between their provisions,[74] the CJEU has consistently upheld that, prior to establishing such a conflict, EU secondary law needs to be interpreted as far as possible in a manner consistent with an EU international agreement on the same issue.[75]

Against this background, the EU – Canada Comprehensive Economic and Trade Agreement (CETA) defines a state enterprise as 'an enterprise that is owned or controlled by a Party', without distinguishing between these two elements.[76] Meanwhile, other FTAs and IIAs concluded at EU level (with or without Member State participation) consider as state-owned any enterprise, over which a state exercises a decisive degree of control, through its ownership structure or otherwise. This is the case, for example, with the EU – Vietnam FTA,[77] Article 11.1 of which provides that

> '[S]tate-owned enterprise' means an enterprise, including any subsidiary, in which a Party, directly or indirectly:
>
> owns more than 50 per cent of the enterprise's subscribed capital or controls more than 50 per cent of the votes attached to the shares issued by the enterprise;

*Relations Law*, 2nd edn (Oxford, OUP, 2011) 67. This obligation constitutes a specific application of the Member States' duty of loyalty under Art 4(3) TEU, see E Neframi, 'The Duty of Loyalty: Rethinking Its Scope Through Its Application in the Field of EU External Relations' (2010) 47 *Common Market Law Review* 323, 349; P Koutrakos, *EU International Relations Law* (Oxford, Hart Publishing, 2006) 185.

[72] Case C-464/14 *SECIL* [2016] ECLI:EU:C:2016:52, Opinion of AG Wathelet, para 41; Case C-366/10 *Air Transport Association of America et als* [2011] ECLI:EU:C:2011:864, para 50; Case C-308/06 *Intertanko et als* [2008] ECLI:EU:C:2008:312, para 42; Case C-344/04 *IATA and ELFAA* [2006] ECLI:EU:C:2006:10, para 35; Case C-311/04 *Algemene Scheeps Agentuur Dordrecht* [2006] ECLI:EU:C:2006:23, para 25; Case C-61/94 *Commission v Germany* [1996] ECLI:EU:C:1996:313, para 52.

[73] A Peters, 'The Position of International Law within the European Community Legal Order' (1997) 40 *German Yearbook of International Law* 9, 41.

[74] In the words of Advocate General (AG) Kokott, '[A] conflict between Community and Member States' obligations under international law always raises problems and is likely to undermine the practical effectiveness of the relevant provisions of EU law and/or of international law. It is therefore sensible and dictated by the principle of cooperation between Community institutions and Member States that efforts be made to avoid conflicts, particularly in the interpretation of the relevant provisions', see Case C-308/06 *Intertanko et als* [2007] ECLI:EU:C:2007:689, Opinion of AG Kokott, para 78.

[75] Case C-265/19 *Recorded Artists Actors Performers Ltd v Phonographic Performance (Ireland) Ltd* [2020] ECLI:EU:C:2020:677, para 62; Case C-363/12 *Z.* [2014] ECLI:EU:C:2014:159, para 72; Joined Cases C-320/11, C-330/11, C-382/11 and C-383/11 *Digitalnet* [2012] ECLI:EU:C:2012:745, para 39; Case C-289/09 *Pace* [2009] ECLI:EU:C:2009:572, para 83; Case C-61/94 *Commission v Germany* [1996] ECLI:EU:C:1996:313, para 52.

[76] Chapter 8 (the Investment Chapter) contains a special definition as to what constitutes an enterprise, without specifically referring to a state enterprise.

[77] Free Trade Agreement between the European Union and the Socialist Republic of Viet Nam [2020] OJ L186/3.

> can appoint more than half of the members of the enterprise's board of directors or an equivalent body; or
>
> can exercise control over the strategic decisions of the enterprise.

Article 13(1)(h) of the EU – Japan Economic Partnership Agreement also provides a definition of the notion of an SOE, according to which

> '[S]tate-owned enterprise' means an enterprise that is engaged in commercial activities in which a Party:
>
> directly owns more than 50 per cent of the share capital;
>
> controls, directly or indirectly through ownership interests, the exercise of more than 50 per cent of the voting rights;
>
> holds the power to appoint a majority of members of the board of directors or any other equivalent management body; or
>
> has the power to legally direct the actions of the enterprise or otherwise exercises an equivalent degree of control in accordance with its laws and regulations.[78]

Title XI on 'Level playing field for open and fair competition and sustainable development' of the recent EU – UK Trade and Cooperation Agreement (TCA)[79] similarly intertwines state ownership with the exercise of state control over the enterprise. In particular, Chapter 4, entitled 'State Owned Enterprises, Enterprises Granted Special Rights or Privileges and Designated Monopolies', defines an 'SOE' as:

> [...] an enterprise in which a Party:
>
> (i) directly owns more than 50% of the share capital;
> (ii) controls, directly or indirectly, the exercise of more than 50 % of the voting rights;
> (iii) holds the power to appoint a majority of the members of the board of directors or any other equivalent management body; or
> (iv) has the power to exercise control over the enterprise. For the establishment of control, all relevant legal and factual elements shall be taken into account on a case- by-case basis.

Guidance on the notion of third state ownership in the sense of the FDI Screening Regulation could also be drawn from the proposed definition of an 'SOE' in the context of the Guidelines of the Organisation for Economic Co-operation and Development (OECD) on Corporate Governance of State-Owned Enterprises.[80]

[78] Agreement between the European Union and Japan on an Economic Partnership [2018] OJ L330/3.

[79] Trade and Cooperation Agreement between the European Union and the European Atomic Energy Community, of the one part, and the United Kingdom of Great Britain and Northern Ireland, of the other part, available at ec.europa.eu/transparency/regdoc/rep/1/2020/EN/COM-2020-857-F1-EN-ANNEX-1-PART-1.PDF (accessed 5 January 2021).

[80] OECD (2015), *OECD Guidelines on Corporate Governance of State-Owned Enterprises* (2015 Edition, OECD Publishing Paris) dx.doi.org/10.1787/9789264244160-en (accessed 5 January 2021) 14.

Albeit non-binding recommendations, the OECD Guidelines shed light on how the concept of an SOE is to be construed, being the 'internationally agreed standard for how governments should exercise the state ownership function to avoid the pitfalls of both passive ownership and excessive state intervention'.[81] According to the Guidelines, any corporate entity recognised by national law as an enterprise, and in which the state exercises ownership, should be considered an SOE. The Guidelines affirm the link between state ownership and the exercise of state control over an enterprise, identifying two relevant forms of ownership: first, the state being the ultimate beneficiary owner of the majority of the voting shares; or, second, the state otherwise exercising an equivalent degree of control. In this latter sense, some forms of minority ownership would also suffice in establishing the required degree of state control. These may include cases, where legal stipulations or corporate articles of association confer on the state effective controlling influence over an enterprise (or its board of directors), in which it holds a minority stake, eg though golden shares, or shareholders' agreements.[82]

Apart from direct control via ownership, a third state may also influence an enterprise engaging in FDI within the EU indirectly. Recital 13 of the FDI Screening Regulation lists the receipt of significant funding, including through subsidies, as well as the pursuit of state-led outward programmes among the possible indicators to consider when establishing the exercise of (indirect) state control over an investor. Under the Commission's recent White Paper on Foreign Subsidies, the taxonomy of foreign subsidies may include the direct financing of the enterprise making the investment, for example through the offer of preferential financing, loan guarantees or other means of reducing capital costs; or the provision of indirect financing, including in the form of dedicated tax rebates (income tax reductions) or financing from government supported investment funds or intermediaries.[83] In the same vein, albeit not directly controlled by a state, an investor may nevertheless be considered state-controlled under the FDI Screening Regulation, if it pursues foreign investment as part of a declared government policy.[84]

The exercise of indirect third state control over an enterprise under the FDI Screening Regulation may also be assessed in light of the notion of a 'single economic entity' of EU competition law. This concept is relevant to the application of Article 101 TFEU, for attributing the conduct of a subsidiary to the parent company. The purpose of the notion of a single economic entity is to delineate the scope of Article 101 TFEU rationae personae; agreements between

[81] ibid 3. Advocate General Sharpston has also drawn inspiration from the OECD in interpreting the notion of 'direct investment' in her opinion in Opinion 2/15, see Opinion 2/15 (AG Sharpston) (n 10) para 320.

[82] OECD Guidelines (n 81) 4.

[83] See Commission, 'White Paper on Levelling the Playing Field as Regards Foreign Subsidies' COM(2020) 253 final, 8.

[84] Commission, 'Welcoming Foreign Direct Investment' (n 2) 5.

legal persons within the same economic entity would fall outside of the scope of Article 101 TFEU altogether, as they are not agreements between separate undertakings.[85] Moreover, according to Recital 22 of the EU Merger Regulation, in the public sector, calculation of the turnover of an undertaking concerned in a concentration needs to take account of undertakings making up an economic unit with an independent power of decision, irrespective of the way in which their capital is held or of the rules of administrative supervision applicable to them.[86] Based on settled case-law of the CJEU, a single economic entity would be perceived to exist, in particular, where the subsidiary, despite having a separate legal personality, does not decide independently upon its own conduct on the market but carries out, in all material respects, the instructions given to it by the parent company.[87] Since the *rationale* underlying the concept of a 'single economic entity' in competition law and that of indirect state control under the FDI Screening Regulation is to establish the exercise of decisive influence over an undertaking/investor respectively, the latter concept would also comprise cases, where the foreign investor operates on the market under the instructions of a third state.

Additional inspiration on how to delineate the notion of indirect state control in the sense of the FDI Screening Regulation may also be drawn from customary international law.[88] In particular, Article 8 of the ILC Draft Articles on Responsibility of States for Internationally Wrongful Acts (ARSIWA) provides that

> [T]he conduct of a person or a group of persons shall be considered an act of a State under international law if the person or group of persons is in fact acting on the instructions of, or under the direction or control of, that State in carrying out its conduct.[89]

[85] Case C-48/69 *ICI v Commission* [1972] EC:I:EU:C:1972:70, para 134; Case C-73/95 P *Viho v Commission* [1996] ECLI:EU:C:1996:405, para 17 and further references there; G Meessen, 'Article 101 TFEU'. in M Kellerbauer, M Klamert and J Tomkin (eds), *The EU Treaties and the Charter of Fundamental Rights: A Commentary* (Oxford, OUP, 2019) 998, 1004.

[86] Council Regulation (EC) 139/2004 of 20 January 2004 on the control of concentrations between undertakings [2004] OJ L24/1.

[87] *ICI v Commission* (n 86) paras 132 and 133; Case C-52/69 *Geigy v Commission* [1972] ECLI:EU:C:1972:73, para 44; Case C-6/72 *DEPE-Europemballage and Continental Can v Commission* [1973] ECLI:EU:C:1975:50, para 15, regard being had in particular to the economic, organisational and legal links between those two legal entities (see, by way of analogy, Case C-189/02 P *Dansk Rørindustri and Others v Commission* [2005] ECLI:EU:C:2005:408, para 117, and Case C-280/06 *ETI and Others* [2007] ECLI:EU:C:2007:775, para 49); also Meessen (n 86) 1004; AH Zhang, 'The Single-Entity Theory: An Antitrust Time Bomb For Chinese State-Owned Enterprises?' (2012) 8 *Journal of Competition Law & Economics* 805, 818.

[88] The CJEU and the General Court of the European Union have consistently accepted that the rules of customary international law are applicable within the EU, binding on both the Member States as well as on the EU itself, see Case T-115/94 *Opel Austria v Council* [1997] ECLI:EU:T:1997:3, para 90; *Intertanko* (n 72) para 52; K Schmalenbach, 'Article 26', in O Dörr and K Schmalenbach (eds), *Vienna Convention on the Law of Treaties: A Commentary* (Berlin, Springer, 2018) 475 and further references there.

[89] ILC, 'Draft Articles on Responsibility of States for Internationally Wrongful Acts, with Commentaries' (2001) UN Doc A/56/10, 47.

Under Article 8 ARSIWA, the conduct of a private entity may exceptionally be attributed to a state in two circumstances: first, if said entity is acting on the instructions of that state; or, second, if it is under said state's direction or control. International *fora*, including the International Court of Justice (ICJ), have interpreted the latter notion as encapsulating cases, where the state provides for 'planning, direction and support' to a private entity,[90] exerting 'effective control' over its conduct,[91] in particular where it aims at achieving a particular result;[92] and cases, where the state has the 'overall control' over its operations.[93] Transposed to the FDI Screening Regulation, a foreign investor would also be perceived to be indirectly controlled by a third state, when that state provides for 'planning, direction, and support' to the foreign investor or has the 'overall control' over its operations.[94]

Considering the above, while state-ownership of the enterprise conducting the (envisaged) FDI is not directly relevant to the application of the FDI Screening Regulation, third state control over the investor is one of the factors to be considered when assessing the likely effects of the FDI on security or public order. To the FDI Screening Regulation, a third state directly controls an investor through its ownership structure, when the former is the ultimate beneficiary owner of the majority of its voting shares; or otherwise exercises an equivalent degree of control, including through minority ownership, when corporate or shareholding structures ensure continued state control over the company. A third state may equally be considered to exercise control over the investor indirectly. This form of control would include cases, where the third state grants the investor significant funding, including subsidies; where the investor pursues state-led outward projects or programmes or operates on the market under state instructions; or where the state provides the investor with planning, direction, and support.

## IV. CONCLUSION

During the last decade, the attraction of investment and, in particular, foreign investment has been among the EU's top political priorities, particularly important to the EU's economic recovery from the pervasive effects of the financial crisis and, most recently, the COVID-19 health crisis. The EU's external action

[90] Military and Paramilitary Activities in and against Nicaragua, 1986 ICJ 14, para 86.

[91] ibid para 115.

[92] ARSIWA (n 90) 48 and further references there.

[93] See also *Prosecutor v Duško Tadić*, International Tribunal for the Former Yugoslavia, Case IT-94-1-A (1999) ILM vol 38, No 6 para 145.

[94] See also PM Gadocha, 'Assessing the EU Framework Regulation for the Screening of Foreign Direct Investment – What is the Effect on Chinese Investors?' (2020) 6 *The Chinese Journal of Global Governance* 36, 59.

in the field of trade and foreign investment, together with the openness of its legal framework have made the EU one of the investment-friendliest destinations worldwide.

The increasing prominence of foreign actors and, in particular, foreign SOEs in sectors of strategic importance, as well as the need to open up third-country economies and ensure a level playing field for EU investors in foreign markets made the calls for the introduction of safeguards at the EU level more pressing than ever. While the EU's principled openness to foreign investment is not going to change, being enshrined in its constitutive treaties, the adoption of vigorous policies is necessary to protect the EU's essential interests from the potentially detrimental effects of uncontrolled foreign investment. In the words of former Commission President Jean-Claude Juncker, 'we are not naïve free traders. Europe must always defend its strategic interests'.[95]

Against this background, the FDI Screening Regulation was enacted in 2019, constituting one of the most recent EU trade defence instruments. The Regulation allows the Member States to adopt or maintain national mechanisms for the screening of FDI on grounds of security or public order. The adoption of the FDI Screening Regulation was largely prompted by the rise in the number of investments by foreign SOEs, which explains why third state control (in the sense of this chapter) over the investor conducting the FDI is a factor that may have a bearing on the Member States' assessment of whether said FDI is likely to affect security or public order. However, the FDI Screening Regulation applies irrespective of the ownership status of the investor planning or having made the investment undergoing screening. The same is true of screening mechanisms applicable to other types of cross-border investment, namely intra-EU direct and (intra-EU and extra-EU) portfolio investment, whose compatibility with EU law is assessed under Article 63 TFEU. Since the application of EU law is ownership-neutral, both private investors and SOEs may invoke protection under Article 63 TFEU against unjustified restrictions on the free movement of capital, including against national investment screening regimes.

[95] Jean-Claude Juncker's State of the Union Address 2017 (n 65).

# 7

# *Foreign Investment in Critical National Infrastructure (CNI) by State-Controlled Entities (SCEs) and Investment Screening Mechanisms (ISMs)*

**MANU MISRA**

## I. INTRODUCTION

INVESTMENT SCREENING MECHANISMS (ISMs) have been in a state of flux, both in practice and design, with a dramatic increase in new regulatory frameworks and significant amendments to existing screening systems observed in recent years.[1] Regulatory approaches pertaining to the screening and review of foreign investments, particularly by state-owned and state-controlled enterprises (together, 'SCEs'), is an issue that states have increasingly come to terms

[1] The most recent policy activity related to foreign investment screening have been reported by the UNCTAD Investment Policy Monitor in the following states: Italy (March 2022), United Kingdom (January 2022), France (December 2021), Spain (November 2021), Japan (November 2021), United States (October 2021), South Africa (September 2021), Saudi Arabia (September 2021), Germany (September 2021), Russia (July 2021) and Denmark (July 2021). Although a rise in investment screening was already observable prior to the onset of the COVID-19 pandemic, the latter further boosted policymaking in the field. See www.oecd.org/coronavirus/policy-responses/investment-screening-in-times-of-covid-19-and-beyond-aa60af47/; investmentpolicy.unctad.org/publications/1213/investment-policy-monitor-special-issue---national-security-related-screening-mechanisms-for-foreign-investment-an-analysis-of-recent-policy-developments; investmentpolicy.unctad.org/publications/1224/investment-policy-monitor-no-23. See also SB Danzman and S Meunier, The Big Screen: Mapping the Diffusion of Foreign Investment Screening Mechanisms (28 August 2021). Available at SSRN: ssrn.com/abstract=3913248 or dx.doi.org/10.2139/ssrn.3913248. The authors at page 10 argue that the pandemic gave 'policy entrepreneurs' 'an opening to push through screening because the prior development of 'off the shelf' solutions made it possible to offer investment review as a quick response to the economic and security concerns COVID instantiated', a phenomenon that they argue also contributed to an increase in policy similarity.

with, while several have reconsidered their official stance towards who they partner with in 'critical' sectors and what constitutes their security interests.

Of particular interest to this chapter are ISMs and a set of economic assets collectively referred to as a host state's 'critical national infrastructure' (CNI or 'critical infrastructure') along with the involvement of SCEs as foreign investors in CNI project, how and why such transactions are addressed with increased scrutiny and state intervention and how that reflects on the nature of contemporary ISMs, as a field of foreign investment policy.

The chapter begins by discussing the evolution of the term 'critical infrastructure' as a standalone concept in the broader national security policy debate along with recent observations of the same emerging in foreign investment policymaking. It then discusses why CNI-related foreign investment transactions (particularly those involving foreign SCEs) may invite, and indeed *should* invite, additional scrutiny by national authorities at the pre-establishment stage, while recognising the perils of the same. It does so by arguing that conceptually, ISMs may be understood as primarily being a problem of trust in international relations (IR) theory and that accepting investment proposals involving foreign SCEs in CNI (especially its modern-day variant) inevitably creates the potential for vulnerability, which, then requires a greater level of trust to be afforded to not just the investing SCE, but also to its governing home state. Trust in IR is therefore argued to be a greatly consequential, if not decisive, underlying factor affecting ISMs, which may be seen as a symptom or manifestation of mistrust in their legislative form, and a test of trust, in their individual decisions.

The chapter then makes two related arguments as to the nature of contemporary ISMs.

First, it argues that, while ISMs were in the past justifiably seen with scepticism and known primarily as being disingenuously conceived policy instruments that invoke national security as a mere guise and are intended towards pursuing protectionist or economic nationalist goals, today such scepticism is no longer tenable, certainly not to the same degree. Instead, ISMs have 'turned over a page' and now hold a more bona fide role in foreign investment policy. It bases this argument on at least three factors, including the emergence of novel, technology-driven security risks (and the structural, therefore inevitable vulnerability they create), the selective usage and limited impact on FDI flows observable after the recent rise in ISMs and lastly, the bipartisan support driving ISMs whose recent rise while no doubt instigated by and directed primarily towards SCEs or ultimate beneficiaries from the People's Republic of China (PRC), has neither resulted in a complete ban on PRC investments, nor has been directed at them exclusively.

Second, the chapter cautions against viewing ISMs from a purely legal lens and argues that given the subjective role of trust (towards not just the SCE but also its governing home state) that is embedded within their decision-making (particularly with regard to transactions involving CNI), ISMs essentially and unavoidably serve an executive *political* function and not an administrative *regulatory* one which can (or even should be) judicialised or be subject to judicial review without limitations, if at all. Investment screening is a different animal and not a case of law being politicised but at its core, politics itself. Therefore, while indeed more attention should be paid by states towards enhancing the transparency and democratic accountability of their ISMs, the standard we apply towards qualitatively assessing their procedural design and degree of fairness should reflect this distinction. The chapter then closes with a few concluding remarks and suggestions for future avenues for research on ISMs.

## II. EVOLUTION IN CNI SECURITY: PHYSICAL, CYBER AND ECONOMIC

With the rise in ISMs, the usage of the term critical infrastructure has also expanded, and the concept has received greater attention within the field of foreign investment policy. Prominent recent examples of this include Australia's designation of all 'Responsible entities' and 'direct interest holders' of critical infrastructure assets as 'national security businesses' in which a foreign investor may not gain direct interest without state approval, regardless of nationality or the value of the business,[2] Germany's expansion of the category of businesses designated as operators of critical infrastructure to also include providers (including third-parties) of services (such as IT, finance, insurance and health) to critical infrastructure operators, thereby subjecting any foreign investment transactions they may seek to conclude to mandatory notification obligations under the German ISM[3] or China's 2020 National Security Review measures that expanded the scope of the Chinese ISM 'from national defence-related activities to critical infrastructure, advanced technology and digital content such as personal data'.[4]

As expected, specific formulations of how CNI is defined vary across jurisdictions.[5] However, broadly, the concept tends to cover assets, whether

[2] FIRB, 'Australia's foreign investment policy', The Australian Government the Treasury, Guidance Note, January 2021.

[3] In addition to being subjected to greater cybersecurity-related risk mitigation measures. See the second amendment of the Ordinance on the Designation of Critical Infrastructures under the BSI Act, following the last update (the 17th amendment) to the Foreign Trade and Payments Ordinance (Außenwirtschaftsverordnung, AWV) which entered into effect on 1 May 2020.

[4] KT Yuen and L Yao, 'China's New National Security Screening Rules on Foreign Investment', NUS East Asian Institute Commentary No 24, February 2021, available at research.nus.edu.sg/eai/wp-content/uploads/sites/2/2021/02/EAIC-24-20210204-1.pdf.

[5] The first formal definition of CNI by a federal government is said to originate from the US during the Clinton Administration which established the US National Commission on Critical Infrastructure Protection in 1996. See EXECUTIVE ORDER EO 13010 CRITICAL INFRASTRUCTURE PROTECTION, irp.fas.org/offdocs/eo13010.htm. See also 'White Paper: Clinton Administration's Policy; Critical Infrastructure Protection' clintonwhitehouse4.archives.gov/WH/EOP/NSC/html/documents/NSCDoc3.html. See also C Gallais and E Filiol. 'Critical Infrastructure: Where Do We Stand Today? A Comprehensive and Comparative Study of the Definitions of a Critical Infrastructure' (2017) 16(1) *Journal of Information Warfare* 64–87.

physical or virtual, that are considered vital for the *functioning* of an economy (or a society at large) and the loss or disruption of which would lead to severe economic or social consequences, at a national scale. Energy facilities, utilities, transportation, international ports and telecom networks and are therefore some of the prime examples of assets that are often designated as CNI.[6] Being intrinsically connected to basic human needs therefore, the 'criticality' of such assets is an objectively identifiable and unavoidable trait.[7] While increased references to and greater awareness of the concept of CNI in ISMs (as a component of what is considered as *economic* security) is a relatively recent phenomenon, the debate surrounding the former has been in existence for several decades prior, first with an emphasis mainly on *physical* security and, as greater technological progress took place, evolving largely into a highly technical one focusing more on *cyber* security.

The earlier realm surrounding the *physical* security of CNI has origins in military doctrine and while it also involves protection against natural disasters such as floods and earthquakes, one major preoccupation that also drove its historical development has been protecting critical infrastructure from

[6] In addition to its criticality, another salient feature of CNI worth acknowledging is its 'national' element ie, that the risks associated critical infrastructure, however defined, are ultimately experienced collectively by all within a territorial boundary, at a national level. This 'territorial' nature of the consequences in question evokes a fundamental and primary responsibility of national-level authorities and as a result, also brings forth the primary role of national-level regulations towards mitigating such risks and attaining 'nationally-best' outcomes. While not all governments employ the term CNI specifically (most prominently the UK does, see www.ncsc.gov.uk/section/private-sector-cni/cni) it is argued that this underlying characteristic nonetheless remains true for all states, to mark which hence this chapter uses the term CNI, while considering it interchangeable with shorter term, critical infrastructure. That said, it is worth remembering that marking the national element of critical infrastructure in its designation may be misinterpreted as an invitation for economic nationalism and lead to securitisation, a 'slippery slope' issue which scholars have been wary of in international economic law more broadly. See G Vidigal and SW Schill, 'International Economic Law and the Securitization of Policy Objectives: Risks of a Schmittean Exception' (2021) 48(2) *Legal Issues of Economic Integration* 109–118, kluwerlawonline.com/journalarticle/Legal+Issues+of+Economic+Integration/48.2/LEIE2021007. On the former issue of economic nationalism within the context of SCE investment in CNI and ISMs, the Dubai Ports World controversy is an apt case. See J Kim, 'Fears of Foreign Ownership: The Old Face of Economic Nationalism' (2017) 27(2) *The SAIS Review of International Affairs* 167–177; J van Scherpenberg, 'Economic Nationalism on the Rise, Foreign Direct Investment in the USA after the Dubai Fiasco', German Institute for International & Security Affairs, SWP Comments 10; D Mostaghel, 'Dubai Ports World Under Exon-Florio: A Threat to National Security or a Tempest in a Seaport' (2007) 70 *Albany Law Review* 583.

[7] Most recently highlighted by the COVID-19 pandemic and the additional state scrutiny and intervention on health infrastructure, (including health-related personnel, intellectual property, raw materials, supply chains, data etc), all being designated or re-emphasised as 'critical'. See D Markopoulou, and V Papakonstantinou, 'The Regulatory Framework for the Protection of Critical Infrastructures against Cyberthreats: Identifying Shortcomings and Addressing Future Challenges: The Case of the Health Sector in Particular' (2021) 41 *Computer Law & Security Review* 105502, available at: ssrn.com/abstract=3979511. See also See F Cohen, 'What makes critical infrastructures Critical?' (2010) 3 *International Journal of Critical Infrastructure Protection* 53–54 where the author notes that critical infrastructure are 'keeping modern society from decaying'.

adversarial physical attacks.[8] Conversely, attacking the CNI of the adversary has also been considered an efficient and sought-after military strategy, in part due to the interdependency between various forms of CNI. For example, almost all forms of CNI require energy (and today, internet connectivity) to function and so attacking the former may debilitate others as well, thereby compounding the intended effect beyond the immediate target.

With technological progress and greater connectivity emerging and rising exponentially from the 1980s through to the 2000s, including private/civil usage, IT networks became increasingly integrated into CNI which in turn created new, more sophisticated and discrete channels of foreign attacks that had a profound effect on the debate surrounding CNI. As mentioned before, this integration rendered the debate into a more technical one that now focused primarily on *cyber* security.

It is worth noting that, concurrent with the emergence of greater threat mechanisms, so did a greater perception of threats arise in response to prominent incidents of both domestic and international terrorism that occurred during the same period, especially (but not exclusively) in the US, whose ecosystem has been a major driver of the field.[9]

The combination of both phenomena (ie emergence of cybersecurity and rise in foreign threat perception) occurring together brought greater attention and resources into the development and study of CNI both as a policy practice and a field of study, often with a special emphasis on the 'resilience' of CNI as a subset of IT security.[10] However, the field of CNI protection has now gained greater richness and diversity in its approaches by integrating 'organizational, managerial, social, political, cultural, and human aspects'[11] with related professionals,

[8] See SA Zaharia, "Critical Infrastructure' Concept's Evolution and Prospects Within the Euro-Atlantic Framework' (2012) 45 *Strategic Impact*; Bucharest Issue 59–72. The author notes that 'awareness of the potential vulnerability of modern infrastructure to deliberate attack or natural disaster dates at least to the interwar era when American and British military theorists first speculated that targeting the industrial infrastructure and civilian morale of the Axis powers with long-range strategic bombing might bring victory at a comparatively low cost'. See also TD Biddle, *Rhetoric and Reality in Air Warfare: The Evolution of British and American Ideas About Strategic Bombing, 1914–1945*, vol 17 (New Jersey, Princeton University Press, 2009).

[9] Including the 1993 bombing of the World Trade Centre in New York City, the 1995 Oklahoma City bombing and the 2001 September 11 Attacks which 'had a galvanizing effect on homeland security policy, and, by extension, critical infrastructure protection'. BE Humphreys, 'Critical Infrastructure: Emerging Trends and Policy Considerations for Congress', Congressional Research Service (CRS) Report, R45809. See also TG Lewis, *Critical Infrastructure Protection in Homeland Security: Defending a Networked Nation* (Hoboken, Wiley, 2020). Indeed, some of the 9/11 Commission Report's recommendations were explicitly concerned with critical infrastructure. See 9-11commission.gov/report/.

[10] See, eg, D Gritzalis; M Theocharidou and G Stergiopoulos, *Critical Infrastructure Security and Resilience Theories, Methods, Tools and Technologies* (Cham, Springer, 2019); U Bhatia, S Flynn and RA Ganguly, *Critical infrastructures resilience: Policy and Engineering Principles* (London, Routledge, 2018). S Bologna, 'Cybersecurity of Critical Infrastructures', in A Masys (eds), *Handbook of Security Science* (Cham, Springer, 2018).

[11] AV Gheorghe et al, *Critical Infrastructures, Key Resources, Key Assets: Risk, Vulnerability, Resilience, Fragility, and Perception Governance*' (Cham, Springer, 2018). See also F De Felice and

authorities and systems personnel also interested in 'operations research and management, economics, risk analysis, and defence management'.[12]

By 2008, the OECD had observed how critical infrastructure protection was receiving 'special attention'[13] in the foreign investment policies of several states. The debate on CNI had thus already by then taken on a more pronounced dimension of *economic* security, a term that has persisted and gained greater adoption in national policymaking[14] alongside the already well-established physical and cybersecurity dimensions discussed above.

As the term suggests, within this realm, foreign investment in CNI is viewed less from a market or development-based lens and more from a security-based lens. That is not to say that the former have become any less relevant or applicable. Indeed, given their sheer size and capital-intensive nature, foreign investment projects in CNI may be justifiable in that they hold immense purely commercial value, including valuable industrial or market links. Likewise for the host state, while by no means guaranteed, foreign investment projects in CNI may be justifiable in that it may provide a significant positive development impact as well. Foreign investment in CNI is thus not an uncommon or necessarily disfavoured activity, not least in the developing world where alternatives for sources of capital and technology are often found to be lacking.

A problem of economic security arises however when such foreign investment may also act as a mechanism for geopolitical leverage and economic espionage. In terms of the former, in addition to the strategic commercial value, there may also then exist a strategic *political* value for the foreign investor's home state, particularly when such investor is an SCE and its actions hence directable by its home state.

To begin with, there may already exist a standing incentive on the part of political leaders of a host state to accept foreign investment in CNI as it may

A Petrillo, *Human factors and reliability engineering for safety and security in critical infrastructures: decision making, theory, and practice* (Cham, Springer, 2018).

[12] MM Keupp (ed), *The Security of Critical Infrastructures: Risk, Resilience and Defense*, International Series in Operations Research & Management Science (288) (Cham, Springer, 2020). See also RK Baggett and AL Stout, 'Critical Infrastructure Risk Analysis and Management', in AJ Masys (ed) *Handbook of Security Science* (Cham, Springer, 2022) doi.org/10.1007/978-3-319-51761-2_1-1; S Raß, S Schauer, S König and Q Zhu, *Cyber-security in Critical Infrastructures: A Game-theoretic Approach* (Cham, Springer, 2020. For an interdisciplinary view in the field of legal studies, see A Vedder, J Schroers, C Ducuing and P Valcke, *Security and Law: Legal And Ethical Aspects Of Public Security, Cyber Security And Critical Infrastructure Security*, KU Leuven Centre For IT & IP Law (Cambridge, Intersentia, 2020).

[13] See www.oecd.org/daf/inv/investment-policy/40700392.pdf, noting the same later in 2018 www.oecd.org/investment/Current-trends-in-OECD-NatSec-policies.pdf.

[14] Albeit with doubts on the clarity and feasibility of its substance. For example, in February 2022, the Japanese Government approved an 'economic security promotion bill' (See www.nippon.com/en/news/yjj2022022501325/) after having, in October 2021, created a ministerial position for and a department of 'economic security'. For a critique of the latter, see T Takahashi, 'Japan's opaque economic security policy agenda', East Asia Forum Op-Ed, December 2021, available at www.eastasiaforum.org/2021/12/13/japans-opaque-economic-security-policy-agenda/.

provide an opportunity for them to receive positive media coverage and make grand ambitious statements about prosperity and economic development.[15] For a home state then, this provides an opportunity for presenting foreign investment as a 'diplomatic carrot' that may be exchanged for influence over what otherwise would be the host state's sovereign decisions.

What is worse, if and when such a carrot is accepted ie, the foreign investment is established within the host state's jurisdiction, it may also then act as a 'diplomatic stick' and leveraged as a coercive tool,[16] thus providing a more potent mechanism for the home state to influence host state policies and lock-in certain domestic preferences of the latter in accordance with its own. Such preferences may be contrary to the host state's national interests, however defined, and entail choices which it otherwise may not have independently adopted.[17]

## III. 'GEOECONOMICS', ISMS AND TRUST IN IR

It is therefore the very structural nature of SCE involvement in modern CNI that may lead to a vulnerability or security risks for the host state, which in turn then requires sufficient trust on the part of that host, towards the home state of the SCE.

[15] Corruption and elite interests are also potential ulterior motives that may influence decisions on accepting foreign investment in CNI, again, given their sheer size and strategic commercial value.

[16] TH Moran, *Three Threats An Analytical Framework for the CFIUS Process* (Washington, The Peterson Institute for International Economics, 2009) available at cup.columbia.edu/book/a/9780881324297. See also T Moran, 'Foreign Acquisitions and National Security: What Are Genuine Threats? What Are Implausible Worries?', ch 11 in Z Drabek and PC Mavroidis (eds), *Regulation of Foreign Investment: Challenges to International Harmonization* (Singapore, World Scientific Publishing Co. Pte. Ltd, 2013) 371–393; J Busby, 'Electricity as Coercion: Is There a Risk of Strategic Denial of Service?', Energy Realpolitik, Council on Foreign relations Blog, August 2019, available at www.cfr.org/blog/electricity-coercion-there-risk-strategic-denial-service. See, eg, T Shipman, 'China threatens to pull plug on new British nuclear plants', *The Times* www.thetimes.co.uk/article/china-threatens-to-pull-plug-on-new-british-nuclear-plants-727zlvbzg.

[17] While observations or such 'geoeconomic' behaviour are by no means unprecedented in itself, the rise in the scale and sophistication of such state activity is notable. That, combined with the return of a multipolar world and 'great power competition' between the US and China has given impetus to suggestions that the global economy has recently witnessed structural changes wherein inter alia unfettered market-driven globalisation is no longer considered feasible, even as an ideal, and achieving one's security goals require going beyond securing one's geographical territory and traditional geopolitics. See A Roberts, HC Moraes and V Ferguson, 'Toward a Geoeconomic Order' (2019) 22 *Journal of International Economic Law* 4 655–676; HC Cohen, 'Nations and Markets' (2020) 23 *Journal of International Economic Law*. More broadly see S Scholvin and M Wigell, 'Power politics by economic means: Geoeconomics as an analytical approach and foreign policy practice' (2018) 37(1) *Comparative Strategy* 73–84, DOI: 10.1080/01495933.2018.1419729, A Vihma, 'Geoeconomics Defined and Redefined' (2018) 23(1) *Geopolitics* 47–49, DOI: 10.1080/14650045.2017.1379010, H Farrell and AL Newman, 'Weaponized Interdependence: How Global Economic Networks Shape State Coercion' (2019) 44(1) *International Security* 42–79 www.brookings.edu/book/the-uses-and-abuses-of-weaponized-interdependence/, www.routledge.com/Geo-economics-and-Power-Politics-in-the-21st-Century-The-Revival-of-Economic/Wigell-Scholvin-Aaltola/p/book/9780815397304, www.routledge.com/Advances-in-Geoeconomics/Munoz/p/book/9781857438307, popularised by Luttwak www.jstor.org/stable/42894676?seq=1. For foundational works, see also S Strange 'States and Markets' (London, Bloomsbury Publishing, 2015).

ISMs and trust in international relations (IR) are therefore interrelated in both, theory and practice. More specifically it is argued that ISMs may be seen as a legal 'symptom' or manifestation of mistrust in international relations, in their legislative form, and a 'test' of trust, in their individual decisions, the two being policy acts where ISMs and trust overlap.[18]

Accepting foreign investment proposals, especially in CNI and involving SCEs naturally augments the host state's potential vulnerability,[19] and resultantly, also requires to be compensated by a greater level of trust to be afforded to both, the investor and its governing home state. Once the investment is legally established, it is not just capital that is received into the host state but depending on the nature of the transaction, also a combination of rights, control and access that is in return, legally afforded to the foreign investor.

The unrestricted allowance of foreign state-controlled capital is therefore akin to exercising a 'discretion granting policy',[20] defined as 'policies that grant other states discretion over outcomes previously controlled by the first'.[21] The discretion granted in the context of ISMs is the discretion that the foreign investor enjoys once the investment is legally established and it may then exercise its control and access over its newly-acquired assets, an outcome that, without the involvement of a foreign state-controlled investor and with only domestic entities involved, would have been previously 'controlled' by the government of the host state and its branches. Allowance of FDI may therefore be a position of vulnerability for the host state, especially if the asset in question may be relating to CNI.

This factor, in conjunction with a demonstrable subjective belief on the part of the host state, in the trustworthiness of the foreign state, has been suggested as one possible measure to identify 'trusting relationships' empirically.[22] Nonetheless, in theory, if and when a sufficient level of trust is required but is nonetheless found to be absent, it creates an incentive for the state to prepare for this possibility by means of introducing an ISM or strengthening an existent one which, while intended at blocking threats, also then exists, as a manifestation of that state's mistrust.

Once an ISM is in place or further strengthened, depending on the complexity of the legislation, the substantive criteria and institutional decision-making

[18] Another facet where ISMs and trust may be said to overlap is at the EU supranational 'bloc' level where introduction of an EU-wide ISM has been argued as itself building trust at the intra-EU level. See ecfr.eu/article/commentary_investment_screening_china_eu_victory_for_europe/.

[19] For a theoretical discussion of the types of potential security threats arising from foreign investment, see www.worldscientific.com/doi/abs/10.1142/9789814390842_0011, www.piie.com/bookstore/three-threats-analytical-framework-cfius-process.

[20] AM Hoffman, 'A Conceptualization of Trust in International Relations' (2002) 8(3) *European Journal of International Relations* 375–401, 385.

[21] ibid

[22] ibid. Trusting relationships are 'special forms of cooperation involving discretion-granting policies' but 'measurement issues present the most formidable barriers' for trust scholarship.

process it lays out, typically a multitude of factors (whether either legal, economic, political) pertaining to the proposed transaction (for example, the sector or assets involved, the amount or proportion of equity purchased, the parties or the home state of the foreign investor) would be considered analysed in the form of costs and benefits. However, the amount of weightage decision-makers applied to each of such factors, whether considered a pro or a con, is ultimately a subjective estimate and therefore inevitably and fundamentally, an exercise of legal self-judgement and executive political discretion.[23] This discretion, it is argued, is to a large extent a reflection or a test of existent trust, not just on the investor but also its home state.

If one were to subscribe to this 'post-neoliberal' vision of contemporary global economic order and adopt it as an analytical lens onto the context of foreign investment, then it may be of little surprise to observe states allocating greater resources towards developing or better equipping their institutional regulatory defences against the threats posed by SCEs as foreign investors in CNI, in the form of ISMs. Indeed, the evolution of the debate on CNI, along with the rise in ISM reforms reflect and have reinforced greater acceptance and legitimacy of such suggestions. Nor would it be surprising to note the normative connotations intrinsic in the terminology used in recent years by states to describe inward foreign investment, including 'predatory', 'unwanted', 'opportunistic'[24] and 'malicious'.[25]

## IV. POST-2018 RISE IN ISMS – TURNING A PAGE

The need for the term 'geoeconomics' and its capacity or appropriateness as an analytical lens aside, the question of protecting a state's CNI, which as described before contains multiple interplaying facets, including physical, cyber and economic security, is evidently not one that is theoretical or mere rhetoric.[26]

[23] Thus, as I later argue in more detail, making investment screening not a case of law being politicised but at its core, politics itself.

[24] As observed by the OECD in July 2020, see www.oecd.org/coronavirus/policy-responses/investment-screening-in-times-of-covid-19-and-beyond-aa60af47/

[25] www.gov.uk/government/news/new-powers-to-protect-uk-from-malicious-investment-and-strengthen-economic-resilience.

[26] Reinforcing this view for example is the UK National Cyber Security Centre that warned in February 2022 that it and its 'international partners observe an increase in sophisticated, high-impact ransomware incidents against critical infrastructure organisations': www.ncsc.gov.uk/news/joint-advisory-highlights-increased-globalised-threat-of-ransomware; C Glover, ''A Storm on the Horizon': Five Eyes issue Russian cyberattack warning', *Techmonitor*: techmonitor.ai/technology/cybersecurity/russia-critical-infrastructure-cyberattack-five-eyes. See also the May 2021 Colonial Pipeline ransomware attack that breached and held to ransom the largest fuel pipeline in the US: www.bloomberg.com/news/articles/2021-06-04/hackers-breached-colonial-pipeline-using-compromised-password or the October 2020 Mumbai power outage, confirmed as the result of a cyberattack that sabotaged the city's power infrastructure: indianexpress.com/article/india/maharashtra-minister-suggests-foreign-hack-in-mumbai-outage-7210282/. Most recently, in relation to the Russian invasion of Ukraine, see the President of Ukraine stating that he 'discussed the

On that note, this chapter makes the first of its two related arguments as to the nature of contemporary ISMs.

First, that while ISMs were in the past justifiably seen with scepticism and known primarily as being disingenuously conceived policy instruments that invoke national security as a mere guise and are intended towards pursuing purely protectionist or economic nationalist goals,[27] today such scepticism is no longer tenable.[28] While reasonably justified in the past,[29] ISMs have turned over a page and now hold a more bona fide role in foreign investment policy. This argument is based on at least three factors, including:

(a) the emergence of 'good faith but novel national security claims'[30] that in the context of foreign investment by SCEs in CNI are technology-driven risks that create a structural vulnerability and an inevitable problem of trust, which in turn justifies at least monitoring of transactions and allowing for the possibility for state intervention at the pre-establishment stage, as ISMs provide.[31] One can be entirely unsympathetic to nationalistic urges,

threat to nuclear facilities, shelling of civilian and critical infrastructure' with the President of the European Council: twitter.com/ZelenskyyUa/status/1500810372877590529.

[27] A scepticism that is often tied-in with a certain loyalism to unfettered market-driven globalisation, one that favours greater economic interdependence between states as a goal in and of itself and that perceives ISMs as unnecessary market distortions that are a source of inefficiency that will deter FDI flows. Such a view gained popularity in the 1990s during the US' unipolar moment.

[28] While still visible. See N Lavranos, 'The new EU Regulation on the screening of foreign direct investments: A tool for disguised protectionism?', *efilablog*: efilablog.org/2019/01/22/the-new-eu-regulation-on-the-screening-of-foreign-direct-investments-a-tool-for-disguised-protectionism/; G Pandey, A Smiatacz, 2019 'How Many Barriers Should a Steeple Chase Have? Will the EU's Proposed Regulation on Screening of Foreign Direct Investments Add yet More Delaying Barriers When Getting a Merger Deal through the Clearance Gate, and Other Considerations' (2019) 14(2) *Global Trade and Customs Journal* 56–65. See also Y Bin, Director of the EU Law research office at the European Department of the China Academy of Social Sciences (CASS): 'FDI screening as 'selective trade protectionism' and as an approach which is incompatible with the principle of free movement of capital, enshrined in European treaties'. Y Bin, '《欧盟外资安全审查条例》与资本自由流动原则的不兼容性, (Incompatibility of the EU Regulation on Screening Foreign Direct Investment with the Principle of Free Movement of Capital)', European Studies – 欧洲研究, (2019) 5 *Chinese Journal of European Studies*: kns.cnki.net/kcms/detail/Detail.aspx?dbname=CJFDTEMP&filename=OZZZ201905004&v=.

[29] Often exemplified by French economic nationalism and 'strategic yoghurt policy' wherein the French Government made clear to US multinational corporation Pepsico that Danone, the food products group, popularly known for its dairy products, was only for French ownership. See J Roberts, 'From Yoghurt to Steel: French Economic Nationalism in Defensive Mode' (2006) 41(25) *Economic and Political Weekly* 2531–2533. See also J Wrighton, 'Paris Leaps to Defense Of Danone Against Pepsi' [2005] *The Wall Street Journal*, www.wsj.com/articles/SB112190042717991475. More broadly on 'economic nationalist policies that protect domestic businesses against competition from FDI' see J Jakobsen and TG Jakobsen, 'Economic nationalism and FDI: The impact of public opinion on foreign direct investment in emerging markets, 1990–2005' (2011) 6(1) *Society and Business Review* 61–76. doi.org/10.1108/17465681111105841

[30] JB Heath, 'The New National Security Challenge to the Economic Order' (2019) 129 *Yale Law Journal* 1020, available at ssrn.com/abstract=3361107. See also ch 10, in this volume.

[31] In so long as national cybersecurity and sectoral regulations are insufficient to guarantee against any potential security risks occurring in the absence of an ISM and that there also remains the threat of geopolitical leverage.

economic or otherwise, and yet find ISMs to be a reasonable and rational policy choice, given how a state's CNI ultimately serves to provide the basic human needs (in the form of utilities, communication and transportation etc) required for the survival of that state's society. This 'criticality' of certain economic assets is what characterises the bona fide role of ISMs and remind us that there is genuine protection (and not necessarily protectionism) being conducted. It also serves as a reminder that there is universal value in conceptualising certain economic assets and data as 'critical' within foreign investment policy, regardless of a state's development status or geographical location.

(b) the selective usage and limited impact on FDI are observable after the recent rise in ISMs. Contrary to some suggestions,[32] by focusing on CNI and distinguishing between critical and non-critical assets or sectors, the scope and ultimate impact of modern ISMs on overall investment flows by volume has been limited and their usage has been selective and not indiscriminate.[33] If it was protectionism of economic nationalism driving ISMs, a more widespread impact in terms of notifiable transactions and a higher proportion of conditioned or blocked transaction would have been observed. Also, while certainly there is a transaction cost for private parties arising from compliance with screening regulations and ensuring the clarity and smoothness of ISM procedures is an important goal for policymakers, the time and cost of notification (when required) proven burdensome enough to be a significant deterrent for foreign investors, if at all.

(c) the bipartisan nature of the domestic support driving ISMs[34] whose recent rise while no doubt instigated by and directed primarily towards SCEs

[32] See the suggestion that ISMs 'might unintentionally inhibit economic development' (insidetrade.com/daily-news/analysts-fdi-screening-uptick-worrisome-global-development) or that 'a rise in screening tools is chilling investments' (exportcompliancedaily.com/news/2021/06/11/countries-should-reduce-fdirelated-risks-stemming-from-screening-regimes-expert-says-2106100039).

[33] See the French example, which despite its reputation concerning economic nationalism, between 2017 to 2019 on average only about 15% of transactions were notifiable (meaning 85% of incoming foreign investment was entirely unaffected), out of which a small minority were conditioned, with blocks being rare. N Bonucci, S Crepy and C Paulhac, 'Let the Data Speak: French Foreign Investment Screening Is No Hurdle for M&A Deals', *Paul Hastings* (Feb 2021), available at www.paulhastings.com/insights/international-regulatory-enforcement/let-the-data-speak-french-foreign-investment-screening-is-no-hurdle-for-m#_ftn1. www.tresor.economie.gouv.fr/services-aux-entreprises/investissements-etrangers-en-france.

[34] The observation of bipartisan support runs counter to the presumption of there being a single specific ideological leaning that ISMs serve. Instead, it indicates a 'growing consensus that all foreign investment is not equally beneficial' and that a wider public expectation that the state must exercise greater control over critical assets. J Bonnitcha, 'The Return of Investment Screening as a Policy Tool', IISD, www.iisd.org/itn/en/2020/12/19/the-return-of-investment-screening-as-a-policy-tool-jonathan-bonnitcha. See, eg, the Dutch cross-sectoral ISM that was recently 'passed in the Dutch House of Representatives without a dissenting vote and therefore with widespread political backing' www.cliffordchance.com/insights/resources/blogs/antitrust-fdi-insights/2022/04/antitrust-dutch-cross-sector-fdi-regime-proposal-passed-with-widespread-political-support-in-house-of-representatives.html.

or ultimate beneficiaries originating from the People's Republic of China (PRC),[35] has neither resulted in a complete ban on PRC investments,[36] nor has been directed at them exclusively.[37]

As a caveat, it is certainly not being suggested that protectionism or economic nationalism in the context of ISMs is no longer plausible, or that states are no longer capable of disingenuity in the practice of their foreign investment policy and using national security as a guise.[38] What is being emphasised here is that in light of the empirics of the most recent rise in ISMs, the previously held scepticism towards the policy activity is outdated and no longer tenable, insofar as it is presumed that protectionism or economic nationalism are the only

[35] As Danzman and Meunier note, 'investments from China may have prompted increased screening measures in host countries because of the perception that there is something inherently different about the nature of Chinese FDI and therefore it should not be treated politically like any other foreign investment'. See Danzman and Meunier (n 1). Also, as Meunier has previously argued vis-à-vis the 'novelty' of Chinese investments as a political challenge, 'some of these characteristics include: an emerging economy in need of high technology; a unique political system with state management of the economy, lack of transparency on the nature of investors, and blurring of lines between economic and political objectives; and a non-ally in the security dimension with geopolitical ambitions'. See S Meunier, 'Beware of Chinese Bearing Gifts: Why China's Direct Investment Poses Political Challenges in Europe and the United States' in J Chaisse (ed), *China's Three-Prong Investment Strategy: Bilateral, Regional, And Global Tracks* (Oxford, Oxford University Press, 2019) See also M Babić and AD Dixon, 'Is the China Effect Real? Ideational Change and the Political Contestation of Chinese State-Led Investment in Europe' (2022) 15(2) *The Chinese Journal of International Politics* 111–139 on how 'China effect affects advanced European economies similarly' and how the 'rise of China as a global investor shifts the perceptions of policy-makers away from being a source of investment toward a potential threat to national security'. See also B Canes-Wrone, L Mattioliand S Meunier, 'Foreign direct investment screening and congressional backlash politics in the United States' (2020) 22(4) *The British Journal of Politics and International Relations* 666–678.

[36] See, eg, the US ISM, CFIUS, approving unconditionally the acquisition of a 47% stake in Icon Aircraft Inc., a California-based maker of recreational amphibious planes by a Chinese SCE, Shanghai Pudong Science and Technology Investment Co, www.wsj.com/articles/u-s-panel-finds-no-national-security-concerns-with-chinese-plane-deal-11646158527. CFIUS had earlier also approved, subject to a risk mitigation agreement, 'a greenfield wind farm project in Texas, to be built by GH America Energy, a subsidiary of Shanghai-listed Guanghui Energy Co., Ltd': www.kwm.com/us/en/insights/latest-thinking/cfius-clears-chinese-wind-farm-deal.html?s=09; see also the sale of Dutch firm Royal Philips NV's home appliances business to Beijing-based private equity firm Hillhouse Capital, *Gadgets360*: gadgets360.com/home-appliances/news/philips-home-appliance-unit-sell-hillhouse-capital-eur-3-7-billion-deal-15-years-2399039. In India, government data has revealed that, between April 2020 and June 2022, national authorities have approved at least 80 transactions involving Chinese entities, see economictimes.indiatimes.com/tech/technology/india-approved-80-fdi-proposals-involving-chinese-entities-data/articleshow/92684499.cms.

[37] See, eg, the UK's review of a US origin takeover in the defence sector, *BBC online* www.bbc.co.uk/news/business-49738885.amp, Spain's screening of a mining sector investment by an Australian entity, *Miningweekly.com*: www.miningweekly.com/article/sandfire-completes-matsa-buy-2022-02-02/; a Canadian foreign investor in the Australian telecom sector requiring FIRB approval, *AFR.com*: www.afr.com/chanticleer/tpg-sells-towers-embraces-telstra-20220509-p5ajsd; the UK government reviewing a French investor's stake in British telecom, *Reuters*: www.reuters.com/markets/deals/britain-launches-review-drahis-bt-stake-deal-2022-05-26/.

[38] Nor is trust necessarily the sole factor driving investment screening. Indeed, there may exist multiple motivations that states may hold individually or simultaneously which may induce states to screen investments.

potential explanations for ISM activity. Indeed, the EU's position on investment screening[39] is emblematic that it is possible to be remain conducive to the aim of liberalising foreign investment while maintaining some form of discriminatory treatment in the interest of maintaining 'strategic autonomy'.[40]

## V. ISMS AS POLITICS, EMBEDDED IN LAW

As its second argument as to the nature of contemporary ISMs, the chapter cautions against viewing ISMs from a purely legal lens, contending that, given the subjective role of trust (towards not just the SCE but also its governing home state) that is embedded within their decision-making (particularly with regard to transactions involving CNI), ISMs essentially serve an executive *political* function and not an administrative *regulatory* one which can (or should) be judicialised or be subject to judicial review on merits.

Some of the common grievances held by lawyers against ISMs include that they are vague, 'politicised', 'discriminatory' and self-judging. These complaints, it is argued, are borne out of adopting a purely legal lens to view ISMs and the resultant misconception that ISMs are akin to post-establishment regulatory bodies, for which it is rightly expected that they should function in a non-discriminatory fashion and be subject to judicial review. However, such an understanding (and resultant grievances) towards ISMs are based on what is a misconception regarding the nature of the function that ISMs fulfil.

More specifically, it is worth noting that there does not exist, nor can there exist a precise 'technical' or 'objective' standard that is generally applicable to derive ISM decisions. Indeed, it is entirely plausible that two separate investment proposals with entirely identical sets of technical, legal, and economic characteristics, including that both are made by foreign SCEs, can be decided upon differently by the same ISM, purely on the bases of the nationality of the investing entity and hence its governing home state.

This is because, as discussed earlier, while typically a multitude of factors pertaining to the proposed transaction may be considered and analysed by an ISM in the form of costs and benefits, the amount of weightage decision-makers apply to each of such factors, whether considered a pro or a con, is ultimately a subjective estimate and therefore inevitably and fundamentally, an exercise of self-judgement and executive political discretion revolving around trust in IR.

Therefore, to protest that investment screening is discriminatory is in itself an illogical stance given that exercising discrimination (albeit a highly selective form of it), is by definition in the very nature of investment screening, indeed the

[39] Marked by a move away from the EU Member States being 'naïve free-traders', as the EU Commission President declared in his 2017 State of the Union speech: ec.europa.eu/commission/presscorner/detail/fr/SPEECH_17_1581.

[40] See also ch 6, in this volume.

very point of the exercise, and justified in very specific circumstances, insofar as the risks being protected against are bona fide.[41] Investment screening is thus a distinct animal and not a case of law being politicised but at its core, politics itself. It is for this reason that rightly, the scope for judicial review of ISM decisions is often relatively limited and at times not available at all.[42]

This is not to argue that there is no need or room for reforming ISMs. On the contrary, because of this subjective and effectively unchecked trust-based discretionary power that they hold, in addition to the recent reforms that have boosted the efficiency and capability of ISMs towards achieving their objective of detecting and scrutinising foreign investment in critical sectors,[43] greater efforts are needed towards enhancing the transparency and democratic accountability of ISMs. However, as discussed above, given the nature of their function and the decisions that they render, ISMs essentially serve an executive *political* function, and not a *regulatory* one and hence the standard applicable towards qualitatively assessing their procedural design and degree of fairness should reflect this distinction.

[41] A similar logic already has long applied in the context of immigration policy and issuance of visas, where again, two entirely identical visa applications may nonetheless result in different results, based purely on the nationality of the applicant and the subject level of trust the issuing authority of the visa holds towards the applicant and their home state. Immigration policies too, in design and in practice, have a clear nationality-based discriminatory element to them, one that also depends upon trust as an operative element.

[42] See, eg, in Australia where 'applicants have no right of administrative or judicial review of foreign investment decisions made under the Foreign Acquisitions and Takeovers Act 1975 (FATA) or the policy. The Administrative Decisions (Judicial Review) Act 1977 specifically exempts decisions made under the FATA from judicial review.' 'Australia's foreign investment policy', available at www.aph.gov.au/About_Parliament/Parliamentary_Departments/Parliamentary_Library/pubs/BriefingBook44p/AustForeignInvest. See also China's Foreign Investment Law of People's Republic of China (Promulgated by the National People's Congress on 15 March 2019, effective on 1 January 2020) which, under Art 35, states that 'all decisions made from the review are final and exclude any administrative or judicial recourse'. See also C Bian, 'Foreign Direct Investment Screening and National Security: Reducing Regulatory Hurdles to Investors Through Induced Reciprocity' (2021) 22(4) *The Journal of World Investment & Trade* 561–595: doi.org/10.1163/22119000–12340218.

[43] For example, focusing on indirect state control through significant state-backed funding (rather than merely ownership) and state-led CNI investment programmes, going beyond traditional M&A activity to include non-acquisition transactions such as 5G equipment supply contracts and focusing on the leakage of critical data and intellectual property by all potential means, including non-transactional exchanges such as research collaborations and joint ventures. Special regard has also been expressly made in recent amendments to address foreign SCE involvement in investment proposals related to CNI, typically involving a lower threshold for triggering the ISM and requiring greater scrutiny. See, eg, in Canada, where, according to a parliamentary committee, 'all investments by state-owned enterprises from authoritarian states' may meet the Investment Canada Act's threshold of potentially being 'injurious to national security' and subjected to 'enhanced scrutiny', regardless of value. House of Commons Industry Committee, nationalpost.com/news/politics/investments-in-canadian-assets-by-authoritarian-states-should-trigger-national-security-review-commons-committee. See also A House, C Douglas and C Margison, 'Enhanced Scrutiny of Foreign State-Owned Investors / Critical Infrastructure at the Heart of Canadian National Security Concerns', *Competitionchronicle*: www.competitionchronicle.com/2020/04/enhanced-scrutiny-of-foreign-state-owned-investors-critical-infrastructure-at-the-heart-of-canadian-national-security-concerns/.

## VI. CONCLUSION

With the above conceptualisation and assertions as to the nature of contemporary ISMs, this chapter has sought to declutter the rise of (and give due credit to) a dynamic and potent field of foreign investment policy that intersects with the economic dimension of national security. It shows how the distinction between critical versus non-critical assets, particularly national infrastructure may be a concern of universal value, regardless of development status or regime type, and provide a potential starting point towards limiting policy practice to cases with bona fide security risks.

Emblematically, when it comes to foreign SCEs being involved in CNI, the chapter has also sought to highlight how the potential for vulnerability is inevitable, which in turn calls for a certain level of trust required towards the SCE and its governing home state for such a transaction to be allowable. Trust, therefore, is the new currency for conducting international economic exchanges in critical assets and the rise of ISMs today is a manifestation of greater mistrust in international affairs.

This loss of naivete towards unfettered globalisation is increasingly global, here to stay for the near future and already having long-term material effects in terms of how capital flows and more importantly, in terms of how the control of and access to critical assets, infrastructure, data and personnel, is demarcated along geopolitical lines that marked with trust in IR. That said, while excessive trust may unwittingly expose states to an otherwise unwanted level of risk, as it may have already, excessive distrust may lead to high opportunity costs and unduly forgo development gains.

Greater attention may therefore be paid towards studying trust within the context of ISMs more specifically at area-level and appropriate legal tools that may be adopted to, if not build trust itself, at the very least help mitigate perceived security risks and allow for investment flows to safely continue despite the general presence of mistrust. Equally important would be gaining greater clarity on how and the extent to which the democratic accountability and transparency of ISMs may be enhanced.

# Part III

# Adjudicating State Capitalism

# 8

# *Chinese State-Owned Enterprises and International Investment Law*

MING DU

## I. INTRODUCTION

DESPITE THREE DECADES of extensive state reform and privatisation, recent empirical research shows that state-owned, state-controlled or otherwise state-influenced enterprises and sovereign wealth funds remain an important economic force in the global economy. They are increasingly competing with private firms in global markets for market shares, resources, ideas and intermediate inputs.[1] More recently, in response to the Covid-19 crisis, governments have taken a vast array of measures to support the business sector. In some cases, rescue packages include the acquisition of equity stakes in companies in financial distress, increasing the number and presence of state-owned multinational enterprises (SOEs) to about 1,600 in the global economy in 2020.[2]

SOEs hold a prominent position in China's socialist market economy system.[3] Even market-oriented reforms have enabled China's GDP to grow at an average rate of 9.5 per cent per year over the past 30 years and led to a rapid expansion of the private sector in China, there are still more than 150,000 SOEs in China today and they contributed to 28 per cent of China's GDP and 16 per cent of employment in 2017.[4] In 2021, 143 Chinese firms appeared on the list of

[1] P Kowalski and K Perepechay, 'International Trade and Investment by State Enterprises', OECD Trade Policy Papers No 184 (OECD Publishing, 2015) 7.

[2] UNCTAD, World Investment Report 2021: Investing in Sustainable Economy (2021) 28.

[3] There is no uniform definition of SOEs. The OECD defines it as 'any corporate entity recognized by national law as an enterprise, and in which the state exercises ownership'. Ownership is defined in terms of control, either by the state holding full or majority of voting shares or otherwise exercising an equivalent degree of control. See OECD, *Guidelines on Corporate Governance of State-Owned Enterprises* (2015 edn) 14–15.

[4] C Zhang, 'How Much Do State-owned Enterprises Contribute to China's GDP and Employment?' The World Bank Working Paper (15 July 2019).

Fortune Global 500, among which 82 were SOEs.[5] It is undisputable that SOEs are, and will be, a hallmark of China's socialist market economy model, rather than a transitional phenomenon leading to liberal capitalism as many critics of SOEs had expected.[6]

Chinese SOEs not only play a key role in Chinese domestic economy, they are also a major force in implementing the Chinese Government's ambitious Belt and Road Initiative (BRI) and 'Made in China 2025' industrial policies, both reinforcing the earlier 'Go Global' strategy adopted in 2000. In 2020, global FDI fell by 42 per cent whilst China's outbound foreign direct investment (OFDI) posted a year-on-year increase of 3.3 per cent, reaching US$130 billion.[7] UNCTAD ranked China third in the world in terms of OFDI in 2020, after the US and Japan.[8] This steady growth trend is expected to continue as Chinese companies increasingly realise that overseas investment is an effective strategy for them to upgrade, transform and become more competitive. Earlier statistics showed that at least 80 per cent of all Chinese OFDI has been funded by SOEs.[9] With the growing strength of Chinese private enterprises, however, a smaller proportion of China's increasing OFDI is coming from SOEs. Still, evidence shows that of 650 Chinese investments in Europe since 2010, roughly 40 per cent have moderate to high involvement by state-owned or state-controlled companies.[10] As of October 2018, Chinese SOEs contracted about half of BRI projects by number and more than 70 per cent by project value.[11]

The purpose of this chapter is to critically analyse how international investment law responds to the challenges brought about by the rise of China's SOEs in the global economy. This article is organised as follows. Section II provides an overview of China SOE reforms since former Chinese paramount leader Deng Xiaoping's historical southern tour in 1992 until today, showing how the Chinese Government has implemented drastic reform measures to make SOEs competitive market players, while retaining effective control to ensure that they follow the political line of the Chinese Communist Party (CCP). Section III explains why Chinese SOEs bring about unique regulatory concerns to host countries. Section IV explores the standing of Chinese SOEs before investor-state dispute settlement (ISDS) and the problems associated with national security mechanisms to screen Chinese SOEs' investments. Section V concludes the chapter.

[5] fortune.com/global500/2021/search/?fg500_country=China.

[6] A Gabriele, 'The Role of the State in China's Industrial Development: A Reassessment' (2010) 52(2) *Comparative Economic Studies* 325, 348.

[7] Chinese Ministry of Commerce, Regular Press Conference (24 January 2021), www.mofcom.gov.cn/xwfbh/20210121.shtml.

[8] UNCTAD, 'World Investment Report 2020: International Production beyond the Pandemic' (2020) 15.

[9] A Wooldridge, 'The Visible Hand', *The Economist* (January 2012) 15.

[10] D Michaels, 'Behind China's Decade of European Deals, State Investors Evade Notice', *Wall Street Journal* (30 May 2020).

[11] R Dossani et al, 'Demystifying the Belt and Road Initiative', Rand Working Paper WR-1338 (May 2020) 13–15.

## II. UNTANGLE THE NET: CHINESE SOES AND THE CHINESE PARTY-STATE

### A. China's SOE Reforms

China has practised state capitalism for many years, but its form, function and implications have changed dramatically over the past decade.[12] To grasp the complexity of China's state capitalism, it is essential to understand China's economic and institutional transformation from a socialist planned economy to a socialist market economy. This transformation was deemed to be necessary to reduce economic losses, increase economic growth and raise living standards, from which the CPP derives its governing legitimacy.[13]

The reform of Chinese SOEs lied at the centre of this grand economic transformation. How Chinese SOEs have been reformed from basically production units in the early 1980s to largely autonomous profit-seeking corporations today was extensively addressed in the literature.[14] In brief, after some experiments in the 1980s, SOE reforms after the historic southern tour of Former Chinese paramount leader Deng Xiaoping in 1992 have gone through several distinct stages. At the first stage, SOEs were required to be modern enterprises characterised by 'clear property rights, well-defined power and responsibility, separation of enterprise from government, and scientific management'.[15] In practice, corporatizstion was seen as a means of achieving this reform goal. The first general Chinese Company Law was enacted to provide for the incorporation of SOEs in 1994. Thereafter, newly incorporated SOEs proliferated all over the country. Along with corporatisation, central to SOE reforms in the 1990s was the policy of 'nurturing the large and letting the small go', a reference to the policy of concentrating the government's resources and control on the larger SOEs in strategic sectors, while relaxing state control over smaller SOEs and retreating from labour-intensive competitive sectors.[16] After this round of reform, the SOEs were streamlined and their advantageous position was further reinforced in the upstream and strategic industries.

The second phase of SOE reforms started in 2003 and focused on reforming property rights and corporate governance in large SOEs. Chinese company law and securities law were revised to achieve more congruence between Chinese law and practice and that of countries with more developed capital markets.[17]

[12] M Du, 'China's State Capitalism and World Trade Law' (2014) 63 *International and Comparative Law Quarterly* 409, 413–426.

[13] J Wang, 'The Political Logic of Corporate Governance in China's State-owned Enterprises' (2014) 47 *Cornell International Law Journal* 631, 637.

[14] B Naughton and KS Tsai (eds), *State Capitalism, Institutional Adaptation and the Chinese Miracle* (Cambridge, Cambridge University Press, 2015).

[15] Decision on Issues Regarding the Establishment of a Socialist Market Economic System, para 1(2) finance.ifeng.com/opinion/jjsh/20090906/1199906.shtml.

[16] M Mattlin, 'Chinese Strategic State-Owned Enterprises and Ownership Control' (2010) 4(6) BICCS Asia Paper 8.

[17] J Feinerman, 'New Hope of Corporate Governance in China?' [2007] *The China Quarterly* 590–612.

One key reform was the establishment of the State Assets Supervision and Administration Commission (SASAC), a quasi-governmental, ministerial level agency operating directly under the State Council, to oversee the management of the SOEs. The SASAC was primarily designed to fulfil the state's ownership function, combining the administrative functions previously carried out by various government agencies. The SASAC is recognised as an 'investor' and assigned the legal rights and duties of a shareholder, holding SOE shares on behalf of the state.[18] As an investor, the SASAC enjoys an owner's equity rights and assumes legal liabilities under Chinese Company Law but it does not intervene directly in SOE operations, so that the ownership rights are separated from those of management.[19]

The establishment of the SASAC contains both centralising and decentralising features. On the one hand, the principle of local control over local SOEs was clarified and institutionalised by clearly separating central, provincial and municipal SOEs and handing control over them to SASAC offices at respective jurisdictional levels. On the other hand, the SASAC serves as a unitary holding company for those key central SOEs that have been selected by the government to be China's national champions and future top global companies. When the SASAC was established in 2003, 196 central SOEs were under its oversight. The number was reduced to 96 by June 2021.[20]

The SASAC has a broad mandate that includes drafting laws and regulations regarding state-owned assets, managing and restructuring state assets so that their value develops positively, hiring and firing executives of SOEs under its supervision and pushing forward further reforms of SOEs.[21] Though there have been doubts over whether the SASAC is always able to exercise its authority effectively, the SASAC is a very powerful state agency and since its establishment the SASAC has been pushing forward SOE reforms aggressively.[22] As the 'the world largest controlling shareholder',[23] the SASAC set out a major policy of promoting the concentration of state-owned capital in key fields and enhancing the controlling power of the state-owned economy.

The third stage of SOE reforms have started from the convention of the 18th CPC Congress in November 2012 until now. In this 'Xi Jinping era', the Chinese central authorities have brought unprecedented momentum to reform Chinese SOEs. The core document guiding the overhaul of SOEs, *The Guideline to Deepen Reforms of SOEs*, was issued by the CCP Central Committee and the

[18] Chapter 2 of PRC Law on State-owned Assets of Enterprises.

[19] B Chiu and M Lewis, *Reforming China's State-Owned Enterprises and Banks* (Cheltenham, Edward Elgar Publishing, 2006) 61.

[20] www.sasac.gov.cn/n2588035/n2641579/n2641645/index.html.

[21] SASAC, 'Main Functions and Responsibilities of SASAC', www.sasac.gov.cn/n1180/n3123702/n3123717/n3162319/index.html.

[22] C Walter and F Howie, *Red Capitalism* (Chichester, John Wiley & Sons Ltd, 2012) 189–191.

[23] Boston Consulting Group, 'SASAC: China's Megashareholder' (2007) www.bcgperspectives.com/content/articles/globalization_strategy_sasac_chinas_megashareholder/.

State Council in 2015. This key policy document (the 'One') is supplemented by a wide range of supporting policies (the 'N'). The comprehensive and thorough Chinese SOE reform has been guided by the 'One Plus N' policy framework.

Based on this overall guidance, Chinese SOEs are classified as commercial SOEs and public service SOEs. Commercial SOEs should stick to commercial operations and aim to increase state-owned assets, while public service SOEs exist to improve people's quality of life and provide public goods and services. Commercial SOEs are further divided into perfect competitive sectors and strategic sectors (ie, key industries related to national security and national economic lifelines). Accordingly, different reform measures, growth strategies, regulations, and evaluations are outlined based on this more sophisticated classification of SOEs.[24]

One salient feature of the 'One Plus N' policy framework is that it aims at strengthening the leadership of the CCP in SOEs. For example, SOEs were mandated to incorporate the CPC's leadership role into their Articles of Association. The board of directors also must hear the opinions of the party committee of the company before deciding on important issues. A cross-appointment system for SOE party commitment members to be directors and senior officers was introduced to ensure that party officials hold all key positions and decision-making power. The campaign to insert the CCP into all levels of organisation and decision-making is further institutionalised in *the Trial Regulation on the Work at Primary-Level Party Organization of SOEs* issued by the CCP Central Committee in December 2019.[25] All these measures have closed the gap between SOE boardrooms and the CCP's strategic goals.[26] Other key reform measures during the third stage include the establishment of a mixed ownership structure in SOEs; organisation of state-owned capital investment and operation companies; consolidation of the state-owned SOEs to make them 'stronger, bigger and better', and upgrading corporate governance standards in SOEs in order to entrench their commercial orientation.[27]

As mighty leviathans of the Chinese planned economy, Chinese SOEs were long depicted as 'industrial dinosaurs', 'muscle-bound goons' or the 'relics of a failed economic experiment', and characterised as possessing a lack of managerial flair, little concern for profit, low employee motivation and mobility and a tendency to maximise corporate size.[28] After the extensive reforms

[24] Notice of the SASAC, the Ministry of Finance, and the National Development and Reform Commission on Issuing the Guiding Opinion on Functional Definition and Classification of SOEs (No 170 [2015] of the SASAC (7 December 2015).

[25] CCP Central Committee, The Trial Regulation on the Work at Primary-Level Party Organization of SOEs (30 December 2019).

[26] J Blanchette, 'From 'China Inc.' to 'CCP Inc.': A New Paradigm for Chinese State Capitalism', 66 China Leadership Monitor (1 December 2020) 7.

[27] J Wang and T Cheng-Han, 'Mixed Ownership Reform and Corporate Governance in China's State-Owned Enterprises' (2020) 53 *Vanderbilt Journal of Transnational Law* 1055, 1089–1099.

[28] J Hassard et al., 'China's State-owned Enterprises: Economic Reform and Organizational Restructuring' (2010) 23(5) *Journal of Organizational Change Management* 501.

of the past three decades, it is unrealistic today to uphold the simplistic and pessimistic view of Chinese SOEs as industrial and commercial dinosaurs fit only for dismemberment or bankruptcy. Modern corporate governance systems have been established in Chinese SOEs, some of which can rival the best private companies in the world. Chinese SOEs have evolved into major actors in international trade, foreign direct investment and international capital markets, and formidable competitors of firms around the world.[29]

## B. SOEs and the Chinese Party-State

One core task of SOE reforms in China is the separation of government functions from enterprise management. Following the reforms, government officials are asked not to intervene in the day-to-day business operations of SOEs.[30] Nevertheless, the management of Chinese SOEs continues to be heavily influenced by politics and policy considerations. To understand the behavioural logic of Chinese SOEs in both national and international markets, it is enlightening to look at how the Chinese party-state exercises central authority on Chinese SOEs.

One important channel for the CCP to ensure their control over SOEs is by virtue of its power to appoint, evaluate and remove SOEs' top management.[31] The leaders of SOEs are appointed in accordance with a highly institutionalised cadre management system to ensure the principle of 'absolute control of the (SOE) executives by the party (CCP)'.[32] In practice the executives of Chinese SOEs face two sets of incentives in promoting their career. On the one hand, they want the SOEs they manage to be profitable because their evaluation will be partly based on the financial performance of the enterprises they manage. On the other hand, their career successes are ultimately determined by the CCP which is more concerned with how well the executives carry out the goals of the state. A top SOE executive judged unresponsive to such direction risks not being promoted or even demoted, even if the SOE performs well financially. These dual criteria for evaluating SOE top executives – to deliver profits and serve the government – usually align. However, when financial and state goals are in conflict, the incentives SOE executives face tend to push them to choose state interests over financial interests of the company and other non-state

[29] Li-wen Lin, 'A Network Anatomy of Chinese State-owned Enterprises' (2017) 16(4) *World Trade Review* 583, 593.

[30] W Li and L Putterman, 'Reforming Chinese SOEs: An Overview' (2008) 50 *Comparative Economic Studies* 353–380.

[31] R McGregor, *The Party: The Secret World of China's Communist Rulers* (London, Penguin Books, 2011) 49.

[32] X Jinping, 'Upholding the Party Leadership over SOEs Unwaveringly', *People's Daily* (12 October 2016).

shareholders.[33] Multiple researchers have revealed that the goals of the state are dominant in SOE executives' decision-making processes.[34] Another key mechanism for the CCP to exercise its authority over SOEs is by institutionalising party committees' leadership role in SOE corporate governance.[35] As in described in section II.A above, the party committee now serves a 'leadership core' function as well as a 'political core' function in SOEs. The party committee also has authority to participate in major decisions involving SOEs' operations, personnel affairs, investment, and spending.

The recentralisation of the CCP authority over SOEs since 2012 has sent potentially conflicting messages concerning the development of China's SOE reform. China needs to maintain the momentum of its economic development as a crucial support for its legitimacy and stability against the new normal of the market slowdown. Given their pivotal role in the national economy, SOEs are expected to perform well financially. Indeed, Xi Jinping stated that the criteria for measuring the success of SOE reform should be 'the value increase in state capital, improvement of the state sector's competitiveness, and expansion of state capital control'.[36] Precisely for the purpose of increasing economic efficiency, China's SOE reform was premised on the separation of the CCP's political functions from SOEs' business management. However, the more recent emphasis of the party leadership as a core element of corporate governance clearly demonstrates a significant change of the conventional thinking of Chinese SOE reform. Consequently, the principle of party leadership, which inevitably assigns much greater weight to safeguarding the party-state's interests, requires SOEs to follow the party's political line rather than to the principle of corporate governance such as maximising shareholder value in case there is a conflict.[37]

The fact that Chinese governmental policies have a significant influence on Chinese SOEs' overseas acquisitions is borne out by empirical findings. Before the introduction of the BRI in 2013, Chinese acquirers were less likely to pursue targets in BRI countries. By contrast, the BRI has a material impact on the location choice of cross-border M&As by Chinese SOEs. Similarly, targets in industries identified by Made in China 2025 policy become significantly more likely to be purchased by Chinese SOEs after the policy was introduced in 2015.[38]

[33] A Szamosszegi and C Kyle, 'An Analysis of State-owned Enterprises and State Capitalism in China', Report to U.S. – China Economic and Security Review Commission (2011) 79.

[34] Y Ruilong et al, 'The Promotion Mechanim of 'Quasi-officials': Evidence from Chinese Central Enterprises' (2013) 3 *Management World* 23–33.

[35] W Leutert, 'Firm Control: Governing the State-owned Economy under Xi Jinping' (2018) 27 *China Perspectives* 30–32.

[36] Xi, above n 32.

[37] X Zhang, 'Integration of CCP Leadership with Corporate Governance: Leading Role or Dismemberment?' (2019) 55 *China Perspectives* 58–61.

[38] C Fuest et al, 'What Drives Chinese Overseas M&A Investment? Evidence from Micro Data' (2022) 30 *Review of International Economics* 306, 322.

## III. THE CHALLENGES OF CHINESE SOES TO INTERNATIONAL INVESTMENT LAW

The meteoric rise of OFDI by Chinese SOEs presents to host countries a vexing policy dilemma. On the one hand, the influx of foreign capital would bring much-needed new capital and job growth that would have positive economic and political ramifications to host countries. On the other hand, due to their political ties with the Chinse Government and concentration in strategic sectors, Chinese SOEs' investment can raise some genuine concerns about national security, fair competition, reciprocity and even the function of free market at home.

### A. Levelling the Playing Field

As part of the scheme to support the 'Go Global' strategy, the Chinese Government has offered a range of financial and non-financial incentives to encourage the overseas expansion of Chinese enterprises and particularly SOEs. The financial support takes a number of different forms, including access to loans below market rates, government special funds, direct capital contribution and subsidies associated with the official aid programmes.[39] The funds may come either from government ministries such as Ministry of Finance (MOF) and National Development and Reform Commission (NDRC), China's policy banks, such as the China Development Bank (CDB) and the China Export and Import Bank (Exim Bank), or even state-owned commercial banks.[40]

These government-bestowed benefits have raised concerns that SOEs may cause market distortions in host countries. Indeed, much of the public criticism of Chinese SOEs' takeover bids has focused on the perception that these bids were facilitated by the subsidised financing from the Chinese Government.[41] For example, the NDRC and the Exim Bank jointly announced in 2004 that the Exim Bank would earmark a portion of its budget for OFDI projects supported by the Chinese Government with at least a two per cent interest rate discount and possibly other preferential lending terms. The MOF would cover the gap between the actual market rate and the subsidised rate offered by the Exim Bank.[42] In its

[39] OECD, Foreign Government- Controlled Investors and Recipient Country Investment Policies: A Scoping Paper (2009) 90.

[40] E Downs, *China's Superbank: Debt, Oil and Influence, How China Development Bank is Re-writing the Rules of Global Finance* (Hoboken, John Wily & Sons, 2013) 25–27.

[41] DN Fagan, 'The U.S. Regulatory and Institutional Framework for FDI', *Investing in the United States: A Reference Series for Chinese Investors* (Vale Columbia Centre on Sustainable International Investment, Vol 2, 2008) 19.

[42] NDRC and Exim Bank, Circular on the Supportive Credit Policy on Key Overseas Investment Project Encouraged by the State (October 2004).

bid for Unocal in 2005, China National Offshore Oil Corporation (CNOOC) borrowed US$6 billion from the Industrial and Commercial Bank of China, a Chinese state-owned commercial bank. Another US$7 billion came in the form of subsidised loans from CNOOC's government-owned parent company. For the US$7 billion loan, US$2.5 billion was interest-free for two years with the potential to remain that way for up to 30 years; interest on the remaining US$4.5 billion could be waived by the parent company in the event that CNOOC's credit rating dropped below investment grade.[43] Similarly, investments in the BRI are largely financed by China's state-owned banks.[44]

Empirical research shows that Chinese SOEs' overseas acquisitions have several unique features compared to Chinese private investors. First, while there are fewer acquisitions by Chinese SOEs, they tend to conduct larger deals and predominantly engage in full or majority acquisitions. Second, Chinese private investors tend to invest in countries where the currency depreciates against the RMB, but the reverse holds true for Chinese SOEs. Third, Chinese SOEs tend to acquire less profitable and more indebted targets. These findings suggest that Chinese SOEs may be less financially constrained than other investors because they have financial support from the state-owned banking system which allows them to engage in large-scale transactions and to pursue less cautious investment strategies.[45] However, on the question of acquisition prices, there is no evidence that Chinese SOEs pay higher prices than other investors for targets with comparable characteristics. This contradicts the view that government support enables Chinese companies to outbid other investors in the global M&A market.[46]

Since there is no international treaty on the regulation of M&A subsidies, some states have taken unilateral measures to address potential distortive effects of foreign subsidies in international investment. For example, the European Commission proposed on 5 May 2021 a new instrument under which the Commission will have the power to investigate financial contributions granted by public authorities of a non-EU country which will benefit companies engaging in an economic activity in the EU and redress their distortive effects. If the Commission establishes that a foreign subsidy exists, that it is distortive, and that the negative effects of foreign subsidies outweigh the positive effects, the Commission will have the power to impose redressive measures or accept commitments from the companies concerned that remedy the distortion.[47]

[43] G Hufbauer et al, 'Investment Subsidies for Cross-border M&A: Trends and Policy Implications', United States Council Foundation Occasional Paper No 2 (April 2008) 2.

[44] Dossani et al (n 11) 13–15.

[45] Fuest et al (n 38) 25.

[46] ibid.

[47] European Commission, 'Commission Proposes New Regulation to Address Distortions Caused by Foreign Subsidies in the Single Market' (5 May 2021).

### B. Reciprocity in Market Access

Chinese SOEs' overseas investment spree has caused reciprocity concerns. In the past few years, China has selectively liberalised foreign investment restrictions in some sectors. Accordingly, China's Foreign Direct Investment Regulatory Restrictiveness Index was reduced from 0.43 in 2013 to 0.24 in 2019. Nevertheless, China's FDI regime remained highly restrictive, compared to the OECD average index of 0.06 in the same year.[48] Foreign companies are likely to face various limits to access the Chinese market, especially in key fields and industries that the Chinese Government regards as strategically important for the Chinese political and economy stability.[49] If the Chinese Government would not approve similar investment projects made by foreign investors in China, critics have questioned why a host country should approve such projects launched by Chinese SOE investors. For example, Senator Charles Schumer of New York demanded that when any SOE sought to acquire an American company, an additional study should be performed on reciprocity.[50]

Lifting market access barriers for EU investors in China was therefore one of the EU's key negotiation objectives for China-EU Investment Agreement (CAI).[51] China has made commitments in manufacturing sectors, including electric cars, chemicals, telecommunication equipment and health equipment, and in services sectors, such as cloud services, financial services, private healthcare, environmental services, international maritime transport and air transport-related services.[52] Similarly, in the US- China 'Phase One' deal, China promised to remove restrictions on investment, reduce burdensome regulation, and expeditiously review the pending licence applications of US companies in its domestic banking, credit rating, electronic payments, asset management, insurance and securities industries.[53]

### C. National Security Concerns

Despite the declining share of Chinese OFDI made by SOEs, one of the most popular concerns is that Chinese SOEs may make overseas investment and corporate decisions on political and strategic rather than commercial and

[48] OECD, 'FDI Regulatory Restrictiveness Index', 2019. stats.oecd.org/Index.aspx?datasetcode=FDIINDEX#

[49] Szamosszegi and Kyle (n 33) 84.

[50] J Bussey, 'Playing Hardball with Chinese Investors', *Wall Street Journal* (25 October 2012).

[51] European Commission, 'Impact Assessment Report on the EU-China Investment Relations' (2013) 20.

[52] G Grieger, 'EU-China Comprehensive Agreement on Investment: Levelling the Playing Field with China', European Parliamentary Research Service Briefing (Mach 2021) 9.

[53] US-China Economic and Security Review Commission, 'The U.S.-China 'Phase One' Deal: A Backgrounder' (4 February 2020) 5.

market considerations.[54] Chinese SOEs may effectively serve as 'Trojan horses', through which the Chinese Government may acquire increasing power and influence abroad. This threatens to jeopardise the national security, energy security and economic security of a host country.[55] As a consequence of a general suspicion of Chinese SOEs, a number of high-profile overseas acquisitions launched by Chinese SOEs were forced to discontinue in the face of strong opposition from host countries.

For example, the Canadian Government prohibited the US$1.5 billion acquisition of Canadian construction company Aecon Group Inc., by China Communications Construction Company International Holding Limited (CCCC) for national security reasons in 2018. Aecon is a significant player in the construction of infrastructure, including telecommunications networks, transportation, electricity grids and military facilities, as well as the refurbishment of nuclear power plants, while CCCC is majority owned by the Chinese Government. Aecon itself supported the CCCC acquisition as a means of more effectively competing with large global construction companies. However, the Canadian Federal Government concluded that the combination of CCCC's status as a Chinese SOE and Aecon's work on critical infrastructure made the acquisition a material risk to Canada's national security.[56] Similarly, in early 2021 Australia blocked a US$300 million deal that would have seen the state-owned China State Construction Engineering Corporation acquire a major Australian construction company, Probuild, over national security concerns. This has led the Chinese Embassy to accuse Australia of 'weaponising' national security.[57]

## D. Ideological Struggle

A deep-rooted ideological concern is the inherent suspicion in some Western countries that foreign state capital is a threat to the free market at home. This is especially the case for countries where recently privatised corporate entities face competition or the prospect of takeover by foreign SOE rivals. Where doubts linger about the commercial and financial autonomy of the foreign SOEs this situation has led to concerns about 'renationalisation' of national champions through a foreign government.[58] For example, after the approval of CNOOC's

[54] EJ Drake, 'Chinese State-owned and State-controlled Enterprises: Policy Options for Addressing Chinese State-owned Enterprises', 15 February 2012, Testimony before the US- China Economic and Security Review Commission.

[55] JE Mendenhall, 'Assessing Security Risks Posed by State-owned Enterprises in the Context of International Investment Agreements' (2016) 31(1) *ICSID Review* 36–37.

[56] S Walker, 'Canada Prohibits Chinese SOE Acquisitions of Aecon on National Security Grounds', Dentons (25 May 2018).

[57] L Parsons, 'Furious China Accuses Australia of 'Weaponising national Security' by Blocking a $300 Million Takeover of a Major Building Company', *Daily Mail Australia* (13 January 2021).

[58] OECD, 'SOEs Operating Abroad: An Application of the OECD Guidelines on Corporate Governance of State-Owned Enterprises to the Cross-border Operations of SOEs', 4–5 (2010).

acquisition of Nexen Inc. in December 2012, the Canadian Government announced new policy guidance with respect to future proposed acquisitions by foreign SOEs. Later the Economic Action Plan 2013 Act introduced several further steps in restricting investment by foreign SOEs in Canada in June 2013.[59] In a statement that made clear the Canadian Government's antipathy towards foreign SOEs, Prime Minister Stephen Harper stated in 2012:

> All investments are not equal … purchases of Canadian assets by foreign governments through state-owned enterprises are not the same as other transactions … To be blunt, Canadians have not spent years reducing the ownership of sectors of the economy by our own governments, only to see them bought and controlled by foreign governments instead.[60]

## IV. SELECTED ISSUES IN CHINESE SOES AND INTERNATIONAL INVESTMENT LAW

### A. The Status of Chinese SOEs in International Investment Arbitration

As China is the third-largest source of OFDI in 2020, it is no surprise that Chinese SOEs may increasingly fall back on ISDS mechanisms provided in Chinese BITs, which promise to offer them an enforceable procedural remedy against infringing host states. Given the close links between the Chinese SOEs and the Chinese Government, should Chinese SOEs be considered as qualified 'investors' and allowed access to ISDS against a host state? The status of Chinese SOEs is more complicated in the ICSID context. As reflected in its preamble, the ICSID Convention was developed by the World Bank in significant part to encourage private international investment, as distinguished from the sovereign/government investment, for economic development purposes. Article 25(1) of the ICSID Convention provides that the jurisdiction of the ICSID is confined to dispute 'between a Contracting State and a national of another Contracting State'. In other words, the ICSID has no jurisdiction to arbitrate disputes between two states, nor does it have jurisdiction to arbitrate disputes between two private entities. Even if Chinese SOEs are covered in the definition of 'investors' in ILAs, the question whether Chinese SOEs have standing as 'a national of another Contracting State' to bring an ICSID proceeding must be independently answered.[61] A different but analogous issue was whether a complaint implicating the conduct of a SOE is in fact a dispute with a 'Contracting State'. because the SOE's conduct can be attributed to it.[62]

[59] M Mackenzie et al, *Bill C-60:* A More Restrictive Approach to Foreign State-owned Enterprises Investment in Canada (June 2013).

[60] Statement by the Prime Minister of Canada on Foreign Investment (7 December 2012).

[61] B Nalbandian, 'State Capitalists as Claimants in International Investor-State Arbitration', (2021) 81 *Questions of International Law, Zoom Out* 5, 12.

[62] *Emilio Agustı'n Maffezini v The Kingdom of Spain*, ICSID Case No ARB/97/7, Decision on Objections to Jurisdiction, 25 January 2000, para 79.

The definition of 'investor' in Chinese IIAs can provide substantial guidance on the question. Empirical research of the definition of 'investor' and ISDS clauses in 851 IIAs reveals that, with extremely limited exceptions, SOEs have equivalent standing to their private counterparts as an 'investor' in IIAs. Specifically, the definition of 'investor' is not based on the nature of ownership but rather on whether a legal person was duly constituted in accordance with the law of a contracting party.[63] Similar to this global trend, many Chinese IIAs do not specifically address SOEs in the definition of 'investor'.[64] Moreover, a recent trend is that more and more Chinese IIAs expressly provide that any entity, including 'government-owned or controlled enterprises' or public institutions, fall within the applicable definition of 'investor'.[65] Therefore, as a general matter, investment treaties are available to Chinese SOE claimants.

The same conclusion holds true in the ICSID context. SOEs have frequently acted as claimants and their standing to bring arbitral proceedings in ICSID has been seldom seriously questioned by the respondent and never declined by arbitral tribunals.[66] When determining whether an SOE is 'a national of another Contracting State', the ICSID case law has consistently applied the famous Broches test, as it was first proposed by Aron Broches, the first secretary-general of the ICSID and the principal architect of the ICSID Convention. Broches observed in 1972 that the classical distinction between private and public investment, based on the source of the capital, was no longer meaningful since many SOEs were practically indistinguishable from the completely privately-owned enterprise both in their legal characteristics and in their business activities. He then concluded that '… for purposes of the Convention a mixed economy company or government-owned corporation should not be disqualified as a 'national of another Contracting State' *unless it is acting as an agent for the government or is discharging an essentially governmental function*'.[67] Specifically, the Broches test addresses two situations: conduct by a person acting under state control (acting as an agent) and conduct by a person exercising delegated state authority. However, the Broches test, in itself, does not prescribe *how* to determine whether SOEs are acting as agents for the government or discharging an essentially governmental function or not.

The arbitral tribunal first applied the Broches test in *CSOB v Slovakia* in 1999. The tribunal made several key findings. First, the legislative history of

[63] JE Low, 'State-controlled Entities as 'Investors' under International Investment Agreements' (2012) 80 *Columbia FDI Perspectives* 1–2.

[64] For example, Art 2 of China-Turkey BIT (2015); Art 1(2) of China-Switzerland BIT (2009).

[65] For example, Art 10(1)(f) of RCEP (2020); Art 12 (1) of Australia-China FTA (2015); Art 2(10)(a) of Canada-China BIT (2012); Art 1(b) of China-Mexico BIT (2008).

[66] C Annacker, 'Protection and Admission of Sovereign Investment under Investment Treaties' (2011) 10 *Chinese Journal of International Law* 531, 552–553.

[67] A Broches, *Selected Essays: World Bank, ICSID, and Other Subjects of Public and Private International law* (Dordrecht, Kluwer Academic Publishers, 1995) 202 (emphasis added). *cf* on the Broches test, ch 1, in this volume.

the ISCID indicates that the term 'juridical persons' as employed in Article 25 and, hence, the concept of 'national', was not intended to be limited to privately-owned companies, but to embrace also wholly or partially government-owned companies.[68] Second, the tribunal held that the Czech's majority ownership of and absolute control over CSOB alone would not disqualify it from filing a claim with ICSID.[69] Finally, and most significantly, the tribunal applied a nature test, which looks at the nature of the party's acts at issue, rather than their motive or purpose, in determining whether CSOB exercises governmental functions. As the tribunal articulated:

> [I]t cannot be denied that for much of its existence, CSOB acted on behalf of the State in facilitating or executing the international banking transactions and foreign commercial operations the State wished to support and that the State's control of CSOB required it to do the State's bidding in that regard. But in determining whether CSOB, in discharging these functions, exercised governmental functions, *the focus must be on the nature of these activities and not their purpose*. While it cannot be doubted that in performing the above-mentioned activities, CSOB was promoting the governmental policies or purposes of the State, the activities themselves were essentially commercial rather than governmental in nature.[70]

In determining the nature of the CSOB's activities at issue, the tribunal compared them with what a private entity would do in normal business transactions. The tribunal found that since the steps taken by CSOB to solidify its financial position in order to attract private capital for its restructured banking enterprise did not differ in their nature from measures a private bank might take to strengthen its financial position, they were commercial in nature.[71] In sum, Because the COSB tribunal solely focused on the commercial nature of the activities at issue, the tribunal found that even if the CSOB's activities were driven by state policies or served state interests, this fact did not transform the otherwise commercial nature of these activities into governmental acts.[72]

The CSOB tribunal's sole focus on the nature of the CSOB's acts at issue was heavily criticised as a misapplication of the Broches test. It was suggested that further guidance on how to apply the Broches test should be drawn from the attribution rules in Articles 5 and 8 of the International Law Commission's Draft Articles on State Responsibility (ILC Articles).[73] As will be discussed below, compared with *CSOB v Slovakia*, one particularly noteworthy aspect of ILC Rules is the possibility to consider not only the nature of the SOE's acts but also other factors, including ownership, control, the nature, purposes and

[68] *CSOB v Slovakia*, ICSID Case No ARB/97/4, Decision on Jurisdiction (24 May 1999), para 16.
[69] ibid, para 18.
[70] ibid, para 20.
[71] ibid, para 25.
[72] ibid, paras 21–25.
[73] M Feldman, 'State-owned Enterprises as Claimants in International Investment Arbitration' (2016) 31(1) *ICSID Review* 24, 32–33; P Blyschak, 'State Owned Enterprises and International Investment Treaties' (2011) 6 *Journal of International Law and International Relations* 1, 35.

objectives of the SOE whose actions are under scrutiny, and to the character of the actions taken, when determining whether the SOE's acts should be attributed to the state.[74]

Several arbitral tribunals have explicitly recognised that the ILC Articles are codification of customary international law on the question of attribution for purposes of asserting state responsibility and that the Broches test is the 'mirror image' of Article 5 and 8 of the ILC Articles. Consequently, the ILC Articles have been widely applied in investment arbitration, both to ascertain whether the SOE was a 'national of another Contracting State',[75] and the analogous issue of whether the conduct of SOEs should be attributed to the Contracting State so that the proper respondent was the Contracting State.[76] In contrast to the question of whether an SOE is a 'national of another Contracting State', which is usually decided at the jurisdictional stage of the proceedings, whether an SOE's conduct is in fact attributable to the respondent state is a merits issue unless there is a 'manifest absence of link' between the state entity and the respondent state.[77]

Article 5 of the ILC Articles, relating to the second branch of the Broches test, prescribes that the conduct of an entity is attributable to the state if the entity is empowered by law to exercise elements of governmental authority and is acting in that capacity in the particular instance. The term 'governmental authority' is not defined in the ILC Draft Articles because what is regarded as 'governmental' depends on the particular society, its history and traditions. In the context of investment arbitration, this would entail activities such as granting licences, approve or block commercial transactions, impose quotas, fees or expropriate companies.[78] According to the ILC's commentary, to apply the general standard to varied circumstances, important factors to be considered include the content of the powers, the way such powers are conferred on an entity, the purposes for which they are to be exercised and the extent to which the entity is accountable to government for their exercise. By contrast, how the entity is classified in a given legal system, the existence of a greater or lesser state participation in the entity's capital and the fact that the entity is not subject to executive control are not decisive criteria for the purpose of attribution of the entity's conduct to the state.[79]

[74] *Maffezini v Spain* (n 62) para 76.

[75] ibid, paras 79–80; *Beijing Urban Construction Group Co., Ltd. (BUCG) v Republic of Yemen*, ICSID Case No ARB/14/3, Decision on Jurisdiction (31 May 2017), para 34.

[76] *Jan de Nul and Dredging International v Egypt*, ICSID Case No ARB/04/13, Award (6 November 2008), para 156; *EDF (Services) Limited v Romania*, ICSID Case No ARB/05/13, Award (8 October 2009), para 191.

[77] *Gustav F W Hamester GmbH & Co KG v Republic of Ghana*, ICSID Case No. ARB/07/24, Award (18 June 2010), para 144.

[78] R Mohtashami, F El-Hosseny, 'State-owned Enterprises as Claimants before ICSID: Is the Broches Test on the Ebb?' (2016) (3) *BCDR International Arbitration Review* 371, 381.

[79] Draft Articles on Responsibility of States for Internationally Wrongful Acts, with Commentaries, in Report of the International Law Commission on the Work of its Fifty-third Session, UN Doc A/56/10 (2001) 43.

Article 5 of the ILC Articles was first applied in *Maffezini v Spain*.[80] The analytical framework outlined in *Maffezini v Spain* was later clarified and refined in *EDF v Romania*. The tribunal in *EDF v Romania* clarified that two cumulative conditions must be fulfilled to trigger an attribution. First, the act must be performed by an entity empowered by the internal law of the state to exercise elements of governmental authority. Second, the act in question must be performed by the entity in the exercise of the governmental authority.[81]

The two-step analytical framework under ILC Article 5 has been followed by other investment arbitral tribunals ever since. In *Jan de Nul v Egypt*, the tribunal first found that the Suez Canal Authority (SCA) is a public entity exercising elements of governmental authority because it is empowered to issue the decrees related to the navigation in the canal and to impose and collect charges for passing through the canal.[82] The tribunal then focused on the nature of the SCA's acts at issue, ie awarding a contract through a bidding process and the refusal to grant a time of extension, and concluded that these acts were not attributable to Egypt because they were not performed pursuant to the exercise of governmental authority. [83] In *Tulip v Turkey*, Emlak is a SOE possessing legal personality under Turkish law separate and distinctive from that state. Even if it enjoyed certain preferential treatment from the Turkish Government with regard to getting construction permits and buying land, the tribunal found that Emlak itself did not exercise elements of governmental authority with respect to any other entity or object.[84]

Article 8 of the ILC Articles relates to the first branch of the Broches test, ie, SOEs acting as an agent for the government. Different from Article 5, the attribution under Article 8 is independent of the status of a person and dependent only on whether the person is 'in fact acting on the instructions of, *or* under the direction or control of, that State in carrying out the conduct'. Such acts could therefore be attributable not because they are the result of the use of governmental power, but because they are under the direct command or effective control of the state.[85] The commentary on Article 8 explains that although SOEs are owned by and in that sense subject to the control of the state, they are considered to be separate and that their conduct in carrying out their activities is prima facie not attributable to the state.

However, where there is evidence that the state was using its ownership interest in or control of a corporation specifically in order to achieve a particular

[80] The award was rendered before the formal adoption of the ILC Draft Articles in 2001. However, the tribunal referred to Article 7 of the draft (now Art 5).

[81] *EDF v Romania* (n 76) paras 189–191.

[82] *Jan de Nul v Egypt* (n 76) para 166.

[83] ibid, para 170.

[84] *Tulip Real Estate Investment and Development Netherlands B.V. v Republic of Turkey*, ICSID Case No ARB/11/28 (10 March 2014), Award, para 292.

[85] *Gustav v Ghana* (n 77) para 198.

result, the conduct in question may be attributed to the state.[86] The degree of control which must be exercised by the state in order for the conduct of a person or entity to be attributable is 'effective control', as the ICJ outlined in *Nicaragua v United States of America*.[87] This is a very demanding standard as it requires not only a general direction or control of the state over the entity but also a specific control of the state over the particular act in question. Several investment tribunals confirmed that 'effective control' is the relevant test in interpreting Article 8 of the ILC Articles.[88]

The finding that an entity performs certain acts under the direction and control of the state within the meaning of ILC Article 8 is an issue of examining the evidence on record. In *EDF v Romania*, the evidence on record indicates that the Romanian Ministry of Transportation issued instructions and directions to two SOEs regarding the conduct these two companies should adopt in the exercise of their shareholder rights. Further, the evidence indicates that the Romanian state was using its ownership interest in or control of the two SOEs to achieve the particular result of bringing to an end their contractual arrangements with the foreign investor and the joint venture and to institute instead a system of auctions for commercial spaces at the Otopeni Airport.[89] In the Tribunal's view, such conduct fell within the meaning of the Commentary to Article 8 of the ILC Articles and was attributable to Romania.

In *Tulip v Turkey*, the majority of Emlak's voting shares and the board at all relevant times were controlled by TOKI, a state organ responsible for Turkey's public housing and operating. Accordingly, the Tribunal concluded that TOKI was capable of exerting a degree of control over Emlak to implement elements of a particular state purpose. However, the tribunal stressed that:

> … the relevant enquiry remains whether Emlak was being directed, instructed or controlled by TOKI with respect to the *specific activity* of administering the Contract with Tulip JV in the sense of sovereign direction, instruction or control rather than the ordinary control exercised by a majority shareholder acting in the company's perceived commercial best interests.[90]

Looking at the evidentiary record, the Tribunal concluded that while Emlak was subject to TOKI's corporate and managerial control, Emlak's conduct with respect to the execution, maintenance and termination of the Contract was acting in what it perceived to be its commercial best interest. Due to an absence of proof that TOKI used its control of Emlak as a vehicle directed towards

[86] The ILC Draft Articles (n 79) 48.

[87] Case Concerning Military and Paramilitary Activities in and against Nicaragua (*Nicaragua v United States of America*), Merits, ICJ Judgement of 27 June 1986, para 115.

[88] *Jan de Nul v Egypt* (n 76), para 173; *Tulip v Turkey*, ICSID Case No ARB/11/28, Decision on Annulment (30 December 2015), para 189.

[89] *EDF v Romania* (n 76) paras 213.

[90] *Tulip v Turkey* (n 84) para 309.

achieving a particular result in its sovereign interests, Emlak's conduct was not attributable to the state under Art 8 of the ILC Articles.[91]

Applying the Broches test and ILC Draft Articles to Chinese SOEs, several conclusions may be drawn. First, after three decades of extensive reforms, Chinese SOEs possess legal personality under the domestic law of China separate and distinct from that of the state. They are not part of the governmental structure, and their business activities are subject to the Chinese Civil Code, the capital market regulations and other private law instruments. Therefore, Chinese SOEs are not state organs, so their acts cannot be attributed to the Chinese Government according to ILC Article 4.

Second, Chinese SOEs are not exercising government authority when they make overseas investment. In *CSOB v Slovakia*, when evaluating whether CSOB's activities were an exercise of governmental authority, the tribunal focused only on the nature of the CSOB's activities. As discussed in the section above, the attribution analysis in investment arbitration has become more nuanced since *Maffezini v Spain*. Now it has become an integral part of analysis for tribunals to examine the link between the entity under inquiry and the home state, including ownership structure, chain of control, the nature, purpose, and objectives of the entity. This approach coincides with the commentary to ILC Article 5 which suggests that multiple factors should be considered to decide on attribution. Nevertheless, like *CSOB v Slovakia*, investment tribunals still focus on the ultimate purpose of the Broches Test and ILC Article 5, ie, whether the state-owned entity exercised governmental authority *in the particular investment projects*. SOE activities cannot be attributed to the state if it did not exercise governmental authority in the specific situation which gives rise to the investment dispute. It is difficult to imagine how Chinese SOEs may exercise governmental authority in overseas acquisitions, given that they do not possess any governmental power in the first place. Indeed, in the new round of SOE reforms, it was stressed that the even the SASAC shall abstain from exercising the public administration function of the government and from intervening in the autonomy of management of enterprises.[92]

The focus on the nature of specific activities at issue explains why the tribunal followed the CSOB's approach in *BUCG v Yemen*. Although the tribunal accepted the respondent's description of the BUCG in the broad context of the PRC state-controlled economy, such as the BUCG is expected to advance China's national interest, and the BUCG's key management, operational and strategic decisions are supervised and monitored by the Chinese state, the tribunal found them largely irrelevant. This is because the issue is not the corporate framework of the state-owned enterprise, but whether it functions as an agent of the state

[91] ibid, para 326.

[92] The State Council, 'Several Opinions of the State Council on Reforming and Improving the State-owned Asset Management System', No 63 [2015] of the State Council.

or discharges a PRC governmental function in the fact specific context, namely, the construction of the Sana'a International Terminal project in Yemen.[93] The tribunal concluded that there was no evidence to establish that, in building an airport terminal in Yemen, the BUCG was discharging a PRC governmental function rather than a commercial function.[94]

Third, a successful rejection of Chinese SOEs' standing is more likely based on the first limb of the Broches test, ie, Article 8 of the ILC Articles. If there is evidence showing that the Chinese Government was using its ownership interest in or control of a SOE specifically in order to achieve a particular result, the investment in question may be attributed to the state and the SOE in question will not have standing to bring the arbitration.[95] However, in practice, it is unlikely to happen for three reasons. To begin with, Chinese SOEs, in particular central SOEs, are under the direction and control of the SASAC and therefore the Chinese state and the CCP. However, the ILC Commentary makes clear that the attribution under Article 8 is highly demanding and exceptional. It requires not only a general direction or control of the state over the entity but also a specific control of the state over the particular act in question.[96] Even if the CCP has tightened the political control of SOEs in the past few years, there is little evidence that the Chinese state has intervened into specific investment projects made by SOEs. Indeed, one of the objectives of the new round of SOE reforms is precisely to reduce governmental interference and make SOEs independent market entities.[97] Second, one fundamental transformation to redefine the Party-state's relationship to SOEs is not to see the role of the state as that of owner and regulator of SOEs, but a core investor.[98] In line with the shift in view from 'managing enterprises to managing capital', state-owned capital investment and operation companies are created to take equity stakes and exercise rights as shareholders in SOEs, mixed-ownership and private firms. As an intermediary between SASAC and SOEs, SASAC would have to convey directives directly to state capital investment companies rather than directly to operating firms. Such a system is seen as putting the SASAC at arm's length and further separating the SOEs from the government agencies.[99]

Finally, whether Chinese SOE's acts which give rise to the investment dispute were performed under the direction and control of the Chinese state is an issue of examining the evidence on record. As a legal matter, the level of required

[93] *BUCG v Yemen* (n 75) para 39.

[94] ibid, para 40.

[95] *Gustav v Ghana* (n 77) para 198.

[96] *EDF v Romania* (n 76) para 200.

[97] *The Economist*, 'A Whimper, not a Bang: China's Plan to Reform its Troubled Firms Fails to Impress' (19 September 2015).

[98] H Chen and M Righmire, 'The Rise of the Investor State: State Capital in the Chinese Economy' (2020) 55 *Studies in Comparative International Development* 257, 258.

[99] The State Council, Implementation Opinions of the State Council on Advancing the Pilot Program of the Reform of State Capital Investment and Operation Companies, No 23[2018] of the State Council.

control to support the attribution argument is difficult to prove with prevailing evidence in practice.[100] This is particularly true in view of the labyrinth of Chinese SOE regulation structure and various informal channels through which government influence may be exerted.

## B. Weaponing National Security

For the purpose of managing national security risks originating from foreign investment, some states, such as the US, Australia and Canada, have imposed special national security scrutiny procedures on SOEs. Since the introduction of these special procedures is readily available in the existing literature, it is sufficient to summarise their key features here. First, the threshold to launch an investigation based on national security concerns is very low. For example, in the US, the CFIUS is required to conduct a full investigation of all foreign government-controlled transactions whether or not the initial review shows that these transactions pose a national security concern.[101] In Canada, the government subjects all investment by SOEs (including even private investors assessed as being closely tied to or subject to direction from foreign governments) to enhanced national security scrutiny, regardless of the value or size of the investment.[102] In Australia, the Foreign Investment Review Board (FIRB) will launch an investigation into whenever a SOE acquires a direct interest (usually 10 per cent or more) in an Australian entity or business.[103]

Second, the key terms, including national security itself, are intentionally left undefined in national foreign investment laws. In addition, the legal test used to assess national security implications of a proposed SOE investment is ambiguous because it usually requires weighing and balancing a range of factors. It is not clear how these factors are assessed, which factors are more important and why, and how to draw a conclusion if different factors point to different inferences.[104] As a result, a host country retains almost unlimited discretion to prohibit the proposed investment or requires Chinese SOEs to undertake onerous commitments to alleviate any regulatory concerns that a host country might have.

Third, to challenge a national security decision in domestic courts is frequently fruitless either because such decisions are immune from judicial

[100] *Tulip v Turkey* (n 84), Separate Opinion of Michael Evan Jaffe on the Questions of Attribution under Article 8, ILC Articles.

[101] F Wehrlé and J Pohl, 'Investment Policies Related to National Security – A Survey of Country Practices', OECD Working Papers on International Investment 2016/02, 25.

[102] The Minister of Innovation, Science and Industry, *Guidelines on the National Security Review of Investments* (24 March 2021).

[103] Australian Government, *Australia's Foreign Investment Policy* (1 January 2021) 7.

[104] M Du, 'The Regulation of Chinese State-owned Enterprises in National Foreign Investment Laws: A Comparative Analysis' (2016) 5 *Global Journal of Comparative Law* 118, 137.

review or because domestic courts tend to defer to administrative agencies to make such decisions. For example, in September 2012, President Obama ordered the China-based Ralls Corp to divest four Oregon wind farms it had previously acquired from Innovative Renewable Energy LLC. Ralls Corp brought a suit against the US Government, including President Obama, in the first legal challenge to a CFIUS decision. The US Court of Appeals in July 2014 ruled allowing Ralls to obtain evidence on why its bid for Oregon wind farms was rejected. However, the ruling did not have a major impact on the actual decision made by CFIUS because the Court did not rule that the CFIUS and Obama had no power to block the Ralls Corp deal.[105]

The reference to international legal rules will not solve the problem either. The principle of sovereignty in international law gives states ample leeway to prevent foreign investors from taking over domestic companies. This freedom may be restricted through bilateral investment treaties (BITs). However, an overview of the BITs shows that they largely focus on the question of the extent to which cross-border investments are protected once they have been made, for example, against arbitrary expropriation.[106] Even though some recent BITs extend national treatment to the pre-entry phase of the investment, countries undertaking such commitments regularly include reservations and exemptions for the protection of national security.[107]

One may wonder whether intensified scrutiny of investments from SOEs on national security grounds is justified. First, the vague standard and lack of transparency in the national security review process may render the scrutiny of Chinese SOEs' investment a tool of economic protectionism.[108] Rather than addressing real regulatory concerns, unrestricted political interference based on political gamesmanship and irrational fears have resulted in a chilling effect on potential foreign SOE investors.[109] The botched attempt by CNOOC, a Chinese SOE, to acquire Unocal in 2005 was a typical example. With the benefit of hindsight, it is clear that the US had overreacted.[110] The main concern that CNOOC might divert Unocal's energy supplies exclusively to meet Chinese needs was not supported by any sensible facts. By 2005, Unocal was no longer a major player

[105] S Tiezzi, 'Chinese Company Wins Court Case against Obama', *The Diplomat* (17 July 2014).

[106] A Heinemann, 'Government Control of Cross-Border M&A: Legitimate Regulation or Protectionism' (2012) 15(3) *Journal of International Economic Law* 843, 855.

[107] UNCTAD, *Bilateral Investment Treaties 1995–2006: Trends in Investment Rulemaking* (New York and Geneva 2007) 142. For a distinction between then distinguishes between 'Limited Entry' BITs and 'Liberalisation' BITs, see ch 5, in this volume.

[108] S Lubman, 'China's State Capitalism: The Real World Implications', *The Wall Street Journal* (1 March 2012); P Rose, 'Sovereigns as Shareholders' (2008) 87 *North Carolina Law Review* 83, 117.

[109] Y Feng, 'We Wouldn't Transfer Title to the Devil: Consequences of the Congressional Politicization of Foreign Direct Investment on National Security Grounds' (2009) 42 *New York University Journal of International Law and Politics* 253, 255.

[110] JW Casselman, 'China's Latest 'Threat' to the United States: The Failed CNOOC-Unocal Merger and its Implications for Exon-Florio and CFIUS' (2007) 17 *Indiana International and Comparative Law Review* 155.

in the energy industry. In 2004, the year before the transaction, Unocal produced less than one per cent of the US natural gas consumption.[111] It possessed no refineries in the US and its most valuable assets were located primarily overseas, which was the primary reason why CNOOC found it so attractive in the first place. To assuage the national security concerns, CNOOC had announced its willingness to divest itself of Unocal's American holdings.[112] Even if CNOOC rerouted all Unocal's US production to China, which is economically penalising for CNOOC and its controller, it would not harm the US interest because US buyers could easily replace Unocal's miniscule production with imports from the international market, leaving net imports and US balance of payments in energy unchanged.[113]

Second, all the current national investment regulations seem to treat all Chinese SOEs in the same way. One may wonder whether such a legal criterion is not too crude. As discussed in section II above, Chinese SOEs are not created equal. Though by definition, all SOEs are controlled by the state, significant variations exist in their organisational structure, relations with the state, sectors in which they operate and management of SOEs. For example, the SASAC serves as a unitary holding company for central SOEs (*yang qi*) that were formerly under the control of various government agencies. In 2017, the total assets and turnover of central enterprises reached RMB55 trillion, a 73.8 per cent increase over 2012, and RMB26.4 trillion, or 33 per cent of that year's national GDP.[114] In view of their importance to the national economy, central SOEs are a different beast from local SOEs as they are closer to the political centre. Similarly, though Chinese SOEs currently operate in many industries and sectors, the Chinese Government maintains control only in strategic fields through either sole ownership or an absolute controlling stake. By comparison, the state's role in other non-strategic sectors will be significantly smaller and the number of SOEs in these sectors will be drastically reduced. Precisely because of these differences, Chinese SOEs should be approached in a more nuanced manner. Variations concerning SOEs' distance from the political centre, the percentage and density of state ownership, the competitiveness and political saliency of the sectors in which they mainly operate, and even certain leadership characteristics inevitably cause SOEs' behavioural differences in cross-border investment and dispute resolution.[115]

[111] DK Nanto et al., 'China and the CNOOC Bid for Unocal: Issues for Congress', CRS Report for Congress (2005) 9.

[112] CNOOC Ltd. Press Release, 'CNOOC Limited Proposes Merger with Unocal Offering USD $67 Per Unocal Share in Cash' (June 23, 2005).

[113] TH Moran, 'Foreign Acquisition and National Security: What are Genuine Threats? What are Implausible Worries', paper presented at OECD Global Forum on International Investment (December 2009) 5.

[114] Zhang (n 37) 57.

[115] J Li, 'State-owned Enterprises in the Current Regime of Investor- State Arbitration', in S Lalani and RP Lazo (eds), *The Role of the State in Investor- State Arbitration* 380 (Leiden, Brill, 2014) 380, 385.

## V. CONCLUSION

This chapter concludes that, after three decades of reforms, Chinese SOEs no longer exercise any governmental functions. They have independent decision-making power, and they are run on a commercial basis. Still, there is no doubt that Chinese SOEs are an integral part of the Chinese Party-state, and they are under the direction and control of the Chinese Government. However, such general direction and control, in itself, cannot be a basis to deny a Chinese SOE from accessing ISDS as a claimant. Moreover, it is submitted that the national security screening procedures may be weaponised with Chinese SOEs as targets, and that a more nuanced mechanism differentiating different types of Chinese SOEs may be warranted.

As Howson pointed out, Chinese companies investing abroad represents a new phase of China's changing entanglement with foreign and international legal, commercial and governance norms. Both the Chinese Government and the Chinese SOEs were forced for the first time to play by internationally accepted rules not only during the whole investment phase but also with respect to internal corporate governance at the firms themselves.[116] In this sense, Chinese SOEs' cross-border investments have started a socialisation process bringing value to both China and the global economy. On the one hand, it is simply a bad policy choice, both economically and politically, to reject Chinese SOE investments not on legitimate grounds but under the influence of misinformed populism and protectionism. On the other hand, the recent spotlight on Chinese SOEs may serve as an external incentive for the Chinese Government to push forward its market-oriented SOE reforms. These reform measures will not only reduce suspicion and misunderstanding when Chinese SOEs make OFDI, but also help them become truly competitive global champions.

[116] NC Howson, 'China's Acquisitions Abroad- Global Ambitions, Domestic Effects' [2006] *Law Quadrangle Notes* 73, 74.

# 9

# *Due Diligence and State-Controlled Entities in the Age of State Capitalism*

SEBASTIÁN MANTILLA BLANCO

## I. INTRODUCTION

IN THE IMMEDIATE aftermath of the Cold War, the world economy was dominated by private investment, privatisation policies, and an increasingly restrained role of the sovereign state in economic affairs.[1] The past decades have witnessed a radical turnaround in economic and investment policy, with states actively participating as competitors in the market through state-controlled entities (SCEs).[2] As an observer puts it, 'State capitalism is omnipresent in the global economy.'[3] SCEs control assets worth trillions of dollars.[4] In 2017, an Organisation for Economic Co-operation and Development (OECD) study about the presence of SCEs in 40 economies revealed that they employed over nine million workers and managed portfolios exceeding US$2.4 trillion.[5]

In a globalised world, government-controlled entities look far beyond their own internal market and pursue massive investments abroad.[6] The United Nations Conference on Trade and Development (UNCTAD) has reported substantial investments of Russian SCEs in Africa and registered the leading

[1] I Bremmer, 'State Capitalism Comes to Age – The End of the Free Market' (2009) 88 *Foreign Affairs* 40, 40–41.

[2] ibid 40ff. In this chapter, the term 'state-controlled entity' (SCE) is used to refer to any entity that is under corporate control of a state.

[3] Y Wu, *Reforming WTO Rules on State-Owned Enterprises in the Context of SCEs Receiving Various Advantages* (Singapore, Springer, 2019) 2. See also J Kurlantzick, *State Capitalism: How the Return of Statism is Transforming the World* (Oxford, OUP, 2016) 3ff.

[4] UN Human Rights Council / Working Group on the Issue of Human Rights and Transnational Corporations and Other Business Enterprises, Report, A/HRC/32/45 (4 May 2016) [12].

[5] OECD, The Size and Sectoral Distribution of State-Owned Enterprises (OECD 2017) 3, 13.

[6] See generally P Kowalski et al., 'State-Owned Enterprises: Trade Effects and Policy Implications' (2013) 147 *OECD Trade Policy Papers* 1, 9.

role of Chinese SCEs in extractive industries.[7] Moreover, a side effect of the COVID-19 pandemic has been the rise of public investments in sectors of enhanced national interest, such as the air transport industry.[8] In part due to rescue packages adopted in response to the Coronavirus pandemic, there was an overall increase of seven per cent in state-owned multinational enterprises in 2020.[9]

The growth of public investments in the past decades runs parallel to the development of an increasingly dense network of instruments about corporate social responsibility (CSR).[10] These instruments typically require enterprises to exercise due diligence to prevent their operations from turning into vehicles for corruption, environmental damage, or human rights violations.[11] The G-20 Leader's Declaration of 8 July 2017 expressed a commitment to '[create] policy frameworks [...] such as national action plans on business and human rights and underline the responsibility of businesses to exercise due diligence'.[12] Moreover, UNCTAD has identified the goal of 'sustainable development through responsible investment' as one of the key features of 'new generation investment policies'.[13] This overall objective entails 'placing social and environmental goals on the same footing as economic growth and development objectives'.[14]

This chapter addresses the intersection of these two phenomena. It explores the standards of diligence applicable to SCEs under CSR instruments and the potential impact of such standards on investment claims. The first section discusses the conceptual underpinnings of due diligence. The second section presents selected *soft law* and *hard law* instruments establishing due diligence standards of conduct relevant for SCEs. In this vein, it distinguishes between due diligence of SCEs as such and due diligence duties of states in respect of their SCEs. The third section focuses on investment treaty claims. It identifies possible effects of foreign investors' due diligence on jurisdictional objections, claims about 'full protection and security' (FPS), and alleged breaches of 'fair and equitable treatment' (FET). This section also addresses differences in the assessment of due diligence of public and private investors. Lastly, a final section draws some concluding remarks.

[7] UNCTAD, *World Investment Report 2020*, UNCTAD/WIR/2020 (UN Publications 2020) 25, 58.
[8] ibid 92.
[9] UNCTAD, *World Investment Report 2021*, UNCTAD/WIR/2021 (UN Publications 2021) xi, 27.
[10] See generally J Ruggie, 'Business and Human Rights: The Next Chapter' (2013) 1(4) *Dovenschmidt Quarterly* 168, 168–170. For the notion of CSR and a description of major CSR instruments see B Spießhofer, *Unternehmerische Verantwortung* (Munich, Beck, 2017) 45ff; J You, *Legal Perspectives on Corporate Social Responsibility* (New Delhi, Springer, 2015) 4ff.
[11] See generally B Fasterling, 'Human Rights Due Diligence as Risk Management: Social Risk Versus Human Rights Risk' (2017) 2 *Business and Human Rights Journal* 225, 225–247.
[12] G-20 Leader's Declaration (8 July 2017) [online] www.g20.utoronto.ca/2017/2017-G20-leaders-declaration.html (accessed 28 February 2022).
[13] UNCTAD, Investment Policy Framework for Sustainable Development (UNCTAD 2015) 17.
[14] ibid.

## II. DUE DILIGENCE: CONCEPTUAL UNDERPINNINGS

The notion of 'due diligence' is well-entrenched in international investment law. From a formal standpoint, 'due diligence' may be best described as a *standard*.[15] Roscoe Pound explained in 1919 that 'standards are devised for special situations in which we are compelled to take special circumstances into account'.[16] Pound emphasised that standards refer to 'classes of cases in which each is necessarily unique', noting that '[f]or such cases we must rely on the common sense of the common man as to common things'.[17] Due diligence can hence not be translated into rule-like syllogistic formulas.[18] Rather, it provides a flexible yardstick for the evaluation of conduct, leaving room for the assessment of the circumstances of each individual case.[19]

Due diligence is omnipresent in international law, from environmental law to investment law.[20] In these contexts, due diligence normally describes the content of a primary norm imposing an obligation on the state.[21] In contrast, in the CSR context, due diligence refers chiefly, albeit not exclusively, to the conduct of a private or public company.[22] Scholars have observed that the function of due diligence in CSR instruments is twofold.[23] In one sense, it designates 'a [business] process of investigation conducted by a business to identify and manage commercial risks'.[24] In a second sense, it is a 'standard of conduct required to

[15] The author has discussed the normative structure and nature of standards (and specifically due diligence) elsewhere: S Mantilla Blanco, *Full Protection and Security in International Investment Law* (Cham, Springer, 2019) 146–154 and 456–457 (relying inter alia on the works of Roscoe Pound).

[16] R Pound, 'The Administrative Application of Legal Standards' (1919) 42 *Annual Report of the American Bar Association* 445, 463.

[17] Ibid.

[18] *cf* ibid See also S Mantilla Blanco, *Full Protection and Security in International Investment Law* (Cham, Springer, 2019) 146–154, 456–457.

[19] On the flexibility and adaptability of due diligence with examples from international law see: ILA Study Group on Due Diligence in International Law, Second Report (2016) 2–3; J Kulesza, *Due Diligence in International Law* (Leiden, Brill, 2016) 1, 264. See also S Mantilla Blanco, *Full Protection and Security in International Investment Law* (Cham, Springer, 2019) 375ff, 456ff (particularly referring to the obligation to protect foreigners under the customary law of aliens and the application of the FPS standard in ISDS proceedings).

[20] For an overview see ILA Study Group on Due Diligence in International Law, First Report (2014). *cf* also N McDonald, 'The Role of Due Diligence in International Law' (2019) 68 *International and Comparative Law Quarterly* 1041, 1041ff. For a similar observation see S Mantilla Blanco, *Full Protection and Security in International Investment Law* (Cham, Springer, 2019) 375.

[21] *cf* N McDonald, 'The Role of Due Diligence in International Law' (2019) 68 *International and Comparative Law Quarterly* 1041, 1042, 1044ff.

[22] B Spießhofer, *Unternehmerische Verantwortung* (Munich, Beck, 2017) 102–105 (particularly referring to the *Ruggie Principles*).

[23] J Bonnitcha and R McCorquodale, 'The Concept of 'Due Diligence' in the UN Guiding Principles on Business and Human Rights' (2017) 28(3) *European Journal of International Law* 899, 902–906.

[24] ibid 901.

discharge an obligation'.[25] While CSR instruments primarily refer to companies' due diligence, they also provide due diligence standards for the state's exercise of regulatory authority and ownership rights over SCEs.[26]

Most CSR codes of conduct provide non-binding standards of diligence, which have the character of mere recommendations.[27] Courts and other dispute settlement bodies could however use those instruments as a reference framework for assessing corporate conduct.[28] This practice entails a 'hardening of soft law', in the sense that soft law gains features and functions commonly associated to 'hard law'.[29] Companies could also be subject to due diligence obligations, properly so-called, the source of which usually is either domestic law or a binding contract.[30]

## III. DUE DILIGENCE IN CONNECTION WITH THE ACTIVITIES OF SCES

SCEs act within a large network of principles, rules, and recommendations set forth in numerous instruments about responsible business conduct. As shown in this section, due diligence standards are a firmly-etched element of this normative network. Section III.A discusses examples of *soft law* and *hard law* due diligence duties applicable to SCEs' operations under major CSR instruments. Thereafter, section III.B addresses due diligence duties of States with respect to entities they own or control.

### A. Due Diligence of SCEs

Due diligence duties under CSR instruments refer to manifold subjects, ranging from environmental impact assessments to human rights due diligence. Most of these duties are applicable to both private and public companies. There are, however, a few instruments that specifically address the activities of government-controlled entities or particular types of SCEs.

[25] ibid 902.

[26] See section III.B.

[27] See section III.A.

[28] See, eg, the use of the UN Guiding Principles in Rechtbank Den Haag, *Milieudefensie v Royal Dutch Shell*, Judgment, 26.5.2021, C/09/571932 / HA ZA 19-379, ECLI:NL:RBDHA:2021:5339, [4.1.11]. See also fn 29 below.

[29] C Macchi and J van Zeben, 'Business and human rights implications of climate change litigation: Milieudefensie et al. v Royal Dutch Shell' (2021) 30(3) *Review of European, Comparative & International Environmental Law* 409, 409ff; L Roorda, 'The Netherlands: A Wide Open Window for Human Rights Norms?', in E Aristova and U Grušić (eds), *Civil Remedies and Human Rights in Flux* (Oxford, Hart, 2022) 245, 264. See also M Herdegen, *The Dynamics of International Law in a Globalised World* (Frankfurt, Vittorio Klostermann, 2016) 83–85.

[30] See section III.A.

### *i. The Santiago Principles and Guidelines by Individual SWFs*

The *Santiago Principles* of the International Working Group of Sovereign Wealth Funds (IWG) are a compilation of 'generally accepted principles and practices' (GAPP) for Sovereign Wealth Funds (SWF).[31] GAPP 15 provides that 'SWF operations and activities in host countries should be conducted in compliance with all applicable regulatory and disclosure requirements of the countries in which they operate'.[32] The language of the *Santiago Principles* is strikingly vague.[33] It is arguable that compliance with GAPP 15 requires conducting a pre-investment due diligence process to gather information about the relevant regulatory framework. This process should encompass all pertinent aspects of domestic law, including environmental and labour standards. This is consistent with the 'guiding objectives' of the *Principles*, which include the goal of ensuring compliance with domestic regulations and of creating 'a transparent and sound governance structure that provides for adequate operational controls, risk management, and accountability'.[34] Due diligence processes are also a tool for a proper management of SWFs' assets, as indicated in GAPP 19.[35] The Commentary to this provision indicates that '[t]he SWF should manage its assets and discharge its other duties with care, skill, and diligence'.[36]

Some SWFs have developed guidelines to prevent investments in companies involved in human rights violations or environmental breaches. As a rule, the effective application of these policies requires proper due diligence on the part of the SWF. Thus, for example, the *Guidelines for Observation and Exclusion of the Government Pension Fund* in Norway establish criteria under which a company can be barred from the Fund's portfolio.[37] These criteria may be either product-based or conduct-based.[38] A product-based criterion is, for instance, the exclusion of companies which 'develop or produce weapons or key components of weapons that violate fundamental humanitarian principles through their normal use'.[39] Conduct-based criteria cover situations of 'unacceptable risk' regarding a company's direct or indirect involvement in severe human rights violations, environmental harm, corruption, among others.[40]

[31] The introduction to the Santiago Principles defines SWF as 'special-purpose investment funds or arrangements that are owned by the general government'. IWG, Sovereign Wealth Funds: Generally Accepted Principles and Practices / Santiago Principles (October 2008) 3.

[32] ibid, 19 (GAPP 15).

[33] On the vagueness of the principles see F Bassan, *The Law of Sovereign Wealth Funds* (Cheltenham, Elgar, 2011) 51. *cf* also Bassan's critical analysis of the Principles at 46–52.

[34] IWG, Sovereign Wealth Funds: Generally Accepted Principles and Practices / Santiago Principles (October 2008) 4.

[35] ibid, 22 (GAPP 19).

[36] ibid, 22.

[37] Government Pension Fund (Norway), *Guidelines for Observation and Exclusion of the Government Pension Fund* (updated as of 19 November2021), ss 1(1), 2.

[38] ibid, ss 3, 4.

[39] ibid, s 3(1)(a).

[40] ibid, s 4. For an author discussing a previous version of these Guidelines see D Palombo, *Business and Human Rights. The Obligations of the European Home States* (Oxford, Hart, 2019) 252.

### *ii. The OECD Guidelines on Corporate Governance of State-Owned Enterprises*

While the *Santiago Principles* only refer to SWFs, other instruments have a broader scope of application. The *OECD Guidelines on Corporate Governance of State-Owned Enterprises* (2015) use a broad definition of State-Owned Enterprise (SOE), which covers 'any corporate entity recognised by national law as an enterprise, and in which the state exercises ownership'.[41] The *Guidelines* pertain primarily to the exercise of the controlling state's ownership rights in SOEs.[42] At the same time, they provide guidance regarding basic expectations about SOEs' standards of conduct, which controlling states should implement through their influence over corporate organs.[43]

The 2015 *Guidelines* depart from the fundamental premise that 'SOEs should observe high standards of responsible business conduct'.[44] Guideline V(D) states that '[e]xpectations established by the government in this regard should be publicly disclosed and mechanisms for their implementation be clearly established'.[45] The *Annotations* to the *Guidelines* indicate that observance of high CSR standards allows SOEs to appear as 'good corporate citizens' and reduce 'reputational risks'.[46] SOEs are further expected to 'acknowledge the importance of stakeholder relations for building sustainable and financially sound enterprises'.[47] The *Annotations* mention a broad spectrum of standards in areas such as human rights, labour relations, health, and environmental protection.[48] In this vein, they refer to other CSR instruments, which are in turn applicable to both SOEs and privately-owned companies:

> [SOEs] actions should be guided by relevant international standards, including: the *OECD Guidelines for Multinational Enterprises*, which have been adopted by all OECD member countries and reflect all four principles contained in the *ILO Declaration on Fundamental Principles and Rights at Work*; and the *UN Guiding Principles on Business and Human Rights*.[49]

Some states have adopted ownership policies which reflect the spirit of the 2015 OECD *Guidelines* and specifically require SOEs to abide by broader CSR instruments. For instance, the 2020 *State Ownership Policy and Principles for State-Owned Enterprises* of the Swedish Government provide that 'State-owned enterprises *have to* act responsibly and work actively to follow international guidelines on environmental and climate consideration, human rights, working

[41] OECD Guidelines on Corporate Governance of State-Owned Enterprises (OECD 2015) 14.
[42] See section III.B.
[43] *cf* OECD Guidelines on Corporate Governance of State-Owned Enterprises (OECD 2015) 14, 23.
[44] ibid, 23.
[45] ibid.
[46] ibid, 60.
[47] ibid, 57.
[48] ibid, 60.
[49] ibid.

conditions, anti-corruption and business ethics.'[50] The *Policy* characterises relevant CSR instruments of the UN and the OECD as 'material for state-owned enterprises'.[51]

### *iii. The Ruggie Principles*

The *UN Guiding Principles on Business and Human Rights* (*Ruggie Principles*) require business enterprises to create 'policies and processes' to ensure compliance with their 'responsibility to respect human rights'.[52] These policies include '[a] human rights due diligence process to identify, prevent, mitigate and account for how they address their impacts on human rights'.[53] Guiding Principle 17 develops the notion of 'human rights due diligence'.[54] It recommends ongoing due diligence regarding direct and indirect human rights impacts of corporate activities and operations.[55] Due diligence must be adapted to the dimension and operational context of each company.[56]

The Commentary to Guiding Principle 17 clarifies that, while human rights due diligence may be an element of 'broader enterprise risk-management systems', it is expected to consider not only the company's interests, but also those of other stakeholders.[57] The Commentary further emphasises that proper human rights due diligence is a tool which could help reduce the risk of civil actions based on complicity in human rights violations.[58] Guiding Principles 18 through 21 provide further orientation for human rights due diligence.[59] Guiding Principle 22 addresses scenarios where a company's activities effectively resulted in 'adverse impacts', in which case it 'should provide for or cooperate in their remediation through legitimate processes'.[60]

### *iv. The OECD Guidelines for Multinational Enterprises*

The *OECD Guidelines for Multinational Enterprises* (2011) provide no definition of 'multinational enterprise' and expressly clarify that '[o]wnership may be private, State or mixed'.[61] They further explain that 'State-owned multinational

[50] Emphasis added. Government of Sweden, *State Ownership Policy and Principles for State-Owned Enterprises 2020* (Government Offices of Sweden 2020) [5.1.3].
[51] ibid.
[52] Guiding Principles on Business and Human Rights, HR/Pub/11/04 (United Nations 2011), GP 15.
[53] ibid, GP 15(b).
[54] ibid, GP 17.
[55] ibid, GP 17(a), (c).
[56] ibid, GP 17(b).
[57] ibid, GP 17 (Commentary).
[58] ibid.
[59] ibid, GP 18–21.
[60] ibid, GP 22.
[61] OECD Guidelines for Multinational Enterprises (OECD 2011) 17.

enterprises are subject to the same recommendations as privately-owned enterprises, but public scrutiny is often magnified when a State is the final owner'.[62] In this sense, the *Guidelines*' provisions on environmental and human rights due diligence are fully applicable to SOEs. The 2011 *Guidelines* further contain detailed recommendations to prevent bribery, including duties of transparency and vigilance over agents in charge of transactions with state organs or SOEs.[63] In order to facilitate the voluntary implementation of the *Guidelines*' recommendations on due diligence, the OECD launched the *OECD Due Diligence Guidance for Responsible Business Conduct*, which provides detailed descriptions of best practices in voluntary due diligence processes.[64]

The *Guidelines* are bolstered by implementation procedures, including complaints before the National Contact Point (NCP) of the company's home jurisdiction.[65] NCPs are agencies within the states that have adhered to the *Guidelines*.[66] Their functions include mediation and conciliation between different stakeholders.[67] They prepare reports and statements about complaints and make recommendations for the adequate implementation of the *Guidelines*.[68]

NCPs have consistently held that the *Guidelines* are applicable with regard to 'business or commercial activities'.[69] Thus, the Swiss NCP stated in 2018 that '[t]he key question should be whether an entity is involved in commercial activities, independently of its legal form, its sector of activity or its purpose (profit or non-profit)'.[70] The Swiss NCP understands 'commercial activities' as a broad notion to be assessed in light of the specific circumstances of each case.[71] Based on such broad understanding, it has applied the *Guidelines* even to NGOs that obtain funds from 'trading activities'.[72]

SCEs have occasionally challenged the applicability of the OECD Guidelines on grounds that their operations could not be characterised as 'commercial activities'. Thus, the Korean NCP rejected in 2019 a complaint filed against the Korean Export-Import Bank (KEXIM), a state-owned entity which provides funding for investment transactions abroad.[73] KEXIM granted a public loan

[62] ibid, 22.
[63] ibid, 48.
[64] OECD Due Diligence Guidance for Responsible Business Conduct (OECD 2018) 20ff.
[65] For an overview see K Weidmann, *Der Beitrag der OECD-Leitsätze für multinationale Unternehmen zum Schutz der Menschenrechte* (Berlin, Duncker, 2014) 236ff.
[66] OECD Guidelines for Multinational Enterprises (OECD 2011) 3.
[67] ibid, 3, 18, 72–73, 86–87.
[68] ibid, 82ff.
[69] Switzerland NCP, *TuK Indonesia v Roundtable for Sustainable Palm Oil*, Initial Assessment (31 May 2018) 4–5.
[70] ibid, 5.
[71] *cf* Switzerland NCP, *Survival International v World Wide Fund for Nature*, Initial Assessment (20 December 2016) 8.
[72] ibid (applying the *Guidelines* to WWF because it engages in 'trading activities', such as selling of items with its logo, and is present in more than 80 jurisdictions).
[73] Korea NCP, *Jalaur River for the People's Movement et al. v KEXIM and Daewoo E&C*, Initial Assessment (18 January 2019) 3.

for the Jalaur Dam Project, a major infrastructure venture of the Philippine Government.[74] The complainants alleged that KEXIM was aware that the government was violating indigenous rights, including the right to prior consultation and proper compensation for farmland.[75] The Korean NCP observed that '[t]he project funded by KEXIM is not an investment activity but a public project promoted by the Philippine government' that was moreover labelled as 'non-commercial'.[76] Holding that 'the project is not considered to be an international investment or a commercial activity', the NCP found that the *Guidelines* were inapplicable to the case.[77] The NCP left the door open to the application of the *Guidelines* to KEXIM in future cases, depending on the functions it performs.[78] Hence, it said, '[t]he Guidelines may not be applicable to KEXIM as a loan provider to developing countries, but applicable to KEXIM as an export credit agency of a commercial nature'.[79]

In 2020, the British NCP received a complaint against the export credit agency of the British Government, UK Export Finance (UKEF).[80] The case concerned UKEF's alleged failure to properly assess the 'climate impact of its financial investments'.[81] The NCP rejected the complaint, noting that UKEF 'does not strictly engage in commercial activity'.[82] The NCP specifically underlined that UKEF 'does not have a separate corporate legal personality, but rather exists as a government department having its legal personality as the Secretary of State for International Trade'.[83]

In 2016, the New Zealand NCP rejected a complaint against Southern Response Earthquake Services Ltd and New Zealand Permanent Trustees Ltd (NZPT) for alleged breaches of human rights in connection with repair and construction projects in the aftermath of the earthquakes of Canterbury in 2010–2011.[84] The New Zealand NCP concluded that neither of the respondents fell within the scope of the *Guidelines*.[85] It noted that 'Southern Response is entirely owned by the New Zealand Government, and only operates in New Zealand [...] It does not compete in the insurance market, has a purely

[74] ibid.
[75] ibid, 2.
[76] ibid, 5.
[77] ibid.
[78] ibid, 6.
[79] ibid. *cf* also the Korean NCP's discussion of cases before other NCPs at 4–5, including Finland NCP, *CEDHA v Finnvera*, Communication on The Orion Paper Mill Factory Project (12 October 2006) 1–2 (rejection of a complaint based on the 'special nature of Finnvera Oyj as a provider of state's export guarantees' and the idea that '[t]he OECD Guidelines cannot be considered to refer to state's export guarantee activities').
[80] UK NCP, *Global Witness v UK Export Finance*, Complaint (16 March 2020) 1.
[81] ibid, 8.
[82] UK NCP, *Global Witness v UK Export Finance*, Initial Assessment (9 September 2020) 8.
[83] ibid.
[84] New Zealand NCP, *Mr and Ms C v Southern Response and NZPT* (9 September 2016) 1.
[85] ibid, 1–2.

domestic operation, and does not have a transnational focus'.[86] As regards to NZPT, the NCP underlined that it was 'wholly owned by Public Trust (a Crown entity)', which could not be characterised as a multinational enterprise on account of its functions.[87]

Other cases against SCEs have been rejected because the complaint focused more on general policy issues at the inter-state level than on the specifics of their commercial activities. In 2011, the Norwegian NCP rejected a complaint against Statoil ASA, an SCE.[88] The complainants referred to the company's engagement in the Canadian oil sands industry, which they deemed incompatible with the Kyoto Protocol.[89] The complaint argued that SCEs have 'a particular responsibility to withdraw from extractions that undermine other Norwegian climate obligations'.[90] The NCP concluded, however, that 'the complaint is aimed more at the policy of Canada to allow the development of oil sands rather than at the manner in which Statoil acts within the framework of this policy'.[91]

Notwithstanding these challenges, the OECD Guidelines remain applicable to SCEs as a matter of principle. There are numerous scenarios in which due diligence standards from the *Guidelines* could be used to evaluate SCEs' conduct. For example, the Norwegian NCP received in December 2019 a complaint against Telenor, a major telecommunications company owned by Norway.[92] According to the complaint, snipers used a tower belonging to Telenor in the vicinity of Alethankyaw to shoot at Rohingya civilians.[93] The complainants specifically argued that Telenor failed to conduct proper due diligence, as required under the *Guidelines*.[94] The complaint highlighted the fact that Telenor is an SOE, noting that 'Norway has a particular obligation to investigate fairly and without bias Telenor's connection to the killing.'[95] In October 2020, the NCP resolved to 'proceed with the complaint', as the case 'raises issues that merit further consideration'.[96]

Human rights due diligence is also relevant for decisions to disengage from business operations. The OECD Due Diligence Guidance provides specific recommendations on responsible disengagement.[97] This aspect of due diligence

[86] ibid, 2.
[87] ibid.
[88] Norway NCP, *Climate Network et al. v Statoil*, Initial Assessment (13 March 2012).
[89] ibid, 1–2.
[90] ibid, 2.
[91] ibid, 6.
[92] Committee Seeking Justice for *Alethankyaw v Telenor*, Complaint (16 December 2019).
[93] ibid, 2.
[94] ibid, 2ff.
[95] ibid, 1.
[96] Norway NCP, *Committee Seeking Justice for Alethankyaw v Telenor*, Initial Assessment (28 October 2020) 9. As of February 2022, the case was still pending: complaints.oecdwatch.org/cases/Case_562 (accessed 28 February 2022).
[97] OECD Due Diligence Guidance for Responsible Business Conduct (OECD 2018) 30f. (see section IV.B).

is particularly important for SCEs. For instance, a company's ties to a foreign state could create a de facto shield of protection for its employees and customers against authoritarian or abusive regimes. Thus, in a new complaint with the Norwegian NCP, 474 civil society groups from Myanmar moved against Telenor's plans to sell its stockholding in Telenor Myanmar to a Lebanese corporation.[98] The complainants contend that the Military Junta of Myanmar forced operators to allow intervention of private communications.[99] According to them, 'Telenor has gained a reputation as the sole reliable mobile operator in the country [...] largely due to the company's links to the Norwegian state.'[100] Hence, the planned sale could arguably endanger fundamental rights of over 18 million users of Telenor Myanmar.[101] The complaint was declared admissible in 2021.[102]

NCPs can even consider complaints against state-owned credit agencies, provided their activities are recognised as 'commercial'.[103] In *Forum Suape v ADSB* (2016), the Dutch NCP assessed a case concerning two dredging projects in Brazil.[104] The complainants argued, among others, that ADSB 'failed to use its influence' to ensure that project operators complied with the *Guidelines*, thus contributing to social and environmental detriments.[105] The NCP noted that ADSB 'issues export credit insurance policies and guarantees to businesses on behalf of and for risk of the State of the Netherlands [...] The State of the Netherlands in this regard acts as insurer and ADSB maintains these export credit insurance policies and guarantees as the State's agent'.[106] The NCP specifically rejected the state's argument that the *Guidelines* were not applicable to export credit agencies.[107] One of the key issues in the case was whether ADSB fell short of its due diligence commitments under the *Guidelines*, both prior to the issuance of insurance policies for the project and during the project's operation.[108] The NCP concluded that the contractors of the project 'could have done a better job in their due diligence activities', including 'active consultation with local communities'.[109] As to ADSB, the Dutch NCP found that 'it may not have quite fulfilled its duty to use its leverage [...] to prevent or mitigate these possible adverse impacts'.[110]

[98] Norway NCP, *SOMO v Telenor*, Complaint (27 July 2021) 3ff.
[99] ibid, 8.
[100] ibid.
[101] ibid, 8–9.
[102] Norway NCP, *SOMO v Telenor*, Initial Assessment (27 September 2021) 9.
[103] On this subject, cf. also the complaints against KEXIM and UKEF, discussed above in this section.
[104] Netherlands NCP, *Both Ends et al. v ADSB*, Final Statement (30 November 2016) 1–2.
[105] ibid, 2.
[106] ibid, 3.
[107] ibid, 4.
[108] ibid, 6.
[109] ibid, 7.
[110] ibid.

### *v. Towards Hard Law Obligations of Due Diligence?*

While due diligence duties of public and private corporations are usually embedded within *soft law* instruments, legally binding duties of responsible business conduct are on the rise. In practice, *hard law* due diligence obligations of investors are predominantly contractual. For instance, the *Model Hydrocarbon Exploration and Exploitation Contract* of the Colombian National Hydrocarbon Agency provides:

> In the execution of its activities, the Contractor shall carry out *social and environmental due diligence*, respect human rights norms and principles, and prevent, reduce, mitigate, and give appropriate management to social, environmental, and economic risks negatively affecting the environment and communities that inhabit the municipalities where [such activities] are executed. [...].[111]

Investment treaties are another possible, albeit far less usual, source of *hard law* diligence obligations. In 2016, Morocco and Nigeria signed a bilateral investment treaty (BIT) establishing far-reaching obligations of diligence for covered investors and their investments.[112] The BIT specifically requires pre-investment 'environmental assessment screening and assessment processes'.[113] Such processes must comply with the laws of the host or the home jurisdiction, 'whichever is more rigorous'.[114] Investors are also expected to conduct a pre-investment 'social impact assessment'.[115] Relatedly, the BIT includes post-establishment obligations, such as the obligations to 'maintain an environmental management system'[116] and to respect labour and human rights.[117] It also comprises rules on 'corporate governance and practices'.[118] Article 20 subjects investors to civil liability in their home jurisdiction for their conduct in the host territory.[119]

International investment agreements (IIAs) occasionally use language that is at the edge between *hard law* and *soft law*. An example would be Article 12 of the Kyrgyzstan-India BIT, whereby 'investors *shall endeavor to voluntarily*

[111] Emphasis added. Author's translation. Agencia Nacional de Hidrocarburos (Colombia), Minuta – Contrato de Exploración y Producción de Hidrocarburos E&P [online] www.anh.gov.co/Asignacion-de-areas/Minuta%20EP%20Continental/1%20Minuta%20de%20Contrato%20de%20EyP%20Continental%2004-03-2019.pdf, Clause 61.1.3 (accessed 28 February 2022).

[112] Morocco-Nigeria BIT (signed 3 December 2016) Arts 14–20. For a more detailed discussion of this BIT see N Zugliani, 'Human Rights in International Investment Law: The 2016 Morocco-Nigeria Bilateral Investment Treaty' (2019) 68 *International and Comparative Law Quarterly* 761, 765–770.

[113] Morocco-Nigeria BIT (signed 3 December 2016) Art 14.1.

[114] ibid.

[115] ibid, Art 14.2.

[116] ibid, Art 18.1.

[117] ibid, Arts 18.2, 18.3. *cf* also Art 18.4.

[118] ibid, Art 19.

[119] ibid, Art 20.

*incorporate* standards of corporate social responsibility in their practices and internal policies'.[120]

Domestic law is another possible source of *hard law* duties of diligence for SCEs. Several states have adopted legislation imposing due diligence obligations on companies under their jurisdiction.[121] Legislation may target specific human rights abuses. That is the case of the Dutch Child Labor Duty of Care Act, approved in 2019, which creates due diligence duties to prevent the produce of child labour from accessing the Dutch market.[122] In the Netherlands, this effort runs parallel with ongoing debates on more ambitious proposals.[123]

Other states have already introduced far-reaching duties of diligence. The German Corporate Due Diligence Duties in Supply Chains Act of 2021 offers a recent example.[124] The Act protects legal positions derived from specific human rights treaties, listed in an Annex.[125] It defines 'human rights risks' as situations where violations of certain human rights tenets (eg prohibition of slavery) are 'sufficiently likely'.[126] The Act also covers environmental risks, including those associated with waste management.[127] It imposes on corporations fairly specific obligations regarding risk management, preventive measures, remedial action, complaint procedures, and indirect suppliers.[128] Parliament additionally introduced procedural provisions for civil action before German courts, allowing domestic unions and NGOs to represent victims.[129]

[120] Emphasis added. Kyrgyz Republic-India BIT (adopted 3 June 2019) Art 12. *cf* also Morocco Model BIT (2019) Art 20.3.

[121] For representative examples see European Coalition for Corporate Justice, 'Corporate due diligence laws and legislative proposals in Europe' (2021) [online] corporatejustice.org/wp-content/uploads/2021/07/Corporate-due-diligence-laws-and-legislative-proposals-in-Europe-June-2021.pdf (accessed 28 February 2022).

[122] Wet van 24 oktober 2019 houdende de invoering van een zorgplicht ter voorkoming van de levering van goederen en diensten die met behulp van kinderarbeid tot stand zijn gekomen (Wet zorgplicht kinderarbeid) [online] zoek.officielebekendmakingen.nl/stb-2019-401.html (particularly at Arts 4, 5) (accessed 28 February 2022). The Child Labor Duty of Care Act is not yet in force. For an overview of the contents and status of the Act see J Wilde-Ramsing, 'Going Dutch: Four things you should know about the Netherlands' new law to eliminate child labour' (24 August 2020) [online] www.business-humanrights.org/en/blog/going-dutch-four-things-you-should-know-about-the-netherlands-new-law-to-eliminate-child-labour/ (accessed 28 February 2022).

[123] See, eg, Wet verantwoord en duurzaam internationaal ondernemen [online] www.tweedekamer.nl/kamerstukken/wetsvoorstellen/detail?cfg=wetsvoorsteldetails&qry=wetsvoorstel%3A35761 (accessed 28 February 2022). For detailed a discussion of this initiative, which could end up absorbing the Child Labor Duty of Care Act, see A Hoff, 'A Bill for Better Business Dissecting the new Dutch Mandatory Human Rights Due Diligence Initiative' (5 May 2021) Völkerrechtsblog [online] voelkerrechtsblog.org/de/a-bill-for-better-business/ (accessed 28 February 2022).

[124] Gesetz über die unternehmerischen Sorgfaltspflichten in Lieferketten (16 July 2021), BGBl. 2021 I, 2959.

[125] ibid, §2(1), Anlage.

[126] ibid, §2(2).

[127] ibid, §2(3).

[128] ibid, §3(1).

[129] ibid, §11(1).

At the global level, the UN Human Rights Council tasked a Working Group in 2014 with the preparation of a legally binding instrument on business and human rights.[130] The Working Group presented a first draft in 2018.[131] Revised versions were launched in 2019,[132] 2020,[133] and 2021.[134]

The current Draft covers 'business activities',[135] ie 'any economic or other activity [...] undertaken by a natural or legal person, including State-owned enterprises, financial institutions and investment funds [...]'.[136] Article 6(1) requires states to adopt measures to prevent human rights abuses of enterprises 'within their territory, jurisdiction, *or otherwise under their control*'.[137] This language suggests that state control over a company is one of the triggers of the obligations envisioned in the instrument. The Draft envisages an obligation on states to introduce mandatory human rights due diligence requirements.[138] It describes the contents of such due diligence and related domestic implementation procedures.[139] The Draft further seeks to provide victims an 'adequate, timely and effective remedy'.[140] This would entail domestic law 'legal liability' for companies and individuals.[141]

This Draft represents the most ambitious initiative worldwide to create legally binding CSR obligations. Further mechanisms are under discussion in other fora. The International Law Association (ILA) has considered the idea of a model law fostering homogeneous domestic CSR regulations.[142] In 2022, the European Commission presented its Proposal for a Directive on Corporate Sustainability Due Diligence.[143]

[130] UN Human Rights Council, Resolution 26/9 – Elaboration of an international legally binding instrument on transnational corporations and other business enterprises with respect to human rights, A/HR/C/RES/26/9 (14 July 2014) No 1.

[131] Zero Draft (16.07.2018) [online] www.ohchr.org/Documents/HRBodies/HRCouncil/WGTransCorp/Session3/DraftLBI.pdf (accessed 28 February 2022).

[132] OEIGWG Chairmanship Revised Draft (16.07.2019) [online] www.ohchr.org/Documents/HRBodies/HRCouncil/WGTransCorp/OEIGWG_RevisedDraft_LBI.pdf (accessed 28 February 2022).

[133] OEIGWG Chairmanship Second Revised Draft (06.08.2020) [online] www.ohchr.org/Documents/HRBodies/HRCouncil/WGTransCorp/Session6/OEIGWG_Chair-Rapporteur_second_revised_draft_LBI_on_TNCs_and_OBEs_with_respect_to_Human_Rights.pdf (accessed 28 February 2022).

[134] OEIGWG Chairmanship Third Revised Draft (17.08.2021) [online] www.ohchr.org/Documents/HRBodies/HRCouncil/WGTransCorp/Session6/LBI3rdDRAFT.pdf (accessed 28 February 2022).

[135] ibid, Art 3(1).

[136] ibid, Art 1(3).

[137] Emphasis added. ibid, Art 6(2).

[138] ibid, Art 6(3).

[139] ibid, Arts 6(4)–6(7).

[140] ibid, Art 7(1).

[141] ibid, Art 8(1).

[142] See ILA Business and Human Rights Study Group, Working Session Report (20 August 2018) 5; ILA Business and Human Rights Study Group, Final Report (16 November 2018) 11.

[143] European Commission, Proposal for a Directive of the European Parliament and of the Council on Corporate Sustainability Due Diligence and amending Directive (EU) 2019/1937, COM(2022) 71 final, 2022/0051(COD) (23 February 2022).

## B. Due Diligence of States in Respect of the Activities of SCEs

### *i. Soft Law Initiatives*

Activities of SCEs involve not only CSR duties of government-owned entities, but also duties of states. These duties refer mainly to the exercise of ownership rights or corporate influence over SCEs. The *OECD Guidelines on Corporate Governance of State-Owned Enterprises* of 2015 are the single most significant instrument on this subject. According to their Foreword, the *Guidelines* are 'the internationally agreed standard for how governments should exercise the state ownership to avoid the pitfalls of both passive ownership and excessive state intervention'.[144] The *Guidelines* posit that state ownership should serve the public interest and be based on a clear 'ownership policy'.[145] In addition, '[t]he state should act as an informed and active owner, ensuring that governance of SCEs is carried out in a transparent and accountable manner [...]'.[146] The *Guidelines* recommend states to adopt ownership policies that properly acknowledge the duties of government-owned companies towards stakeholders.[147] These policies should envisage reporting systems about relations with stakeholders,[148] disclosure of the state's expectations about responsible business practices,[149] and implementation of both ethical standards and compliance programmes (eg against corruption).[150]

The *Ruggie Principles* offer another example of *soft law* instruments addressing the relation of governments to enterprises under their influence or control.[151] Under Guiding Principle 4:[152]

> States should take *additional steps* to protect against human rights abuses by business enterprises that are owned or controlled by the State, or that receive substantial support and services from State agencies such as export credit agencies and official investment insurance or guarantee agencies, including, where appropriate, by requiring human rights due diligence.

As acknowledged in the Commentary to the *Ruggie Principles*, control over a company provides states with a privileged position to advance their own human rights commitments.[153] Even where the acts of an SCE cannot be attributed to the state under international law, the influence of the state over the

[144] OECD Guidelines on Corporate Governance of State-Owned Enterprises (OECD 2015) 3.
[145] ibid, 17 (ch I, A, B).
[146] ibid, 18 (ch II).
[147] ibid, 23 (ch V).
[148] ibid (ch V, B).
[149] ibid (ch V, D).
[150] ibid (ch V, C).
[151] Guiding Principles on Business and Human Rights, HR/Pub/11/04 (United Nations 2011) GP 4–6.
[152] Emphasis added. ibid, GP 4.
[153] ibid, 7.

company allows greater control over potential human rights impacts.[154] In this spirit, the *Principles* recommend states to introduce human rights due diligence requirements for SCEs.[155]

In its Report of May 2016, the Working Group on Business and Human Rights analysed the 'additional steps' required under Guiding Principle 4.[156] The Report is based on the maxim that government-owned companies should 'lead by example'.[157] The Working Group observed that most states do not yet impose SOEs obligations to adopt fully-fletched due diligence processes.[158] It therefore recommended that 'States define the criteria under which they will require State-owned enterprises to conduct human rights due diligence.'[159] Said criteria may include 'the size of the enterprise, the type of enterprise and its operations, the political and human rights context and the industry sector in which it operates'.[160] Alternatively, states could impose a general, far-reaching due diligence requirement applicable to every SOE.[161]

### *ii. State Responsibility in Connection with the Activities of SCEs*

While the *Ruggie Principles* and the 2015 OECD *Guidelines* are formulated as recommendations, operations of SCEs could also engage the responsibility of the state under international law.[162] International responsibility attaches only where there is an 'internationally wrongful act of a State'.[163] This presupposes that conduct which is attributable to the state is in breach of some obligation of that state under international law.[164] Responsibility for the acts of SCEs is twofold.

*First*, the state could be directly responsible under international law for the wrongful conduct of its SCEs.[165] The acts of an SCE giving rise to responsibility may be not only actions, but also omissions (eg internationally wrongful wants of diligence).[166] This form of responsibility requires that the acts of the SCE

[154] ibid.

[155] ibid, 6–7. See also P Muchlinski, 'Corporations', in the *Max Planck Encyclopedia of Public International Law* (Oxford, Oxford University Press, 2014) [16].

[156] UN Human Rights Council / Working Group on the Issue of Human Rights and Transnational Corporations and Other Business Enterprises, Report, A/HRC/32/45 (4 May 2016) [2].

[157] ibid, [45ff], particularly [52].

[158] ibid, [75].

[159] ibid, [77].

[160] ibid.

[161] ibid.

[162] Guiding Principles on Business and Human Rights, HR/Pub/11/04 (United Nations 2011) 7 (addressing this scenario of state responsibility in the Commentary).

[163] ILC, 'Responsibility of States for Internationally Wrongful Acts. General Commentary' (2001) 2 *ILC Yearbook* 31, 32, Art 1.

[164] ibid, 34, Art 2.

[165] *cf* UN Human Rights Council / Working Group on the Issue of Human Rights and Transnational Corporations and Other Business Enterprises, Report, A/HRC/32/45 (4 May 2016) [32–34].

[166] See ILC, 'Responsibility of States for Internationally Wrongful Acts. General Commentary' (2001) 2 *ILC Yearbook* 31, 34, Art 2.

are attributable to the state.[167] Attribution does not follow directly from corporate control or ownership.[168] Where an SCE cannot be characterized as a de jure or de facto organ of the state,[169] attribution typically requires that it 'exercises elements of governmental authority'.[170] Another possibility for attribution is that the acts of an SCE take place under instructions, direction, or control of the state.[171] In the latter case, analysis focuses on the link of the state to a specific action or omission rather than its general relation to the SCE.[172]

State responsibility will only attach if the actions or omissions of the SCE are in breach of an international obligation of the controlling state.[173] In cases involving investments made outside said state's territory, this form of responsibility thus requires identifying an international obligation with extraterritorial reach.[174]

*Second*, even where the acts of an SCE are not attributable to the state, the latter remains responsible for its own conduct with regard to the administration of the SCE and the exercise of ownership rights.[175] The UN Working Group on Human Rights and Transnational Corporations has noted that '[t]he State could be held responsible for not taking all reasonable steps to prevent, mitigate and remediate the abuse [of human rights]'.[176] Responsibility will likely refer to breaches of customary or treaty-based positive obligations, which are often defined in terms of due diligence.[177] To be sure, this scenario does not entail a form of indirect responsibility for the acts of others, but a form of direct responsibility: the state is responsible for its own want of diligence, that is to say, for

[167] ibid. On the question of attribution and the scenarios discussed below (on the basis of the ILC-Articles) see J Dereje, *Staatsnahe Unternehmen* (Baden-Baden, Nomos, 2015) 111ff, 433ff. *cf* also M Karavias, 'Shared Responsibility and Multinational Enterprises' (2015) 62 *Netherlands International Law Review* 91, 96ff (focusing on privately-owned companies and discussing situations where they perform public functions, such as prison administration).

[168] P Muchlinski, 'Corporations' in the *Max Planck Encyclopedia of Public International Law* (Oxford, Oxford University Press, 2014) [49]. *cf* also R McCorquodale and P Simmons, 'Responsibility Beyond Borders' (2007) 70(4) *Modern Law Review* 598, 606ff (also addressing scenarios of attribution).

[169] ILC, 'Responsibility of States for Internationally Wrongful Acts. General Commentary' (2001) 2 *ILC Yearbook* 31, 34, Art 4.

[170] ibid, 34, Art 5.

[171] ibid, 34, Art 8.

[172] *cf* J Dereje, *Staatsnahe Unternehmen* (Baden-Baden, Nomos 2015) 436.

[173] ILC, 'Responsibility of States for Internationally Wrongful Acts. General Commentary' (2001) 2 *ILC Yearbook* 31, 34, Art 2.

[174] On the question of extraterritoriality see R McCorquodale and P Simmons, 'Responsibility Beyond Borders' (2007) 70(4) *Modern Law Review* 598, 603ff.

[175] See generally J Schönsteiner, 'Attribution of State Responsibility for Actions or Omissions of State-Owned Enterprises in Human Rights Matters' (2019) 40(4) *University* of *Pennsylvania Journal of International Law* 895, 900ff.

[176] UN Human Rights Council / Working Group on the Issue of Human Rights and Transnational Corporations and Other Business Enterprises, Report, A/HRC/32/45 (4 May 2016) [31].

[177] *cf* ICtHR, Advisory Opinion OC-23/17 – The Environment and Human Rights (15 November 2017) [123ff.].

an omission, which is directly attributable to it and distinguishable from the SCE's wrongful conduct.[178]

Some investment treaties contain obligations concerning SOEs. A prominent example is Article 22(1) of the Energy Charter Treaty (ECT), according to which the Contracting Parties have an obligation to 'ensure' that their state enterprises conduct activities consistently with the ECT's provisions on investment.[179] Notably, Article 22 ECT covers activities conducted in the 'Area' of the controlling state. Thus, it applies to operations of state enterprises of the *host* state in the *host* territory, as opposed to investments abroad.

Still, positive obligations of states often have extraterritorial reach.[180] The American Convention on Human Rights (ACHR) offers a representative example in this regard. In its Advisory Opinion on the Environment and Human Rights (2017), the Inter-American Court of Human Rights (ICtHR) held that 'States are obliged to respect and to ensure the human rights of all persons subject to their jurisdiction, even though such persons are not within their territory.'[181] Specifically, the Court considered that 'it is understood that individuals whose rights under the Convention have been violated owing to transboundary harm are subject to the jurisdiction of the State of origin of the harm'.[182] The reason is that '[said] State exercises effective control over the activities carried out in its territory or under its jurisdiction'.[183] This approach results in positive extraterritorial obligations for the prevention of environmental harm.[184] Following this rationale, failure to prevent environmental damage abroad through the exercise of ownership rights over government-owned investors could potentially entail a breach of the ACHR.

[178] On direct responsibility for omissions in the exercise of due diligence *cf* generally: T Becker, *Terrorism and the State* (Oxford, Hart 2006) 24ff; S Mantilla Blanco, *Full Protection and Security in International Investment Law* (Cham, Springer, 2019) 411ff. *cf* also ICtHR, *Velásquez Rodríguez v Honduras*, Sentencia–Fondo (29 July 1988) [172].

[179] Energy Charter Treaty (adopted 17 December 1994, in force 16 April 1998) 2080 UNTS 100, Art 22(1). This provision has not been interpreted as a rule attributing acts and omissions of SOEs to the host state, but rather as an autonomous positive obligation of conduct. *cf Al-Bahloul v Tajikistan*, SCC Case No V064/2008, Partial Award on Jurisdiction and Liability (2 September 2009) [172], quoting *AMTO v Ukraine*, SCC Case No 080/2005, Final Award (26 March 2008) [12]. *cf* also *Petrobart v Kyrgyz Republic*, SCC Case No 126/2003, Arbitral Award (29 March 2005) [VIII.8.25]. For an overview of arbitral practice on this provision see C Grasso and T Hunter, 'Article 22. State and Privileged Enterprises' in R Leal-Arcas (ed), *Commentary on the Energy Charter Treaty* (Cheltenham, Elgar, 2018) 299, 299ff.

[180] Extraterritorial obligations could include, for example, duties to exercise influence over private parties with regard to their investments abroad. *cf* Maastricht Principles on Extraterritorial Obligations of States in the Area of Economic, Social and Cultural Rights (2011) [online] www.etoconsortium.org/nc/en/main-navigation/library/maastricht-principles/?tx_drblob_pi1%5BdownloadUid%5D=23 (accessed 28 February 2022) Art 9(c). *cf* also fn 174 above.

[181] See ICtHR, Advisory Opinion OC-23/17 – The Environment and Human Rights (15 November 2017) [104(c)].

[182] See ibid, [244(4)].

[183] See ibid.

[184] See ibid, [244(5)].

CSR instruments could provide guidance in the assessment of state responsibility for breaches of due diligence obligations. The ICtHR has relied on the *Ruggie Principles* as an orientation regarding systems of accountability and information which states must implement to fulfil positive obligations under the ACHR.[185]

## IV. SCE'S DUE DILIGENCE AND INVESTMENT TREATY CLAIMS

The previous sections have provided an overview of due diligence duties of SCEs and of states in connection with the activities of SCEs. This section discusses the possible implications of these developments for investment arbitral proceedings. As most known cases have so far referred to privately-owned investors, a first subsection examines the relevance of investors' due diligence for the assessment of investment treaty claims from a general perspective. The second subsection analyses specific issues concerning SCEs.

This section does not address the attribution of SCEs' wants of diligence to their home states. The reason is that, as a rule, tribunals in treaty-based investment arbitration have no jurisdiction to decide on the responsibility of foreign states exercising control over covered investors. By submitting a claim to arbitration, the investor accepts an offer to arbitrate made by the host state in a BIT.[186] While the home state is a party to the BIT containing the offer to arbitrate, it is not a party to the arbitration agreement between the investor and the host state.

In the specific context of the ICSID Convention, cases archetypically refer to situations where the acts of the investor are *not* attributable to a state.[187] In *BUCG v Yemen*, the Tribunal explained that '[a]rticle 25(1) of the ICSID Convention is not a State-to-State dispute resolution mechanism and is not open to State-owned companies as claimants when acting as agents of the State or when engaged in activities where they exercise governmental functions'.[188] ICSID tribunals will typically reject jurisdiction where the investor 'is acting as an agent for the government or discharging an essentially governmental function' (so-called '*Broches test*').[189]

[185] See ibid, [154–155]. In the Advisory Opinion, the Court also refers to its decision in ICtHR, *Case of the Kaliña and Lokono Peoples v Suriname*, Judgment–Merits, Reparations and Costs (25 November 2015) [223–226].

[186] See generally Z Douglas, *The International Law of Investment Claims*, 4th printing (Cambridge, CUP 2009, 2012) 75, 115 and 470–471.

[187] There is no provision expressly and specifically excluding such entities from ICSID jurisdiction, albeit the Preamble to the Washington Convention uses the phrase 'private direct investment'. See generally S Konrad, 'Protection of Investments Owned by States', in M Bungenberg et al. (eds), *International Investment Law* (Munich, Beck, 2015) 545, 550–553.

[188] *Beijing Urban Construction Group v Yemen*, ICSID Case No ARB/14/30, Decision on Jurisdiction (31 May 2017) [31].

[189] A Broches, 'The Convention on the Settlement of Disputes between States and Nationals of Other States' 1972(II) *Recueil des cours – Collected Courses of the Hague Academy of International Law* 331, 355.

If the *Broches Test* is followed, jurisdiction excludes attribution to the home state and vice-versa.[190]

## A. Investors' Due Diligence in Investment Arbitration

In a steadily growing number of cases, arbitral tribunals have dealt with allegations that the investor failed to exercise due diligence, either prior to the making of the investment or after the investment was made. Contentions about investors' wants of diligence appear in the most varied procedural contexts, ranging from objections to the jurisdiction of the tribunal or the admissibility of the claims to defences on the merits of the case.[191]

Due diligence does not usually appear as a fully-fletched obligation of foreign investors, but rather as an expression of what some authors would call 'behavioural expectations' relevant for the assessment of claims.[192] A host state's counterclaim based on a violation of due diligence duties of a foreign investor, while theoretically possible, would require the existence of a *hard law* obligation of diligence under the investment treaty, domestic law, or a contract.[193] In addition, it would need to meet stringent procedural requirements.[194] The present section will therefore not deal with the scenario of a counterclaim, focusing on those procedural settings that are most common in practice.

### *i. Investors' Due Diligence and Illegality Objections*

Numerous investment agreements require that investments comply with applicable domestic regulations of the host country.[195] New IIAs sometimes extend the legality requirement to compliance not only with the national law of the host state, but also with relevant domestic regulations of the home state.[196]

[190] *cf Beijing Urban Construction Group v Yemen*, ICSID Case No ARB/14/30, Decision on Jurisdiction (31 May 2017), particularly at [34] (observing that 'the Broches factors are the mirror image of the attribution rules in Articles 5 and 8 of the ILC's Articles on State Responsibility' and noting that 'the Broches test lays down markers for the non-attribution of State status').

[191] For an overview see J Viñuales, 'Investor Diligence in Investment Arbitration: Sources and Arguments' (2017) 32(2) *ICSID Review* 346, 356ff.

[192] On 'behavioural expectations' regarding foreign investors' conduct see K Nowrot, 'Obligations of Foreign Investors', in M Bungenberg et al. (eds), *International Investment Law* (Munich, Beck, 2015) 1155, 1174.

[193] On the possible sources of *hard law* obligations of diligence see section III.A. A respondent state's counterclaim needs to be based on an obligation that is legally binding for the investor. *cf Teinver et al. v Argentina*, ICSID Case No ARB/09/11, Award (21 July 2017) [1064, 1066].

[194] See generally Y Kryvoi, 'Counterclaims in Investor-State Arbitration' (2011) 8 *LSE Law, Society and Economy Working Papers* 1, 4ff.

[195] See K Diel-Gligor and R Hennecke, 'Investment in Accordance with the Law', in M Bungenberg et al. (eds), *International Investment Law* (Munich, Beck, 2015) 566, 566ff; S Schill, 'Illegal Investments in Investment Treaty Arbitration' (2012) 11 *Law and Practice of International Courts and Tribunals* 281, 283ff.

[196] For an example see Slovak Republic-UAE BIT (adopted 22 September 2016, in force 5 February 2018) Art 17(2).

Failure to fulfil such requirements may lead to a finding that the tribunal lacks jurisdiction.[197] Even where there is no explicit legality clause, illegality could render the claims inadmissible or affect the tribunal's decision on the merits.[198] The burden of proof falls on the respondent state asserting the illegality objection.[199] The threshold for a successful objection is high. It depends on the language of the treaty and the nature of the breach of municipal law (eg whether it is material to the investment).[200]

Provided that there is a solid basis for an objection, the investor cannot rely on its own ignorance of the applicable law to obtain protection of an illegal or otherwise tainted investment.[201] Pre-investment due diligence processes are therefore a tool for investors to avoid subsequent disqualification of the investment from the scope of protection of the BIT. In *Churchill Mining v Indonesia* (2016), an ICSID tribunal found that a series of forged documents obtained through corrupt practices formed a 'fraudulent scheme' which 'permeated' the investment.[202] Evidence was insufficient to attribute such fraud to the foreign investors.[203] Still, the record clearly pointed to one of their business partners.[204]

The tribunal observed that '[i]nvestors must exercise a reasonable level of due diligence, especially when investing in risky business environments'.[205] It also explained that the requirement of due diligence 'includes ensuring that a proposed investment complies with local laws, as well as investigating the reliability of a business partner'.[206] The investors were aware of corruption and pervasive administrative disorder in relevant Indonesian agencies.[207] The tribunal concluded that, notwithstanding their knowledge of the situation, 'Claimants did not engage in proper due diligence in their dealings with their partners.'[208] The award underscored that 'an investor aware of the risks of investing in a certain environment [is expected] to be particularly diligent in

[197] *cf* R Moloo and A Khachaturian, 'The Compliance with the Law Requirement in International Investment Law' (2011) 34(6) *Fordham International Law Journal* 1473, 1499.

[198] ibid. For a critical perspective see Z Douglas, 'The Plea of Illegality in Investment Treaty Arbitration' (2014) 29(1) *ICSID Review* 155, 177ff. See also the diagram at 186.

[199] See generally F Fontanelli, *Jurisdiction and Admissibility in Investment Arbitration* (Leiden, Brill, 2018) 142ff.

[200] *cf* S Schill, 'Illegal Investments in Investment Treaty Arbitration' (2012) 11 *Law and Practice of International Courts and Tribunals* 281, 283ff and 291ff.

[201] See J Viñuales, 'Investor Diligence in Investment Arbitration: Sources and Arguments' (2017) 32(2) *ICSID Review* 346, 356–360 (also discussing the *Churchill Mining* case at 360).

[202] *Churchill Mining and Planet Mining v Indonesia*, ICSID Cases No ARB/12/14 and 12/40, Award (6 December 2016) [507]. See also the analysis at [466, 476].

[203] ibid, [475].

[204] ibid, [476, 528].

[205] ibid, [506]. *cf* also [518–519].

[206] ibid, [506].

[207] ibid, [517].

[208] ibid, [518].

investigating the circumstances of its investment'.[209] The claims were therefore inadmissible.[210]

### *ii. Investors' Due Diligence and Full Protection and Security (FPS) Claims*

The standard of 'full protection and security' entails an obligation of due diligence, which requires the host state to protect foreign investors against risks that are par excellence external to the state (eg mob violence).[211] While FPS pertains to due diligence by the state, investors' due diligence could also play a role in the assessment of FPS claims.[212] This holds true both for the investor's conduct prior to the making of the investment and for its acts after the investment was made. Investors have the burden of gathering information about the circumstances of the place where they intend to invest. Thus, the decision to make an investment in a war zone or politically instable area entails an assumption of risk.[213] The investor cannot entirely transfer such risks to the host state.

In *Mamidoil v Albania*, the investor alleged that Albanian authorities failed to prevent illegal conduct by third parties who adulterated fuel, evaded taxes, and smuggled merchandises.[214] The arbitrators noted that these circumstances were known to the investor at the moment when the investment was made.[215] According to the tribunal, there was a 'general insecurity' which 'was part of the general business environment and investment conditions'.[216] The arbitrators concluded that[217]

> While Claimant might have been entitled to expect that the general conditions of insecurity would improve over time, it was not entitled to expect that Respondent would protect its investment against the general insecurity that was inherent to the investment climate as opposed to specific instances of harassment.

As stated above, the investor is not only expected to be diligent prior to making an investment but also after the investment is made. In *Al Tamini v Oman* the tribunal considered that the host state was not responsible for failing to prevent vandalism in a quarry site that was abandoned by the investor.[218] According to the arbitrators, '[t]o the extent that the Claimant was willing to abandon his

[209] ibid.
[210] ibid, [528].
[211] S Mantilla Blanco, *Full Protection and Security in International Investment Law* (Cham, Springer, 2019) 207ff.
[212] ibid, 471ff (discussing these and other cases in detail).
[213] ibid, 471–472.
[214] *Mamidoil Jetoil Greek Petroleum Products v Albania*, ICSID Case No ARB/11/24, Award (30 March 2015) [824].
[215] ibid, [823].
[216] ibid, [823–824].
[217] ibid.
[218] *Adel A Hamadi Al Tamini v Oman*, ICSID Case No ARB/11/33, Award (3 November 2015) [450].

property, he cannot equally assert that the Respondent failed to take steps to preserve it'.[219] Other situations where reckless conduct by the investor could impair success of FPS claims involve, for example, failure to report incidents or risks to competent local authorities.[220] The underlying rationale is that the investor cannot reasonably expect that the host state displays a greater degree of diligence in the protection of the investment than that which the investor has exercised in its own affairs.[221]

### *iii. Investors' Due Diligence and Fair and Equitable Treatment (FET) Claims*

Virtually every investment treaty case involves an alleged breach of the host state's obligation to provide a 'fair and equitable treatment' to the investment.[222] The vast majority of FET claims concern the protection of foreign investors' legitimate expectations.[223] Where acts attributable to the host state have created an objective expectation on the foreign investor and said expectation motivated the decision to make an investment, subsequent frustration of such legitimate expectation entails a breach of FET.[224] The adjudication of claims about legitimate expectations requires determining what the investor either knew or should have reasonably known about the social, legal, political, and economic environment of the investment.[225]

This usually leads to an analysis of the investor's due diligence.[226] The reason is that, as observed in *InfraRed v Spain*, there is an interplay between the notion

[219] ibid, [451].

[220] For an indicative example see *Tenaris et al. v Venezuela*, ICSID Case No ARB/11/26, Award (29 January 2016) [446, 449].

[221] S Mantilla Blanco, *Full Protection and Security in International Investment Law* (Cham, Springer, 2019) 471ff.

[222] On the importance of the standard see R Kläger, *'Fair and Equitable Treatment' in International Investment Law* (Cambridge, CUP, 2011) 1–2; R Dolzer and C Schreuer, *Principles of International Investment Law*, 2nd edn (Oxford, OUP, 2012) 130.

[223] On legitimate expectations in the context of the FET standard see FM Palombino, *Fair and Equitable Treatment and the Fabric of General Principles* (Heidelberg, Springer, 2018) 85ff. See also ET Laryea, 'Legitimate Expectations in Investment Treaty Law: Concept and Scope of Application', in J Chaisse et al. (eds), *Handbook of International Investment Law and Policy* (Singapore, Springer, 2020) 1, 2ff.

[224] *cf Stadtwerke München et al. v Spain*, ICSID Case No ARB/15/1, Award (2 December 2019) [263].

[225] *cf SunReserve Luxco Holdings et al. v Italy*, SCC Case No V 2016/32, Final Award (25 March 2020) [714]; *Antartis Solar et al. v Czech Republic*, PCA Case No 2014-01, Award (2 May 2018) [360]; *Steag v Spain*, ICSID Case No ARB/15/4, Decision on Jurisdiction, Liability, and Principles of Quantum (8 October 2020) [524ff.].

[226] See, eg, *Cavalum SGPS S.A. v Spain*, ICSID Case No ARB/15/34, Decision on Jurisdiction, Liability, and Directions on Quantum (31 August 2020) [443–447, 516–538]. For an overall analysis see Y Levashova, 'Fair and Equitable Treatment and Investor's Due Diligence under International Investment Law' [2020] *Netherlands International Law Review* [online] doi.org/10.1007/s40802-020-00170-7 (particularly at ss 2–3). For a discussion of relevant ECT cases see Y Levashova, 'The Role of Investor's Due Diligence in International Investment Law: Legitimate Expectations of Investors' (22 April 2020) Kluwer Arbitration Blog [online] arbitrationblog.kluwerarbitration.com/2020/04/22/the-role-of-investors-due-diligence-in-international-investment-law-legitimate-expectations-of-investors/ (accessed 28 February 2022).

of due diligence and foreseeability, as adjudicators must establish whether a proper due diligence process would have allowed a 'reasonably prudent investor' to foresee the acts that give rise to the claim.[227] For these purposes, tribunals normally apply an objective 'standard of reasonable diligence' in respect of the investor's conduct prior to the making of the investment.[228]

Tribunals are generally reluctant to require investors to conduct an all-encompassing and detailed pre-investment due diligence process.[229] The question is not whether the investor was diligent on an abstract level, but whether its expectations are reasonable in light of the information available at the time of the investment.[230] In this context, due diligence appears more as a burden of the investor than as an obligation, properly so-called.[231] As expressed by a Dissenting Arbitrator in an ECT case, '[d]ue diligence is only relevant in a case such as this if it would have provided the Claimants with information that contradicted their asserted expectations [...] An investor is under no abstract duty to conduct due diligence'.[232]

This analysis confirms that the exercise of due diligence is not an actionable positive obligation, but only a factor in the assessment of the investor's claims.[233] The host state should bear no responsibility for investment decisions that reflect unrealistic expectations, which could have been avoided through an adequate due diligence process on the part of the foreign investor.[234] Following this line of argument, the tribunal in *SolES de Badajoz v Spain* explained:[235]

> The Tribunal considers that a formal due diligence process is not a precondition to a successful claim of legitimate expectations. However, an investor cannot benefit from gaps in its subjective knowledge of the regulatory environment because, under an objective standard, the investor's legitimate expectations are measured with reference to the knowledge that a hypothetical prudent investor is deemed to have had as of the date of the investment.

Expectations must exist at the moment when the investment was made, so that the relevant time for the assessment of expectations is the date of the

[227] *InfraRed Environmental Infrastructure et al. v Spain*, ICSID Case No ARB/14/12, Award (2 August 2019) [362, 371].

[228] *cf SunReserve Luxco Holdings et al. v Italy*, SCC Case No V2016/32, Final Award (25 March 2020) [714]; *Gavrilovic et al. v Croatia*, ICSID Case No ARB/12/39, Award (28 July 2018) [829, 986, 1010–1011, 1016]. *cf* also Croatia's argument at [980].

[229] See the analysis in *Isolux Infrastructure Netherlands v Spain*, SCC Case No V2013/153, Laudo (17 July 2016) [781].

[230] *cf* ibid.

[231] *cf Antartis Solar GmbH et al. v Czech Republic*, PCA Case No 2014-01, Dissenting Opinion/ Gary Born (2 May 2018) [73–74].

[232] *cf* ibid.

[233] Somewhat inaccurately, some arbitral tribunals have acknowledged an 'obligation to conduct due diligence'. *Eurus Energy Holdings Corp. v Spain*, ICSID Case No ARB/16/4, Decision on Jurisdiction and Liability (17 March 2021) [423(a)].

[234] See *MTD Equity et al. v Chile*, ICSID Case No ARB/01/7, Award (25 May 2004) [167].

[235] *SolEs Badajoz v Spain*, ICSID Case No ARB/15/38, Award (31 July 2019) [331].

investment decision.[236] Even where investors' expectations have changed with the passage of time, they must objectively determine a decision related to the investment (eg expansion or reorganisation of assets).[237] Thus, the absence or insufficiency of due diligence *prior* to the making of the investment could lead a tribunal to declare that the investor's claimed expectations were illegitimate.[238] This does not however mean that investors are not expected to act diligently in the period subsequent to the making of the investment.[239] Neither does it mean that every want of diligence attributable to the claimant has the same bearing on its FET claims.

Negligence – either prior to the investment or in the operation of the investment – could justify a reduction of damages for contributory fault under Article 39 of the ILC Articles on State Responsibility.[240] Thus, the tribunal in *MTD v Chile* declared a breach of the FET standard, but found that the investors' 'business judgement' was the cause of a portion of the alleged damages.[241] The arbitrators explained that 'BITs are not an insurance against business risk' and underscored that 'Claimants should bear the consequences of their own actions as experienced businessmen'.[242] Accordingly, the tribunal reduced compensable damages by 50 per cent.[243] Using a similar argument, the tribunal in *Steag v Spain* reduced damages by 25 per cent.[244]

Similarly, non-fulfilment of CSR standards could justify a reduction of compensable damages. Thus, the Netherlands Model BIT of 2019 provides:[245]

> Behavior of the investor. Without prejudice to national administrative or criminal law procedures, a Tribunal, in deciding on the amount of compensation, is expected to take into account non-compliance by the investor with its commitments under the UN Guiding Principles on Business and Human Rights, and the OECD Guidelines for Multinational Enterprises.

[236] See *SunReserve Luxco Holdings et al. v Italy*, SCC Case No V/2016/32, Award (20 March 2020) [715ff], particularly at [720].

[237] ibid, [722–725], quoting *Crystallex v Venezuela* at [722] and referring to other cases at [723ff].

[238] *cf RWE Innology et al. v Spain*, ICSID Case No ARB/14/34, Decision on Jurisdiction, Liability and Certain Issues of Quantum (30 December 2019) [507ff].

[239] *cf Rusoro Mining Ltd. v Venezuela*, ICSID Case No ARB(AF)/12/5, Award (22 August 2016) [525] (requiring 'pre-investment due diligence' and 'proper conduct both before and during the investment').

[240] On this scenario see J Viñuales, 'Investor Diligence in Investment Arbitration: Sources and Arguments' (2017) 32(2) *ICSID Review* 346, 364–366 (discussing relevant cases, including *MTD v Chile*). See also *Gemplus et al. v Mexico*, ICSID Cases Nos ARB(AF)/04/3 & ARB(AF)/04/4, Award (16 June 2010) [11.12].

[241] See *MTD Equity et al. v Chile*, ICSID Case No ARB/01/7, Award (25 May 2004) [242].

[242] See ibid, [178].

[243] See ibid, [243].

[244] *Steag v Spain*, ICSID Case No ARB/15/4, Decision on Jurisdiction, Liability, and Principles of Quantum (8 October 2020) [796].

[245] Netherlands Model BIT (2019) Art 23. On the new Netherlands Model BIT see K Duggal and L van de Ven, 'The 2019 Netherlands Model BIT: Riding the New Investment Treaty Waves' (2019) 35 *Arbitration International* 347, 357ff.

A tribunal constituted under a treaty using this language will likely analyse the investor's conduct through the prism of CSR *soft law* instruments. Failure to fulfil those standards could therefore impact the amount of compensation.

## B. Specific Issues Concerning Due Diligence of State-Controlled Investors

There is a basic expectation that a private or public investor seeking protection under an international treaty conducts a process of due diligence prior to the making of the investment. So far, arbitral tribunals have not considered possible differences between private and public investors' due diligence in this context. For instance, in *Stadtwerke München v Spain* (2019), the tribunal rejected the investors' FET claim, noting that their expectations were neither 'legitimate' nor 'reasonable'.[246] The arbitrators observed that 'a prudent investor, having conducted an appropriate due diligence, would not have reasonably formed an expectation of a legally stable income stream'.[247] The fact that one of the investors was wholly-owned by the city of Munich played no role whatsoever in the assessment of the claims. This seems consistent with the tribunal's decision on a jurisdictional objection, where it stated that 'the ECT does not provide that companies owned by States are to be treated differently from companies owned by private individuals and entities'.[248] This section submits that state control could have at least two implications for the evaluation of foreign investors' conduct.

*First*, adjudicators could be warranted to consider documents or information stemming from agencies of the state that controls the investment. Knowledge about a risk by the investor's parent company could indicate risk awareness on the part of the investor. Thus, for example, in *Isolux v Spain* the parent company of one of the investors had filed a claim before Spanish courts years before the investment, relying on the Spanish Supreme Tribunal's jurisprudence on economic rights of renewable energy producers.[249] For the arbitrators, this circumstance indicated that the investor (ie, a subsidiary) was 'perfectly aware' of the Supreme Tribunal's decisions in question.[250]

[246] *cf Stadtwerke München et al. v Spain*, ICSID Case No ARB/15/1, Award (2 December 2019) [308].

[247] *cf* ibid.

[248] *cf* ibid. The arbitrators only considered the public nature of Stadtwerke München GmbH in connection with a jurisdictional objection based on Article 344 TFUE which, in Spain's view, precluded the submission to arbitration of an investment dispute between two EU Member States (at [132]). The tribunal held that Stadtwerke München 'should [not] be equated to the Federal Republic of Germany' and noted that the company qualified as a protected investor under the ECT (at [133–134]).

[249] *Isolux Infrastructure Netherlands v Spain*, SCC Case No V2013/153, Laudo (17 July 2016) [796].

[250] ibid.

This form of attribution of knowledge or risk awareness could gain significance in cases involving SCEs. In principle, state-controlled investors cannot claim that they were ignorant about planned reforms or political circumstances that were known to the controlling state's organs, such as ministries, agencies, and embassies or consulates in the host state. Even if the acts of an SCE are considered not to be attributable to the controlling state under the general rules of state responsibility, the relationship between said state and the company is part of the factual matrix of the case. Tribunals could examine reports or warnings issued by organs of the controlling state regarding the political or economic situation of the country where the SCE's investment was planned, as they reveal information that was or should have been available to the investor. This analysis must necessarily consider whether relevant pieces of information were confidential or otherwise subject to access restrictions.

*Second*, the higher standards of diligence CSR instruments devise for SCEs could be used as a means to substantiate the expectation that the investor acts diligently. This holds particularly true where the government holding control over an SCE has adhered to key OECD and UN instruments on CSR. In such scenarios, it can be assumed that those instruments crystallise the standards of conduct that the government considers reasonable for the activities of its own enterprises. In fact, SCEs are generally expected to 'lead by example'.[251] The state's commitment under the *Ruggie Principles* to take 'additional steps' to minimise human rights risks associated to the activities of SCEs reinforces this idea.[252]

Where the controlling state has adhered to the OECD Guidelines on Corporate Governance of SOEs, it should have a clear ownership policy that reveals in transparent terms the government's expectations regarding conduct of its SOEs.[253] Arbitrators can use those policies as guidelines for assessing the investor's due diligence processes. A state company cannot present itself as a diligent investor if it has failed to comply with the standards set by its own controlling government.

Investor-state dispute settlement (ISDS) proceedings could thus become a forum for testing and applying *soft law* standards of conduct, particularly in cases involving SCEs. While so far only a few arbitral tribunals have considered CSR instruments,[254] CSR is likely to gain importance as a new generation of investment agreements containing express references to CSR codes of conduct expands. Some new model BITs combine legally binding language regarding compliance of municipal law, on the one hand, and broader references to CSR

[251] *cf* section III.B.

[252] Guiding Principles on Business and Human Rights, HR/Pub/11/04 (United Nations 2011), GP 4.

[253] OECD Guidelines on Corporate Governance of State-Owned Enterprises (OECD 2015) 23 (ch V, D).

[254] For a tribunal addressing CSR see *Urbaser et al. v Argentina*, ICSID Case No ARB/07/26, Award (8 December 2016) [1165] and fn 434 (examining, in the analysis of a counterclaim, whether investors are bound by human rights).

instruments on the other.[255] Other treaties simply refer to the promotion of CSR and responsible business practices as a goal of the contracting parties.[256] Some of these instruments mention specific codes of conduct.[257]

While these references to CSR do not turn *soft law* instruments into sources of *hard law* obligations for covered investors, they facilitate their use in the assessment of prospective investment claims. The argument for the use of such CSR standards is stronger where the claimant is an SCE. The contracting states' commitment to the promotion of CSR and sustainable development serves as an anchor for the use of such standards in the analysis of due diligence. There is merit to the idea that conduct of a government-controlled investor can be evaluated against the due diligence standards that the controlling state has agreed to promote.

## V. CONCLUDING REMARKS

This chapter has provided an overview of due diligence duties applicable to the activities of government-controlled entities. The focus was set not only on *soft law* instruments about corporate social responsibility, but also on initiatives aiming to create legally binding obligations of diligence for state-controlled investors. These developments show a growing consensus that SCEs are subject to higher standards of conduct than private investors. Such standards are not only a matter of policy, but also a means for the controlling state to fulfil its own commitments under international law.

The study has further shown that investors' due diligence plays an increasingly important role in ISDS. State control over the investor is a factual circumstance relevant for the assessment of its business conduct. In the appropriate circumstances, CSR standards can aid investment tribunals in the evaluation of investors' due diligence, particularly where the controlling state is a party to relevant CSR instruments. Ongoing developments hence reveal that the expansion of state capitalism is not only a challenge but also an opportunity for fostering socially responsible investments. Government-controlled investments provide the controlling state with a unique opportunity to put into practice the CSR standards it has endorsed, offering an example of best practices of implementation.[258]

[255] See, eh, Belgium-Luxembourg Economic Union Model BIT (2019) Art 18.1 (investors' obligation to comply with domestic law, including 'administrative guidelines and policies') and 18.2 (Parties' agreement 'to promote CSR and RBC in line with international guidelines and principles'). Arts 2.10 and 2.11 of the Model BIT define both 'corporate social responsibility' (CSR) and 'responsible business conduct' (RBC). For another example, see Netherlands Model BIT (2019) Arts 7.1 and 7.2. Other treaties merely mention the Parties' adherence to the 2011 OECD Guidelines. See, eg, Colombia-Israel FTA (adopted 30 September 2013, in force 11 August 2020) Art 10.3(4).

[256] See, eg, Korea-Indonesia Comprehensive Economic Partnership Agreement (adopted 18 December 2020) Art 7.18. This aim is sometimes mentioned in the treaty's preamble. See Czech Republic Model BIT (2016) Preamble, [4].

[257] See, eg, USMCA Agreement (signed 30 November 2018, in force 1 July 2020) Art 14.17.

[258] This chapter was last updated in February 2022.

# 10

# *Sovereign Investors and National Security Exceptions in WTO and Investment Law*

PANAGIOTIS DELIMATSIS AND OLGA HRYNKIV*

## I. INTRODUCTION

SECURITY-RELATED RHETORIC IS omnipresent in the trade and investment fora of political or judicial nature. Such a trend constitutes a shift from a protracted period of self-restraint regarding the invocation of security exceptions before international trade and investment courts. In that sense, we witness the end of innocence: an era of relatively stable international commercial relations with mutually advantageous – but admittedly unbalanced – results is followed by an era that reveals the unpleasant face of trade regulation, reminding us how inextricably connected foreign policy and power politics are with trade.

The evolving geoeconomic environment has raised the stakes of international competition and new forms of economic warfare.[1] Trade flows are being instrumentalised, as states look to turn the increasing dependence of businesses on global markets and supply chains into leverage and choose to use tariffs and blockades aimed to protect their national security interests as instruments of choice in pressure campaigns.[2] This is the result of a gradual reversal of a centuries-long reality of virtual exclusivity of foreign direct investment (FDI) flows from the developed world to the developing world, coupled with an

* The authors are grateful to the participants at the Colloquium on 'International Investment Law and State Capitalism' on 15–16 October 2020 for their comments and suggestions. Remaining errors are of the authors' alone.

[1] JC Zarate, *Treasury's War: The Unleashing of a New Era of Financial Warfare*, 1st edn (New York, PublicAffairs, 2013) 385.

[2] HG Cohen, 'Nations and Markets' (2020) 23(4) *Journal of International Economic Law* 793, 797.

important rise of FDIs from emerging economies, such as China.[3] The renewed trend for the creation of national industry champions and the procurement of overseas natural resources by the Chinese Government arguably reinforce a broader politically-driven agenda of economic nationalism focused on issues of national security and autonomy, geopolitical positioning, and national competitiveness.[4]

The concerns raised are in particular related to the FDIs of State-Owned Enterprises (SOEs), Sovereign Wealth Funds (SWFs) and other state-influenced entities (collectively understood as 'sovereign investments'). These concerns stem from the fear that such investments might no longer follow a strictly market-based logic but rather be utilised for geopolitical ends.[5] As a result, host states increasingly reconsider their approach vis-à-vis the design of investment agreements in particular so that they shift from investment protection towards creating sufficient regulatory margin of manoeuvre for the state.[6] Along with more flexibility in the interpretation and enforcement of investment agreements, states also adopt investment screening mechanisms.

Protectionist discourse and a new form of contemporary mercantilism have unleashed such forces that consider every economic transaction as potentially having an impact on national security interests. This does not mean that security was never a subject of heated discussions at the international economic order. On the contrary, much of the Cold War period brims full of such instances at political fora. Nevertheless, such discussions remained outside any judicial scrutiny. More recently, though, security considerations came back to the fore, calling for revisiting the concept, scope, and limits of national security exceptions.

The concept of national security has evolved to address a range of threats, including non-state actors and non-military and non-human threats, such as economic crises, cybersecurity, terrorism, infectious disease, and climate change.[7] In particular, some states are vigorously expanding the notion of

[3] M Steinitz, 'Foreign Direct Investment by State-Controlled Entities at a Crossroad of Economic History: Conference Report of the Rapporteur', in KP Sauvant et al. (eds), *Sovereign Investment: Concerns and Policy Reactions* (Oxford, OUP, 2012) 539.

[4] See chs 4 and 8, in this volume. See also LC Backer, 'Sovereign Investing in Times of Crisis: Global Regulation of Sovereign Wealth Funds, State-Owned Enterprises, and the Chinese Experience' (2010) 19 *Transnational Law & Contemporary Problems* 3, 106.

[5] GR Elgueta and B Mauro, 'The Paradoxical Relationship between 'Foreign Direct Investment Screening' and International Investment Law: What Role for Investor-State Arbitration?' (2018) Kluwer Arbitration Blog arbitrationblog.kluwerarbitration.com/2020/04/30/the-paradoxical-relationship-between-foreign-direct-investment-screening-and-international-investment-law-what-role-for-investor-state-arbitration/ (accessed 6 October 2021).

[6] See M Sornarajah, *The International Law of Foreign Investment*, 4th edn (Cambridge, Cambridge University Press, 2018) 536.

[7] JB Heath, 'The New National Security Challenge to the Economic Order' (2019) 129 *Yale Law Journal* 1020, 1024.

national security to include economic security, protection of critical infrastructure, communications assets, advanced technology, and data.[8]

The concept of national security, arguably, cannot be viewed in the abstract. Rather, the well-established rationale of security exceptions to preserve countries' freedom of action in areas relating to national defence and security has to be viewed within the confines that substantive obligations in international economic agreements impose. It involves a balancing exercise that puts obligations of non-discrimination, due process, predictability, and transparency at the other end of the spectrum.

Many modern free trade agreements (FTAs) contain not only rules with respect to trade, but also rules related to investment.[9] Global value chains have also reinforced the organic links between trade and investment.[10] Both regimes limit governmental measures that are adopted in the public interest but also affect commercial entities, and in this respect, perform common functions.[11] Furthermore, as a basic principle, exception clauses under all international economic agreements are to be interpreted according to the customary rules of treaty interpretation enshrined in the Vienna Convention on the Law of Treaties (VCLT), no matter what the substance of the individual treaty is.[12]

Consequently, in light of the general intent by the international community to address global problems on a multilateral basis, this chapter argues for a coherent approach to the review of security exceptions under international trade and investment law. First, it sketches the form and structure of security exceptions under both regimes. Second, it discusses the most important issues arising from the adjudication of national security disputes and the choice of the standard of review. Third, it explores the trends in the interpretation of security exceptions in the World Trade Organization (WTO) and investment law and their implications for sovereign investors. This chapter concludes that the clarification of the scope of the security exceptions clauses and their coherent application by

[8] See, for instance, European Commission, 'Shared Vision, Common Action: A Stronger Europe – A Global Strategy for the European Union's Foreign and Security Policy', (2016) eeas.europa.eu/archives/docs/top_stories/pdf/eugs_review_web.pdf (accessed 6 October 2021); or National Security Strategy of the United States of America (2017) trumpwhitehouse.archives.gov/wp-content/uploads/2017/12/NSS-Final-12-18-2017–0905.pdf (accessed 6 October 2021); and the Interim National Security Strategic Guidance published by the Biden administration in March 2021 www.whitehouse.gov/wp-content/uploads/2021/03/NSC-1v2.pdf (accessed 20 February 2022). See also ch 7, in this volume.

[9] J Ma, 'International Investment and National Security Review' (2019) 52(4) Vanderbilt Journal of Transnational Law 899, 927.

[10] S Cho and J Kurtz, 'Convergence and Divergence in International Economic Law and Politics' (2018) 29 *European Journal of International Law* 169, 181.

[11] AD Mitchell and C Henckels, 'Variations on a Theme: Comparing the Concept of 'Necessity' in International Investment Law and WTO Law' (2013) 14(1) *Chicago Journal of International Law* 93, 95.

[12] D Eisenhut, 'Sovereignty, National Security and International Treaty Law The Standard of Review of International Courts and Tribunals with Regard to 'Security Exceptions'' (2010) 48(4) *Archiv des Völkerrechts* 431, 458.

international adjudicators under both regimes could help tame the unleashed opportunistic forces by catalysing domestic legal and policy developments that would ensure a certain level of self-restraint and scrutiny in the application of protectionist measures. In particular, it could promote trade and investment liberalisation while preventing sovereign investments from becoming political battlefields and means of circumventing diplomacy.

## II. NATIONAL SECURITY EXCEPTIONS IN WTO AND INVESTMENT LAW

To date, much of the conversation has been refracted through a series of legal rules that might define the relationships between international economic law and security. Within the trade regime, for example, the relationship between trade and national security is governed primarily by Article XXI General Agreement on Tariffs and Trade 1994 (GATT), Article XIV$^{bis}$ General Agreement on Trade in Services (GATS), and Article 73 Agreement on Trade-Related Aspects of Intellectual Property Rights (TRIPs Agreement). Together with general exceptions under respective agreements (such as Article XX GATT), they embody potential getaways for states wishing to protect non-trade legitimate policy goals.

Article XXI GATT entails a broad carve-out, as it states that 'nothing in this Agreement' shall be construed to prevent WTO Members from taking measures 'which it considers necessary' as defined under this provision. All the WTO law provisions relating to national security essentially adopt the same language, irrespective of structural differences in their subject matter and application to goods, services, and intellectual property rights, respectively. Several FTAs also echo the wording and structure of Article XXI GATT.[13]

Furthermore, security is a term found in bilateral investment treaties (BITs) and investment chapters of FTAs (together – international investment agreements or IIAs). It is more often than not used to denote the obligation of the host state to protect the investor and its investment from adverse effects. Such clauses are typically encapsulated under the overarching term 'full protection and security' to physically protect from infringements by state organs[14] or private actors.[15]

[13] See, for instance, Art 19 Singapore – Australia FTA (2003) www.dfat.govau/trade/negotiations/safta/chapter_7.pdf (accessed 6 October 2021); or Art 17.13 RCEP (2020) www.dfat.govau/sites/default/files/rcep-chapter-17.pdf (accessed 6 October 2021).

[14] *Asian Agricultural Products v Sri Lanka*, ICSID Case No ARB/87/3 Award (27 June 1990) paras 45–53, 78 www.italaw.com/sites/default/files/case-documents/ita1034.pdf (accessed 6 October 2021).

[15] *Wena Hotels Ltd. v Arab Republic of Egypt*, ICSID Case No ARB/98/4 Award (8 December 2000) para 84 www.italaw.com/sites/default/files/case-documents/ita0902.pdf (accessed 6 October 2021).

As things stand, the text of Article XXI GATT relating to security exceptions that can be invoked to restrict trade in goods is among the most elaborate to date. This is not always the case in international investment law. Traditionally, BITs did not contain general or security exceptions of the kind prescribed in Articles XX and XXI GATT.[16] Yet, as a matter of newer treaty practice, security exceptions in the IIAs have been promulgated in a binary manner: either IIAs (notably concluded by the United States (US)) include a broad, undefined carve-out vis-à-vis any treaty obligations if a state's essential security interest is at stake[17] or IIAs incorporate a more elaborated exceptions clause, often by way of cross-references to WTO law or by including provisions modelled on WTO law, thereby tying the two regimes together and making commonality of interpretation inevitable. Yet, in other agreements we also witness parties' willingness to add as much guidance as possible to the arbitrator, combining wording from WTO law and other jurisdictions such as the EU.[18]

Having said this, in both cases, even if the drafters want to be more precise and circumscribe parties' discretion to act unilaterally, they lack the necessary information to draft a complete contract for all potential future emergencies. Granting host states the sufficient – and sometimes excessive – scope for discretion to react to external or internal economic or political shocks and crises without compensating foreign investors shifts more risk to the investor but can be essential for upholding the implementation and efficiency of the agreement in the long term.[19]

In light of this, three forms of security exceptions under international economic agreements can be identified: exceptions allowing a state to take security measures as 'it considers necessary' subject to good faith scrutiny (WTO-style exceptions);[20] exceptions subject to the full scrutiny of the

[16] L Knight and T Voon, 'The Evolution of National Security at the Interface between Domestic and International Investment Law and Policy: The Role of China' (2020) 21(1) *Journal of World Investment & Trade* 104, 108.

[17] For instance, Art 32.2 USMCA provides that nothing in the agreement precludes a party from applying measures it considers necessary for the fulfilment of its obligations regarding the maintenance or restoration of international peace or security, or the protection of its own essential security interests: USMCA (2020) ustr.gov/trade-agreements/free-trade-agreements/united-states-mexico-canada-agreement/agreement-between (accessed 8 October 2021).

[18] See Art 12 of Colombia-China BIT 2008: '1. Nothing contained in this Agreement shall be construed so as to prevent a Party from adopting or maintaining measures intended to preserve public order including measures to protect the essential security interests of the State, provided that such measures: a) are only applied where a genuine and sufficiently serious threat is posed to one of the fundamental interests of society; b) are not applied in a manner constituting arbitrary discrimination; c) do not constitute a disguised restriction on investment; d) are proportional to the objective they seek to achieve; e) are necessary and are applied and maintained only while necessary; and f) are applied in a transparent manner and in accordance with the respective national legislation. For greater clarity, nothing under this paragraph shall be construed to limit the review by an arbitral tribunal of a matter when such exception is invoked.'

[19] A van Aaken, 'International Investment Law Between Commitment and Flexibility: A Contract Theory Analysis' (2009) 12(2) *Journal of International Economic Law* 507, 509, 525–526.

[20] See, for instance, Art 17.13 RCEP (2020) www.dfat.govau/sites/default/files/rcep-chapter-17.pdf (accessed 6 October 2021).

adjudicator;[21] and exceptions that expressly exclude any security measures from judicial review (self-judging).[22] Within the first two groups, the wording of the different provisions under trade and investment agreements is virtually uniform allowing adjudicators to deduce a common standard of scrutiny for the two sorts of exceptions under international trade and investment law.[23] The third group of security exceptions used in an array of BITs appears to push any security measure completely outside the purview of arbitral review even with regard to the question of whether it was adopted in good faith.[24] To date, no tribunal has been precluded from the review of the dispute because of the explicit, self-judging language of security exceptions. This might suggest that if the parties are clear about their intention to prevent adjudication of security measures, they are reluctant to invoke security exceptions during the proceedings.

## III. ADJUDICATION OF NATIONAL SECURITY DISPUTES

When seized with the issue, the International Court of Justice (ICJ), WTO panels, and investment tribunals have accepted jurisdiction in disputes under economic agreements in order to determine whether questions of national security were at stake and whether adopting the measures that deviated from the state's international legal commitments in question was justified or not. *Djibouti v France* is notable particularly for being the first case[25] in which the ICJ has been called upon to review a self-judging clause under Article 2(c) Mutual Assistance Convention stating that the assistance in criminal proceedings 'may be refused [...] if the requested State considers that the execution of the request is likely to prejudice its sovereignty, its security, its ordre public or other of its essential interests'.[26] Notwithstanding the 'State considers' wording,[27] the ICJ has reviewed the actions of France which confirms that a

[21] See, for instance, Art XI US – Argentina BIT allowing for the measures that are necessary (1991) investmentpolicy.unctad.org/international-investment-agreements/treaties/bit/162/argentina---united-states-of-america-bit-1991- (accessed 6 October 2021).

[22] See, eg, the US – Republic of Korea FTA specified in footnote 2 to Art 23.2 that 'For greater certainty, if a Party invokes Article 23.2 [Security Exceptions] in an arbitral proceeding initiated under Chapter Eleven (Investment) or Chapter Twenty–Two (Institutional Provisions and Dispute Settlement), the tribunal or panel hearing the matter shall find that the exception applies': US – Republic of Korea FTA (2007) ustr.gov/trade-agreements/free-trade-agreements/korus-fta/final-text (accessed 6 October 2021).

[23] See Eisenhut (n 12) 457.

[24] P Ranjan, 'Non-Precluded Measures in Indian International Investment Agreements and India's Regulatory Power as a Host Nation' (2012) 2 *Asian Journal of International Law* 21, 42.

[25] R Briese and S Schill, 'Djibouti v France: Self-Judging Clauses before the International Court of Justice' (2009) 10(1) *Melbourne Journal of International Law* 308.

[26] Convention on Mutual Assistance in Criminal Matters between the Djiboutian Government and the French Government (1986).

[27] *Case Concerning Certain Questions on Mutual Assistance in Criminal Matters (Djibouti v France)* Judgment (4 June 2008) ICJ Reports para 148 www.icj-cij.org/public/files/case-related/136/136-20080604-JUD-01-00-EN.pdf (accessed 6 October 2021).

self-judging language is not sufficient to grant full discretion to states invoking the exception.

On a couple of instances, the ICJ had to decide on the application of security exceptions that did not use self-judging language. In *Nicaragua v United States*, the ICJ also rejected the absolute self-judging nature of security exception under the treaty between the US and Nicaragua[28] stating that it 'does not restrict [the Court's] jurisdiction in the present case, but is confined to affording the Parties a possible defence on the merits to be used should the occasion arise'.[29] In *Oil Platforms*[30] and *Iran v United States*,[31] the ICJ commented on an identical provision found in the treaty between the US and Iran allowing for the measures 'necessary to protect [State's] essential security interests'. In *Oil Platforms*, the ICJ, following the precedent of its earlier Nicaragua judgment, asserted its jurisdiction on measures taken for security reasons.[32] Likewise, in *Iran v United States*, the ICJ stated that the security exception analysis might raise the question of the existence of 'essential security interests', as well as the reasonableness and necessity of the measures which can be conducted only at the merits stage.[33]

In 2019, the WTO Panel in *Russia – Traffic in Transit* made the first attempt to answer certain questions related to the interpretation of Article XXI(b) GATT using 'it considers necessary' language. Similar to the ICJ practice, it rejected Russia's argument supported by the US that the security exception clause is totally self-judging, or non-justiciable.[34] The Panel asserted that it has a significant role to play in reviewing security measures that affect international trade and proposed a flexible and politically sensitive framework for adjudicating security matters. It highlighted that it had 'inherent jurisdiction'

[28] *Military and Paramilitary Activities in and against Nicaragua (Nicaragua v United States of America)* Judgment (26 November 1984) ICJ Reports para 222 www.icj-cij.org/public/files/case-related/70/070-19860627-JUD-01-00-EN.pdf (accessed 6 October 2021).

[29] Treaty of Friendship, Commerce and Navigation between the United States of America and Nicaragua (1956) treaties.un.org/doc/Publication/UNTS/Volume%20367/v367.pdf (accessed 6 October 2021).

[30] *Oil Platforms (Islamic Republic of Iran v United States of America)* Judgment (12 December 1996) ICJ Reports para 11 www.icj-cij.org/public/files/case-related/90/090-19961212-JUD-01-00-EN.pdf (accessed 6 October 2021).

[31] *Alleged Violations of the 1955 Treaty of Amity, Economic Relations, and Consular Rights (Islamic Republic of Iran v United States of America)* Judgment (3 February 2021) ICJ Reports para. 98 www.icj-cij.org/public/files/case-related/175/175-20210203-JUD-01-00-EN.pdf (accessed 6 October 2021).

[32] *Oil Platforms (Islamic Republic of Iran v United States of America)* Judgment (12 December 1996) ICJ Reports para 21 www.icj-cij.org/public/files/case-related/90/090-19961212-JUD-01-00-EN.pdf (accessed 6 October 2021).

[33] *Alleged Violations of the 1955 Treaty of Amity, Economic Relations, and Consular Rights (Islamic Republic of Iran v United States of America)* Judgment (3 February 2021) ICJ Reports para 112 www.icj-cij.org/public/files/case-related/175/175-20210203-JUD-01-00-EN.pdf (accessed 6 October 2021).

[34] Panel Report, *Russia: Measures Concerning Traffic in Transit* (5 April 2019) WT/DS512/R para 7.102.

over the dispute as a result of its 'adjudicative function',[35] in particular, since the Dispute Settlement Understanding (DSU) contains no special or additional rules for Article XXI disputes. The text of security exceptions does not call directly for an a priori denial of competence to a WTO panel regarding cases involving the application of exceptions. In light of this, once a panel is established, it has the jurisdiction to consider a complaint and to address all the legal issues relating to that dispute, even when one party to the dispute invokes security exceptions. The Panel also stated that the existence of the circumstances enumerated in the subparagraphs of Article XXI(b) was subject to an objective determination.[36] The approach adopted in *Russia – Traffic in Transit* was followed by the Panel in *Saudi Arabia – IPRs*.[37]

Investment tribunals also reject the approach that a state's invocation of national security ipso facto deprives any adjudicator of jurisdiction and generally admit at least some review of security exceptions.[38] In several cases arising from the claims against Argentina following its response to the economic crisis in 2001–2002 (Argentinean cases),[39] Argentina invoked Article XI US – Argentina BIT providing the security exception for the measures 'necessary for … the protection of [Argentina's] essential security interests'.[40] Comparing Article XI US – Argentina BIT with differently worded provisions such as Article XXI GATT, the CMS Tribunal highlighted that when states intended to preserve a right to unilaterally determine the legitimacy of security measures, they did so expressly.[41] Following the same line, in *Continental Casualty v Argentina*, the Tribunal underscored that 'caution must be exercised in allowing a party unilaterally to escape from its treaty obligations in the absence of clear textual or contextual indications'.[42] Accordingly,

> '[t]his is especially so if the party invoking the allegedly self-judging nature of the exemption can thereby remove the issue, and hence the claim of a treaty breach by the

[35] ibid, para 7.53.

[36] ibid, para 7.101.

[37] WTO Panel Report, *Saudi Arabia – Measures Concerning the Protection of Intellectual Property Rights* (16 June 2020) WT/DS567/R.

[38] D Desierto, 'Protean 'National Security' in Global Trade Wars, Investment Walls, and Regulatory Controls: Can 'National Security' Ever Be Unreviewable in International Economic Law?' (*Blog of the European Journal of International Law*, 2 April 2018) www.ejiltalk.org/national-security-defenses-in-trade-wars-and-investment-walls-us-v-china-and-eu-v-us/ (accessed 7 October 2021).

[39] See, eg, *Sempra Energy International v Argentina*, ICSID Case No ARB/02/16, Award (18 September 2007) www.italaw.com/sites/default/files/case-documents/ita0770.pdf (accessed 6 October 2021); or *Enron Corporation v Argentina*, ICSID Case No ARB/01/3, Award (22 May 2007) www.italaw.com/sites/default/files/case-documents/ita0293.pdf (accessed 6 October 2021).

[40] Art XI US – Argentina BIT (1991) investmentpolicy.unctad.org/international-investment-agreements/treaties/bit/162/argentina---united-states-of-america-bit-1991- (accessed 6 October 2021).

[41] *CMS Gas Transmission Co. v Republic of Argentina*, ICSID Case No ARB/01/8 Award (12 May 2005) paras 370–373 www.italaw.com/sites/default/files/case-documents/ita0184.pdf (accessed 6 October 2021).

[42] *Continental Casualty Co. v Argentine Republic*, ICSID Case No ARB/03/9, Award (5 September 2008) para 187 ita.law.uvic.ca/docu ments/ContinentalCasualtyAward.pdf (accessed 6 October 2021).

> investor against the host State, from arbitral review. This would conflict in principle with the agreement of the parties to have disputes under the BIT settled compulsorily by arbitration'.[43]

In more recent cases, *Deutsche Telekom v India*[44] and *CC/Devas v India*,[45] the Tribunals followed the approach of Argentinean cases while interpreting security exception clauses under the Germany – India BIT and Mauritius – India BIT. Both BITs use the language of security exception compatible with Article XI US – Argentina BIT and allow for the measure 'to the extent necessary for'[46] or 'which is directed to' the protection of either party's essential security interests.[47] In *Deutsche Telekom v India*, the Tribunal held that Article 12 Germany – India BIT is not self-judging.[48] Likewise, in *CC/Devas v India*, the Tribunal stated that 'unless a treaty contains specific wording granting full discretion to the State to determine what it considers necessary for the protection of its security interests, national security clauses are not self-judging'.[49]

It is not uncommon for exception clauses in other regimes to incorporate a less stringent nexus requirement permitting a state to take action that 'it considers' or 'it determines to be necessary' rather than that is 'necessary'. Similar to Article XXI(b) GATT, Article 346(1)(b) Treaty on the Functioning of the European Union (TFEU) allows any EU Member State 'to take such measures as it considers necessary for the protection of the essential interests of its security which are connected with the production or trade in arms, munitions and war material'.[50] In this respect, in *Commission v Finland*, the Court of Justice of the European Union (CJEU) noted that although the exception refers to measures which a Member State may 'consider necessary' for the protection of the essential interests of its security, it cannot, however, be read in such a way as to confer on EU Member States a power to depart from the provisions of the agreement based on no more than reliance on those interests. Rather, the Member State must show the necessity of such derogation for the protection of its essential

[43] ibid.

[44] *Deutsche Telekom AG v Republic of India*, PCA Case No 2014–10, Interim Award (13 December 2017) www.italaw.com/sites/default/files/case-documents/italaw10496.pdf (accessed 6 October 2021).

[45] *CC/Devas (Mauritius) Ltd v Republic of India*, PCA Case No 2013–09, Award on Jurisdiction and Merits (25 July 2016) www.italaw.com/sites/default/files/case-documents/italaw9750.pdf (accessed 6 October 2021).

[46] Art 12 Germany – India BIT (1995) investmentpolicy.unctad.org/international-investment-agreements/treaty-files/1340/download (accessed 6 October 2021).

[47] Art 11 Mauritius – India BIT (1998) investmentpolicy.unctad.org/international-investment-agreements/treaty-files/1577/download (accessed 6 October 2021).

[48] *Deutsche Telekom AG v Republic of India*, PCA Case No 2014–10, Interim Award (13 December 2017) paras 231, 238 www.italaw.com/sites/default/files/case-documents/italaw10496.pdf (accessed 6 October 2021).

[49] *CC/Devas (Mauritius) Ltd v Republic of India*, PCA Case No 2013–09, Award on Jurisdiction and Merits (25 July 2016) para 219 www.italaw.com/sites/default/files/case-documents/italaw9750.pdf (accessed 6 October 2021).

[50] Consolidated Versions of the Treaty on European Union and the Treaty on the Functioning of the European Union [2016] OJ C202/1.

security interests.[51] In *Schiebel Aircraft*, the CJEU relied on the established case law concerning derogations from fundamental freedoms, according to which Article 346 TFEU, just like any other exception under EU law, must be narrowly construed.[52] However, the EU is a sui generis legal order whereby the *telos* of the EU Treaties calls for a level of judicial scrutiny for such claims that is generally higher than in other areas of international law.

Exception clauses in certain BITs allow parties to take measures for the protection of *its* essential security interests without however calling for the application of a necessity test.[53] In *Naumchenko and others v India*, the arbitral tribunal had to review an investor claim brought about by the cancellation of Letters of Intent for the issuance of 2G licences in five telecommunications circles in India. In reviewing the scope of the BITs India concluded with Russia and Cyprus, whereby despite their differences both agreements refer to the protection of safeguarding its essential security interests,[54] the tribunal found that the measures in question called for a marginal review of the discretion of India to invoke the essential security clause.

Self-judging wording of the essential security exception is rare but does occur. BITs of this category appear to preclude even a good faith review of the measure at issue. For example, certain BITs concluded by the US foresee the non-justiciability of those measures for which either party invokes the security exception.[55] A similar approach, for all practical purposes, is followed in the India-Singapore Comprehensive Economic Cooperation Agreement, whereby the parties went a step further in that they underscored the self-judging and non-justiciable character of the essential security exception.[56]

Thus, the mere invocation of essential security concerns as a justification for a given measure that potentially affects an investment would suffice for the arbitral tribunal to decline jurisdiction and declare the underlying investment claim non-admissible.[57] Quite paradoxically at first blush, this type of absolute

[51] Case C-284/05 *Commission* v *Finland* [2009] ECR I-11705 para 47.

[52] Case C-474/12 *Schiebel Aircraft GmbH v Bundesminister für Wirtschaft, Familie und Jugend* [2014] EU:C:2014:2139 para 33.

[53] See Art 12.2 Russia – Cyprus BIT (2002).

[54] ibid; and Art 3.3 Russia – India BIT (1994).

[55] See, for instance, Art 22.2 of US-Peru Trade Promotion Agreement (2006) and accompanying footnote 2; and Art 22.2 of US-Colombia Trade Promotion Agreement (2006) and accompanying footnote 2. Although around the same time period, the US included self-judging essential security exceptions in various BITs such as the ones concluded with Bahrain or Oman, the BIT with Peru heralded a new era for the US BIT model, which attempts to explicitly anticipate and prevent any judical second-guessing of a party's own determination regarding essential security. This approach was replicated in the US BITs with Panama and Korea. For the political background in introducing additional clarity through a clarifying footnote to enhance the self-judging character of the provision, see J Mendenhall, 'The Evolution of the Essential Security Exception in U.S. Trade and Investment Agreements', in K Sauvant, L Sachs and WPF Schmit Jongbloed (eds), *Sovereign Investment: Concerns and Policy Reactions* (Oxford, Oxford University Press, 2012) 310, 336ff.

[56] See Art 6.12.1-4 of the India-Singapore CECA (2005).

[57] See J Alvarez, 'Sovereign Concerns and the International Investment Regime', in Sauvant et al (n 55) 273.

clarity of the essential security exception may indeed lead parties to a BIT to exhibit high levels of self-restraint in invoking the exception, taking into account that it opens a dangerous Pandora's box; inconsiderate invocation of the security defence would undermine the very existence of that investment agreement and the rule of law rationale that it purportedly served. This would be because it would make the investors worse off compared to the protection they enjoyed before the BIT-related landscape started expanding, whereby their home countries could potentially protect their investors active abroad by pursuing a denial of justice claim or a violation of customary law.

Such an analysis is not a mere theoretical exercise. The ICSID tribunal in the case of *Seda and others v Republic of Colombia*[58] will soon have the opportunity to review the scope, contours and limits of the security exception enshrined in Article 22.2 of the US-Colombia TPA, as Colombia invoked it in these proceedings. The case relates to the alleged expropriation without compensation of a large real estate development project. Interestingly, Colombia did not invoke the security defence in its first respondent submission but only in its rejoinder.[59] The respondent claims that the invocation of the security exception laid down in Article 22.2 of the TPA is necessary because the laws at stake are the very expression of Colombia's effort to combat organised crime, drug trafficking and money laundering. Reminding the self-judging character of the wording of Article 22.2, Colombia therefore asked the tribunal to recognise that it has no jurisdiction and dismiss the case – or in the alternative accept the well-founded basis of the defence.[60] The respondent subsequently challenged the belated invocation of the defence on good faith grounds but the tribunal decided to accept as admissible of the jurisdictional objection brought forward by Colombia.[61]

To sum up, the case law analysed earlier suggests that the discussion around national security disputes involving WTO-style exceptions or exceptions that refer to the necessity as such has shifted from questioning the jurisdiction of the judicial body and justiciability of national security matters to the applicable standard of review.[62] Such a shift does not necessarily indicate the triumph of objective determination over the subjective appreciation of states in national security matters. Still, it confirms that the invocation of security exceptions shall not per se preclude the jurisdiction of an adjudicator and that the interpretation of exceptions clauses irrespective of the presence of 'it considers' language has become a matter of the standard of review. As to the exceptions that expressly

[58] ICSID Case No ARB/19/6 (pending).

[59] See Colombia's rejoinder, available at: /www.italaw.com/sites/default/files/case-documents/italaw16514.pdf.

[60] ibid, para 23.

[61] See Procedural Order No 9 of 28 March 2022, para 11.

[62] G-D Balan, 'On Fissionable Cows and the Limits to the WTO Security Exceptions' (2019) 14(1) *Global Trade and Customs Journal* 2, 10.

exclude the measures adopted in the interests of national security from any judicial review, the existing practice suggests that in any event the parties' intention to deliberately limit the intensity of any judicial review or overall exclude such review under international economic agreements cannot be presumed a priori but shall be determined based on the language used in each specific provision.

## IV. CHOICE OF STANDARD OF REVIEW

In the international context, the standard of review determines the extent of discretionary powers enjoyed by national authorities in making certain decisions and affects the allocation of power between national and international levels. While the legal doctrine concerning standards of review arises from common law, the concept of margin of appreciation is rooted in the European legal tradition. In the international context, the margin of appreciation concept can be defined as the breadth of deference that the adjudicator is willing to grant to the decisions of national decision-makers and is normally associated with international human rights law.[63] The two concepts, the standard of review and margin of appreciation, may be regarded as referring to the same thing, although in reverse fashion (ie a wide margin of appreciation equals a low standard of review, and vice versa), and may be used by international adjudicators while interpreting security exceptions.

For WTO disputes, the standard of review becomes an issue whenever a panel or the Appellate Body reviews the measure of a WTO Member's compliance with WTO obligations according to Article 11 DSU. The standard of review determines the depth and intensity with which the WTO judicial organ reviews the national measure of the WTO Member. Consequently, this defines the margin of discretion and vertical power allocation enjoyed by the WTO Members. However, on its face, Article 11 does not address when adjudicators should review a matter de novo or when a more deferential attitude is warranted.[64]

According to WTO practice to date, the pendulum of security exceptions appears to be tilting closer to deference. The Panel rulings in *Russia – Traffic in Transit* and *Saudi Arabia – IPRs* confirmed that WTO-style security exceptions deal with different issues and some of them are self-judging. The consensus emerging from these rulings is that the appropriate standard of review to apply to self-judging parts of security exceptions is that of good faith.[65] WTO Members

[63] L Gruszczynski and W Werner, 'Introduction', in L Gruszczynski and W Werner (eds), *Deference in International Courts and Tribunals* (Oxford, OUP, 2014) 4.

[64] T-F Chen, 'To Judge the 'Self-Judging' Security Exception Under the GATT 1994 – a Systematic Approach' (2017) 12(2) *Asian Journal of WTO and International Health Law and Policy* 311, 328.

[65] See section V.B. below.

in their submissions in *Russia – Traffic in Transit* have also acknowledged that security exceptions are different from other non-deferential provisions under WTO Agreements, and thus a certain degree of deference shall be granted to the state invoking the exceptions. In its third-party submission, for example, Singapore considers that the language 'it considers necessary' in Article XXI(b) indicates that the invoking Member is allowed to determine 'with a significant degree of subjectivity' what action it considers necessary to protect its essential security interests.[66]

The concept of standard of review is arguably far less developed and consistent in international investment law compared to other areas of public international law.[67] States have a right to regulate commercial and business activities within their territory which stems from the principle of state sovereignty.[68] Especially in times of economic crisis, investment tribunals are often called upon to measure the regulatory powers of host states against the guarantees conferred by IIAs on foreign investors. In any such balancing process, tribunals are expected to give due weight to the sovereign functions of a state due to the hybrid (public/private) nature of investment arbitration, in which the principle of equality of the parties shall be mitigated by the presence of a sovereign entity.[69]

In particular, based on the police power doctrine, a measure that falls within the state's police power resulting in loss of property does not constitute indirect expropriation and can justify the non-payment of compensation to a foreign investor.[70] According to Black's Law Dictionary, the state's police power is the 'power of the State to place restraints on the personal freedom and property rights of persons for the protection of the public safety, health, and morals or the promotion of the public convenience and general prosperity'.[71] It is too early to say whether there exists enough evidence of an emerging trend towards the affirmation of the police power doctrine by international tribunals.[72] Yet, even in the cases where tribunals relied on the police power doctrine, they treated it as limited in scope and effect and subject to certain conditions.[73] To illustrate,

[66] WTO, *Russia: Measures Concerning Traffic in Transit* (5 April 2019) WT/DS512/R para 7.48.

[67] V Vadi, 'Standards of review in investment treaty arbitration', in V Vadi (ed), *Proportionality, Reasonableness and Standards of Review in International Investment Law and Arbitration* (Cheltenham, Edward Elgar Publishing, 2018) 225.

[68] BF Mostafa, 'The Sole Effects Doctrine, Police Powers and Indirect Expropriation under International Law' (2008) 15 *Australian International Law Journal* 267, 269.

[69] G Zarra, 'Right to Regulate, Margin of Appreciation and Proportionality: Current Status in Investment Arbitration in Light of Philip Morris v Uruguay' (2017) 14 *Brazilian Journal of International Law* 95, 112.

[70] C Titi, 'Police Powers Doctrine and International Investment Law', in F Fontanelli, A Gattini and A Tanzi (eds) *General Principles of Law and International Investment Arbitration* (Leiden, Brill, 2018).

[71] BA Garner, *Black's Law Dictionary*, 6th edn (Eagan, West Publishing Co. 1990).

[72] Zarra (n 69) 104.

[73] G Born, D Morris and S Forrest, ''A Margin of Appreciation': Appreciating Its Irrelevance in International Law' (2020) 61(1) *Harvard International Law Journal* 65, 126.

tribunals independently assessed whether the state was actually motivated by the asserted public policy in adopting the challenged regulatory measure and whether the measure was reasonable and/or proportionate to the objective pursued.

The question of whether treaty-based exceptions, including security exceptions, substitute or supplement existing police power doctrine was discussed in *Bear Creek Mining Corporation v Republic of Peru*.[74] Certain scholars even see that treaty-based exceptions codify the police power doctrine. This proposal, however, is not widely accepted given that if treaty-based exceptions could effectively substitute for the doctrine, the question arises why they were needed in the first place, particularly in treaties that additionally define and limit the notion of indirect expropriation. Moreover, treaty-based exceptions, unlike the police power doctrine, could apply to a wider array of obligations that are not normally considered outside the police power context, such as most favoured nation (MFN) provisions.[75]

Nevertheless, without mentioning the police power doctrine, tribunals still allowed for a certain level of deference to the states invoking security exceptions even when exceptions clauses used no self-judging language and referred to the necessity as such. To illustrate, the Tribunal in *Continental Casualty v Argentina*, agreed that Argentina was entitled to what the Tribunal termed a 'significant margin of appreciation' under Article XI US – Argentina BIT stating that '[an] objective assessment must contain a significant margin of appreciation for the State applying the particular measure: a time of grave crisis is not the time for nice judgments, particularly when examined by others with the disadvantage of hindsight'.[76] The Tribunal reasoned that 'its own security interests' under Article XI implied that 'a margin of appreciation must be afforded to the Party that claims 'in good faith' that the interests addressed by the measure are essential security interests or that its public order is at stake'.[77] Despite referring to a margin of appreciation, and stating that it had no mandate to 'censure Argentina's sovereign choices as an independent State', the Tribunal went on to apply various objective standards of review, including a less-restrictive means analysis, to determine whether Argentina's plea of necessity under Article XI was well-founded.

In *CC/Devas v India*, the Tribunal also acknowledged that it might not sit in judgment on national security matters as on any other factual dispute

[74] *Bear Creek Mining Corporation v Republic of Peru*, ICSID Case No ARB/14/21 Award (30 November 2017) paras 473–474 www.italaw.com/sites/default/files/case-documents/italaw9381.pdf (accessed 7 October 2021).

[75] W Alschner and K Hui, 'Missing in Action: General Public Policy Exceptions in Investment Treaties', in L Sachs, L Johnson and J Coleman (eds), *Yearbook on International Law and Policy* (Oxford, OUP, 2018).

[76] *Continental Casualty Co. v Argentine Republic*, ICSID Case No ARB/03/9 Award (5 September 2008) para 181 ita.law.uvic.ca/docu ments/ContinentalCasualtyAward.pdf (accessed 6 October 2021).

[77] ibid.

arising between an investor and a state.[78] Accordingly, an investor challenging a state decision in that respect 'faces a heavy burden of proof, such as bad faith, absence of authority, or application of measures that do not relate to essential security interests'.[79] In *Deutsche Telekom v India*, the Tribunal also recognised a margin of deference to the host state's determination of 'essential security interests' and necessity, given the state's proximity to the situation, expertise, and competence.[80] Thus, the Tribunal decided not to review de novo the state's determination nor adopt a standard of necessity requiring the state to prove that the measure was the 'only way' to achieve the stated purpose. According to the Tribunal, 'the deference owed to the State cannot be unlimited, as otherwise unreasonable invocations of Article 12 would render the substantive protections contained in the Treaty wholly nugatory'.[81]

Investment tribunals have not had a chance yet to interpret the security exception that contains the term 'that it considers necessary', what is deemed the textual hallmark of a self-judging clause. The application of a security exception of this kind has radical and far-reaching consequences, especially given that some tribunals characterise security exceptions as limiting the scope of the treaty obligations.[82] In particular, the CMS Annulment Committee put forward the view that where the requirements of the exception are met, the 'substantive obligations under the Treaty do not apply'.[83] This view was also confirmed in *Deutsche Telekom v India*.[84] Further, the *El Paso* Tribunal suggested that measures necessary for the protection of essential security interests 'are not in breach of the relevant BIT'.[85] In other words, following such an approach, the security exception confirms the drafters' intention that the measures that meet the

[78] *CC/Devas (Mauritius) Ltd v Republic of India*, PCA Case No 2013–09 Award on Jurisdiction and Merits (25 July 2016) paras 5–7 www.italaw.com/sites/default/files/case-documents/italaw9750.pdf (accessed 6 October 2021).

[79] ibid, para 245.

[80] *Deutsche Telekom AG v Republic of India*, PCA Case No 2014–10 Interim Award (13 December 2017) para 238 www.italaw.com/sites/default/files/case-documents/italaw10496.pdf (accessed 6 October 2021).

[81] *Deutsche Telekom AG v Republic of India*, PCA Case No 2014–10 Interim Award (13 December 2017) para 238 www.italaw.com/sites/default/files/case-documents/italaw10496.pdf (accessed 6 October 2021).

[82] C Henckels, 'Scope Limitation or Affirmative Defence?: The Purpose and Role of Investment Treaty Exception Clauses', in L Bartels and F Paddeu (eds), *Exceptions in International Law* (Oxford, OUP, 2020) 366.

[83] *CMS Gas Transmission Co. v Republic of Argentina*, ICSID Case No ARB/01/8 Decision of the Ad Hoc Committee on the Application for Annulment of the Argentine Republic (25 September 2007) para 129 www.italaw.com/sites/default/files/case-documents/ita0187.pdf (accessed 6 October 2021).

[84] *Deutsche Telekom AG v Republic of India*, PCA Case No 2014–10 Interim Award (13 December 2017) para 227 www.italaw.com/sites/default/files/case-documents/italaw10496.pdf (accessed 6 October 2021).

[85] *El Paso Energy International Company v The Argentine Republic*, ICSID Case No ARB/03/15 Award (31 October 2011) para 553 www.italaw.com/sites/default/files/case-documents/ita0270.pdf (accessed 7 October 2021).

requirements of the exception will not be captured by the treaty obligations.[86] In this case, if the security exception applies, the investor is deprived of the BIT's protection, including the treaty's full protection and security standard. Thus, the potential danger to the rights of investors posed by security exceptions of this kind is considerable.[87]

Such a view contradicts the approach of other investment tribunals in Argentinean cases, as well as the approach of the WTO panels and the Appellate Body, viewing general exceptions and security exceptions under investment treaties and the WTO Agreements respectively as an affirmative defence that operates to justify measures that are inconsistent with WTO Members' obligations. It implies that a state relying on the exception would accept that it had failed to observe its treaty obligations but would be exempted from the consequences of such a breach by proving that it was protecting the interests permitted by the clause.[88]

Thus, to date, no investment tribunal has set out a coherent framework for determining the appropriate standard of review to apply to disputes involving the exercise of public power by states in the interests of national security,[89] although tribunals have generally referred to the desirability of deference in their decision-making and adopted a more deferential approach to the interpretation of security exceptions even if the clause does not use 'it considers necessary' wording.

## V. TRENDS IN THE INTERPRETATION OF SECURITY EXCEPTIONS IN WTO AND INVESTMENT LAW

### A. The Evolving Concept of National Security

The concept of 'essential security interests' is a key to the interpretation of security exceptions under the WTO Agreements. Irrespective of the view of WTO Members on the scope of their national security, the terms 'essential', 'security', and 'interest' have ordinary meanings. The 'interest' means '[t]he relation of being involved or concerned as regards potential detriment or (esp.) advantage', while 'security' refers to '[t]he condition of being protected from or not exposed to danger'.[90] The definitions of 'essential' include '[t]hat is such in the

[86] Henckels (n 82) 365.

[87] C Schreuer, 'The Protection of Investments in Armed Conflicts', in F Baetens (ed), *Investment Law within International Law: Integrationist Perspectives* (Cambridge, Cambridge University Press, 2013) 18.

[88] Henckels n 82) 366.

[89] C Henckels, 'The Role of the Standard of Review and the Importance of Deference in Investor–State Arbitration', in Gruszczynski and Werner (n 63) 118.

[90] The New *Shorter Oxford English Dictionary*, 4th edn, L Brown (ed) (Clarendon Press, 1993) (excerpts) referred to by the US in the First Written Submission of the United States of America in WTO, *United States: Origin Marking Requirements* (2021) DS597, para 39 ustr.gov/sites/default/files/enforcement/DS/DS597/US.Sub1.fin.pdf (accessed 7 October 2021).

absolute or highest sense' and '[a]ffecting the essence of anything; significant, important'.[91] Therefore, not every interest relates to the security of a nation, nor will every security interest qualify as being 'essential'. The security exception requires a qualified interest in the absence of which restrictions cannot be imposed.

In *Russia – Traffic in Transit*, the Panel regarded 'essential security interests' as referring to 'those interests relating to the quintessential functions of the State, namely, the protection of its territory and its population from external threats, and the maintenance of law and public order internally'.[92] The designation of essential security interests is left, in general, to the WTO Member since '[t]he specific interests that are considered directly relevant to the protection of a State from such external or internal threats will depend on the particular situation and perceptions of the State in question, and can be expected to vary with changing circumstances'.[93] Thus, while military security, for instance, can generally be deemed essential, non-military security can equally be regarded as essential due to new threats and technologies.[94]

Still, the unfettered discretion of the WTO Members to determine their essential security interests is limited by the obligation of good faith. In particular, the obligation of good faith requires that WTO Members not use the security exception as a means to circumvent their obligations under the WTO Agreements. A glaring example of this, according to the Panel in *Russia – Traffic Transit*, would be where a Member sought to release itself from the structure of 'reciprocal and mutually advantageous arrangements' that constitutes the multilateral trading system simply by re-labelling trade interests that it had agreed to protect and promote within the system, as 'essential security interests', falling outside the reach of that system.[95]

The interpretive context provided by other GATT provisions supports this interpretation of 'essential security interests'. General exceptions provision under WTO law accord to WTO Members a degree of autonomy to adopt measures in order to achieve particular non-trade legitimate objectives during peacetime. Such general exceptions also carve out important economic exceptions, such as the measures relating to the conservation of exhaustible natural resources. Thus, given that under WTO law economic exceptions are already covered by other provisions, Article XXI GATT should serve only for distinct purposes.[96]

[91] ibid.

[92] Panel Report, *Russia: Measures Concerning Traffic in Transit* (5 April 2019) WT/DS512/R para 7.130.

[93] ibid, para 7.131.

[94] See European Commission, Interpretative Communication on the Application of Article 296 of the Treaty in the Field of Defence Procurement (SEC(2006) 1554) (SEC(2006) 1555), COM(2006) 779 final, 7 December 2006, 5.

[95] Panel Report, *Russia: Measures Concerning Traffic in Transit* (5 April 2019) WT/DS512/R para 7.133.

[96] W Weiß, 'Interpreting Essential Security Exceptions in WTO Law in View of Economic Security Interests', in W Weiß and C Furculita (eds), *Global Politics and EU Trade Policy: Facing the Challenges to a Multilateral Approach* (Cham, Springer International Publishing, 2020) 270.

BITs are often devoid of a general exceptions provision similar to the one found in Article XX GATT.[97] The initial generations of BITs were focused exclusively on investor rights and at least until the 1990s incorporated no reference to social issues, such as labour and the environment.[98] Since a bifurcated specification of general and security exceptions is often lacking in the investment treaty context, one may argue that the use of the term 'essential security interests' in the investment realm is meant to embrace economic dimensions, in addition to security purposes.[99] Nevertheless, the recent trend towards the generalised inclusion of clauses related to public policy objectives in IIAs and the current evolution towards the inclusion of WTO-style exceptions in these agreements illustrate the changes in the understanding that states have of investment treaties and the exceptions thereunder.

Recent state policy and practice demonstrate that the concept of national security has also grown in the context of both domestic review of foreign investments and international investment law, particularly in response to Chinese industry expansion and Chinese Government policies. In addition to addressing concerns directly related to conventional military-related activities, the notion of 'national security' increasingly encompasses, in the vast majority of states, the protection of domestic industries or sectors considered as vital or strategic; critical infrastructure; and natural resources.[100] Telecommunications, transportation, energy, and the water supply are now frequently incorporated in the list of strategic sectors, sometimes together with education and health services.[101] Furthermore, perceived threats posed by competing ideologies; value systems and geopolitical contestation are increasingly seen as falling under the umbrella of national security in the investment context.[102]

The Argentinean cases have addressed the question of whether Argentina's economic crisis at the beginning of the new millennium amounted to a threat to the state's national security and whether this could be a valid defence against

[97] WJ Moon, 'Essential Security Interests in International Investment Agreements' (2012) 15(2) *Journal of International Economic Law* 481, 492.

[98] A de Mestral and L Vanhonnaeker, 'Exception Clauses in Mega-Regionals (International Investment Protection and Trade Agreements)', in T Rensmann (ed), *Mega-Regional Trade Agreements* (Cham, Springer 2017).

[99] Moon (n 97).

[100] See, eg, Foreign Investment Risk Review Modernization Act of 2018 (2017–2018) Congress.gov. Text – H.R.5841–115th Congress www.congress.gov/bill/115th-congress/house-bill/5841/text (accessed 7 October 2021); or National Security Law of the People's Republic of China (2015) Standing Committee of the National People's Congress (in English) www.chinalawtranslate.com/2015nsl/?lang=en (accessed 7 October 2021).

[101] F Wehrlé and J Pohl, 'Investment Policies Related to National Security: A Survey of Country Practices' (2016) OECD Working Papers on International Investment, No 2016/02, OECD Publishing, Paris, 22 doi-org.tilburguniversity.idm.oclc.org/10.1787/5jlwrrf038nx-en (accessed 7 October 2021).

[102] K Lai, 'National Security and FDI Policy Ambiguity: A Commentary' (2021) *Journal of International Business Policy* doi-org.tilburguniversity.idm.oclc.org/10.1057/s42214-020-00087-1 (accessed 7 October 2021).

investor allegations that Argentina had violated its obligations under the US – Argentina BIT.[103] Nearly all Tribunals reviewing the regulatory measures undertaken by Argentina, while mitigating the effects of such a crisis, agreed that an economic crisis can implicate a state's 'essential security interests' under Article XI US-Argentina BIT even if there is no military dimension to the threat. To illustrate, the CMS Tribunal stated that 'if the concept of essential security interests were to be limited to immediate political and national security concerns, particularly of an international character, and were to exclude other interests, for example, major economic emergencies, it could well result in an unbalanced understanding of article XI'.[104]

However, the Tribunals disagreed concerning the degree of severity of the crisis required to rely on the security exception. Tribunals in *CMS v Argentina*,[105] *Enron v Argentina*,[106] and *Sempra v Argentina*[107] found that the economic crisis, which befell Argentina, was not of a sufficient magnitude to threaten Argentina's essential interests. In particular, the CMS Tribunal stated that 'the Argentine crisis was severe but did not result in total economic and social collapse'.[108] In contrast, the Tribunal in *LG&E v Argentina* found that the crisis in Argentina was sufficient to imperil an essential interest: '[a]s evidence demonstrates, economic, financial or those interests related to the protection of the State against any danger seriously compromising its internal or external situation, are also considered essential interests'.[109] It found that 'from 1 December 2001 until 26 April 2003, Argentina was in a period of crisis during which it was necessary to enact measures to maintain public order and protect its essential security interests'.[110] The *Continental Casualty* Tribunal, without delimiting the period of crisis, concluded that the invocation of the security exception 'does not require that the situation has already generated into one that calls for the suspension of constitutional guarantees and fundamental liberties'.[111]

[103] United Nations Conference on Trade and Development, 'The Protection of National Security in IIAs' (2009) UNCTAD Series on International Investment Policies for Development 8.

[104] *CMS Gas Transmission Co. v Republic of Argentina*, ICSID Case No ARB/01/8 Award (12 May 2005) para 360 www.italaw.com/sites/default/files/case-documents/ita0184.pdf (accessed 6 October 2021).

[105] ibid, paras 344–352.

[106] *Enron Corporation v Argentina*, ICSID Case No ARB/01/3 Award (22 May 2007) paras 324–326 www.italaw.com/sites/default/files/case-documents/ita0293.pdf (accessed 6 October 2021).

[107] *Sempra Energy International v Argentina*, ICSID Case No ARB/02/16 Award (18 September 2007) para 367 www.italaw.com/sites/default/files/case-documents/ita0770.pdf (accessed 6 October 2021).

[108] *CMS Gas Transmission Co. v Republic of Argentina*, ICSID Case No ARB/01/8 Award (12 May 2005) para 355 www.italaw.com/sites/default/files/case-documents/ita0184.pdf (accessed 6 October 2021).

[109] *LG&E Energy Corp., LG&E Capital Corp., and LG&E International, Inc. v Argentine Republic*, ICSID Case No ARB/02/1 Decision on Liability (3 October 2007) para 251 www.italaw.com/sites/default/files/case-documents/ita0460.pdf (accessed on 7 October 2021).

[110] ibid, para 226.

[111] *Continental Casualty Co. v Argentine Republic*, ICSID Case No ARB/03/9, Award (5 September 2008) para 180 ita.law.uvic.ca/docu ments/ContinentalCasualtyAward.pdf (accessed 6 October 2021).

In *CC/Devas v India*, India argued that it instructed the Indian state-owned company Antrix to terminate the agreement for the lease of S-band electromagnetic spectrum on two satellites with the claimant in the dispute, Devas, for reasons linked to the state's 'essential security interests'.[112] The Tribunal confirmed that national security issues shall 'relate to the existential core of a State'[113] and that India's actions fell outside the security exception under the Mauritius – India BIT since they addressed not only military-related but also other concerns. In particular, in the view of the Tribunal, the inclusion of 'other public utility services and for societal needs' and 'the country's strategic needs' or 'strategic requirements' covers a whole range of government activities (such as economic strategies, public health strategies, energy strategies, etc) 'which went far beyond the military or paramilitary sectors or the 'essential security interests' of [India]'.[114] In *Deutsche Telekom v India*, the Tribunal mentioned that the 'essential security interests' required for a successful invocation of security exceptions 'must protect something of higher value than any 'public interest''.[115] Accordingly, no reasonable reading of security exceptions 'could include the other societal needs such as train tracking, disaster management, tele-education, tele-health, and rural communication, without distorting the natural meaning of the term 'essential security interests''.[116]

Thus, in the current state of affairs, WTO adjudicators and investment tribunals prefer to apply a narrow interpretation of 'essential security interests' that generally covers the military and defence sectors while dealing with both WTO-style exceptions and exceptions that refer to the necessity as such.

## B. Good Faith Review

As it transpired from the galleries of cases of international courts and tribunals, the function of good faith does not appear to be that of setting a precise rule of conduct but to serve as an interpretative principle which would be essential in the interpretation and application of the applicable rules, both procedural and substantive.[117] As a doctrine that hovers above the law, good faith may have

[112] *CC/Devas (Mauritius) Ltd v Republic of India*, PCA Case No 2013–09 Award on Jurisdiction and Merits (25 July 2016) paras 5–7 www.italaw.com/sites/default/files/case-documents/italaw9750.pdf (accessed 6 October 2021).

[113] ibid, para 245.

[114] ibid, paras 315–58.

[115] *Deutsche Telekom AG v Republic of India*, PCA Case No 2014–10 Interim Award (13 December 2017) para 236 www.italaw.com/sites/default/files/case-documents/italaw10496.pdf (accessed 6 October 2021).

[116] ibid, para 281.

[117] A Tanzi, 'The Relevance of the Foreign Investor's Good Faith', in A Gattini, A Tanzi and F Fontanelli (eds), *General Principles of Law and International Investment Arbitration* (Leiden, Brill, 2018) 218.

a corrective and harmonising role to play that is essential while dealing with security measures, especially given the inconsistencies that abound in the law as a result of different approaches to the interpretation of security exceptions.

WTO adjudicators have derived from the rule of *pacta sunt servanda* articulated in Article 26 VCLT a presumption that WTO Members have acted in good faith in carrying out their WTO obligations.[118] In *US – Continued Suspension*, the Appellate Body clarified that

> 'the presumption of good faith attaches to the actor, but not to the action itself. Thus, whilst the presumption of good faith concerns the reasons for which a Member acts, such a presumption does not answer the question whether the measure taken by the implementing Member has indeed brought about substantive compliance'.[119]

The Panel in *Russia – Traffic in Transit* recalled that the obligation of good faith is a general principle of law and a principle of general international law that underlies all treaties, as codified in Article 31(1) VCLT.[120] While reviewing the measures that Russia attempted to justify under Article XXI GATT, the Panel found that the obligation of good faith produces two legal hurdles for a state seeking to justify a measure under security exceptions: to articulate the essential security interests sufficiently to prove their veracity and to demonstrate that the security measures are not implausible as protective of these interests.

First, the veracity of whether it's in a Member's 'essential security interests' will be determined on a case-by-case basis given that the further the 'emergency' is removed from armed conflict or other 'hard core' emergency, the greater the level of specificity is required for the articulation of 'essential security interests'. Second, the connection between the protection of 'essential security interests' and the measure at issue is subject to good faith review. The Panel explained that in this case, good faith meant '… that the measures at issue meet a minimum requirement of plausibility in relation to the proffered essential security interests'.[121] Specifically, a panel must determine 'whether the measures are so remote from, or unrelated to, the … emergency that it is implausible that [the respondent] implemented the measures for the protection of its essential security interests arising out of the emergency'.[122] In *Saudi Arabia – IPRs*, for example, the Panel did not find any connection between the non-application of criminal procedures and penalties to the company, which infringed the IP rights of the Qatari broadcaster, and the protection of essential security interests of Saudi Arabia.

[118] T Cottier and J Paul Müller, '*Estoppel*', in *Max Planck Encyclopedia of Public International Law* (Rüdiger Wolfrum edn, Oxford, OUP, 2007) para 1.

[119] Appellate Body Report, *United States-Continued Suspension of Obligations in the EC – Hormones Dispute* (16 October 2008) WT/DS320/AB/R para 315.

[120] Panel Report, *Russia-Measures Concerning Traffic in Transit* (5 April 2019) WT/DS512/R para 7.132.

[121] Panel Report, *Saudi Arabia-Measures Concerning the Protection of Intellectual Property Rights* (16 June 2020) WT/DS567/R para 7.138.

[122] ibid, para 7.135.

Security exceptions under certain IIAs expressly refer to the principle of good faith.[123] In *LG&E v Argentina*, the Tribunal suggested in the context of the non-self-judging clause in Article XI US – Argentina BIT that even if it were to conclude that this clause is self-judging, 'Argentina's determination would be subject to a good faith review anyway, which does not significantly differ from the substantive analysis [the Tribunal] presented'.[124] This statement by the Tribunal seems to suggest that a good faith review would not differ significantly from a substantive review, however, it does not exclude that the Tribunal, in light of the subject matter of the clause, would nevertheless grant Argentina a certain amount of deference. The presence of a self-judging clause, in this view, would merely make explicit and compulsory the granting of a margin of appreciation that would otherwise be a question of judicial self-restraint and deference. This approach, however, does not adequately clarify the precise criteria for ascertaining whether the good faith standard for security measures is met.[125]

Investment tribunals facing the security exceptions using 'it considers necessary' language in the future could follow the approach to the good faith review adopted in *Russia-Traffic in Transit* and *Saudi Arabia – IPRs* that focuses primarily on the subjective perception of the state invoking security exceptions and stresses the connection with the agreement's object and purpose to prevent protectionism. In addition, tribunals could also take into account the equal treatment required by the MFN principle while considering whether more than one state poses a substantially similar threat to the essential security interests of another state, and if so whether or not similar measures have been imposed against all such states. If similar measures have not been imposed, so as to lead to discrimination between states posing a similar threat, this fact would be an indicator of the existence of bad faith.[126] While it can be argued that the considerations of reasonableness or proportionality can also be added to a good faith review allowing for stricter international control on the appropriateness of the means employed to achieve security objectives,[127] such an approach will make it difficult for international adjudicators to avoid second-guessing a state's judgment as to what constitutes its national security interest

[123] To illustrate, Art 12 Netherlands – India BIT allows for prohibitions or restrictions to the extent necessary for the protection of its essential security interests given that they are applied in accordance with the laws of the contracting party, in good faith, and on a non-discriminatory basis. Netherlands – India BIT (1995) (terminated) investmentpolicy.unctad.org/international-investment-agreements/treaty-files/1584/download (accessed 8 October 2021).

[124] *LG&E Energy Corp., LG&E Capital Corp., and LG&E International, Inc. v Argentine Republic*, ICSID Case No ARB/02/1 Decision on Liability (3 October 2007) para 214 www.italaw.com/sites/default/files/case-documents/ita0460.pdf (accessed on 7 October 2021).

[125] S Schill and R Briese, "If the State Considers': Self-Judging Clauses in International Dispute Settlement' (2009) 13(1) *Max Planck Yearbook of United Nations Law Online* 61, 124.

[126] ibid 108.

[127] E Cannizzaro, 'Proportionality and Margin of Appreciation in the Whaling Case: Reconciling Antithetical Doctrines?' (2016) 27(4) *European Journal of International Law* 1061, 1068.

and to respect the intention of the parties drafting the exception to limit judicial intervention.

Ultimately, evidential and procedural controls can be seen primarily as a method of reviewing the good faith behind a security measure.[128] Among others, this implies that a state relying on security exceptions provides the information necessary for an adjudicator to make the findings within its competence. Notably, if the state concerned acting in good faith refuses to disclose such information relying on Article XXI(a) GATT or similarly-drafted provisions under other agreements,[129] the exercise of this legitimate right must not be used against it in the ensuing decision on the merits.[130]

### C. Necessity of Security Measures

The concept of necessity is used in many legal systems to delimit permissible from prohibited measures where such measures negatively affect the regime's values.[131] As noted earlier, exceptions under many economic agreements specify a 'necessity' nexus between the government action and the permissible objective, such as 'necessary to protect' or that 'it considers necessary to protect' certain interests, or 'necessary for the fulfillment' of certain obligations, to protect its security interests.[132] The necessity component of the treaty exception asks a question of the closeness or appropriate fit between the chosen means and the asserted regulatory purpose of the state in question.[133] In many regimes, the necessity criterion regulates only means and requires an adjudicative body to ask an essentially factual question: whether the objective could have been achieved in some other way that would have involved a more modest restriction of the conflicting right.[134]

Notably, a different understanding by tribunals of the relationship between security exceptions and the customary defence of necessity under Article 25

[128] I Cheyne, 'Deference and the Use of the Public Policy Exception in International Courts and Tribunals', in Gruszczynski and Werner (n 63) 57.

[129] Under Art XXI(a), Members retain the right to derogate from any GATT obligation which requires them to supply any information which, if disclosed, would be deemed contrary to their essential security interests.

[130] HL Schloemann and S Ohlhoff, ''Constitutionalization' and Dispute Settlement in the WTO: National Security as an Issue of Competence' (1999) 93 *American Journal of International Law* 424, 448.

[131] See Mitchell and Henckels (n 11) 93.

[132] C Henckels, 'Investment treaty security exceptions, necessity and self-defence in the context of armed conflict', in KF Gómez, A Gourgourinis and C Titi (eds), *International Investment Law and the Law of Armed Conflict* (Cham, Springer, 2019).

[133] J Kurtz, 'Adjudging the Exceptional at International Law: Security, Public Order and Financial Crisis' (2010) 59 *International and Comparative Law Quarterly* 325, 365.

[134] M Elliott, 'Proportionality and Deference: The Importance of a Structured Approach' (2013) University of Cambridge Faculty of Law Research Paper No 32/2013 SSRN dx.doi.org/10.2139/ssrn.2326987 (accessed 7 October 2021).

International Law Commission's Draft Articles on State Responsibility (ARSIWA) resulted in the application of a stricter (customary law-based) standard of review to the 'necessity' nexus under security exceptions in IIAs.[135] The early Tribunals' decisions on the Argentina crisis (*CMS v Argentina*, *Enron v Argentina*, and *Sempra v Argentina*) assimilate the conditions of the security exception under the US – Argentina BIT and the customary defence of necessity. In particular, the Tribunals viewed Article XI US – Argentina BIT as too imprecise and found that it had to be concretised by reference to the elements of the customary defence of necessity in accordance with Article 25 ARSIWA. This finding of the Tribunals was highly criticised given that the test of necessity under Article XI US – Argentina BIT differs from the test under Article 25 ARSIWA: Article XI does not require that the essential interest be threatened by a grave and imminent peril; nor that the means chosen be the 'only way' to protect the essential interest at issue, nor that a contribution of the state to the emergency exclude reliance on necessity: the measure only has to be 'necessary'.

In *Continental Casualty v Argentina*, the Tribunal abandoned the necessity analysis within the framework of customary international law and instead assessed whether Argentina had no other 'reasonably available alternative' to protect its essential security interests to justify the plea of necessity.[136] Likewise, the CMS Annulment Committee stated that the Tribunal in *CMS v Argentina* misunderstood the scope and function of Article XI US – Argentina BIT when it equated that provision to customary law under Article 25 ARSIWA.[137] Instead, the CMS Annulment Committee suggested an alternative 'separation' or 'two-step' approach to the relationship between treaty-based exceptions and customary defence of necessity while distinguishing between primary and secondary norms in international law.[138]

Investment tribunals have been recently more eager to follow the 'separation' approach to the relationships between security exceptions and the customary defence of necessity. In particular, in *Deutsche Telekom v India*, the Tribunal held that Article 12 Germany – India BIT must be interpreted on its own terms, without incorporating requirements from the customary defence of necessity

[135] C Binder, 'Non Performance of Treaty Obligations in Cases of Necessity – From 'Necessity Knows No Law' via the 'Law(s) of Necessity' to Interfaces Between Different 'Laws of Necessity'' (2011) 13(1) *Austrian Review of International and European Law Online* 1, 27.

[136] *Continental Casualty Co. v Argentine Republic*, ICSID Case No ARB/03/9, Award (5 September 2008) para 199 ita.law.uvic.ca/documents/ContinentalCasualtyAward.pdf (accessed 6 October 2021).

[137] *CMS Gas Transmission Co. v Republic of Argentina*, ICSID Case No ARB/01/8 Decision of the Ad Hoc Committee on the Application for Annulment of the Argentine Republic (25 September 2007) para 132 www.italaw.com/sites/default/files/case-documents/ita0187.pdf (accessed 6 October 2021).

[138] A Gourgourinis, 'General/Particular International Law and Primary/Secondary Rules: Unitary Terminology of a Fragmented System' (2011) 22(4) *European Journal of International Law* 993, 1016.

that were not present in the treaty text.[139] It did not consider that Article 12 is limited to situations of emergency, or that the state must prove that a measure is the 'only one' available, or that it must not have contributed to the situation of necessity;[140] rather, it analysed whether India had 'reasonable alternatives, less in conflict or more compliant with its international obligations'.[141]

Likewise, in *CC/Devas v India*, the Tribunal rejected the claimant's position that security exceptions under the Mauritius – India BIT shall be subject to the more restrictive standards imposed upon the respondent by Article 25 ARSIWA, including that the respondent must demonstrate that 'the wrongful act was the only way to safeguard (India's) essential interest under Article 25'.[142]

It follows that, unless it is clear from the treaty's text, context, subsequent practice, or relevant rules of international law as specified in the treaty, the interpretation treating security exception as intertwined with the customary defence of necessity should not be read into existing investment law. It is for the parties to the treaties to negotiate and provide for these specific legal consequences to the application of security exceptions, and not for vacillating tribunals with opaque interpretive methodologies.[143] Rather, based on the recent practice, tribunals seem to test the necessity nexus between the measure and the protection of national security by determining whether there existed any reasonably available less restrictive alternatives.[144]

At the same time, a different approach to the necessity requirement might be adopted if the necessity nexus is modified by deference, ie referring to the measures '[a State] considers necessary'. Since concerns relating to national security are more sensitive than most other public concerns, to import the interpretation of the word 'necessary' from other provisions into WTO-style security exceptions and to require, for example, the indispensability of security measures or non-availability of less restrictive alternatives, is to set an unduly demanding threshold of legality that ignores the intention of the treaty drafters, the sensitivity of the issue and the responsibility that states have undertaken to protect their security.[145] Considering such concerns, the *Russia-Traffic in Transit* Panel determined that the adjectival clause 'which it considers necessary' under

[139] *Deutsche Telekom AG v Republic of India*, PCA Case No 2014–10, Interim Award (13 December 2017) para 229 www.italaw.com/sites/default/files/case-documents/italaw10496.pdf (accessed 6 October 2021).

[140] ibid.

[141] ibid, para 239.

[142] *CC/Devas (Mauritius) Ltd v Republic of India*, PCA Case No 2013–09, Award on Jurisdiction and Merits (25 July 2016) para 252 www.italaw.com/sites/default/files/case-documents/italaw9750.pdf (accessed 6 October 2021).

[143] DA Desierto, 'Necessity and 'Supplementary Means of Interpretation' for Non-Precluded Measures in Bilateral Investment Treaties' (2010) 31(3) *University of Pennsylvania Journal of International Economic Law* 827, 934.

[144] Kurtz (n 133) 365–70.

[145] A Dapo and W Sope, 'International Adjudication on National Security Issues: What Role for the WTO' (2003) 43(2) *Virginia Journal of International Law* 365, 395.

Article XXI GATT meant that 'it is for Russia to determine the 'necessity' of the measures for the protection of its essential security interests'.[146] Accordingly, 'there is no need to determine the extent of the deviation of the challenged measure from the prescribed norm in order to evaluate the necessity of the measure, ie that there is no reasonably available alternative to achieve the protection of the legitimate interests covered by the exception'.[147]

## D. Review of Objective Criteria

Many security exceptions are limited in their scope *ratione materiae*, being applicable only to certain goods or situations.[148] To illustrate, by invoking Article XXI(b) GATT, a WTO Member can justify trade restrictions which are aimed at the protection of its essential national security interests: (i) relating to the services supplying a military establishment; (ii) relating to nuclear fission and fusion; and/or (iii) adopted in wartime or other emergency in international relations. Thus, whereas national security can be deemed to encompass many areas or domestic industries, Article XXI attempts to narrow down this concept.[149] Difficulties mainly emerge under Article XXI(b)(iii) and the scope of the terms 'other emergency in international relations'. Indeed, the case law reveals that it was under this catch-all provision that most cases were brought before the contracting parties during the GATT years and then before the WTO.

In *Russia – Traffic in Transit*, the Panel concluded that even such a seemingly subjective element, the question of what constitutes 'other emergency in international relations', was amenable to an objective determination by a panel. The Panel observed that war is one example of the larger category of emergency in international relations. In particular, the Panel asserted that: '[a]n emergency in international relations would … appear to refer generally to a situation of armed conflict, or of latent armed conflict, or of heightened tension or crisis, or of general instability engulfing or surrounding a State'.[150] In contrast, the Panel emphasised that political or economic differences between WTO Members are not sufficient, of themselves, to constitute an emergency in international relations.

In assessing whether the challenged measures were 'taken in time of war or other emergency in international relations' within the meaning of Article XXI(b)(iii), the Panel in *Russia – Traffic in Transit* explained that the phrase 'taken in time of …' describes the connection between the action

[146] Panel Report, *Russia: Measures Concerning Traffic in Transit* (5 April 2019) WT/DS512/R para 7.146.

[147] ibid, para 7.108.

[148] See Eisenhut (n 12) 433.

[149] WL Thorp, 'Trade Barriers and National Security' (1960) 50 *American Economic Review* 433, 434.

[150] Panel Report, *Russia: Measures Concerning Traffic in Transit* (5 April 2019) WT/DS512/R para 7.76.

and the events of war or other emergency in international relations in that subparagraph.[151] This temporal link can help avoid retroactive justification of a measure by pointing to a past emergency in international relations, and limits reliance on security exceptions for the duration of the emergency.[152] The EU in its submission as a third party in *Russia – Traffic in Transit* also highlighted that without setting temporal parameters on 'war' or 'emergency in international relations' there could be a never-ending disruption to WTO non-discrimination norms.[153]

The Panel acknowledged that this chronological concurrence is an objective fact, amenable to objective determination.[154] After finding that the Russian identification of a situation of emergency was sufficient in the particular circumstances of the dispute, it confirmed that Russia took measures in the course of the emergency.[155] However, the Panel failed to examine the genuine connection between the duration of the measure at stake and the continued presence of the emergency. In particular, the Panel did not clarify whether there needs to be an expectation that the war or other emergency in international relations ends.[156] Neither did it discuss the importance of a geographical component, such as the proximity to the respective conflict.[157]

## VI. SOVEREIGN INVESTORS AND SECURITY EXCEPTIONS

State capitalism is a global phenomenon, notably if we also take into account, other than direct state ownership, state-driven mechanisms that aim to control allocation of capital based on security interests.[158] In 2020, about 1,600 globally active SOEs exist, increased by seven per cent compared to 2019. The pandemic has led to various governments delaying their privatisation program or becoming shareholders in companies as part of a corporate rescue package. Overall, a longer-term trend of decreasing cross-border activity by SOEs is to

[151] ibid, para 7.70.

[152] JP Meltzer, 'Cybersecurity, Digital Trade, and Data Flows: Re-thinking a Role for International Trade Rules' (2020) 132 *Global Economy & Development WP* 26 ssrn.com/abstract=3595175 or dx.doi.org/10.2139/ssrn.3595175 (accessed 7 October 2021).

[153] Panel Report, *Russia – Measures Concerning Traffic in Transit*, WT/DS512/R/Add.1, ANNEX D-5 para 18.

[154] ibid, para 7.70.

[155] ibid, para 7.124.

[156] M Paulsen, 'The Beginning, End, and Imminence of Invoking Essential Security at the WTO' (*International Economic Law and Policy Blog*, 24 July 2021) ielp.worldtradelaw.net/2021/07/the-beginning-end-and-imminence-of-invoking-essential-security-at-the-wto.html (accessed 7 October 2021).

[157] See Balan (n 62) 8.

[158] See M Babic, 'State Capital in a Geoeconomic World: Mapping State-led Foreign Investment in the Global Political Economy' (2021) *Review of International Political Economy*, DOI: 10.1080/09692290.2021.1993301; and K Kim, 'Locating New "State Capitalism" in Advanced Economies: An International Comparison of Government Ownership in Economic Entities' (2021) *Contemporary Politics*, DOI: 10.1080/13569775.2021.2022335.

be observed.[159] Sovereign investments are originally supposed to be genuinely made for commercial purposes. However, because of a close connection between sovereign investors and government funding, host states often remain suspicious of the true purpose behind such FDIs.[160] The extent to which states are entitled to use commercial channels to pursue strategic, geopolitical purposes lies at the very heart of the ideological divergence between liberal capitalists and state capitalist countries.[161] Even if acting in their private capacity, the pursuance of public policy objectives might still constitute (at least partially) the underlying rationale to sovereign investors' activity, especially given that many of such entities' sponsoring governments are state capitalists in their domestic economic approach.

The majority of IIAs have either been neutral on this issue or have explicitly included protections for sovereign investors and their investments.[162] The common trend in investment arbitration has been to treat sovereign investors as privately owned corporations, apart from the cases when sovereign investors act as agents of states or carry out governmental functions. Even the latter element, however, appears to have been interpreted narrowly to grant access to investment arbitration.[163] To date, no claim for barring sovereign investors from any form of investment treaty protection has been reasonably put forward. Once jurisdiction has been established, sovereign investors would be typically entitled to all the protections that are available to any foreign investor under the applicable treaties.

It can be argued that applying investment treaties to sovereign investors levels the playing field with other investors and prevents host states from politically retaliating against a country by denying sovereign investments.[164] From this perspective, security exceptions under IIAs can play a two-fold role. If the government in control of the sovereign investors truly aspires to exert undue influence over the host state via SWFs or SOEs, security exceptions can be a shield for the host state to block potential threats to its national security. If, however, sovereign investments are made purely for commercial purposes but the host government abuses security exceptions to reject the investment because

[159] See UNCTAD, *World Investment Report 2021*, 28.

[160] J Chaisse, 'Demystifying Public Security Exception and Limitations on Capital Movement: Hard Law, Soft Law and Sovereign Investments in the EU Internal Market' (2015) 37 *University of Pennsylvania Journal of International Law* 583, 599.

[161] B Nalbandian, 'State capitalists as claimants in international Investor-State arbitration' (QIL-QDI, 31 May 2021) < www.qil-qdi.org/state-capitalists-as-claimants-in-international-investor-state-arbitration/ (accessed 7 October 2021).

[162] C Annacker, 'Protection and Admission of Sovereign Investment under Investment Treaties' (2011) 10(3) *Chinese Journal of International Law* 531; See ch 5, in this volume.

[163] See LNS Poulsen, 'Investment treaties and the globalisation of state capitalism: opportunities and constraints for host states', in R Echandi and P Sauvé (eds), *Prospects in International Investment Law and Policy* (Cambridge, CUP, 2013).

[164] M Lippincott, 'Depoliticizing Sovereign Wealth Funds through International Arbitration' (2013) 13(2) *Chicago Journal of International Law* 649.

of political reasons, allowing a tribunal to review the invocation of the exception and to establish its limits can act as a protector to escort sovereign investors through the process.[165] To be able to differentiate between the two scenarios, adjudicators shall read the concept of the state's 'essential security interests' in a quite broad manner, but at the same time closely review the constraints on the invocation of security exceptions imposed by substantive obligations under the treaty in question.

In light of this, the legal test for a successful invocation of security exceptions under IIAs shall be the same irrespective of the legal status of the complainant. Host states shall retain the right to adopt emergency measures when their 'essential security interests' are at stake and to justify them based on security exceptions in the disputes with either private or sovereign investors provided that such measures meet the standards of the international agreements and their exceptions clauses. In this regard, coherent interpretation and application of security exceptions by investment tribunals, potentially using the WTO acquis on similar-drafted provisions as guidance, can prevent host states from increasingly exploiting national security rhetoric while restricting sovereign investments, thereby liberating sovereign investors from being instrumentalised in political battles between governments.

## VII. CONCLUSION

The inclusion of explicit exceptions in international economic agreements is designed to bring more certainty on the regulatory function of states and provide more guidance as to their understanding and application of public policy and national security in international economic relations.[166] This chapter aimed to demonstrate that, in view of the similarities of the treaty language used, such certainty and clarity can be reached if security exceptions, to a certain extent, are interpreted uniformly across different treaty regimes.

The explicit wording of 'it considers necessary for the protection of [State's] essential security interests' indicates the intention of the drafters to limit judicial scrutiny to their application in good faith. Thus, adjudicators should only examine whether the state substantiated its essential security interests sufficiently to prove their veracity and demonstrated the plausibility that the measures were implemented for the protection of the state's essential security interests. Apart from a good faith review focusing on the efforts to control abuse, adjudicators shall also review objective components of the exception clause, if any, such as whether the measure is adopted in the time of 'other emergency in international relations' under Article XXI(b)(iii) GATT.

[165] Chaisse (n 160) 599.
[166] de Mestral and Vanhonnaeker (n 98).

At the same time, the ICJ, in the *Nicaragua* and *Oil Platforms* cases, as well as investment tribunals, reaffirmed that the appropriate standard of review for the assessment of security exceptions without 'it considers necessary' language must be a stricter one. On the one hand, substantive review increases the risk that international courts and tribunals will override states' evolving national security priorities and may re-impose conventional military-related notions of security.[167] On the other hand, as the existing practice demonstrates, international courts and tribunals can and do afford a certain degree of deference to states' judgment through ordinary judicial techniques; for example, while interpreting the ever-evolving term of 'essential security interests' or the concept of 'necessity', which inherently varies depending on the precise facts and its assessment by the state concerned.

In the nearest future, international adjudicators might have to decide on the emerging issues in the area of national security, which notably include global emergencies, climate change, cybersecurity, and pandemics. As it stands now, it can be suggested that the WTO is better equipped to deal with such security matters than investment tribunals. It might use its institutional prerogative to construct security exceptions under the WTO Agreements while interpreting what qualifies as a security defence and therefore balance trade and national security of its Members ensuring uniformity in approaches to the application of security measures on a global scale.

At the same time, the cases decided by international courts and tribunals to date have not satisfactorily or definitively resolved many of the questions arising from the invocation of different forms of security exceptions. For one, the demise of the WTO Appellate Body deprives the multilateral trading system of a reliable jurisprudential stance on the reviewability and scope of Article XXI GATT and other similarly drafted WTO exceptions. Additionally, the express wording in some investment treaties to exclude security measures from arbitral review can pose a serious threat to the functioning and uniform application of these treaty regimes. Finally, at the national level (and similarly at the EU level), accommodating the competing demands of national security and legality requires courts to prompt the political branches to strengthen procedures for imposing trade restrictions thereby facilitating mutual learning and experimentation among courts and governments about what types of procedures can be legitimately expected of the state.[168] It is less clear, however, absent express treaty standards, how international courts or tribunals, often acting alone, would be able to contribute to the development of the appropriate procedures for reviewing states' security measures.

[167] See Heath (n 7) 1070.
[168] ibid 1079.

Consequently, dealing with national security matters in the international economic regime might require a more holistic view that addresses the role of not only adjudicators but also other domestic and international institutions involved in governing economic and security policies. Instead of forcing adjudicators to stretch the ordinary meaning of the term 'national security' under international law, states could rather collaborate more generally to adopt an illustrative list of measures or policy areas that would typically come within the ambit of a permissible derogation from the international economic agreements.[169]

For example, WTO Members could agree on a decision for the interpretation of Article XXI GATT and accompany it with special rules of procedure for such disputes under the DSU, thereby enhancing transparency and predictability of invocation of security exceptions. This could entail a notification and consultation phase and, potentially, a waiver-type system that is time-bound and periodically reviewed. Such a decision might also serve as guidance for investment tribunals eliminating the potential for inconsistent interpretation of security exceptions under international investment law. Arguably, there is nothing that would prevent such a decision from including provisions and commitments specific to sovereign investments. A decision of this type essentially entails a convergence of mind around the use of a good faith test. Such a construct would also mean a vote of trust toward multilateralism: states reluctant to be subject to judicial review policies taken to protect essential security interests would need to change course. Doing so would not only help avoid opening the Pandora's box of non-cooperative outcomes that will leave every state worse off. It would also minimise the scope for forum shopping, whereby, in different treaties signed by a given state, the security exception may be justiciable or not. Working at the multilateral level would have the clear advantage of avoiding fragmentation in approaching such a sensitive issue.

Restoring trust would be a precondition for such a development, which appears unlikely in the current geopolitical environment. In this scenario going back to the whiteboard to clarify the fundamentals of good faith would be important. For instance, how to assess the fact that the state invoking the security exception has created or contributed significantly to an emergency situation, for instance, by initiating an armed conflict or otherwise creating diplomatic tension? None of the WTO panels in *Russia – Traffic in Transit* and *Saudi Arabia – IPRs* were bothered with the question. The same would apply to the issue of duration of application of trade-restrictive measures based on security interests. Equally, the issue of extraterritorial effects (for instance, taking

[169] See also P Delimatsis and O Hrynkiv, 'Article XIVbis GATS', in P-T Stoll and H Hestermeyer (eds), *Commentaries on World Trade Law – the General Agreement on Trade in Services* (Leiden, Brill, 2022).

economic measures impinging on trade or investment due to an emergency that relates exclusively to two different states) poses complicated questions that the adjudicator alone appears to be unable to give a satisfactory answer. As the current conflict between Russia and Ukraine shows, dealing with such questions is not a mere theoretical exercise. Such issues underscore the importance of politics in solving this complicated equation at the international level.

# 11

# *International Commercial Courts in the Age of State Capitalism*

**GEORGIOS DIMITROPOULOS AND MOHAMMED AL-AHMADANI**

## I. INTRODUCTION

EVERY ECONOMIC SYSTEM comes with its own set of institutions. In the system of capitalist production, institutions are influenced by the market and are designed to serve the market.[1] The same is true for political institutions, as well as legal institutions – such as contract and property rights.[2] Market capitalism has developed 'varieties' with their own more distinct institutions.[3] Anglo-Saxon capitalism and continental capitalism come with their sets of political, economic and legal institutions. The Anglo-Saxon variety of capitalism, for example, is said to promote more extensive liberalisation than other varieties of capitalism.[4]

In the course of the twentieth century, capitalism became the dominant paradigm of economic organisation at the international level too.[5] This gave

[1] On market capitalism as the dominant economic system since at least the 19th century see K Polanyi, *The Great Transformation: The Political and Economic Origins of Our Time* (Boston, MA, Beacon Press, 1944, 1957, 2001).

[2] J Getzler, 'Theories of Property and Economic Development' (1996) 26(4) *The Journal of Interdisciplinary History* 639 doi.org/10.2307/205045 (accessed 16 April 2022).

[3] See generally PA Hall and D Sockice (eds), *Varieties of Capitalism: The Institutional Foundations of Comparative Advantage* (Oxford, OUP, 2001); G Menz, *Varieties of Capitalism and Europeanization: National Response Strategies to the Single European Market* (Oxford, OUP, 2005); Bob Hancké (ed), *Debating Varieties of Capitalism: A Reader* (Oxford, OUP, 2009); K Thelen, *Varieties of Liberalization and the New Politics of Social Solidarity* (Cambridge, CUP, 2014); R Westra, D Badeen and R Albritton (eds), *The Future of Capitalism After the Financial Crisis: The Varieties of Capitalism Debate in the Age of Austerity* (London, Routledge, 2015).

[4] See PA Hall and D Sockice, 'An Introduction to Varieties of Capitalism', in PA Hall and D Sockice (eds), *Varieties of Capitalism: The Institutional Foundations of Comparative Advantage* (Oxford, OUP, 2001).

[5] See for an interesting account, Q Slobodian, *Globalists: The End of Empire and the Birth of Neoliberalism* (Cambridge, MA, Harvard University Press, 2018).

rise to institutions such as the International Monetary Fund (IMF), the General Agreement on Tariffs and Trade (GATT) as well as eventually the World Trade Organization (WTO). The main assumption of twentieth-century capitalism was that the market will produce individual and social welfare;[6] it is only important to provide the appropriate conditions to allow for the market to do so. Political institutions should primarily serve this purpose. The state as well as international organisations were meant to operate as facilitators of the market. But the 2008 financial crisis put the system of global market capitalism to the test. Around the same time, 'state capitalism' as a system and ideology emerged.[7]

The existence of a forum for the resolution of disputes between market actors is central in market capitalism. Dispute settlement has acquired a special place and role in the system of international law too.[8] Commercial arbitration became in the post-WWII era the main institution for the resolution of international commercial disputes;[9] investment arbitration became the dominant means for the settlement of international investment disputes.[10]

State capitalism as a new form of capitalism is now producing its own institutions. The chapter focuses on a new institution of state capitalism in the broader area of dispute settlement: International Commercial Courts (ICommCs).[11] ICommCs take their general inspiration from the Commercial Court of England and Wales, and aim at allowing the host jurisdiction to play a similar role as that of the London courts in the world of international business transactions. They often use the English language as the language of proceedings, as well as

[6] See generally J Graafland and H Verbruggen, 'Free-Market, Perfect Market and Welfare State Perspectives on "Good" Markets: an Empirical Test' (2022) 17 Applied Research in Quality of Life 1113 link.springer.com/content/pdf/10.1007/s11482-021-09946-2.pdf (accessed 21 April 2022) 1116.

[7] I Bremmer, 'State Capitalism Comes of Age: The End of the Free Market' (2009) 88 *Foreign Affairs* 40; see also N Ferguson, 'We're All State Capitalists Now' (2012) 9 *Foreign Policy*; L-W Lin and CJ Milhaupt, 'We are the (National) Champions: Understanding the Mechanisms of State Capitalism in China' (2013) 65 *Stanford Law Review* 697; M Du, 'China's State Capitalism and World Trade Law' (2014) 63 *International & Comparative Law Quarterly* 409.

[8] While at the end of the 19th century, scholarship and practice favoured international arbitration, this started changing during the 20th century with the increasing adoption of permanent courts; see M Mazower, *Governing the World: The History of an Idea, 1815 to the Present* (London, Penguin Books, 2012).

[9] The New York Convention is remarkable for the extent of its adoption since 1958.

[10] The ICSID Convention has been in force since 1966, and has been ratified by 156 states.

[11] See generally P Bookman, 'The Adjudication Business' (2020) 45 *Yale Journal of International Law* 227; MS Erie, 'The New Legal Hubs: The Emergent Landscape of International Commercial Dispute Resolution' (2020) 60 *Virginia Journal of International Law* 228; A Roberts, 'Introduction to the Symposium on Global Labs of International Commercial Dispute Resolution' (2021) 115 *AJIL Unbound* 1 (as well as the other contributions in the 'Global Labs of International Commercial Dispute Resolution' symposium); G Dimitropoulos, 'International Commercial Courts in the "Modern Law of Nature": Adjudicatory Unilateralism in Special Economic Zones' (2021) 24 *Journal of International Economic Law* 361 (hereinafter: Dimitropoulos, ICommCs in the 'Modern Law of Nature'); S Brekoulakis and G Dimitropoulos (eds), *International Commercial Courts: The Future of Transnational Adjudication* (Cambridge, CUP 2022).

base their applicable law and rules of procedure on English (common) law.[12] At the same time, ICommCs may qualify as state capitalist institutions. First, they have, so far, been established predominantly in state capitalist economies. Second, they largely serve state capitalist goals in that they form part of broader efforts to use government institutions to help develop market relationships. China, for example, established in 2019 the China International Commercial Court (CICC) for the primary purpose of facilitating disputes arising out of the Belt and Road (BRI) initiative.[13]

The chapter looks into the interplay between state capitalism as a new variety of capitalism, and the institution of ICommCs. The aim of the chapter, however, is not to provide a description of these courts. It seeks to present the various aspects of the relationship between ICommCs and state capitalism – focusing on the international dimensions of state capitalism. The chapter is structured as follows: section II discusses ICommCs as state capitalist institutions. But ICommCs are not only state capitalist institutions; they are also involved in international state capitalist projects themselves. Section III discusses ICommCs as part of broader international state capitalist projects. Section IV engages with the other side of the coin of the questions addressed in sections II and III, namely the extent to which state capitalists will eventually find themselves as parties before ICommCs. Section V concludes.

## II. INTERNATIONAL COMMERCIAL COURTS AS STATE CAPITALIST INSTITUTIONS

State capitalism as an ideological, political and eventually legal paradigm at the domestic and international levels of governance has started developing an intermediate layer of institutions that are grounded in domestic law, but have an international outlook. ICommCs are the prime example of such institutions – alongside Special Economic Zones (SEZs). ICommCs have been developed by state capitalist economies in the West, East and Central Asia with a view to serving two main goals: attracting foreign capital and serving as global and/

[12] The AIFC Court, for example, is self-described as 'an independent common law court operating to the highest international standards'; see court.aifc.kz/. See generally G Dimitropoulos, 'The Design of International Commercial Courts: From Organizational Hybridity to Functional Interoperability', in S Brekoulakis and G Dimitropoulos (eds), *International Commercial Courts: The Future of Transnational Adjudication* (Cambridge, CUP 2022) 251 (hereinafter: Dimitropoulos, The Design of ICommCs).

[13] 'Opinion Concerning the Establishment of the Belt and Road International Commercial Dispute Resolution Mechanism and Institutions', which was then adopted by China's Leading Group for Deepening Overall Reform; see also S Zhang 'China's International Commercial Court: Background, Obstacles and the Road Ahead' (2020) 11 *Journal of International Dispute Settlement* 150; Sir W Blair 'The New Litigation Landscape: International Commercial Courts and Procedural Innovations' (2019) 9(2) *International Journal of Procedural Law* 212, 221.

or regional dispute settlement hubs.[14] This section of the chapter discusses ICommCs as an institution of state capitalism – as a new variety of capitalism.

### A. Different Forms of Capitalism

Institutions such as commercial courts and ICommCs are never established in a vacuum. They develop in response to the political economy of the state in question, the institutions that operate within it, and the policy sets resulting from that mix.

Peter Hall and David Soskice provide a thorough account of what they describe as two broad types of capitalism: Coordinated Market Economies (CMEs) and Liberal Market Economies (LMEs).[15] According to Hall and Soskice, a CME can broadly be defined as a system whereby firms that operate within it are heavily dependent on non-market relationships to coordinate their efforts with other actors as well as construct their core competencies.[16] The non-market coordination that firms are dependent on in such a system comes with extensive relational contracting, network monitoring based on the exchange of private information inside networks, and reliance on collaborative relationships to build the competencies of a firm. Equilibria in a CME are achieved through strategic interactions among private firms and other actors.[17]

This is quite different from LMEs like the US and the UK, where firms primarily coordinate their activities through competitive market arrangements and hierarchies.[18] Market relationships in such a system can be identified by the exchange of goods and services in a competitive setting and formality of contractual regimes. Actors within the system adjust their willingness according to demand and adjust the supply of goods and services based on price signals generated from the markets for such goods and services. This tends to be done in line with marginal calculations found in neoclassical economic literature – unlike CMEs, where equilibria are attained through strategic interactions among private firms and other actors.[19]

In order to understand the difference between CMEs and LMEs, and the reasons some states may have – broadly speaking – chosen one approach to capitalism over the other, one must account for what Hall and Soskice call, 'institutional complementaries'. Institutions can be considered complementary if the presence (or efficiency) of one increases the return from (or the efficiency of)

[14] See Dimitropoulos, ICommCs in the 'Modern Law of Nature' (n 11) 371–372.

[15] P Hall and D Soskice, Introduction, in *Varieties of Capitalism: The Institutional Foundations of Comparative Advantage* (Oxford, OUP, 2001) (hereinafter Hall and Soskice, Introduction to Varieties of Capitalism).

[16] Hall and Soskice, Introduction to Varieties of Capitalism (n 15) 8.

[17] ibid.

[18] ibid.

[19] ibid, 8.

the other.[20] Take, for example, labour-management relationships in Germany which is used as an example of a CME by the authors. Firms in a CME make use of production strategies that depend on having a highly skilled workforce that is given a significant amount of work autonomy and encouraged to constantly share information they acquire in the process to generate continuous improvements in a given product and/or service and the process by which such goods and/or services are produced and delivered. Companies operating within such a system are vulnerable to 'hold up' by the employees of the company and having their skilled workers 'poached' by other firms. Furthermore, employees who share information they have gained at work with management risk exploitation.[21]

In Germany, such issues are addressed by having wages set through industry-level bargains between trade unions and employer associations. The equalising of wages at equivalent skill levels across a given industry makes it difficult for rival firms to poach the employees and provides assurance to employees that they are receiving the highest feasible wages in return for their deep commitment to their company, while mitigating the inflationary effects of wage settlements. Workers' councils encourage employees to invest in company-specific skills and extra effort, as a result of their ability to protect employees from arbitrary lay-offs and changes in working conditions.[22] Trade unions, employer associations and workers' councils are, therefore, complementary, since they mitigate the risks of employee 'hold up' and poaching, while ensuring a higher standard of living for employees and enhancing firm specific skills.

LMEs, on the other hand, deal with similar matters in very different ways. Unlike CMEs, where lay-offs and the issue of 'poaching' are handled through industry-wide national trade unions, employers' associations, and company level works councils, and the relationship between such institutions, LMEs tend to rely on the market relationship between individual workers and the employer to organise relations with their labour force. Upper management in a firm generally has unilateral control over the firm, which includes substantial rights to hire and fire. In this system, it is difficult to achieve economy-wide wage coordination due to the lack of cohesion between trade unions and employers. This means that LMEs' ability to control wages and inflation is more heavily dependent on market competition and macroeconomic policy.[23]

## B. State Capitalism: A New Form of Capitalism Between the State and Market?

The analysis of Hall and Soskice is primarily focused on the more traditional forms of capitalism in North America and Europe. It does not account for the

[20] ibid 17 (references omitted).
[21] ibid 24.
[22] ibid.
[23] ibid 29.

rise of state capitalism, and its place within the aforementioned forms of market economies. The present section discusses state capitalism as a new variety of capitalism focusing on China and the Gulf Region. The analysis highlights the international dimensions of state capitalism. In the same way that neoliberalism became a global economic and institutional system, state capitalism is becoming a global economic system with its own international(ised) institutions.[24] China and the Gulf Region have their own versions of state capitalism. Leveraging their state capitalist models, they go beyond simply meeting their internal economic interests and policies; their forms of state capitalism have also taken on an international dimension in order to meet these states' foreign interests.

### *i. China*

In December 2018, China commemorated the 40th anniversary of Reform and Opening.[25] China has adopted a model of (state) capitalism that, in many ways, is a deviation from the CME and LME models put forward by Hall and Soskice. At the end of the 1970s, China introduced under Deng Xiaoping a policy reform and liberalisation program with a view to opening its economy to the world.[26] Market-oriented reforms were introduced in selected SEZs[27] that initially took the form of Export-Processing Zones (EPZs).[28] By the mid-2000's and following decades of multi-faceted, non-linear, and sometimes contested reforms which involved – among others – the privatisation and downsizing of the state-owned sector, China's state capitalism was defined by the management of the remaining large SOEs to contribute to economic growth, create wealth for the Party-state, and look out for its economic and strategic interests at home and internationally.[29] China's adoption of its current form of state

[24] See also A Roberts, HC Moraes and V Ferguson, 'Toward a Geoeconomic Order in International Trade and Investment' (2019) 22 *Journal of International Economic Law* 655 (discussing the rise of a new 'geoeconomic order'). On IIL as a neoliberal form of capitalism, see ch 2, in this volume.

[25] See X Jinping, speech commemorating the 40th anniversary of Reform and Opening, December 2018. Margret Pearson, Meg Rithmire, and Kellee S. Tsa have detailed the evolution of China's approach to state capitalism from one that was in line with 'familiar depictions of State-Directed economies' to 'distinctly party-driven incarnation'; M Pearson, M Rithmire and KS Tsai, 'Party-State Capitalism in China' [2020] HBS Working Paper 21-065, 4 (hereinafter: Pearson, Rithmire and Tsai, Party-State Capitalism).

[26] This was especially the case at the 3rd Plenary Session of the 11th Central Committee of the Communist Party of China in December 1978.

[27] Chinese Paramount leader Deng Xiaoping is said to have coined the term 'special zones' for these first zones; see CD Stoltenberg 'China's Special Economic Zones: Their Development and Prospects' (1984) 24 (6) Asian Survey 637; see also section II.C. below

[28] Slobodian (n 5) 236 (with further references); on EPZs, see P Neveling, 'The Global Spread of Export Processing Zones and the 1970s as a Decade of Consolidation', in K Andersen and S Müller (eds), *Changes in Social Regulation: State, Economy, and Social Protagonists since the 1970s* (Oxford, Berghahn Books, 2017) 23–40; see also II.C. and III.A. below.

[29] Pearson, Rithmire and Tsai, Party-State Capitalism (n 25) 2.

capitalism has been motivated by the following justifications: first, an effort to mitigate the less desirable effects of capitalism, such as inequality, business cycles, and/or an inability to plan long term; second, manage industrial growth and global competition; and third, the use of state ownership and government intervention to bolster geo-strategic and/or economic competition in globalised sectors of the economy.[30]

In more recent years, the government has made a more concerted effort to exert its authority and play a more active role – organisationally, financially and politically – in domestic and foreign economic relations. The state expanded its institutional capacity and role within the economy to go beyond mere public ownership of large companies in key industries.[31] Second, the government has expanded its capital beyond companies that are majority owned by the state. Since 2003, the ownership of firms has been institutionalised in the State Asset Supervision and Administrative Commission (SASAC) – a body that appoints managers and generally acts like a 'capitalist asset manager' rather than a classic state owner.[32] The Party has also encouraged the creation of 'state-owned capital investment companies' that would 'invest in non-state-owned enterprises in "various ways" to further the state's industrial policy goals and provide capital to non-state firms with "strong growth potential"'.[33] Third, China has further extended industrial policy to the private sector through the *Made in China 2025* strategic plan. The plan was launched in 2015 to encourage indigenous innovation, technological self-reliance, and industrial upgrading. The state made more of an effort to involve private companies, both as beneficiaries of such policies and as the means of enacting them.[34]

As part of a broader effort to play a more active role in international relations, China has expanded its role in international trade and investment through the BRI – formerly known as One Belt One Road (OBOR). The BRI is a massive economic policy initiative on the part of the Chinese Government that aims to revive the 'iconic land and maritime Silk Road via a trade and infrastructure network spanning East Asia to Western Europe and South through Africa.

[30] ibid 2–3.

[31] H Yue, 'The Private Sector: Challenges and Opportunities During Xi's Second Term' (China Leadership Monitor. 1 March 2019) www.prcleader.org/hou (accessed 23 February 2021) (hereinafter, Hou); see also L Lucas, 'China Government Assigns Officials to Companies Including Alibaba' *Financial Times* (London, 23 September 2019). (This has been supplemented with assignments to new oversight offices, by (SASAC) and key municipalities, in major firms, including major tech firms like Alibaba).

[32] Hou (n 31).

[33] Pearson, Rithmire and Tsai, Party-State Capitalism (n 25) 10.

[34] People's Republic of China (PRC) Ministry of Industry and Information Technology, 'Guiding Opinions of 16 Departments including the Ministry of Industry and Information Technology on Giving Full Play to the Role of Private Investment to Promote the Implementation of the Strategy of Manufacturing Power' [2017]; see also B Naughton, 'Financialisation of the State Sector in China', in Y Zheng and SY Tong (eds), *China's Economic Modernization and Structural Changes: Essays in Honour of John Wong* (Singapore, World Scientific, 2019) 167–185.

It consists of roads, railways, ports, pipelines and everything in between'.[35] A number of policy reasons drive the government's ambitious plan. First, China is looking to use infrastructure investments as a means of building up and projecting regional influence.[36] Second, it is a means of advancing China's goal of regional economic integration and promoting greater economic reliance on China.[37] Third, and most importantly, it is a means of addressing structural challenges afflicting China's growth model, particularly its reliance on SOEs and state subsidised finance that has led to over-investment and an undeveloped services sector.[38]

The BRI is intended to allow China to continue pursuing its growth model through exposure to new markets by developing new infrastructure projects using SOEs and state finance.[39] Furthermore, the objective of the BRI is to redirect government investments through SOEs and state subsidised finance in a manner that is more efficient, mitigating the risk of over-investment domestically, while still focusing domestically on developing other critical sectors of the state's economy such as new technologies. Therefore, the BRI, and the above-mentioned actions by the Chinese Government are part of a larger project to adapt its economy, develop critical sectors locally, and leverage its SOEs and financing tools to exert economic influence globally.

#### *ii. GCC*

The states that form the Gulf Cooperation Council (GCC) adopted models of state capitalism that were more in line with the approach taken by Singapore under long time Prime Minister Lee Kuan Yew. The focus in this section is on the approaches taken by Qatar and the UAE – in particular, Dubai and Abu Dhabi.

Qatar and the UAE have been influenced in policy making by the East Asian model of the developmental state in general, and its implementation in Singapore in particular.[40] Similar to Singapore, both states have leveraged their centralised forms of governance to overcome limitations inherent to many small states with a view to diversifying into knowledge-based and highly globalised economies. This model pragmatically combined private market initiatives with state intervention and traditional forms of local governance.[41]

[35] C Campbell, 'China Says It's Building the New Silk Road. Here Are Five Things to Know Ahead of a Key Summit' (*Time*, 12 May 2017) time.com/4776845/china-xi-jinping-belt-road-initiative-obor/ (accessed 12 January 2021).

[36] JP Meltzer, '*China's One Belt One Road initiative: A view from the United States*' (Brookings Institute, 19 June 2017) www.brookings.edu/research/chinas-one-belt-one-road-initiative-a-view-from-the-united-states/ (accessed 12 January 2021)

[37] ibid.

[38] ibid.

[39] ibid.

[40] KC Ulrichsen, *The Gulf States in International Political Economy*, 1st edn (Basingstoke, Palgrave 2016) 69 (hereinafter Ulrichsen).

[41] See M Hvidt, 'The Dubai Model: An Outline of Key Development-Process Elements in Dubai' (2009) 41(3) *International Journal of Middle East Studies* 397, 412.

Even though there are differences between Qatar and the UAE in their macroeconomic approaches and sector-specific focus, their economic approaches have many similarities. Both states have established a number of highly successful State-Owned Enterprises (SOEs) that operate across a variety of strategic economic sectors – ranging from oil and gas production to telecommunications and hospitality. These SOEs have largely gained a reputation for strong corporate management, which are consistent with 'international standards of corporate governance, efficiency and leadership'.[42] The boards of such companies are made up of representatives from both the private and public sectors, and tend to include senior members of the ruling family of that state along with a number of influential personalities from the business world. Given the make-up of the boards, these SOEs have access to the top of the decision-making structure and can mobilise key state assets in support of particular policies.[43]

Furthermore, given the strategic role they have in the local economy, they are also aligned with the national economic and vision plans of these states, and are thus recipients of targeted forms of state support. One example of such a plan is the Qatar National Vision 2030 (QNV 2030).[44] QNV 2030 was rolled out in 2008. It identified five major policy challenges that Qatar would face during a period of growth driven by the extraction and sale of natural gas. Two of the most fundamental challenges are, first, to meet the needs of both current and future generations, and second, to align economic growth with social development and environmental management. In order to meet the challenges, QNV 2030 focuses on four interdependent pillars: human, social, environmental and economic development.[45]

Qatar and the UAE have expanded their role in international trade and investment in two broad ways. First, they have created two of the world's largest Sovereign Wealth Funds (SWFs) to facilitate investment of their excess fossil fuel revenues. Both vehicles invest in international markets across all asset classes – equities, fixed income and treasury, infrastructure, real estate, private equity and alternatives. Second, both states have formed a number of SEZs with the aim of attracting Foreign Direct Investment (FDI) into their markets, while also utilising them as a means of supporting their wider economic policies.[46] Both Qatar and the UAE established financial centres – the Qatar Financial Centre (QFC) and the Dubai International Financial Centre (DIFC) respectively, with the hopes of further developing their financial markets, supporting their

[42] Ulrichsen (n 40) 69.

[43] ibid 70.

[44] 'Qatar National Vision 2030' (General Secretariat for Development Planning, July 2008) www.gco.gov.qa/wp-content/uploads/2016/09/GCO-QNV-English.pdf (accessed 12 January 2021).

[45] QNV was accompanied by the *Qatar National Development Strategy 2011–2016* – as well as the follow up development strategy – to help align macroeconomic and institutional reforms with specific short-term projects that were already in the pipeline. The winning of the hosting right to the 2022 FIFA World Cup introduced another element into planning considerations due to the scale of the infrastructure projects associated with hosting such an event; Ulrichsen (n 40) 66.

[46] See sections II.C. and III.A. below.

respective state's financial regulation reform efforts, and attracting foreign financial firms by providing them with a regulatory and legal system that is both familiar to them and independent.[47]

## C. Intermediate Institutions of State Capitalism

State capitalism at the international level can be seen as a response to neoliberalism. International state capitalism has started producing its own institutions. Internationally-oriented state capitalist policies and projects have produced an intermediate layer of institutions that are grounded in domestic law, but have an international outlook. A prime example of such institutions – that has close links to ICommCs – are Special Economic Zones.[48] SEZs are, according to the World Bank, areas within a state that are geographically limited and, usually, physically secured; that include a 'single management or administration; determine eligibility for benefits based upon physical location within the zone; and offer a separate customs area (duty-free benefits) and streamlined procedures'.[49] SEZs are established by states in the hope of achieving one or more of the following policy goals:[50]

1. *To attract foreign direct investment (FDI)*: Virtually all zone programs, from traditional EPZ to China's large-scale SEZs aim, at least in part, to attract FDI.
2. *To serve as "pressure valves" to alleviate large-scale unemployment*: The SEZ programs of Tunisia and the Dominican Republic are frequently cited as examples of programs that have remained enclaves and have not catalyzed dramatic structural economic change, but that nevertheless have remained robust, job-creating programs.
3. *In support of a wider economic reform strategy*: In this view, SEZs are a simple tool permitting a country to develop and diversify exports. Zones reduce anti-export bias while keeping protective barriers intact. The SEZs of China, the Republic of Korea, Mauritius, and Taiwan follow this pattern.
4. *As experimental laboratories for the application of new policies and approaches*: China's large-scale SEZs are classic examples. FDI, legal, land, labor, and even pricing policies were introduced and tested first within the SEZs before being extended to the rest of the economy.

[47] See, eg, P Bookman, 'The Adjudication Business' (2020) 45(2) *Yale Journal of International Law* 227.

[48] See J Chaisse and G Dimitropoulos, 'Special Economic Zones in International Economic Law: Towards Unilateral Economic Law' (2021) 24 *Journal of International Economic Law* 229.

[49] T Farole and G Akinci, 'Special Economic Zones: Progress, Emerging Challenges, and Future Directions' (World Bank, 1 August 2011) openknowledge.worldbank.org/bitstream/handle/10986/2341/638440PUB0Exto00Box0361527B0PUBLIC0.pdf?sequence=1&isAllowed=y (accessed 15 April 2022) 3.

[50] ibid.

SEZs are thus often established by states as a means of furthering their state capitalist policies. Since the 1970s, zones have been used to attract foreign investors. The year after the opening of the economy of China to the rest of the world, the state established the first of six SEZs, with the goal of attracting foreign investment and accelerating industrialisation, while simultaneously serving as a catalyst for the large-scale economic reforms the government would later implement throughout the country.[51] Middle Eastern states established such SEZs as part of their overall policy of 'catalysing export-oriented diversification' in order to become less dependent on the extraction of fossil fuels such as oil and natural gas.[52]

One of the key characteristics of SEZs is that they are areas that operate under a different set of business, trade and/or financial laws that tend to be more liberal than those of the jurisdiction where such zones are established. This is, in part, a recognition by the enacting state, that in order to attract foreign investors, it would need to provide a legal infrastructure that is familiar to the industries and industry actors it hopes to attract – such as the financial free zones in the GCC that provide an English (common) law-based legal framework.

ICommCs are also intermediate institutions of state capitalism. Lord Denning MR, in *The Atlantic Star* stated the following to illustrate his confidence in the superiority of English Courts situated in London:[53]

> No one who comes to these courts asking for justice should come in vain … The right to come here is not confined to Englishmen. It extends to any friendly foreigner. He can seek the aid of our courts if he desires to do so. You may call this 'forum-shopping' if you please, but if the forum is England, it is a good place to shop in, both for the quality of the goods and the speed of service.

Lord Denning viewed English courts as the forum of choice for international commercial actors looking to settle commercial disputes. The Commercial Court in London was established in the late nineteenth century as part of the Queen's Bench Division of the High Court. The Commercial Court is now part of the Business and Property Courts – which are part of the High Court of Justice in London. Britain's historical political power, together with London being a global destination for international commerce, banking and trade has allowed for a significant number of the cases in the Commercial Court in London to continue to have a foreign dimension to them.[54]

[51] ibid 5.

[52] ibid 5.

[53] *The Atlantic Star* [1973] QB 364, 382,

[54] Although there is no exact equivalent in the US, the United States District Court for the Southern District of New York (situated in Manhattan, New York City, also referred to as 'the Mother Court') has become the de facto 'International Commercial Court' for the US given the fact that New York City, since the early to mid-20th century, has become the world's financial hub and, therefore, the centre of some of the world's most significant commercial disputes.

Almost 50 years after Lord Denning's statement, not only has the Commercial Court remained a forum of choice for many commercial parties in resolving their disputes; it has, moreover, served as a model replicated by a wide variety of jurisdictions. Modern day ICommCs can trace their origins back to the establishment of the Commercial Court.[55] There are nowadays ICommCs established within a financial free zone; ICommCs that have a stand-alone nature; as well as international chambers within ordinary courts.[56]

The courts of the first category are predominantly English (common) law based – irrespective of whether the host state is a common or civil law jurisdiction.[57] The DIFC Courts, the Qatar International Court and Dispute Resolution Centre (QICDRC) of the QFC, the Abu Dhabi Global Markets (ADGM) Courts and the Astana International Financial Centre (AIFC) Court are established in a zone that draws its rules from the common law tradition – while the regular jurisdiction of the state is civil law-based. The jurists that make up the roster of judges for these ICommCs are also mostly from the common law world.[58]

The second category of ICommCs are established in two of the countries that have championed state capitalism and international state capitalism as an economic system. The Singapore International Commercial Court (SICC) is one very important piece of the puzzle of the overall effort of the government of Singapore to establish Singapore as a dispute resolution hub for Asia and the world. The CICC is part of China's grand plan towards developing the BRI and its institutions.[59]

Even states that Hall and Soskice would characterise as CMEs, like Germany and France, have established International Commercial Chambers within their existing judicial systems. The International Chambers at the Paris Commercial Court and the Paris Court of Appeals resolve disputes where contracting parties have selected Paris as their preferred forum. Most often in such cases, the defendant is a non-resident, or the governing law is foreign. Judges sitting in the International Chamber are bilingual (French/English) and most have studied

[55] See S Menon, 'International Commercial Courts: Towards a Transnational System of Dispute Resolution' (*DIFC Courts Lecture Series* 2015) www.supremecourt.gov.sg/docs/default-source/default-document-library/media-room/opening-lecture---difc-lecture-series-2015.pdf (accessed 15 April 2022); G Dimitropoulos and S Brekoulakis, 'International Commercial Courts: The Future of Transnational Adjudication – An Introduction', in S Brekoulakis and G Dimitropoulos (eds), *International Commercial Courts: The Future of Transnational Adjudication* (Cambridge, CUP, 2022) 1.

[56] Dimitropoulos, The Design of ICommCs (n 12) 254–262.

[57] Former Chief Justice of the DIFC Courts and Head of the DRA, Dr Michael Hwang, has called, for example, the DIFC in 2008 'a common law island in a civil law ocean' referring to the operation of the DIFC Courts within the United Arab Emirates – a civil law jurisdiction; see M Hwang, 'The Courts of the Dubai International Finance Centre – A Common Law Island in a Civil Law Ocean' (DIFC Courts, 1 November 2008) www.difccourts.ae/2008/11/01/the-courts-of-the-dubai-international-finance-centre-a-common-law-island-in-a-civil-law-ocean/ (accessed 30 August 2020).

[58] See section III.A. below.

[59] See section III.B. below.

or worked in English-speaking countries.[60] Additionally, the Chamber can turn to judges from the other specialised chambers of the Paris Commercial Court who have specific expertise in the case at hand. Unlike the ICommCs of the first category, the International Chamber of the Paris Commercial Court is not separate from the larger French judicial system, but a part of it. These chambers are an effort on the part of the state to extend its judicial reach to international commercial disputes, while drawing upon its existing judicial infrastructure to resolve such matters.

ICommCs are intermediate institutions of state capitalism in that they create international institutional complementarities. They are established through domestic legislation and form part of larger state capitalist projects.[61] Their outlook, however, is international as they handle cases involving foreign commercial parties, or those in which the parties simply agree to resolve their commercial disputes in that forum. ICommCs provide parties with an alternative to international arbitration, while simultaneously filling in the gaps that exist in the current systems of international dispute resolution.[62]

The chapter focuses next on ICommCs established as part of larger state capitalist projects.

## III. INTERNATIONAL COMMERCIAL COURTS AS PART OF STATE CAPITALIST PROJECTS

ICommCs are not only institutions of state capitalism as a variety of capitalism; they are also involved in state capitalist projects themselves. ICommCs often form part of SEZs. A prime example of a state capitalist project that mobilises domestic resources to achieve international goals is the BRI.[63] The BRI engages a variety of dispute resolution mechanisms that are analysed in this section of the chapter while highlighting the role of ICommCs.

### A. International Commercial Courts and SEZs

The GCC states are examples of states that developed their ICommCs as part of a specific subset of state capitalist projects. The QICDRC, the DIFC Courts

[60] Standing International Forum of Commercial Courts, 'Le Tribunal de Commerce de Paris – Paris Commercial Court' sifocc.org/countries/france/ (accessed 27 July 2022).

[61] See section III.A. below.

[62] Dimitropoulos, ICommCs in the 'Modern Law of Nature' (n 11); Dimitropoulos, The Design of ICommCs (n 12).

[63] On the BRI objectives see State Council of the People's Republic of China, 'Full text of the Vision for Maritime Cooperation under the Belt and Road Initiative' (State Council of the People's Republic of China, 20 June 2017) english.www.gov.cn/archive/publications/2017/06/20/content_281475691873460.htm (accessed 27 July 2022).

and the ADGM Courts have been established as part of larger financial centre initiatives by Qatar and the UAE.

The DIFC was set up as a free zone by the Government of the Emirate of Dubai in the UAE in 2004 under DIFC Law No 10 of 2004 to serve as a hub for financial services in the region. It has its own independent regulatory framework and legal system and offers companies 100 per cent ownership without the need for a local partner.[64] A year later, Qatar established the Qatar Financial Center (QFC) through Law No 7 of 2005, for the purposes of – much like the DIFC – attracting foreign investors and providing a legal and business infrastructure for financial services. Like its counterpart in Dubai, the legislative framework of the QFC provides entities established in the QFC with a range of legislative guarantees, including the ability to repatriate profits, realise investments and allowing for 100 per cent ownership by individuals or legal entities that are not nationals or resident in the State of Qatar.[65] It also provides for an entire legal system based on the English (common) law system (as is the case with the DIFC), which includes legislation dealing with employment, data protection, financial services regulations, contract law, trusts, insolvency, single family offices, companies and special companies.[66]

The integrity of a financial centre (or more generally any financial system) is dependent on its court system and its ability to resolve disputes effectively and efficiently – while maintaining regulatory soundness. ICommCs are part of broader legislative and institutional frameworks that aim to attract international investors and financial services, and have been critical to the success of both the DIFC in Dubai and the QFC in Qatar – and increasingly the ADGM in Abu Dhabi – and the AIFC in Kazakhstan.

## B. International Commercial Courts and the BRI

China is another example of a state that developed its ICommCs as part of a much larger state capitalist project, the BRI. China has gone beyond merely relying on its existing network of BITs with its BRI partners, taking active steps to address potential lack of adjudicatory institutions that would deal specifically with disputes arising from the BRI. This section discusses the role of the CICC in the broader BRI institutional framework and closes with a discussion of the (at least aspired) role of other ICommCs in the BRI.

[64] Further, legislation governing the day-to-day operations and requirements of various types of financial institutions, companies and individuals have been enacted including, but not limited to: Companies Law DIFC Law No 5 of 2018; Contract Law DIFC Law No 6 of 2004; Employment Law DIFC Law No 2 of 2019; Insolvency Law No 1 of 2019. There is also legislation that provides clarity on the application of civil and commercial laws within the DIFC's jurisdiction; see Z Al Abdin Sharar and M Al Khulaifi, 'The Courts in Qatar Financial Centre and Dubai International Financial Centre: A Comparative Analysis' (2016) 46 *Hong Kong Law Journal* 529.

[65] Oxford Business Group, *The Report: Qatar2014*, 1st edn (Oxford Business Group, 2014) 117.

[66] ibid 69.

### *i. CICC and the BRI*

China is currently the world's second largest recipient and exporter of FDI – just behind the US.[67] This is expected to be reversed, however, in the coming years as China continues to invest in the BRI. The BRI is, as discussed above, is a development strategy adopted by the Chinese Government that involves infrastructure development and investments in countries in Europe, Asia and Africa.[68]

China's approach to international law with regard to the BRI has been a source of growing literature.[69] The Chinese Government has adopted many strategies to help finance the projects that fall under the BRI. One example of such a financing mechanism is the Asian Infrastructure Investment Bank (AIIB) established in 2016.[70] President Xi Jinping explicitly instructed policymakers that the AIIB is to be primarily tasked with the provision of capital for BRI projects. In addition to the AIIB, China has created a new US$40 billion 'Silk Road fund'[71] and has injected another US$31 billion in China's policy banks to support the BRI.[72]

China's approach to dispute settlement in the BRI context has been a source of growing literature too.[73] Beyond the existing BIT network between China and its BRI partner countries,[74] China has also taken the additional step of establishing courts and tribunals to specifically adjudicate potential disputes that could arise from the BRI. It began by expanding the jurisdiction of the existing arbitral

[67] UNCTAD, 'World Investment Report 2020' (United Nations, 2020) unctad.org/system/files/official-document/wir2020_en.pdf (accessed 14 April 2022) 15.

[68] 'Belt' refers to the overland routes for road and rail transportation, called the 'Silk Road Economic Belt'; 'road' refers to the sea routes, or the 21st century Maritime Silk Road. See generally J Chaisse, 'China's 'Belt and Road' Initiative: Mapping the World's Normative and Strategic Implications' (2018) 52 *Journal of World Trade* 163; J Chaisse (ed), *China's International Investment Strategy: Bilateral, Regional, and Global Law and Policy* (Oxford, Oxford University Press, 2019).

[69] See, eg, MR Dahlan, 'Envisioning Foundations for the Law of the Belt And Road Initiative: Rule of Law and Dispute Resolution Challenges' (2020) 62 *Harvard International Law Journal*.

[70] N Lichtenstein, *A Comparative Guide to the Asian Infrastructure Investment Bank* (Oxford, OUP, 2018).

[71] 'China to Speed up Construction of New Silk Road' (*China Daily*, 6 November 2014) www.chinadaily.com.cn/china/2014-11/06/content_18880708.htm (accessed 14 April 2022).

[72] Z Yuzhe, 'Policy Banks Linked to 'Belt and Road' Plans Said to Get US$ 31 Bln' (*Caixin Online*, 21 July 2015) www.caixinglobal.com/2015-07-21/policy-banks-linked-to-belt-and-road-plans-said-to-get-us-31-bln-101012319.html (accessed 14 April 2022).

[73] See J Wang, 'China's Governance Approach to the Belt and Road Initiative (BRI): Relations, Partnership, and Law' (2019) 14(5) *Global Trade and Customs Journal* 222; H Wang, 'China's Approach to the Belt and Road Initiative: Scope, Character and Sustainability' (2019) 22(1) *Journal of International Economic Law* 29; J Chaisse and M Matsushita, 'China's "Belt And Road" Initiative: Mapping the World Trade Normative and Strategic Implications' (2018) 52(1) *Journal of World Trade* 163; M Feldman, 'A Belt and Road Dispute Settlement Regime' (13 June 2019) papers.ssrn.com/sol3/papers.cfm?abstract_id=3403846 (accessed 15 April 2022).

[74] The investment arbitration mechanisms in BITs between China and BRI countries are generally viewed as not providing sufficient protection. Most of these treaties are very conservative on the scope of disputes that can be submitted to international arbitration; see S Zhang, 'China's Approach in Drafting the Investor–State Arbitration Clause: A Review from the "Belt and Road' Regions" Perspective' (2017) 5(1) *The Chinese Journal of Comparative Law* 79.

institutions to include disputes arising from foreign investments. In 2016, the Shenzhen Court of International Arbitration (SCIA) updated its rules to allow it to deal with foreign investment disputes – making it the first Chinese arbitral institution to take up Investor-State Dispute Settlement (ISDS) cases.[75] It also adopted guidelines to allow for the administration of cases under the UNCITRAL Arbitral Rules.[76] The China International Economic and Trade Arbitration Commission (CIETAC) did the same a year later.[77]

China has gone a step further by developing joint arbitration centres with other regions – and specifically in those regions where China has invested heavily. One example is the China-Africa Joint Arbitration Centre (CAJAC), which was established by the Chinese Government and 50 African countries at the Johannesburg Summit and the Sixth Ministerial Conference of the Forum on China-Africa Cooperation in 2015. The institution currently has five centres in both China and Africa – in Shanghai, Beijing, Shenzhen, Johannesburg and Nairobi.[78]

In a 2015 Opinion, the Supreme People's Court (SPC) recognised the need for Chinese courts to improve their adjudicatory functions to effectively deal with issues arising from such an ambitious policy as the BRI:[79]

> They shall pay close attention to such international economic cooperation as the building of the New Asia-Europe Continental Bridge Economic Corridor, try foreign-related civil and commercial cases concerning infrastructure development, economic and trade exchanges, industrial investment, energy resource cooperation, financial services, ecological environment, intellectual property rights, freight transport, and labor cooperation in a timely manner, and positively guarantee the implementation of the 'bringing in' and 'going out' strategies according to the law. They shall pay close attention to the construction of such maritime strategic channels as major ports and shipping hubs, properly try maritime cases concerning port construction, shipping finance, carriage of goods by sea, and marine ecological protection in a timely manner, and promote the maritime power strategy according to the law. They shall accurately comprehend and grasp the relevant provisions and policies on the 'pre-access national treatment' and 'negative list' related to the construction of free trade zones, properly handle the relationship between the party autonomy and the administrative approval, amend and adjust the relevant judicial policies in a timely manner, strictly restrict the scope of determining the invalidity of contracts, and promote opening to the outside world. They shall strictly implement the principle of equal

[75] M Erie, 'The New Legal Hubs: The Emergent Landscape of International Commercial Dispute Resolution' (2020) 60(2) *Virginia Journal of International Law* 225, 292.

[76] Shenzhen Court of Int'l Arbitration, Guidelines for the Administration of Arbitration under the UNCITRAL Arbitration Rules (effective 1 December 2016).

[77] CIETAC, 2017 Investment Arbitration Rules (effective 1 October 2017).

[78] D Welgemoed, 'CAJAC: A New International Arbitration Centre' (Keating Chambers) www.keatingchambers.com/wp-content/uploads/2017/12/DW-CAJAC.pdf (accessed 19 November 2021).

[79] Supreme People's Court, Several Opinions of the Supreme People's Court on Providing Judicial Services and Safeguards for the Construction of the 'Belt and Road' by People's Courts (No 9 [2015] of the Supreme People's Court, 16 June 2015).

> protection of Chinese and foreign parties and adhere to the equal litigation status, equal application of law, and equal legal liability of various market players.

In particular, it committed the adjudication of international commercial disputes to the principle of 'equal protection of the lawful rights and interests of Chinese and foreign parties'.[80] The SPC views courts as an institutional investment in view of its objectives of increasing regionalism in East and Central Asia, and promoting interregional cooperation and coordination. This process of judicialisation may also be seen as part of the government's effort to underwrite the transaction risks of the large numbers of Chinese firms actively participating in BRI trade and investment projects.[81]

China took steps to establish new courts dedicated to the resolution of international commercial disputes.[82] The SPC established the First International Commercial Court in Shenzhen and the Second International Commercial Court in Xi'an in June 2018; they are supervised by the Fourth Civil Division of the SPC.[83] Even though these courts were initially intended to deal exclusively with cases arising out of the BRI, their mandate evolved to include other types of commercial disputes.

Under Article 2 of the Provisions of the Supreme People's Court on Several Issues Concerning the Establishment of the International Commercial Court (CICC Provisions), the CICC has jurisdiction over five types of cases:[84]

1. First instance international commercial cases in which the parties have chosen the jurisdiction of the SPC according to Article 34 of the Civil Procedure Law, with an amount in dispute of at least 300,000,000 Chinese yuan.

[80] ibid.

[81] See L Ang, 'International Commercial Courts and the Interplay Between Realism and Institutionalism: A Look at China and Singapore' (2020) *Harvard International Law Journal* Online harvardilj.org/2020/03/international-commercial-courts-and-the-interplay-between-realism-and-institutionalism-a-look-at-china-and-singapore/ (accessed 20 May 2021).

[82] China Council for the Promotion of Int'l Trade (China Chamber of Int'l Commerce), China International Economic and Trade Arbitration Commission International Investment Arbitration Rules (For Trial Implementation) (effective 1 October 2017).

[83] CICC, 'Opinion Concerning the Establishment of the Belt and Road International Commercial Dispute Resolution Mechanism and Institutions' (CICC, 27 June 2018) cicc.court.gov.cn/html/1/219/208/210/819.html (accessed 15 November 2019). In June 2018, the SPC adopted the 'Provisions of the SPC on Several Issues Regarding the Establishment of the International Commercial Court' (hereinafter, 'Provisions on Several Issues'). CICC, 'Provisions of the SPC on Several Issues Regarding the Establishment of the International Commercial Court' (CICC, 27 June 2018) cicc.court.gov.cn/html/1/219/208/210/817.html (accessed 10 October 2020). See generally Z Mollengarden, 'One-Stop' Dispute Resolution on the Belt and Road: Toward an International Commercial Court with Chinese Characteristics' (2019) 36(1) *UCLA Pacific Basin Law Journal* 65; W Cai and A Godwin, 'Challenges and Opportunities for the China International Commercial Court' (2019) 68 *International & Comparative Law Quarterly* 869.

[84] Provisions of the Supreme People's Court on Several Issues Regarding the Establishment of the International Commercial Court (promulgated by the Sup. People's Ct., 27 June 2018, effective 1 July 2018), Art 2, 2018 CICC, China.

2. First instance international commercial cases which are subject to the jurisdiction of the higher people's courts who nonetheless determine that the cases should be tried by the SPC, for which permission has been obtained.
3. First instance international commercial cases that have a nationwide significant impact.
4. Cases involving applications for preservation measures in arbitration, for setting aside or enforcement of international commercial arbitration awards according to Article 14 of these Provisions.
5. Other international commercial cases that the SPC considers appropriate to be tried by the CICC.

Judges at the CICC, as opposed to other ICommCs, are exclusively Chinese nationals, who must have experience in international commerce, along with the ability to work in both English and Chinese – unlike all other ICommCs of jurisdictions that operate under the state capitalist system such as the DIFC Courts, QICDRC, ABGM Courts and the SICC. The CICC has, instead, opted to constitute an 'International Commercial Expert Committee' (ICEC) consisting mainly of foreign legal experts from other jurisdictions along the BRI and beyond. The aim of such a committee is to involve foreign legal experts who will provide advice during the dispute settlement process and assist CICC judges in ascertaining the content of foreign laws as well as preside over mediation.[85]

### *ii. Other ICommCs and the BRI*

There has also been a recent trend on the part of several ICommCs and SEZs to position themselves in a manner whereby they may be viewed as institutions commercial actors may turn to when looking to resolve disputes arising out of investments connected to the BRI – and attract Chinese state driven investment in their respective jurisdictions. As discussed above, China has already taken steps to invest in institutions that would provide both Chinese and foreign commercial actors with the means of resolving disputes connected to the BRI; other ICommCs aspire to achieve the same.

The AIFC with its court system was established by the Government of Kazakhstan with a view to also attracting BRI business.[86] The DIFC Courts also aspire to attract BRI disputes. The Dispute Resolution Authority (DRA) of the DIFC, which incorporates the DIFC Courts, has signed an MoU with

[85] China International Commercial Court, *The Decision on the Establishment of International Commercial Expert Committee of the Supreme People's Court* (24 August 2018) cicc.court.gov.cn/html/1/219/235/243/index.html (accessed 27 July 2022).

[86] Blair (n 13) 221 ('Sometimes, geopolitical considerations are also involved. The China International Commercial Court was set up with a view to China's Belt and Road Initiative, and the AIFC Court in Kazakhstan is seen as strategic both as regards BRI and the development of commerce and finance in Central Asia generally').

the University of Oxford's China Centre to 'pool expertise on legal certainty, protection and contract enforcement needed for Chinese and other international investors to secure participation in China's five trillion Dollar Belt and Road Initiative'. Michael Hwang SC, former Chief Justice of the DIFC Courts and Head of the DRA, stated the following on the day of the MoU signing:[87]

> As goods and services travel across the world along the BRI, they will seamlessly cross borders – so we shall need a seamless legal platform, based on legal convergence, that can start to do the same. This aim can partly be fulfilled by the near-universality of the New York Convention for recognition and enforcement of international arbitral awards, but the ideal legal platform should also include a robust regime of enforceable court judgments outside the boundaries of the issuing court. The answer is to make sure that when a dispute is resolved, court systems can deliver a judgment that can be executed across the full extent of the belt and road. Building up connectivity and enforceability will remove many of the roadblocks that could threaten the success of the Belt and Road Initiative.

Furthermore, ADGM opened a representative office in Beijing around the same time. In doing so, ADGM also entered into new collaborations with key Chinese authorities and institutions to augment the BRI growth plans, which include the UAE-China Industrial Co-operation Demonstration Zone, a feasibility study with the Shanghai Stock Exchange, the Asian Financial Co-operation Association, and Guo-Tai Jun-An Securities. The opening of the representative office is also an effort on the part of the UAE Government to support the RMB internationalisation strategy and build up an offshore RMB centre serving the MENA region via ADGM.[88]

These examples demonstrate that states operating under a state capitalist economic paradigm do not simply leverage ICommCs to further their domestic economic and legal policies; they also use them as a means of advancing their state capitalist projects with the state capitalist projects of other states.

## IV. STATE CAPITALISTS BEFORE INTERNATIONAL COMMERCIAL COURTS

Article 2 of the CICC Provisions clarifies that the court shall not have jurisdiction over investor-state cases – that is, cases brought against a state by an investor under a bilateral or multilateral investment treaty.[89] Articles 8(3)(c) of

[87] DIFC, *New Alliance to Enhance Legal Protection along China's Belt and Road* (28 May 2018), www.difc.ae/newsroom/news/new-alliance-enhance-legal-protection-along-chinas-belt-and-road/ (accessed 27 July 2022).

[88] ADGM, *ADGM establishes its 1st representative office in Beijing, capital of the People's Republic of China* (11 May 2018) www.adgm.com/media/announcements/adgm-establishes-its-1st-representative-office-in-beijing (accessed 27 July 2022).

[89] M Puchyna and J Kelly, 'Investment protection and dispute resolution on the Belt and Road' (*Arbitration Journal*, 15 November 2019) journal.arbitration.ru/ru/analytics/investment-protection-and-dispute-resolution-on-the-belt-and-road/ (accessed 12 April 2022); see also CICC, 'The State

Law No 7 of 2005[90] and Article 5(A) of Law No 12 of 2004[91] concerning the jurisdiction of the QICDRC and the DIFC Courts, respectively, also clarify that both courts, much like the CICC, shall not have jurisdiction over investor-state cases. The statutes of other ICommCs may potentially more easily allow investor-state disputes. The SICC is a case in point. The broad interpretations of the terms 'international' and 'commercial' adopted by the SICC may possibly allow such disputes.[92]

The above provisions do not seem though to explicitly exclude contractual disputes between a private party and a state actor. The CICC could admit such disputes if the minimum value threshold is met and the parties agree to the jurisdiction of the court contractually. The same may also happen with other ICommCs such as the DIFC Courts.[93] The DIFC Courts' legislation allows parties not registered in the DIFC to expressly agree to take their dispute to the DIFC Courts.[94] There are, however, some differences between the jurisdictional approaches adopted by the legislators in Qatar and Dubai. The QFC legislation specifically states that one of the parties to a dispute must be registered with the QFC.[95] Still, an SOE could be registered with the QFC.

The status of states as respondents in commercial disputes has been addressed in commercial arbitration under major arbitral institutional rules. When a state enters into a commercial contract – which includes an arbitration clause – with a private commercial actor, one important issue for both sides to consider is whether the party in question truly represents the state. The law applicable to the contract and seat may vest certain state agencies or instrumentalities with separate legal personality, which would allow the state to hedge its legal risks when entering into commercial contracts. The applicable law may also provide a state party with an opportunity to avoid such liabilities, especially in situations when a state agency is not given the legal right to own and dispose of assets. The private party must consider whether the entity named as the party to the contract by the state is, from both a legal and a commercial perspective, the proper party to the contract.

Arbitral tribunals and courts that have dealt with such cases have taken one of the following two approaches: first, extend the applicability of the arbitration clause to the non-signatory state; second, respect the corporate veil between the

Council Information Office Held a Press Conference on the "Opinion on the Establishment of 'The Belt and Road' International Commercial Dispute Settlement Mechanism and Institutions"' (28 June 2018) cicc.court.gov.cn/html/1/219/208/210/769.html (accessed 1 November 2020).

[90] QFC No 7 of 2005, as amended by Law No 2 of 2009 and Law No 14 of 2009, Art 8(3)(c).

[91] Dubai Law No 12 of 2004, amended by Dubai Law No 16 of 2011, Art 5(A).

[92] See A Godwin, I Ramsay and M Webster, 'International Commercial Courts: The Singapore Experience' (2017) 18 *Melbourne Journal of International Law* 219, 226.

[93] See also M Beer, 'Belt and Road Initiative: One Vision of Justice' (13 May 2018), www.difccourts.ae/2018/05/13/belt-and-road-initiative-one-vision-of-justice/ (accessed 27 July 2022).

[94] Art 5 of Law No (16) of 2011 Amending Certain Provisions of Law No (12) of 2004 Concerning Dubai International Financial Centre Courts.

[95] Art 8(3) of Law No (7) of 2005.

'core' state and state agencies and instrumentalities which possess a separate legal personality.[96] Arbitral tribunals have shown a tendency to adopt the first approach, while national courts tend to sustain the challenges of arbitral awards based on the argument that they improperly extend the jurisdiction of the arbitral tribunal to a non-signatory.[97]

In the final award rendered by the tribunal in ICC Case No 9762, where the claimant had named as respondents, inter alia, a ministry of the country as well as the 'government', the arbitral tribunal decided to extend the arbitration agreement to cover the 'state'. It did so despite that the contract in dispute had been concluded only with the Ministry, which under the applicable law of the contract had a separate legal personality. The arbitral tribunal pointed to the claimant's reference to the 'government', and stated that it should be considered as a reference to the 'state' given the circumstances of the case.[98]

In *Svenska Petroleum Exploration AB v Lithuania*, another ICC case, the contract in question was entered into on the part of the state by AB Geonafta, a state corporation. One interesting detail in this case is that the contract was also signed by government officials and contained a statement above their signatures whereby the government approved the agreement and 'acknowledge[d] itself to be legally and contractually bound as if the Government were a signatory to the Agreement'.[99] The tribunal found that the government was, therefore, bound by the agreement. When Svenska sought to enforce the award in England, the state challenged the award on grounds that it was entitled to immunity from process. English courts dismissed the challenge and upheld the award rendered by the tribunal.[100]

In *Southern Pacific Properties (Middle East) Ltd v Egypt*, *Dallah v Pakistan* and *Bridas SAPIC v Turkmenistan*, the tribunals adopted the second line of case law, respecting the corporate veil between the 'core' state and state agencies and instrumentalities which possess a separate legal personality. In the SPP case, the agreement in question was signed by EGOTH, a state organisation with separate legal personality, as well as the Minister of Tourism of Egypt, which signed the contract underneath the words 'approved, agreed and ratified'.[101] Although the tribunal ruled that the state was indeed bound by the arbitration agreement through the aforementioned signature, the Court of Appeal of Paris considered

[96] V Heiskanen, 'State as a Private: The Participation of States in International Commercial Arbitration' (April 2010) 7(1) *Transnational Dispute Management* 6 www.lalive.law/data/publications/vhe_State_as_a_Private;_The_Participation_of_States_in_International_Commercial_Arbitration.pdf (accessed 27 July 2022).

[97] ibid.

[98] ICC Case No 9762, Final Award of 22 December 2001, 29 Y.B. INT'L COM. ARB. 26 (2004).

[99] *Svenska Petroleum v Lithuania*, [2006] APP.L.R. 11/13, 1.

[100] ES Romero, 'Are States Liable for the Conduct of Their Instrumentalities', in E Gaillard and J Younan (eds), *State Entities in International Arbitration* (Huntington, Juris Publishing, 2008) 49–52.

[101] *Southern Pacific Properties (Middle East) Ltd v Egypt*, 16 Feb 1983, 3 ICSID REP. 79, 87.

that the words did not imply the government's intention to be bound by the arbitration agreement; they simply meant that the government had approved the agreement. Accordingly, the Court set aside the award.[102]

The *Dallah* case arose out of an agreement between Dallah, a Saudi Arabian company, and the Awami Hajj Trust, a body set up by the Ministry of Religious Affairs of Pakistan to accept deposits from prospective Hajj pilgrims and invest them for the purpose of covering the costs of the pilgrimage. Like the *SPP* case, the arbitral tribunal found that it had jurisdiction over the Pakistani Ministry of Religious affairs.[103] The Ministry challenged the award in London and argued that it was not bound by the arbitration agreement given its non-signatory status. The High Court upheld the challenge, finding that under French law (the law governing the arbitration agreement, in the absence of a choice of law clause) Pakistan was not bound. The decision was subsequently upheld by the Court of Appeals.[104]

Similarly, in the *Bridas* case, the tribunal upheld its jurisdiction over both the relevant state entity, Turkmenneft, and the Government of Turkmenistan, even though the latter was not formally a party to the underlying contract, on grounds, inter alia, that the contract contained undertakings which only the government could fulfil. Bridas, following the decision, moved to enforce the award in the US. The Government of Turkmenistan argued that the arbitral tribunal exceeded its jurisdiction when it found that it had jurisdiction over the government. The US Court of Appeals for the 5th Circuit rejected all the theories pursued by Bridas, with the exception of the alter ego doctrine. When the District Court vacated the award, the matter again ended up at the Court of Appeals, which this time upheld the award on the basis of the alter ego theory.[105]

Based on the above discussion, depending on the circumstances of a transaction and/or contract, an SOE, state Ministry and even the state itself may end up as a party to a dispute before an ICommC. There are already examples of SOEs appearing as parties before an ICommC. The Regulatory Authority of the QFC (QFCRA), for example, commenced legal proceedings against The First Abu Dhabi Bank (FAB), which is 53.2 per cent owned by Mubadala – the Sovereign Wealth Fund of Abu Dhabi – and members of the Abu Dhabi Ruling Family. The QFCRA had commenced an investigation in March 2018 into suspected manipulation by FAB (along with Samba Bank of Saudi Arabia) of the Qatari Riyal, Qatari Government securities and related financial instruments. FAB – via its QFC branch – was served notice to produce certain documents and information held by the bank at any of its branches or offices. FAB, however, refused

[102] ibid 91.

[103] *Dallah Estate and Tourism Holding Co. v The Ministry of Religious Affairs, Government of Pakistan* [2009] EWCA Civ 755.

[104] G Born, 'Enforcement of International Arbitral Awards in England and the New York Convention', Kluwer Arbitration Blog, 22 August 2009.

[105] *Bridas S.A.P.I.C. v Government of Turkmenistan*, 345 F.3d 347 (5 Cir. 2003).

to submit documents that were held by the bank's head office in Abu Dhabi. Following FAB's refusal, the QFCRA commenced legal proceedings in the First Instance Circuit in July 2018 and obtained an order to comply with the notice to produce.[106]

The two most important questions for our purposes that the Court addressed are the following: first, whether the QFCRA had jurisdiction to commence an investigation into matters that took place outside the QFC, and as such issue a notice to the bank to produce documents and provide information on these matters; second, whether the QFCRA's jurisdiction extended beyond the QFC branch of the bank, as well as whether this jurisdiction extended to mandating the production of documents held outside Qatar.

The Appellate Division of the QICDRC rejected the first ground of appeal due to the fact that Article 26 of the Financial Services Regulations did not extend the actual jurisdiction conferred by the QFC Law (which established the QFCRA 'for the purpose of regulating, licensing and supervising banking, financial and insurance-related business carried on *in or from* the QFC').[107] The pertinent question, according to the Court, was whether there was an evidential basis for the QFCRA's request for the documents and whether information was required from FAB. The Court stated that the QFCRA needed to demonstrate whether the activities in question: (i) related to a firm active in the QFC; and (ii) were capable of affecting confidence in the financial system operating in the QFC or the firm's fitness and propriety. The Court concluded that the activities carried on outside the QFC related to the activities of the branch of the bank in the QFC.[108]

In dealing with the second issue, the Court considered the following three questions: (i) whether the QFC Law and Regulations gave the Regulatory Authority jurisdiction to require the production of documents held outside Qatar; (ii) whether the case law on the distinction between a bank and its branch is relevant; and (iii) the rationale for treating a branch as distinct for regulatory purposes where this is the case.[109] For the first question, the Court stressed that in order for the QFCRA to carry out its regulatory duties, it must at times exercise powers in the QFC relating to matters occurring or documents and information held outside the territory of Qatar, and that the QFC Laws and Regulations enable the QFCRA to do so. The Court, therefore, held that the QFCRA's actions did not infringe the principle of territoriality.[110] Concerning the second point, the Court relied on two DIFC Court cases applying the well-established principle that a branch is no more than a part of the larger company

[106] *Qatar Financial Centre Regulatory Authority v First Abu Dhabi Bank P.J.S.C.* [2019] QIC (A) 3, 27.

[107] ibid, 21, 24.

[108] ibid, 30.

[109] ibid, 38.

[110] ibid, 42–49.

similar to a division of the company.[111] The Court also denied FAB's arguments concerning the separability of the branch from the main bank for regulatory purposes.[112]

Based on awards of various tribunals in international commercial arbitration, the jurisdictional requirements outlined in the acts governing the relevant ICommCs, as well as QICDRC case law, commercial actors may indeed bring claims arising out of contracts against SOEs, state agencies/ministries and, even, the state itself.

## V. CONCLUSION

The 2008 global recession gave rise to what Ian Bremmer dubbed 'state capitalism'. State capitalism, as detailed above, does not fall under the two broad types of capitalism outlined by Peter Hall and David Soskice – CMEs and LMEs. State capitalism is developing as an economic system with domestic and international economic as well as institutional implications.

ICommCs may be seen as institutions of a new variety of international state capitalism. The relationship between ICommCs and state capitalism is multifaceted. ICommCs can operate without the need for domestic institutional complementarities. ICommCs have the potential of establishing international institutional complementarities. A number of ICommCs are not only institutions of state capitalism as a variety of capitalism, but are also involved in international state capitalist projects themselves. Many ICommCs are established either as part of an SEZ or as part of a larger state capitalist strategy like China's BRI. They provide an avenue for commercial actors to resolve their disputes, ensuring the integrity of state-backed projects and institutions, and catering for a legal environment that is welcoming to foreign investors as a means of furthering the state's policy ends. At the same time, commercial actors could eventually bring forward claims against SOEs – based on the circumstances of a transaction and/or contract – before an ICommC.

As both state capitalism as an international economic system will continue expanding, and ICommCs will continue proliferating, the greater interconnectedness between them will continue growing too.

[111] ibid, 52, 55.
[112] ibid, 57–64.

# Part IV

# Contextualising State Capitalism

# 12

# *State Capitalism and Global Governance under the Belt and Road Initiative*

QINGXIU BU

## I. INTRODUCTION

MAJOR POWERS INFLUENCE the design and implementation of global rules to their own advantage.[1] Globalisation has led to asymmetric engagement and opportunities, although standard theory would lead one to expect that all countries will benefit evenly. The resulting unequal opportunities under the existing institutions trigger increased nationalist push-back, while a new power is seeking to integrate its own institutional approaches into the global policy architecture. During this geopolitical transformation, the contestations are even sharper in the context of globalising economic orders and legal norms.

With its enormous financial capacity, China has been building up its soft power through a 'Belt and Road Initiative' (BRI),[2] which differs from existing treaty-based integration concepts. It is worth examining whether it signifies a 'global public good' concept and further achieves win-win objectives. At a macro level, this chapter addresses whether the BRI strikes a balance between China's ambitious national goals and its international obligations. At a micro-level, the chapter explores rigorously how China deals with cross-border disputes in accordance with international law. The study proceeds in four steps.

In the context of reshaping global governance, section I conceptualises a state capitalism model vis-à-vis the Washington Consensus. This section seeks

[1] PM Haas and JA Hird, *Controversies in Globalization: Contending Approaches to International Relations,* 2nd edn (Washington, CQ Press, 2012) 40–70, 67.

[2] The two following terms are used interchangeably in this chapter: 'One Belt and One Road (BRI)' and 'Belt and Road Initiative (BRI)'. On the actors, rules and processes of state capitalism in China, see ch 4, in this volume.

to address whether the two models could complement each other, since they may become rival models of influence. The chapter then continues with an application of power transition theory to analyse how China is engaged in global institution-building through creating a new formula of global governance. Section II deals with China's grand BRI strategy. In addition to the exploration of its rationales, it is argued that the BRI differs substantially from that of the 'Marshall Plan'. Section III ascertains whether the establishment of a hybrid global governance regime is dependent on China's unique characteristics and also whether it is compatible with international law. It remains unclear as to whether an ideologically perceived line is becoming increasingly blurred by the market-driven BRI. It is equally essential to look at the EU Foreign Investment Screening Regulation as well as the response from the Organisation for Economic Cooperation and Development (OECD). Their interaction with the BRI provides more insights in terms of the viability of the initiative. Section IV examines barriers to China's implementation of its long-standing principles of equality and cooperation for mutual benefits. The emerging multilateral system embedded in the BRI has been challenged by rising popular nationalist sentiments. This section seeks to mitigate inevitable conflicts from multipronged perspectives. The concluding section affirms that the BRI must be based on universally recognised international norms, otherwise it will be difficult for China to project strategic narratives on the international stage. At stake is whether China can overcome the governance challenge while enhancing its own global influence.

## II. CONCEPTUALISING STATE CAPITALISM VIS-À-VIS THE WASHINGTON CONSENSUS

China's stunning growth rates have corresponded with the rise of state capitalism.[3] It captures China's unique blend of market, finance, government-owned corporations and central control.[4] The re-emergence of capitalism in China after the 2008 financial crisis is fuelling competition between China and other states around the globe for soft power and global influence.[5] Since the mid-2000s, China's political economy has stabilised around a model where most sectors are marketised and increasingly integrated with the global economy.[6] However, strategic industries remain firmly in the control of an elite empire of state-owned

[3] KS Tsai and B Naughton (eds), *State Capitalism, Institutional Adaptation, and the Chinese Miracle* (New York, Cambridge University Press, 2015) 1–24.

[4] ibid.

[5] C McNally, 'Sino-Capitalism: China's Reemergence and the International Political Economy' (2012) 64(4) *World Politics* 741, 776.

[6] KS Tsai and B Naughton (eds), *State Capitalism, Institutional Adaptation, and the Chinese Miracle* (New York, Cambridge University Press, 2015) 240–265.

enterprises (SOEs).[7] It poses a direct challenge to the western concept of the free market and neoliberal capitalism.[8] A variety of inquiries are explored regarding the implications of state capitalism on geopolitical competitiveness and global governance. It is not yet entirely clear to what extent the BRI offers a different version of capitalism.[9] Any approaches via either purely economic or geopolitical and security affairs would be too simplified and incomplete. It is crucial to conceptualise China's BRI in an interdisciplinary context.

## A. The Rise of a Distinct Form of State Capitalism in China

As the primary driver, the rise of state capitalism in China poses a challenge to the free market economies of the developed world, particularly in the aftermath of the 2008 financial crisis.[10] It is a market-driven economic system where the state allows for more direct control of the economy.[11] The sustainability of Chinese capitalism depends upon the extent to which China can address development challenges with adequate resilience and efficient adaptability.[12]

### *i. Legitimacy*

China needs to maintain domestic economic growth, which is the foundation for political stability in the Chinese Communist Party (CCP) regime. This helps to strengthen the role of the CCP as a tool of governance in an authoritarian but market-dominated system.[13] Chinese state capitalism along with its institutional adaption has led to the Chinese miracle.[14] As regards a long-term global strategy of poverty eradication, China's double-digit growth has moved over

[7] M Pearson, 'State-Owned Business and Party-State Regulation in China's Modern Political Economy', in KS Tsai and B Naughton (eds) *State Capitalism, Institutional Adaptation, and the Chinese Miracle* (New York, Cambridge University Press, 2015) 27–45.

[8] S Breslin, 'The 'China model' and the global crisis: from Friedrich List to a Chinese mode of governance?' (2011) 87(6) *International Affairs* 1323, 1343.

[9] A Nordin and M Weissmann, 'Will Trump Make China Great Again? The Belt and Road Initiative and International Order' (2018) 94(2) *International Affairs* 231, 249.

[10] C Calhoun, 'What Threatens Capitalism Now?', in I Wallerstein and C Calhoun, et al. (eds), *Does Capitalism Have a Future?* (Oxford, Oxford University Press, 2013) 131–161.

[11] I Bremmer, 'State Capitalism Comes of Age: The End of the Free Market?' (2009) 88(3) *Foreign Affairs* 40, 55.

[12] 'What Keeps Xi Up at Night: Beijing's Internal and External Challenges' Hearing before the United States-China Economic and Security Review Commission (Washington, 116th Congress, 1st Session, 7 February 2019) www.uscc.gov/sites/default/files/transcripts/February%207%2C%20 2019%20Hearing%20Transcript.pdf.

[13] LY Ruan, 'The Chinese Communist Party and Legitimacy' *The Diplomat* (30 September 2015).

[14] M Frazier, 'The Evolution of a Welfare State under China's State Capitalism', in KS Tsai and B Naughton (eds), *State Capitalism, Institutional Adaptation, and the Chinese Miracle* (New York, Cambridge University Press, 2015) 223–239.

400 million people out of poverty,[15] associated with structural and systemic measures. China holds that its development paradigm would contribute to global economic prosperity as well as security and stability.[16] Given the essential role of the poverty eradication narrative, it remains to be seen to which extent other BRI member states will benefit from the BRI.

### *ii. Geo-economics and Geopolitical Perspectives*

Steadily advancing China's strategic objective of fashioning a Sinocentric order characterises geo-economics.[17] Conceptually, the term 'geo-economics' refers to China's long-standing predilection for a realist or mercantilist style of state–economy relations and foreign economic policy.[18] It means the use of economic instruments to promote national interests, and to produce beneficial geopolitical results,[19] and further to achieve broader foreign policy or geostrategic aims.[20] Ikenberry and Lim provided insights into China's incentives via a theory of external innovation:

(i) offering a new institutional mode of international cooperation within the existing system;
(ii) creating a new tool of statecraft to enhance bilateral or multilateral influence; and
(iii) replacing the prevailing substantive rules and norms within the relevant policy domain.[21]

China may use the BRI to promote its economic system to other countries. Given the long-term geopolitical implications, China's economic might could translate into global political influence.[22] Positively, BRI plays into the narrative laid out by China that its rise will be peaceful and marked by economic relationships.[23]

[15] S Fan and R Kanbur, et al., *The Oxford Companion to the Economics of China* (Oxford, Oxford University Press, 2014) 1–28.

[16] M Ferchen, 'China, Economic Development, and Global Security: Bridging the Gaps' (Carnegie–Tsinghua Center for Global Policy, December 2016) carnegieendowment.org/files/CP_289_Ferchen_China_Final2.pdf, 1.

[17] ibid, 6.

[18] H Harding, 'Has U.S. China Policy Failed?' (2015) 38(3) *Washington Quarterly* 95, 122.

[19] R Blackwill and J Harris, *War by Other Means: Geoeconomics and Statecraft* (Cambridge, MA, Harvard University Press, 2016) 20.

[20] G Grieger, 'One Belt, One Road (BRI): China's Regional Integration Initiative' (European Parliamentary Research Service, Briefings, July 2016) www.europarl.europa.eu/RegData/etudes/BRIE/2016/586608/EPRS_BRI(2016)586608_EN.pdf.

[21] J Ikenberry and D Lim, 'China's Emerging Institutional Statecraft: The Asian Infrastructure Investment Bank and the Prospects for Counter-Hegemony' *Brookings* (April 2017) www.brookings.edu/wp-content/uploads/2017/04/chinas-emerging-institutional-statecraft.pdf, 8.

[22] Global Agenda Council on Geo-Economics, 'Geo-Economics with Chinese Characteristics: How China's Economic Might Is Reshaping World Politics' (World Economic Forum, January 2016) www3.weforum.org/docs/WEF_Geoeconomics_with_Chinese_Characteristics.pdf.

[23] J Sidaway and CY Woon, 'Chinese Narratives on 'One Belt, One Road' in Geopolitical and Imperial Contexts' (2017) 69(4) *The Professional Geographer* 591, 603.

It is worth examining the extent to which these logics and pathways of influence align with China's practical objectives.[24]

## III. BRI

China's BRI was launched in 2013 to boost economic integration with its neighbours and various trading partners.[25] Morgan Stanley has predicted that China's investment in BRI member states will increase by 14 per cent annually, and the total investment amount could double to US$1.2–1.3 trillion by 2027.[26] The strategy is designed largely to fund projects from China's west through Central Asia to the Middle East and Europe.[27] As the vanguard for Beijing's reach for global power,[28] the BRI has the potential to be perhaps the world's largest institutional platform for regional collaboration. The implementation of the BRI involves complex interactions among the economic, geopolitical and security dimensions of China's relations with the rest of the world.[29] Economically and strategically expanding its global influence, the BRI marks a new stage in the growing salience of geopolitical considerations in Chinese foreign policy.[30] It is intended to promote infrastructure, enhance complementarity of development strategies and boost interconnected development to achieve common prosperity.[31]

### A. Overcapacity and Energy Security

China's domestic economy is at a critical juncture in its development trajectory, facing a challenging transition from an investment-led to consumption-led model of growth.[32] Overcapacity is one of China's comprehensive economic and

[24] J Ikenberry and D Lim, 'China's Emerging Institutional Statecraft: The Asian Infrastructure Investment Bank and the Prospects for Counter-Hegemony' *Brookings* (April 2017) www.brookings.edu/wp-content/uploads/2017/04/chinas-emerging-institutional-statecraft.pdf.

[25] 'China's Belt and Road Initiative (BRI)' (Chatham House London, The Royal Institute of International Affairs) www.chathamhouse.org/research/topics/china-belt-and-road-initiative-bri.

[26] Morgan Stanley, 'Inside China's Plan to Create a Modern Silk Road' (14 March 2018) www.morganstanley.com/ideas/china-belt-and-road.

[27] 'One Belt One Road' (Oxford, Faculty of Law, Oxford University) www.law.ox.ac.uk/one-belt-one-road.

[28] W Hawkins, 'China's Belt and Road Initiative: Globalisation as Imperialism' *Selous Foundation for Public Policy Research* (2 August 2017).

[29] J-MF Blanchard and C Flint, 'The Geopolitics of China's Maritime Silk Road Initiative' (2017) 22(2) *Geopolitics* 223, 245.

[30] C Hughes, 'Reclassifying Chinese Nationalism: The Geopolitik Turn' (2011) 20(71) *Journal of Contemporary China* 601, 620.

[31] 'Chinese President Xi's Address at APEC CEO Summit' *Xinhua* (11 November 2017) www.xinhuanet.com/english/2017-11/11/c_136743492.htm.

[32] F Zilibotti, 'Growing and Slowing Down Like China' (2017) 15(5) *Journal of the European Economic* 943, 988.

geopolitical motives. There is great potential for China to use the BRI to absorb some of its surplus.[33] The BRI-orientated infrastructure projects offer outlets to relieve overcapacity in major industrial sectors, where domestic returns have been declining.[34] Given trade and infrastructure are inextricably linked, the goal of the BRI is to provide energy security and access to global markets for Chinese products. Such strategic moves could shape a more pliable regional security and political environment for the country.[35]

There is overcapacity in many sectors, which squeezes corporate profits, increases debt levels and makes China's financial system more vulnerable.[36] Dealing with China's excess capacity has become one of the top economic priorities, and is considered the sword of Damocles hanging over its head.[37] Cutting down overcapacity would involve slashing jobs, shutting down plants and closing factories.[38] The BRI serves as an initiative to drain some of China's excess production.[39] More specifically, investment in infrastructure and investment in poverty eradication are two of the most pressing public-policy issues.[40] The world faces a global infrastructure deficit of US$2 trillion per year over the next 20 years.[41] The absence of adequate infrastructure represents a key structural factor that holds back local economic development. China has relatively advanced technologies as well as abundant capital. Its global extraction of oil and other resources has created a formidable capability in construction and engineering. During the last four decades, infrastructure development abroad has represented the cornerstone of China's rise. The lure has been almost irresistible to countries which do not have these resources.[42]

Another projected benefit is the energy security that will come through the construction of BRI-funded transport routes.[43] For instance, China's energy

[33] D Dollar, 'The AIIB and the 'One Belt, One Road'' *Brookings* (Summer 2015) www.brookings.edu/opinions/the-aiib-and-the-one-belt-one-road/.

[34] J Ikenberry and D Lim, 'China's Emerging Institutional Statecraft: The Asian Infrastructure Investment Bank and the Prospects for Counter-Hegemony' *Brookings* (April 2017) www.brookings.edu/wp-content/uploads/2017/04/chinas-emerging-institutional-statecraft.pdf, 10.

[35] J Zhou, K Hallding and G Han, 'The Trouble with China's 'One Belt One Road' Strategy' *The Diplomat* (26 June 2015).

[36] P Cai, 'Understanding China's Belt and Road Initiative' (Lowy Institute for International Policy, March 2017).

[37] ibid.

[38] J Zhou, K Hallding and G Han, 'The Trouble with China's 'One Belt One Road' Strategy' *The Diplomat* (26 June 2015).

[39] A Chatzky and J McBride, 'China's Massive Belt and Road Initiative' (Washington D.C., The Council on Foreign Relations, 21 May 2019) www.cfr.org/backgrounder/chinas-massive-belt-and-road-initiative.

[40] M Dunford and W Liu, 'Chinese Perspectives on the Belt and Road Initiative' (2019) 12(1) *Cambridge Journal of Regions, Economy and Society* 145, 167.

[41] World Economic Forum, 'The Global Competitiveness Report 2015–2016', reports.weforum.org/global-competitiveness-report-2015-2016/infrastructure-and-connectivity/.

[42] W Hawkins, 'China's Belt and Road Initiative: Globalisation as Imperialism' *Selous Foundation for Public Policy Research* (2 August 2017).

[43] T Greer, 'One Belt, One Road, One Big Mistake' *Foreign Policy* (6 December 2018).

security can be enhanced by creating alternative trade routes across land bridges in economic corridors linking China's south-western provinces directly to the Indian Ocean.[44] A flagship project of the China–Pakistan Economic Corridor provides China with energy resources as well as growing consumer markets.[45] The BRI features prominently, alongside China's reliance on SOEs for the country's efforts to guarantee access to energy and other global commodities.[46] It can be reconceptualised as the cornerstone of China's future global vision. Thus, China may gain a more viable return on its foreign exchange reserves, create new overseas business opportunities for Chinese firms, create new markets for industries currently experiencing overcapacity, and stimulate economic development in poorer regions of China.[47] As such, seen as a quick solution to the problem of overcapacity, Chinese companies are incentivised to go abroad by expanding their access to overseas markets.

### B. BRI vis-à-vis 'Marshall Plan'

Compared with the US Marshall Plan for Europe,[48] the BRI could serve as a twenty-first century version of the 'Marshall Plan', with huge infrastructure projects and enhanced trade and investment schemes underpinning new forms of Chinese leverage.[49] The 'Chinese Marshall Plan' risks, however, prolonging China's state capitalism, with its SOEs and state-owned policy banks playing a major role in the BRI's implementation, even though China has pledged to allow the market to play a decisive role in resource allocation.[50] It will present China with strategic opportunities in expanding its global influence, given that state capitalism may cross national boundaries through the BRI.[51] It is important to explore how each national context affects the operations of the SOEs and

[44] G Grieger, 'One Belt, One Road (BRI): China's Regional Integration Initiative' (European Parliamentary Research Service, Briefings, July 2016) www.europarl.europa.eu/RegData/etudes/BRIE/2016/586608/EPRS_BRI(2016)586608_EN.pdf.

[45] A Rafiq 'China's $62 Billion Bet on Pakistan' *Foreign Affairs* (24 October 2017).

[46] M Ferchen, 'China, Economic Development, and Global Security: Bridging the Gaps' (Carnegie–Tsinghua Center for Global Policy, December 2016) carnegieendowment.org/files/CP_289_Ferchen_China_Final2.pdf, 6.

[47] P Haenle and A Gabuev, et al., 'The Belt and Road Initiative: Views from Washington, Moscow, and Beijing' (Carnegie-Tsinghua Center for Global Policy, 8 April 2019) carnegietsinghua.org/2019/04/08/belt-and-road-initiative-views-from-washington-moscow-and-beijing-pub-78774.

[48] S Tiezzi, 'The New Silk Road: China's Marshall Plan?' *The Diplomat* (6 November 2014).

[49] S Shen, 'How China's 'Belt and Road' Compares to the Marshall Plan' *Diplomat* (6 February 2016).

[50] G Grieger, 'One Belt, One Road (BRI): China's Regional Integration Initiative' *European Parliament Briefing* (July 2016) www.europarl.europa.eu/RegData/etudes/BRIE/2016/586608/EPRS_BRI(2016)586608_EN.pdf.

[51] P Le Corre, 'China's Rise as a Geoeconomic Influencer: Four European Case Studies' (Carnegie Endowment for International Peace, 15 October 2018) carnegieendowment.org/2018/10/15/china-s-rise-as-geoeconomic-influencer-four-european-case-studies-pub-77462.

thus shapes idiosyncratic models of state capitalism being developed in the BRI member states.[52]

Similarly, the two grand schemes share a common context of market failure or global power vacuum.[53] China does not share the US's belief in limited state intervention, which plays an important role via markets.[54] As the BRI projects boost local economic growth, Chinese investors will be in a position to take advantage of new opportunities and further expand their foreign direct investment holdings. The initiative seems to put common development over power politics,[55] but the strategic purpose of the BRI goes beyond merely economic gain.[56] Rolland provides testimony:[57]

> … BRI's different components serve Beijing's vision for regional integration under its helm. It is a top-level design for which the central government has mobilised the country's political, diplomatic, intellectual, economic and financial resources … it is a grand strategy.

Vines points to potential risks: 'The Belt and Road initiative might conceivably become no more than a gigantic instrument of supply-chain management for China, creating the kind of jobs that drive an enormous Chinese production machine.'[58] Echoed by Dunford and Liu, it is just the old 'division of labour' common to imperialism, despite the fact that it was claimed to be a win-win situation.[59]

## IV. RESHAPING THE GLOBAL GOVERNANCE LANDSCAPE?

Power transition theory deals with the emergence of global power transformations and their effects on the structure of global governance.[60] The rise of China

[52] 'The Rise of State Capitalism' *The Economist* (21 January 2012); 'Theme and Variations' *The Economist* (21 January 2012).

[53] S Shen and W Chan, 'A Comparative Study of the Belt and Road Initiative and the Marshall Plan' (2018) 4(1) *Palgrave Communications* 32, 32.

[54] D Rediker, 'Who are the Winners and Losers of Geo-economic Competition?' *World Economic Forum* (27 February 2015) www.weforum.org/agenda/2015/02/who-are-the-winners-and-losers-of-geo-economic-competition/.

[55] T Piccone, 'China's Long Game on Human Rights at the United Nations' (Washington, D.C., Brookings, September 2018) www.brookings.edu/wp-content/uploads/2018/09/FP_20181009_china_human_rights.pdf.

[56] A Scobell and B Lin, et al., 'At the Dawn of Belt and Road: China in the Developing World' (Rand Corporation, 2018) www.rand.org/pubs/research_reports/RR2273.html.

[57] N Rolland, 'Testimony before the U.S.-China Economic and Security Review Commission Hearing on: 'China's Belt and Road Initiative: Five Years Later'' (25 January 2018) www.uscc.gov/sites/default/files/Rolland_USCC%20Testimony_16Jan2018.pdf.

[58] D Vines, 'Can Belt and Road Initiative Resurrect a Liberal International Order?' *Daily Mirror* (15 May 2017).

[59] M Dunford and W Liu, 'Chinese Perspectives on the Belt and Road Initiative' (2019) 12(1) *Cambridge Journal of Regions, Economy and Society* 145, 167.

[60] C Layne, 'The US–Chinese Power Shift and the End of the Pax Americana' (2018) 94(1) *International Affairs* 89, 111.

to the status of a global power is one of the seminal developments of the current era.[61] The emerging power dynamics highlight a competition of ideologies about the future constitution of global governance.[62] China inevitably finds itself with growing stakes in how the world is organised, and seeks to reshape the current governance regime.[63] Based primarily upon an ideological perspective, China's economic miracle is often attributed to its unique political and economic policies, which are referred to as the Beijing Model. It is worth examining whether the Model can be replicated by BRI member states and how China is moving to realign the global economy with its interests.[64]

## A. Existing Global Governance Regime

American hegemony, liberal internationalism and the deeper systemic foundations of sovereignty and state primacy are three layers of the existing system.[65] Many of the existing global rules and institutions were established prior to China's ascent and entry into the global system.[66] Reform of the institution entails the redistribution of decision-making authority, facilitating greater influence over operations and potentially a larger share of the gains generated by the reshaping of institutions.[67] Influence may extend to leverage in the pursuit of greater formal authority within existing institutions in the relevant policy domain, thus overlapping with the authority-seeking stakeholder strategy.[68] As Kaya described it, a 'status-quo stakeholder' state accepts the existing rules and norms of the institution or regime, while an 'authority-seeking stakeholder' seeks to gain greater voice and influence in the formal processes of the institution, defined as 'distributive change' via enhanced voting rights and/or greater national representation in the constituent organs based on underlying

[61] DW Larson, 'Will China be a New Type of Great Power?' (2015) 8(4) *The Chinese Journal of International Politics* 323, 348.

[62] Peter Ferdinand, 'Westward Ho-The China Dream and 'One Belt, One Road': Chinese Foreign Policy under Xi Jinping' (2016) 92 (4) International Affairs 941, 957.

[63] X Yan, 'The Age of Uneasy Peace: Chinese Power in a Divided World' *Foreign Affairs* (January/February 2019).

[64] DA Lake, 'Economic Openness and Great Power Competition: Lessons for China and the United States' (2018) 11(3) *The Chinese Journal of International Politics* 237, 270.

[65] J Ikenberry and D Lim, 'China's Emerging Institutional Statecraft: The Asian Infrastructure Investment Bank and the Prospects for Counter-Hegemony' *Brookings* (April 2017) www.brookings.edu/wp-content/uploads/2017/04/chinas-emerging-institutional-statecraft.pdf.

[66] H Feng and K He, 'China's Institutional Challenges to the International Order' (2017) 11(4) *Strategic Studies Quarterly* 23, 49.

[67] J Ikenberry and D Lim, 'China's Emerging Institutional Statecraft: The Asian Infrastructure Investment Bank and the Prospects for Counter-Hegemony' *Brookings* (April 2017) www.brookings.edu/wp-content/uploads/2017/04/chinas-emerging-institutional-statecraft.pdf, 4.

[68] ibid, 7–8.

member characteristics.[69] BRI challenges the still dominating western vision of the international system and could effectively transform the existing structure of the current international order.[70] Development has always entailed social and political change and challenges.[71] Improving the policy coordination necessary for the implementation of such cross-border infrastructure projects remains a challenge.[72] In this regard, China is not seeking to reform the substantive rules and norms of an institution.

### B. Global Governance Characterised with Chinese Elements

The geo-economics paradigm characterises China as a mercantilist power whose state-led economy and increasingly assertive foreign economic initiatives will enhance the country's global power and leverage.[73] Despite China's four-decade economic reforms, it is still labelled as a socialist market economy. The transformation from state socialism to state capitalism helps to legitimise the marketisation of the economy.[74] The China Model attempts to play a levelling role in markets, to ensure that booms and busts are limited and that unbridled capitalism is tempered by the interests of the state and other stakeholders.[75] This appears to indicate that the government uses free market forces to promote the economy, but it still plays a major role in the country's economic development.[76] In the scenario of BRI, democracy and individual rights are largely subservient to economic growth and social stability.[77] As such, the BRI is characterised

[69] A Kaya, *Power and Global Economic Institutions* (New York, Cambridge University Press, 2015) 9.

[70] M Esteban and W Zhou, 'Beyond Balancing: China's Approach Towards the Belt and Road Initiative' (2018) 27(112) *Journal of Contemporary China* 487, 501.

[71] J Horsley, 'Challenging China to Make Good Project Governance a Centerpiece of the Belt and Road Initiative' (Paul Tsai China Center, Yale Law School, December 2018) law.yale.edu/system/files/area/center/china/document/horsley_china_bri-good_governance_infrastructure.pdf.

[72] M Raiser and M Ruta, 'World Bank: Managing the Risks of the Belt and Road' *Caixin* (19 June 2019).

[73] M Ferchen, 'China, Economic Development, and Global Security: Bridging the Gaps' (Carnegie–Tsinghua Center for Global Policy, December 2016) carnegieendowment.org/files/CP_289_Ferchen_China_Final2.pdf, 1.

[74] I Bremmer, 'State Capitalism Comes of Age: The End of the Free Market?' (2009) 88(3) *Foreign Affairs* 40, 55.

[75] D Redike, 'Challenge 3-State Capitalism 2.0' (World Economic Forum: Geo-economics Seven Challenges to Globalization, January 2015) www3.weforum.org/docs/WEF_Geo-economics_7_Challenges_Globalization_2015_report.pdf.

[76] W Morrison, 'China's Economic Rise: History, Trends, Challenges, and Implications for the United States' (Washington D.C., Congressional Research Service, 25 June 2019) fas.org/sgp/crs/row/RL33534.pdf.

[77] C Cheney, 'China's Belt and Road Initiative: Reshaping the Global and Regional Orders' *Political Insights* (9 November 2018).

by an economically liberal and politically illiberal order, which mirrors China's domestic governance architecture.[78]

### *i. China as an Ideological Rival: Paving the Way to a New Global Order?*

Globalisation has helped fuel China's rise as a strategic rival.[79] It is emerging as a near-peer competitor and has begun to project geo-economic influence beyond its vicinity.[80] The advance of the BRI project could trigger a transition of the international system that would move the current US-dominant order to a multipolar, or even China-centric, one.[81] As a new player in global governance, China is committed to being a frontrunner in developing a new kind of multilateralism and in reshaping the global governance system.[82] Critical inquiries arise as to what alternative concepts of order exist and how these concepts may challenge the existing order.[83] Some commentators have respectively labelled China a 'fragile' or 'partial' power.[84] However, British polemicist Martin Jacques speculates about when China will 'rule the world'.[85] Theoretically, China could create a parallel global order with a new model of development, given China's ascendant role in the global economy.[86] It depends largely upon whether China can create new potential rival institutions within the wider context of its engagement with global institutions, and the broader system of existing multilateral rules and institutions.[87] The country is attempting to reshape the geo-economic landscape through the BRI.[88] This ambitious initiative is to be achieved through nurturing China's multinational champions, building infrastructure across continents and creating new markets.

[78] ibid.

[79] P Mishra, 'The Rise of China and the Fall of the Free Trade Myth' *The New York Times* (7 February 2018).

[80] T Cavanna, 'What Does China's Belt and Road Initiative Mean for US Grand Strategy?' *The Diplomat* (5 June 2018).

[81] S Saran, 'Is a China-Centric World Inevitable?' *YaleGlobal Online* (25 July 2017).

[82] H Moynihan, 'Engage China to Uphold Multilateralism – But Not at Any Cost' (Chatham House, The Royal Institute of International Affairs, 12 June 2019) www.chathamhouse.org/expert/comment/engage-china-uphold-multilateralism-not-any-cost#.

[83] N Godehardt, 'No End of History: A Chinese Alternative Concept of International Order?' (Berlin, SWP Research Paper 2, January 2016) www.swp-berlin.org/fileadmin/contents/products/research_papers/2016RP02_gdh.pdf.

[84] S Shirk, *China: Fragile Superpower* (New York, Oxford University Press, 2007) 107.

[85] M Jacques, *When China Rules the World: The Rise of the Middle Kingdom and the End of the Western World*, 2nd edn (New York, Penguin Group, 2009) 364–414.

[86] J Ikenberry, 'The Rise of China and the Future of the West: Can the Liberal System Survive?' (2008) 87(1) *Foreign Affairs* 23, 37.

[87] J Ikenberry and D Lim, 'China's Emerging Institutional Statecraft: The Asian Infrastructure Investment Bank and the Prospects for Counter-Hegemony' *Brookings* (April 2017) www.brookings.edu/wp-content/uploads/2017/04/chinas-emerging-institutional-statecraft.pdf, 2.

[88] P Ferdinand, 'Westward Ho – The China Dream and 'One Belt, One Road': Chinese Foreign Policy under Xi Jinping' (2016) 92(4) *International Affairs* 941, 957.

### *ii. A Hybrid Model: State's Dominance vis-à-vis Private Actors' Emerging Roles*

China's BRI may give rise to a hybrid model of transnational governance.[89] Its state-driven aspects contribute to the BRI's ambition. The government uses its ownership of companies and financial institutions to further its strategic goals.[90] The state still dominantly shapes rulemaking, and SOEs advancing state policy play a key role in the implementation of BRI projects. States often create national investment portfolios via sovereign wealth funds, which are used to help finance state capitalism.[91] Large SOEs and government policy banks provide more than 95 per cent of BRI funding.[92] The privileged relationship between the state and Chinese SOEs allows the former to secure control over key strategic sectors and resources, thereby ensuring stable energy supplies and providing national stability.[93] The highly centralised model seems to make a lot of these projects viable. However, there is substantial challenge in dealing with the issues in the state-driven side of the hybrid governance model. Entering a phase of relatively slower growth, China needs to adapt to new challenges and party-state priorities.[94]

To build an effective and sustainable hybrid model of transnational governance, a number of strategies can be pursued. It is essential to develop a diversified financing system and facilitate greater cooperation between government and private capital.[95] State-affiliated multinational corporations (MNCs) serve to promote national developmental agendas. Some powerful non-state actors, such as MNCs, play increasingly significant roles in the BRI framework. In response, they are expected to increase their level of engagement with non-state entities on BRI-related issues. It is notable that the interface between state and market is complex and multifaceted.[96] It remains uncertain whether this hybrid model

[89] M Feldman, 'China's Belt and Road Investment Governance: Building a Hybrid Model' (Columbia FDI Perspectives on Topical Foreign Direct Investment Issues No. 244, Columbia Centre for Sustainable Investment, 28 January 2019) ccsi.columbia.edu/files/2018/10/No-244-Feldman-FINAL.pdf.

[90] D Zhang and J Yin, 'China's Belt and Road Initiative, from the Inside Looking Out' (Sydney, Lowy Institute, 2 July 2019) www.lowyinstitute.org/the-interpreter/china-s-belt-and-road-initiative-inside-looking-out.

[91] I Bremmer, 'State Capitalism Comes of Age: The End of the Free Market?' (2009) 88(3) *Foreign Affairs* 40, 55.

[92] T Greer, 'One Belt, One Road, One Big Mistake' *Foreign Policy* (6 December 2018).

[93] 'State-Owned Enterprises in the Chinese Economy Today: Role, Reform, and Evolution' (China Institute, University of Alberta, 2018).

[94] KS Tsai and B Naughton (eds), *State Capitalism, Institutional Adaptation, and the Chinese Miracle* (New York, Cambridge University Press, 2015) 1–24.

[95] M Feldman, 'China's Belt and Road Investment Governance: Building a Hybrid Model' (Columbia FDI Perspectives on Topical Foreign Direct Investment Issues No. 244, Columbia Centre for Sustainable Investment, 28 January 2019) ccsi.columbia.edu/files/2018/10/No-244-Feldman-FINAL.pdf.

[96] E-U Petersmann, 'Trade and Investment Adjudication Involving 'Silk Road Projects': Legal Methodology Challenges' (EUI Working Paper LAW 2018/02) cadmus.eui.eu/bitstream/handle/1814/51225/LAW_2018_02.pdf?sequence=1.

could be effective and sustainable in dealing with unprecedentedly complicated legal issues. High standards of labour and environmental protection, among other things, need to be highly prioritised.[97] It is necessary that both public and private actors adhere to principles of transparency and social standards for BRI projects.

## C. Compatibility vis-à-vis Transplantation

China is not just trying to export higher-end goods through the BRI but also to encourage the acceptance of Chinese standards.[98] More precisely, China is exporting the idea of 'market authoritarianism', whose appeal rests largely in its challenge to the basic tenets of the Washington Consensus.[99] One is through ideology and another is through institutional methods, despite the indefinite overlap between these. Authoritarian states seek to emulate China's growth model, given that the CCP has managed to retain its power not only politically but also economically.[100] It remains uncertain as to whether state-directed development in other emerging market economies will be compatible with China's model of state capitalism.[101] This viability is of utmost importance when Chinese approaches are translated into local institutions in foreign societies.

Strong governance can promote BRI projects, especially in the absence of appropriate local standards. The BRI serves as a vehicle for using the Chinese model of state capitalism to develop the world's poorer regions. The BRI member states may benefit from some potentially positive spillover effects to advance their economic development. An inclusive approach to governance has won support due to its voluntary nature and its embrace of the principle of 'common but differentiated responsibilities'.[102] However, there is heterogeneity across countries in terms of institutions and thus experience from China cannot be directly transferred elsewhere.[103] As Ikenberry argued, 'the liberal international characteristics of order, openness, rules, multilateral cooperation, are

[97] D Vines, 'One Belt, One Road: China's 21st Century Marshall Plan?' *Caixin* (17 May 2017).

[98] A Nordin and M Weissmann, 'Will Trump Make China Great Again? The Belt and Road Initiative and International Order' (2018) 94(2) *International Affairs* 231, 249.

[99] J Reardon-Anderson, *The Red Star and the Crescent: China and the Middle East* (Oxford, Oxford University Press, 2018) 79.

[100] D Shullman, 'Protect the Party: China's Growing Influence in the Developing World' (Washington, DC., Brookings, 22 January 2019) www.brookings.edu/articles/protect-the-party-chinas-growing-influence-in-the-developing-world/.

[101] J Harris, 'China's Road from Socialism to Global Capitalism' (2018) 39(9) *Third World Quarterly* 1711, 1726.

[102] D Ollapally, 'India and the International Order: Accommodation and Adjustment' (2018) 32(1) *Ethics & International Affairs* 67, 74.

[103] R Hoskisson and M Wright, et al., 'Emerging Multinationals from Mid-Range Economies: The Influence of Institutions and Factor Markets' (2013) 50(7) *Journal of Management Studies* 1295, 1321.

deeply rooted and likely to persist'.[104] BRI involves diverse political, economic and social factors and regulatory regimes that impact implementation. The involvement of foreign financing, foreign companies and foreign investment makes the typical infrastructure governance challenges more complicated.[105] The scenarios become even more complicated when considering such factors as environmental and social impact, and the interests of the local populations.[106]

## D. The Chinese BRI: An Alternative Concept of International Order?

The narrative of China's rise questions the hegemony of western powers in global governance. Influence comes via wielding substantial authority over the operations of the new institution and the status conferred by institutional leadership. It remains a significant inquiry as to whether the growing global interdependence of China's economy is translating into greater Chinese geopolitical influence. The BRI helps to increase the leverage for China to push forward alternative ideas of global governance.[107] China's influence on the global economy and creation of new relations with other developing economies presents a growing challenge to US hegemony.[108] Mouffe argued that the world is a pluriverse and to accept diversity of political forms of organisation will be more conducive to peace and stability than the enforcement of a universal model.[109] The complexity is expressed in a competition over ideologies about international order and a multifaceted understanding of power.[110]

### *i. Is Thucydides' Trap Inevitable?*

China is adjusting to an international system that was developed in its absence.[111] The current global governance system has generally been slow to adjust, and

[104] J Ikenberry, 'Why the Liberal World Order Will Survive' (2018) 32(1) *Ethics & International Affairs* 17, 29.

[105] JP Horsley, 'Challenging China to Make Good Project Governance a Centerpiece of the Belt and Road Initiative' (Paul Tsai China Centre, Yale Law School, December 2018) law.yale.edu/system/files/area/center/china/document/horsley_china_bri-good_governance_infrastructure.pdf.

[106] A Hoare, L Hong and J Hein, 'The Role of Investors in Promoting Sustainable Infrastructure under the Belt and Road Initiative' (Chatham House, The Royal Institute of International Affairs, May 2018) www.chathamhouse.org/sites/default/files/publications/research/2018-05-11-role-investors-sustainable-infrastructure-belt-and-road-hoare-hong-hein.pdf.

[107] M Beeson and F Li, 'China's Place in Regional and Global Governance: A New World Comes into View' (2016) 7(4) *Global Policy* 491, 499.

[108] T Greer, 'One Belt, One Road, One Big Mistake' *Foreign Policy* (6 December 2018).

[109] C Mouffe, 'Democracy in a Multipolar World' (2009) 37(3) *Millennium: Journal of International Studies* 549, 561.

[110] N Godehardt, 'No End of History: A Chinese Alternative Concept of International Order?' (Berlin, SWP Research Paper 2, January 2016) www.swp-berlin.org/fileadmin/contents/products/research_papers/2016RP02_gdh.pdf.

[111] R Blackwill and A Tellis, *Revising U.S. Grand Strategy Toward China* (Washington, DC, Council on Foreign Relations, 1 April 2015) 16.

slow to grant China a voice commensurate with its growing stature.[112] China's approach will not involve a singular decision either to 'engage and integrate into' existing regional and global institutions, or 'oppose and undermine' these institutions.[113] On the one hand, Chinese state capitalism selectively integrates aspects of the Washington Consensus, while maintaining strong political control over key strategic sectors. On the other hand, China attempts to build a network of 'counter-hegemonic' institutions that seeks to challenge, oppose and undermine the US-led global and regional institutions and the order they help sustain.[114] As an innovative institution, the BRI serves as a great example for 'counter-hegemonic' purposes. Trump's national populism and protectionist trade policies have effectively undermined the very liberal order that once justified US leadership.[115] It appears that the BRI is a radical departure from the crude mercantilism of 'my country first' trade governance.[116] As Russel observed:[117]

> It's the risk that the US might curtail its global leadership and participation in international institutions, while China approaches global engagement and international institutions largely as a means to satisfy so-called core interests and national goals.

China's BRI is even viewed by some as a major challenge to US global economic interests.[118] Through fostering a strategic dialogue, international institutions should seek to mitigate and circumvent historical patterns, such as the Thucydides Trap.

### *ii. Is the Creation of a Rival International Order Viable Under the BRI?*

Institutions should work to facilitate better resolution of cross-border disputes and develop the capacity to set forward-looking agendas to deal with future challenges. Chinese policymakers are actively trying to develop a new international order through the creation of new institutions, such as the BRI blueprint for international trade and investment centred on China.[119] The weakening of

[112] D Russel, 'Not a Zero-Sum Game: Global Governance Must Adapt to the New US-China Equation' *South China Morning Post* (17 January 2018).
[113] J Ikenberry and D Lim, 'China's Emerging Institutional Statecraft: The Asian Infrastructure Investment Bank and the Prospects for Counter-Hegemony' *Brookings* (April 2017) www.brookings.edu/wp-content/uploads/2017/04/chinas-emerging-institutional-statecraft.pdf, 3.
[114] ibid.
[115] D Araya, 'China's Grand Strategy' *Forbes* (14 January 2019).
[116] D Drache, 'Systemic Challenges to Global Trade Governance – No Way Out?' *TLI Think! Paper* 80/2017 (24 March 2017).
[117] D Russel, 'Not a Zero-Sum Game: Global Governance Must Adapt to the New US-China Equation' *South China Morning Post* (17 January 2018).
[118] W Morrison, 'China's Economic Rise: History, Trends, Challenges, and Implications for the United States' (Washington D.C., Congressional Research Service, 25 June 2019) fas.org/sgp/crs/row/RL33534.pdf 37.
[119] M Beeson and F Li, 'China's Place in Regional and Global Governance: A New World Comes into View' (2016) 7(4) *Global Policy* 491, 499.

the West's global domination and the growing unwillingness on the part of the US to defend the liberal order have increased the importance of regional-level international politics.[120] China increasingly presents itself as an alternative to the western democratic model,[121] conceived as a 'revisionist' power.[122] The BRI will create new impetus in world economic growth and lay the foundations of regional peace and stability.[123] Its focus on infrastructure-led development domestically became the catalyst for its rapid industrialisation and ascendant rise as regional hegemon in the last 40 years.[124] China has been attempting to create some institutions to propagate rules, principles and norms that could form the basis of a rival international order.[125] It remains unclear as to whether China's strategy is one of portfolio diversification or the replacement of institutions and systems.[126] Further inquiry is necessary to ascertain whether China can remain a unique epicentre with a growing sphere of influence and core interests to counterbalance the US sole superpower.[127] The BRI serves as a touchstone to demonstrate whether China can use the Initiative to advance its strategy. The above approaches could present various sorts of challenges to the existing system of rules and institutions. In the global governance arena, arguably, there is a long way to go for China to become the global leader and hegemonic power of the Asian Century.[128] After all, China's ability to wield new institutions as 'instruments' of its geopolitical goals has limits.[129] While using counter-hegemonic institutional strategies, China faces substantial challenges, like ideological and normative competition, to achieve them in the short term.

[120] M Kaczmarski, 'Non-Western Visions of Regionalism: China's New Silk Road and Russia's Eurasian Economic Union' (2017) 93(6) *International Affairs* 1357, 1376.

[121] X Yan, 'How China Can Defeat America' *New York Times* (20 November 2011).

[122] P Le Corre, 'China's Rise as a Geoeconomic Influencer: Four European Case Studies' (Carnegie Endowment for International Peace, 15 October 2018) carnegieendowment.org/2018/10/15/china-s-rise-as-geoeconomic-influencer-four-european-case-studies-pub-77462.

[123] F Godement and M Rudolf, et al., 'The United Nations of China: A Vision of the World Order' (European Council for Foreign Relations, April 2018) www.ecfr.eu/page/-/the_united_nations_of_china_a_vision_of_the_world_order.pdf.

[124] M Wu, 'The 'China, Inc.' Challenge to Global Trade Governance' (2016) 57(2) *Harvard International Law Journal* 261, 324.

[125] J Ikenberry and D Lim, 'China's Emerging Institutional Statecraft: The Asian Infrastructure Investment Bank and the Prospects for Counter-Hegemony' *Brookings* (April 2017) www.brookings.edu/wp-content/uploads/2017/04/chinas-emerging-institutional-statecraft.pdf.

[126] P Le Corre, 'China's Rise as a Geoeconomic Influencer: Four European Case Studies' (Carnegie Endowment for International Peace, 15 October 2018) carnegieendowment.org/2018/10/15/china-s-rise-as-geoeconomic-influencer-four-european-case-studies-pub-77462.

[127] T Zimmerman, 'The New Silk Roads: China, the U.S., and the Future of Central Asia' (University of New York, October 2015) cic.nyu.edu/sites/default/files/zimmerman_new_silk_road_final_2.pdf.

[128] J-MF Blanchard and C Flint, 'The Geopolitics of China's Maritime Silk Road Initiative' (2017) 22(2) *Geopolitics* 223, 245.

[129] J Ikenberry and D Lim, 'China's Emerging Institutional Statecraft: The Asian Infrastructure Investment Bank and the Prospects for Counter-Hegemony' *Brookings* (April 2017) www.brookings.edu/wp-content/uploads/2017/04/chinas-emerging-institutional-statecraft.pdf.

### *iii. Too Early to Conclude*

In terms of the policy implications of the BRI, it is essential to examine how other states and stakeholders align their interests in response to the challenges. The OECD has set ground rules designed to preserve capitalist rule, in response to which China supported calls for a New World Economic Order.[130] With the EU sensitive about big powers trying to play divide-and-rule within its sphere, China's dealings have caused concern in Brussels.[131] Upon China's rising global prominence, the EU initiated the Euro–Asian Connectivity Strategy in September 2018 in a move to increase investments in Asia. The EU plans to address sustainability issues and has expressed that it will adopt a comprehensive, rules-based and transparent approach.[132] The European Parliament approved the EU Foreign Investment Screening Regulation on 14 February 2019.[133] It is aimed at harmonising and coordinating the various national foreign investment screening mechanisms. The Regulation set out to strengthen the EU's tools for dealing with the challenges while reaping the opportunities stemming from the BRI. As of 11 October 2020, the Regulation became binding on all 27 Member States, it may catalyse the BRI to become a truly two-way-street initiative for China and the EU.

Such institutions should draw states to greater convergence around shared interests.[134] It is up to those states that value the current liberal, rules-based international order to 'ensure that the illiberal values China is exporting under the guise of the BRI do not take root across the globe'.[135] This will require constructive global leadership and engagement from states that have benefited most from the current global and regional governance architectures.[136] As Ikenberry observed, the success of a Chinese-centred order would depend on its ability to outcompete liberal internationalism over the long term.[137] Democratic

[130] J Bader, 'How Xi Jinping Sees the World … and Why' *Foreign Policy at Brookings* (Asian Working Group, February 2016).

[131] J Kynge and M Peel, 'Brussels Rattled as China Reaches out to Eastern Europe' *Financial Times* (27 November 2017); Gde Jonquières, 'The European Union's China Policy: Priorities and Strategies for the New Commission' (European Centre for International Political Economy (ECIPE), April 2015) ecipe.org/publications/the-european-unions-china-policy-priorities-and-strategies-for-the-new-commission/?chapter=all.

[132] European Parliamentary Research Service, 'Prospects for EU-Asia Connectivity: The 'European Way to Connectivity'' *Briefing* (October 2018) www.europarl.europa.eu/RegData/etudes/BRIE/2018/628265/EPRS_BRI(2018)628265_EN.pdf.

[133] Regulation (EU) 2019/452 establishes a framework for screening of foreign direct investments into the European Union.

[134] J Keith and Z Xiaotong, 'From Wealth to Power: China's New Economic Statecraft' (2017) 40(1) *The Washington Quarterly* 185, 203.

[135] R Fontaine and D Kliman, 'On China's New Silk Road, Democracy Pays A Toll' *Foreign Policy* (16 May 2018).

[136] C Cheney, 'China's Belt and Road Initiative: Reshaping the Global and Regional Orders' *Political Insights* (9 November 2018).

[137] J Ikenberry, 'Why the Liberal World Order Will Survive' (2018) 32(1) *Ethics & International Affairs* 17, 29.

constitutionalism is conducive to limiting abuse of power and enhancing legitimacy of law and governance.[138] The lack of rule of law creates injustice at every level of society.[139] During its incomplete transition to a market economy, China is using access to its own market as a point of leverage in negotiations with the West, while the latter seeks to use laws, standards and trade agreements to set the rules of the game by which China and its firms must play.[140] Efficient global governance cannot occur without greater government transparency, a system of checks and balances, and an independent judiciary.[141]

Despite the challenges, it is worth exploring how China seeks to address the above-mentioned barriers to pursue multi-win ends in the following section. To address potential disputes, it is inadequate to rely purely on legal and regulatory mechanisms. An approach that embodies transparency and inclusiveness will efficiently mitigate potential conflicts as well. A key issue is who will be reshaping the global governance rules in the long-standing competition between China and the West.

## V. GOING BEYOND A GEOPOLITICAL POWER PLAY

China could use the BRI as part of a strategy to increase its influence and authority within the existing system of institutions and liberal international order.[142] Nevertheless, the BRI-oriented investment brings not only golden opportunities, but also a series of risks and challenges that may lead to low returns on investment and weak profitability.[143] The BRI is in need of better governance mechanisms, including higher social standards, greater transparency and more local engagement.[144] These include establishing responsible financial, environmental and labour standards for projects under the initiative, and ensuring that projects are transparent and inclusive with open and competitive bidding.[145]

[138] M Rosenfeld, 'The Rule of Law and the Legitimacy of Constitutional Democracy' (2001) 74 *Southern California Law Review* 1307, 1351.

[139] I Bremmer, 'How China's Economy Is Poised to Win the Future' *Time* (2 November 2017).

[140] M Ferchen, 'China, Economic Development, and Global Security: Bridging the Gaps' (Carnegie-Tsinghua Center for Global Policy, December 2016) carnegieendowment.org/files/CP_289_Ferchen_China_Final2.pdf, 12.

[141] TN Hale, 'Transparency, Accountability, and Global Governance' (2008) 14(1) *Global Governance* 73, 94.

[142] J Ikenberry and D Lim, 'China's Emerging Institutional Statecraft: The Asian Infrastructure Investment Bank and the Prospects for Counter-Hegemony' *Brookings* (April 2017) www.brookings.edu/wp-content/uploads/2017/04/chinas-emerging-institutional-statecraft.pdf.

[143] J Horsley, 'Challenging China to Make Good Project Governance a Centerpiece of the Belt and Road Initiative' (Paul Tsai China Centre, Yale Law School, December 2018) law.yale.edu/system/files/area/center/china/document/horsley_china_bri-good_governance_infrastructure.pdf.

[144] J Horsley, 'Can China Deliver a Better Belt and Road?' *Foreign Policy* (22 April 2019).

[145] C Lagarde, 'BRI 2.0: Stronger Frameworks in the New Phase of Belt and Road' (Washington, D.C., IMF, 26 April 2019).

### A. Strategic Focus: Geopolitical Manoeuvrings vis-à-vis Economic Enhancement

BRI is truly transformative in its strategic vision.[146] The initiative could provide a big boost to China's economy and soft power image.[147] In principle, the BRI member states' economic interdependence with China is leading to new patterns in the latter's economic and political influence. As a form of economic imperialism, the BRI gives China enormous leverage over other BRI member states.[148] China may use its growing leverage to push forward an alternative model of global governance.[149] The BRI can be regarded as a proactive Chinese response to the growing complexity in the world that has the potential to turn into an alternative concept for how international politics could be organised in the future.[150] It remains unclear as to how China's international economic links interact with its geopolitical ambitions.

#### *i. Geopolitical Influence and Perceptions*

The mark of a global superpower is the ability to shape geopolitics through long-term strategies.[151] Under the BRI framework, China is endeavouring to move towards being a superpower that is trying to shape the global governance regime. As a domestic economic strategy but with geopolitical effects, the BRI is also a massive exercise in soft power projection.[152] A rising China would integrate into, and share responsibility for leading, the world's governance institutions.[153] It remains uncertain as to whether the BRI could lay the groundwork for a Sinocentric global order or for the emerging multipolar world order.[154] The ultimate success of the BRI will depend largely upon whether issues of debt sustainability and terms of financing and competition for projects are properly

[146] W Hawkins, 'China's Belt and Road Initiative: Globalisation as Imperialism' *Selous Foundation for Public Policy Research* (2 August 2017).

[147] W Morrison, 'China's Economic Rise: History, Trends, Challenges, and Implications for the United States' (Congressional Research Service, 5 February 2018) fas.org/sgp/crs/row/RL33534.pdf.

[148] L Kuo and N Kommenda, 'What is China's Belt and Road Initiative?' *Guardian* (30 July 2018).

[149] M Beeson and J Zeng, 'The BRICS and Global Governance: China's Contradictory Role' (2018) 39(10) *Third World Quarterly* 1962, 1978.

[150] N Godehardt, 'No End of History: A Chinese Alternative Concept of International Order?' (Berlin, SWP Research Paper 2, January 2016) www.swp-berlin.org/fileadmin/contents/products/research_papers/2016RP02_gdh.pdf.

[151] A Holland, 'China's One Belt, One Road: An Ambitious Strategy Challenging the U.S.' *American Security Project* (25 May 2017) www.americansecurityproject.org/chinas-one-belt-one-road-an-ambitious-strategy-challenging-the-u-s/.

[152] E Albert, 'China's Big Bet on Soft Power' (Washington, DC, Council for Foreign Relations, 9 February 2018) www.cfr.org/backgrounder/chinas-big-bet-soft-power.

[153] J Ikenberry, 'The Rise of China and the Future of the West: Can the Liberal System Survive?' (2008) 87(1) *Foreign Affairs* 23, 37.

[154] A Nordin and M Weissmann, 'Will Trump Make China Great Again? The Belt and Road Initiative and International Order' (2018) 94(2) *International Affairs* 231, 249.

addressed.[155] In this regard whether the impetus behind the BRI is more economic or more political is less significant, given that they are inseparable.[156]

While using the BRI in favour of China's own firms, the initiative could saddle some member states with large debts. Friedman uses the expression 'golden straitjacket' to refer to a situation where individual countries must sacrifice some degree of economic sovereignty to global institutions, such as the BRI.[157] Using its leverage to extract concessions, China is taking a strategic approach to pragmatic solutions.[158] Dependencies may develop, with political leverage applied to poorer nations.[159] The initiative could pose financial risks if borrowers cannot repay loans.[160] China could use debt-trap diplomacy to gain footholds in some of the world's most strategic places.[161] There are some subtle triggers in the financing that result in financing default. In the long run, China hopes to channel capital into areas where it will gain the largest long-term benefit and make cumulative infrastructure improvements possible. For instance, a US$1 billion transaction in Sri Lanka in 2017 illustrates how the state-driven aspects of the BRI can result in controversy. China signed a 99-year lease to control a port in Sri Lanka after the government was unable to maintain it.[162] After struggling to make repayments, Sri Lanka agreed to transfer control over and leased the strategic port to a Chinese company in exchange for a reduced debt burden. The deal should have been scrutinised in terms of debt sustainability.

Arguably, BRI projects are shaped first and foremost by the political incentives. The CCP even enshrined the BRI in the party constitution when it was revised in October 2017, reinforcing the political importance of the BRI.[163] Infrastructure projects that are driven more by political considerations than commercial needs bring added risk to the banks funding them.[164] If an investment failed, the SOE director could face disciplinary action or court, even after

[155] J Kynge, 'China's Belt and Road Projects Drive Overseas Debt Fears' *Financial Times* (7 August 2018).

[156] K Pethiyagoda, 'What's Driving China's New Silk Road, and How Should the West Respond?' (Washington, DC Brookings, 17 May 2017).

[157] T Friedman, *The Lexus and the Olive Tree* (New York, Farrar, Straus Giroux, 2000) 101–111.

[158] S Breslin, 'China and the Global Order: Signalling Threat or Friendship' (2013) 89(3) *International Affairs* 615, 634.

[159] S van der Meer, 'Demystifying Debt Along China's New Silk Road' *The Diplomat* (6 March 2019).

[160] W Morrison, 'China's Economic Rise: History, Trends, Challenges, and Implications for the United States' (Congressional Research Service, 5 February 2018) fas.org/sgp/crs/row/RL33534.pdf.

[161] C Cheney, 'China's Belt and Road Initiative: Reshaping the Global and Regional Orders' *Political Insights* (9 November 2018); H Davidson, 'Warning Sounded over China's 'Debtbook Diplomacy'' *Guardian* (15 May 2018).

[162] 'China Tries to Calm Jitters about the 'Belt and Road' Initiative' *The Economist* (25 April 2019).

[163] B Goh and J Ruwitch, 'Pressure on as Xi's 'Belt and Road' Enshrined in Chinese Party Charter' *Reuters* (27 October 2017).

[164] D Weinland, 'China Warned of Risk to Banks from One Belt, One Road Initiative' *Financial Times* (26 January 2017).

retirement.[165] Nevertheless, many investment decisions often seem to be driven by geopolitical needs instead of sound financial sense.[166] Most of them have likely been prioritised from a geopolitical perspective. Thirty-two per cent of the total value of all the BRI projects in south and southeast Asia has been put on hold because of problems with financial viability.[167] The BRI has the potential to stimulate global growth, and should not involve geopolitical manoeuvrings.[168] A touchstone is whether all the BRI member states benefit from the initiative as an essential part of the global poverty eradication narrative.[169] It would be more sustainable if China does not intend to exert undue political influence but to enhance economic understanding between the BRI member states.[170]

## B. Promote More Transparent and Inclusive Procedures

The world would benefit if the BRI could pursue high standards for projects and governance and avoid non-transparent competition and inequality.[171] At a micro level, BRI projects have a substantial impact on local communities. Both public and private actors are expected to strive to ensure high standards for engaging with those affected local communities. A challenge is to address how national and regional markets can use locational theory to create new opportunities.[172]

### *i. Theory of Localisation*

The BRI must align closely with localised needs and conditions in order to create a sustainable strategy.[173] The importance of local engagement cannot be overstated in implementing this ambitious development programme.[174] This could help China ensure more successful projects to benefit the people in other

[165] D Thomas and M Price, 'When Deals Go Bad: China State Firm Managers Spooked by New Liability Rules' *Reuters* (27 September 2016).

[166] A Chatzky and J McBride, 'China's Massive Belt and Road Initiative' (Washington DC, The Council on Foreign Relations, 21 May 2019) www.cfr.org/backgrounder/chinas-massive-belt-and-road-initiative.

[167] T Greer, 'One Belt, One Road, One Big Mistake' *Foreign Policy* (6 December 2018).

[168] AA Wong, 'How Asia Could be the Winner in the US and China's Belt and Road Race' (Genève, The World Economic Forum, 16 January 2019) www.weforum.org/agenda/2019/01/china-the-us-and-the-great-asean-infrastructure-race/.

[169] C Lynch, 'China Enlists U.N. to Promote Its Belt and Road Project' *Foreign Policy* (10 May 2018).

[170] D Tweed, 'China's New Silk Road' *Bloomberg* (16 April 2019).

[171] D Vines, 'One Belt, One Road: China's 21st Century Marshall Plan?' *Caixin* (17 May 2017).

[172] P Krugman, *Geography and Trade* (Cambridge, Mass, MIT Press, 1993) 22.

[173] H Feldshuh, 'China Debates the Belt and Road' *The Diplomat* (8 September 2018).

[174] H Lu and C Rohr, et al., 'China Belt and Road Initiative: Measuring the Impact of Improving Transportation Connectivity on Trade in the Region' (Rand Europe, 2018) www.rand.org/pubs/research_reports/RR2625.html.

member states while realising China's economic and other strategic goals.[175] Cross-border infrastructure projects under the BRI framework are more challenging than those based in one jurisdiction. Enthusiasm among development partners could wane if projects are organised in a circular way with all spokes directed toward China.[176] This is reflected in concerns regarding the environmental and social sustainability of BRI projects, which directly affects local populations.[177] An established governance regime must involve collaboration with not only public and private actors, but also those that have been negatively affected. Many projects are not deemed viable in regard to problems with local employment, environmental protection and so on.[178] Local opposition can stall or derail the best-intended of projects.[179] Strong public opposition has led to the suspension and even cancellation of many major BRI infrastructure projects.[180] This has put China's huge investment at risk. As some commentators noted:[181]

> The embryonic China-led international order has not yet shown any signs of credible constraint on China's power, and this lack of check on the arbitrary use of its predominant strength undermines not only China's relations with its periphery but also the broader international community's acceptance of a China-centric system.

Geopolitical and financial risk considerations mean China will need to ensure more widespread participation in projects.[182] On the other hand, well-executed consultation processes can enhance the legitimacy of the project within the community and foster a sense of shared ownership.[183] Furthermore, effective transparency and local public consultation mechanisms must be incorporated as a requirement for the financing, development and implementation of all BRI projects.[184] Such approaches can ensure that local concerns are dealt with properly.

[175] J Horsley, 'Challenging China to Make Good Project Governance a Centerpiece of the Belt and Road Initiative' (Paul Tsai China Centre, Yale Law School, December 2018) law.yale.edu/system/files/area/center/china/document/horsley_china_bri-good-governance.infrastructure.pdf, 3.

[176] D Vines, 'One Belt, One Road: China's 21st Century Marshall Plan?' *Caixin* (17 May 2017).

[177] J Ewing, 'Making the Belt and Road Environmentally Sustainable' *The Diplomat* (3 May 2019).

[178] D Tweed, I Marlow and D Li, 'Souring Deals Put China's Belt and Road Dreams under Pressure' *Bloomberg* (29 January 2019).

[179] H He, 'The 'Belt and Road' Projects China Doesn't Want Anyone Talking About' *South China Morning Post* (8 August 2017).

[180] C Balding, 'Why Democracies Are Turning Against Belt and Road' *Foreign Affairs* (24 October 2018).

[181] Columbia-Harvard China and the World Programme, 'The One Belt One Road Project and China's Foreign Relations' (13 April 2016).

[182] 'Embracing the BRI Ecosystem in 2018: Navigating Pitfalls and Seizing Opportunities' *Deloitte Insights*, www2.deloitte.com/content/dam/insights/us/articles/4406_Belt-and-road-initiative/4406_Embracing-the-BRI-ecosystem.pdf.

[183] OECD, 'Getting Infrastructure Right: The Ten Key Governance Challenges and Policy Options' 2016, www.oecd.org/gov/getting-infrastructure-right.pdf.

[184] J Horsley, 'Can China Deliver a Better Belt and Road?' *Foreign Policy* (22 April 2019).

### *ii. Transparency Facilitation*

The process of implementation of projects should be transparent,[185] given that high standards of governance are crucial to success. There should be transparency throughout the project life, including information disclosure, procurement processes and project implementation.[186] It is necessary to make government procurement for BRI projects transparent and open to qualified companies from around the world. However, in many BRI member states, public tendering is opaque and unestablished. In theory, all eligible enterprises can be involved in building the BRI, regardless of their background.[187] In reality, roughly 60–80 per cent of overseas projects funded by Chinese state banks have been awarded to Chinese companies.[188] Nearly 89 per cent of contracts for China-funded transport infrastructure projects in 34 Asian and European countries were awarded to Chinese contractors.[189] This partly attributes to the fact that foreign loans will have strings attached mandating the hiring of Chinese firms to design, build and even operate the new infrastructure.[190] Nevertheless, the downside is that the Chinese model of development creates ill feeling locally and nurtures the rise of anti-Chinese sentiment.[191] To address this asymmetry, a variety of initiatives are examined below.

China's highly advocated 'Open Government' emphasises transparent, participatory, service-oriented and accountable government.[192] Relevant information must be disclosed by different levels of government, including environmental assessment, licensing, budget, government procurement and contracts. The government could be sued for failing to disclose information.[193] In addition, the Chinese scheme of Provisional Major Administrative Decision-Making requires transparency and public participation in major project decisions.[194]

[185] W Morrison, 'China's Economic Rise: History, Trends, Challenges, and Implications for the United States' (Congressional Research Service, 5 February 2018) fas.org/sgp/crs/row/RL33534.pdf.

[186] J Horsley, 'Challenging China to Make Good Project Governance a Centerpiece of the Belt and Road Initiative' (Paul Tsai China Centre, Yale Law School, December 2018) law.yale.edu/system/files/area/center/china/document/horsley_china_bri-good_governance_infrastructure.pdf, 4.

[187] X Wei, 'China Will Work to Ensure Belt, Road Transparent' *China Daily* (4 July 2018).

[188] C Devonshire-Ellis, 'EU Ambassadors, China Policy Advisors' Myopia Misses the Point of Belt and Road' *Silk Road Briefing* (25 April 2018).

[189] J Kynge, 'Chinese Contractors Grab Lion's Share of Silk Road Projects' *Financial Times* (24 January 2018).

[190] A Chatzky and J McBride, 'China's Massive Belt and Road Initiative' (Washington DC, The Council on Foreign Relations, 21 May 2019) www.cfr.org/backgrounder/chinas-massive-belt-and-road-initiative.

[191] M Ferchen, 'China, Economic Development, and Global Security: Bridging the Gaps' (Carnegie–Tsinghua Center for Global Policy, December 2016) carnegieendowment.org/files/CP_289_Ferchen_China_Final2.pdf.

[192] J Horsley, 'China Promotes Open Government as it Seeks to Reinvent Its Governance Model' *Freedominfo* (22 February 2016) law.yale.edu/system/files/china-lawdocuments/2016_horsley_china_promotes_open_government.pdf.

[193] J Horsley, 'China's FOIA Turns Eight' *Freedominfo* (28 April 2016).

[194] Provisional Regulations on Major Administrative Decision Procedures were issued by the State Council for Public Comment on 9 June 2017.

Furthermore, projects must be open to participation by both local and Chinese companies in project procurement and development. To make BRI projects more truly transparent and inclusive, the National Development and Reform Commission Regulations on Approving and Recording Overseas Investment require overseas Chinese investors to do business in good faith, and avoid any act of unfair competition.[195] This is in line with the World Trade Organisation (WTO) Agreement on Government Procurement, which establishes rules for open, competitive and transparent international competition. This helps to minimise the opportunity for corruption and ensure better, more cost-effective projects.[196] The Foreign Investment Law 2019 guarantees fair participation and equal treatment in government procurement activities with respect to non-Chinese enterprises.[197] As such, foreign companies can compete on a level playing field for BRI-related government procurement contracts funded by the Chinese Government and its policy banks.[198] In order to secure more BRI projects, Chinese companies must increase their global competitiveness, and China's manufacturing sector must move up the value chain to keep up with increased labour costs and foreign competition.[199] However, a fundamental issue is still in the way because China still provides heavy subsidies to its own companies, which constitutes an advantage over foreign competitors.[200]

## C. Legal and Regulatory Framework in Response to Other Concerns

Legal regulation and institutions are indispensable instruments for effective global governance. There have been concerns that the BRI does not guarantee international standards of transparency and equal opportunities for all investors. This, to some extent, inevitably results in undermining China's diplomatic and strategic goals for the BRI. On the other hand, the judicial interpretations issued by the Supreme People's Court (SPC) illustrate how China is bound by

[195] The *NDRC Regulations on Approving and Recording Overseas Investment* took effect on 1 March 2018.

[196] J Horsley, 'Challenging China to Make Good Project Governance a Centerpiece of the Belt and Road Initiative' (Paul Tsai China Centre, Yale Law School, December 2018) law.yale.edu/system/files/area/center/china/document/horsley_china_bri-good_governance_infrastructure.pdf 13.

[197] Foreign Investment Law of the People's Republic of China 2019 (中华人民共和国外商投资法) Chapter II Investment Promotion Art 16.

[198] C Devonshire-Ellis, 'China's New Foreign Investment Law and the Impact on the Belt & Road Initiative' *Silk Road Briefing* (25 June 2019).

[199] W Hawkins, 'As U.S. Balks at Rebuilding Infrastructure, China Advances 'Silk Road Economic Belt' Strategy to Dominate Eurasia Africa' *World Tribune* (17 May 2017).

[200] J Hillman, 'China's Belt and Road Initiative: Five Years Later' (Centre for Strategic and International Studies (CSIS), 25 January 2018) www.csis.org/analysis/chinas-belt-and-road-initiative-five-years-later-0.

its international obligations. It must treat foreign parties on an equal basis. The SPC Opinions[201] to be analysed below represent China's progress in international rulemaking during its integration into the global market.

### *i. Provisions and Guidelines*

As early as 2008, the Chinese State Council adopted National Regulations on Contracting Foreign Projects, which require Chinese contractors to protect the local environment, and promote local economic and social development.[202] The Ministry of Commerce Rules on Overseas Investment issued in 2014 require both state-owned and private enterprises to honour social responsibilities.[203] Another legally binding multi-agency government guideline calls for the fostering of a culture of compliance with Chinese and local law, relevant international treaties, internal rules and self-disciplinary regulations and codes of professional ethics.[204] In 2012, the China Banking Regulatory Commission, China's bank regulator, issued a legally binding guideline that focuses on 'green credit' in dealing with environmental and social concerns.[205] As such, banks are required to strengthen environmental and social risk management for overseas projects, to ensure they abide by laws and regulations on environmental protection.[206] Finally, a catch-all regulation provides that an investor may be ordered to suspend or cease the relevant project, and the project may be terminated if the project is deemed to injure China's national interests or security.[207] In practice, BRI projects should be mandated to release regular reports on their corporate social responsibility and sustainable development performance.

[201] SPC, '*Several Opinions on the Provision by the People's Courts of Judicial Services and Safeguards for the Construction of the 'One Belt One Road*'' promulgated on and effective since 16 June 2015.

[202] *State Council Regulations on Administering Foreign Contracting Projects* (对外承包工程管理条例, 21 July 2008) Art 4, www.mofcom.gov.cn/article/swfg/swfgbi/201101/20110107352097.shtml.

[203] Ministry of Commerce (MOFCOM), *Measures for the Administration of Overseas Investment* (境外投资管理办法, 6 September 2014) Art 20, www.mofcom.gov.cn/article/b/c/201409/20140900723361.shtml.

[204] National Development and Reform Commission (NDRC), Ministry of Foreign Affairs (MFA), Ministry of Commerce (MOFCOM), People's Bank of China (PBoC), State-owned Assets Supervision and Administration Commission (SASAC), State Administration of Foreign Exchange (SAFE), and All-China Federation of Industry and Commerce (ACFIC) jointly issued *Guidelines for Enterprise Compliance Management of Overseas Operations* (企业海外经营合规管理指引) on 26 December 2018 www.ndrc.gov.cn/gzdt/201812/t20181229_924456.html.

[205] China Banking Regulatory Commission, *Green Credit Guidelines* (12 February 2012).

[206] J Horsley, 'Challenging China to Make Good Project Governance a Centerpiece of the Belt and Road Initiative' (Paul Tsai China Centre, Yale Law School, December 2018) law.yale.edu/system/files/area/center/china/document/horsley_china_bri-good_governance_infrastructure.pdf, 8.

[207] NDRC Regulations on Approving and Recording Overseas Investment took effect on 1 March 2018. Arts 55, 56.

*ii. The SPC's Judicial Interpretations*

The question of a legal response to the BRI was addressed by the SPC in the 2015 'Several Opinions on the Provision by the People's Courts of Judicial Services and Safeguards for the Construction of the 'Belt and Road Initiative'' (SPC Opinions).[208] In the legally binding SPC Opinions, the SPC sets out the need for increased capability in the courts in relation to the creation of a fair and impartial judicial environment for business investment[209] and an increase in judicial assistance and cooperation.[210] In addition, the SPC adjusts judicial policies, strictly limits jurisdictional scope for finding contracts invalid, and promotes transparency in the case of foreign matters. The measures embodied in the SPC Opinions help to promote the use of Chinese dispute resolution centres and the application of Chinese law. This holds particularly true when Chinese investors are involved in forum shopping in countries with relatively weak legal systems.[211] The SPC urges Chinese courts' application of international treaties to which China and other BRI member states are parties pursuant to the principles of international law.[212] Judicial support should be provided for the performance of obligations under investment treaties and free trade agreements.[213] The SPC Opinions also include exhortations for the courts to emphasise equality before the law and equal treatment of Chinese and foreign parties, and to strengthen criminal trials with an international element.[214] Institutionally, the SPC has established specialised divisions, ie International Commercial Courts (ICCs), to handle major cross-border litigation over the increasing number of BRI-related international disputes.[215] In order to facilitate application of the ICCs, the SPC also issued 'Rules of Procedure for the China International Commercial Courts'. Given that disputes are arising in multi-jurisdictional projects, a new Committee of International Business Experts will aid judges in ascertaining applicable foreign law.[216] It is worth noting that China has established internet courts, making these services more accessible for far-flung litigants.[217]

[208] SPC, '*Several Opinions on the Provision by the People's Courts of Judicial Services and Safeguards for the Construction of the 'One Belt One Road*'' promulgated on and effective since 16 June 2015.

[209] SPC Opinions Art 4.

[210] SPC Opinions Arts 5 and 6.

[211] H Wang, 'China's Approach to the Belt and Road Initiative: Scope, Character and Sustainability' (2019) 22(1) *Journal of International Economic Law* 29, 55.

[212] SPC Opinions Art 7.

[213] SPC Opinions Art 8.

[214] SPC Opinions Arts 2 and 3.

[215] SPC, '*Provisions of the Supreme People's Court on Several Issues Concerning the Establishment of the International Commercial Courts*' became effective on 1 July 2018; MS Erie, 'The China International Commercial Court: Prospects for Dispute Resolution for the 'Belt and Road Initiative'' *ASIL Insights* (31 August 2018) www.asil.org/insights/volume/22/issue/11/china-international-commercial-court-prospects-dispute-resolution-belt.

[216] Supreme People's Court, *Working Rules of the International Commercial Expert Committee of the Supreme People's Court* (for trial implementation) was adopted on 21 November 2018.

[217] C Yin, 'World's First Internet Court Goes Online in Hangzhou' *China Daily* (18 August 2017).

*iii. (In)adequate?*

It is essential to ensure that Chinese MNCs comply with local and Chinese national as well as international laws.[218] In the absence of local legal requirements, they are to observe the standards of international organisations and multilateral institutions instead.[219] It is in China's interests for Chinese MNCs to adhere, at a minimum, to basic domestic standards in their overseas business as well.[220] It is essential to improve standards for the conduct of Chinese public and private actors in overseas financing, project contracting and investment.[221] The above practices are conducive to gradually changing the behaviour of Chinese SOEs, as well as public expectations.[222] It would not only make BRI projects sustainable, but also help promote China's soft power.

Given its non-treaty-based initiative, the BRI allows for considerable flexibility in its implementation.[223] At a macro level, global constitutionalism helps to limit abuses of power and justify third-party adjudication by following due process of law. China, as a founding member state, lacks an overarching law governing BRI-related cross-border transactions, most of which are still regulated through the interplay of policy and legally enforceable regulations.[224] At the current stage, the legitimacy of BRI-related governance is still dependent upon multilevel respect for the legal settings of all the BRI member states.[225] China may set contractual terms and conditions for each BRI project; meanwhile, it uses law of contracts as a powerful lever. Concession-bargaining serves to build friendly *guanxi* (interrelationships) for political and solidaristic purposes by offering large-scale financing of infrastructural deals at discount rates.[226] Each bilateral agreement is negotiated without a one-size-fits-all template. This flexibility differs from the WTO with its precise rules and rigid legal codes. It does result in a substantial space of soft power. It is essential to work out more innovative solutions to reinforce more constructive interaction between China and

[218] J Horsley, 'Challenging China to Make Good Project Governance a Centerpiece of the Belt and Road Initiative' (Paul Tsai China Centre, Yale Law School, December 2018) law.yale.edu/system/files/area/center/china/document/horsley_china_bri-good_governance_infrastructure.pdf 7.

[219] Y Wang, 'SOE Foreign Investment Risk Curbed' *China Daily* (29 December 2017).

[220] J Horsley, 'Challenging China to Make Good Project Governance a Centerpiece of the Belt and Road Initiative' (Paul Tsai China Centre, Yale Law School, December 2018) law.yale.edu/system/files/area/center/china/document/horsley_china_bri-good_governance_infrastructure.pdf 18.

[221] ibid 6.

[222] ibid 5.

[223] H Wang, 'China's Approach to the Belt and Road Initiative: Scope, Character and Sustainability' (2019) 22(1) *Journal of International Economic Law* 29, 55.

[224] J Horsley, 'Challenging China to Make Good Project Governance a Centerpiece of the Belt and Road Initiative' (Paul Tsai China Centre, Yale Law School, December 2018) law.yale.edu/system/files/area/center/china/document/horsley_china_bri-good_governance_infrastructure.pdf, 6.

[225] E-U Petersmann, 'Trade and Investment Adjudication Involving 'Silk Road Projects': Legal Methodology Challenges' (EUI Working Paper LAW 2018/02) cadmus.eui.eu/bitstream/handle/1814/51225/LAW_2018_02.pdf?sequence=1.

[226] D Drache, AT Kingsmith and D Qi, *One Road, Many Dreams: China's Bold Plan to Remake the Global Economy* (New York, Bloomsbury, 2019) 37–75.

all the BRI member states. The realisation of the ambitious BRI will depend, inter alia, on multilevel legal regulation. It is critical for the BRI member states to acquire shared institutions and values.

Furthermore, many of the official documents regulating Chinese overseas investment do not impose legally enforceable obligations.[227] Legally binding laws and regulations on overseas activities are increasingly important not only for addressing environmental and social risk considerations, but also for projecting decision-making within China.[228] In terms of transnational corporate crime, the corrosive effects of BRI-project-related corruption might be reduced through strengthening and enforcing China's criminalisation of overseas bribery.[229] The move is in line with the US Foreign Corrupt Practices Act[230] and adherence to the OECD Anti-Bribery Convention,[231] to bolster the general commitments China has already made pursuant to the United Nations Convention against Corruption.[232] However, the People's Court may not be able to decide disputes independently.[233] Another concern is that China may pressure recipient countries to agree to submit to the jurisdiction of the ICCs and to the application of Chinese law.[234]

## D. Who Will Write the New Global Order?

China, with substantial investments in infrastructure, could emerge as a leader in setting rules and standards for global governance.[235] The BRI may propagate new norms that could form the basis of a rival international order.[236] They are well embodied in such innovations as 'Global Community of Common Destiny' and the China-led Asian Infrastructure Investment Bank (AIIB). The ideology and the financial institution could serve as a vehicle for China to write

[227] J Horsley, 'Challenging China to Make Good Project Governance a Centerpiece of the Belt and Road Initiative' (Paul Tsai China Centre, Yale Law School, December 2018) law.yale.edu/system/files/area/center/china/document/horsley_china_bri-good_governance_infrastructure.pdf, 9.

[228] ibid 7.

[229] China's amended Art 164 of the Criminal Law in 2011 includes providing money or property to foreign officials or officers of public international organisations in order to derive improper commercial benefits.

[230] The Foreign Corrupt Practices Act of 1977, as amended, 15 U.S.C. §§78dd-1, et seq.

[231] OECD Convention on Combating Bribery of Foreign Public Officials in International Business Transactions.

[232] China ratified the United National Convention against Corruption in 2006.

[233] N Chandran, 'China's Plans for Creating New International Courts Are Raising Fears of Bias' *CNBC* (1 February 2018).

[234] J Horsley, 'Challenging China to Make Good Project Governance a Centerpiece of the Belt and Road Initiative' (Paul Tsai China Centre, Yale Law School, December 2018) law.yale.edu/system/files/area/center/china/document/horsley_china_bri-good_governance_infrastructure.pdf, 12.

[235] D Dollar, 'China as a Global Investor' (Washington DC, Brookings, May 2016) www.brookings.edu/wp-content/uploads/2016/07/China-as-a-Global-Investor_Asia-Working-Paper-4-2.pdf.

[236] J Ikenberry and D Lim, 'China's Emerging Institutional Statecraft: The Asian Infrastructure Investment Bank and the Prospects for Counter-Hegemony' *Brookings* (April 2017) www.brookings.edu/wp-content/uploads/2017/04/chinas-emerging-institutional-statecraft.pdf, 2.

new rules, establish institutions that reflect Chinese interests, and reshape soft infrastructure.[237]

### *i. The UN's Endorsement of Global Community of Common Destiny*

The BRI is somewhat compatible with the goal of the G20 and should be seen as part of a new and inclusive globalisation.[238] Since the initiative represents an alternative mode of interstate cooperation in the creation of mutual gains, it may ultimately entail future global economic growth.[239] The BRI helps to relieve the infrastructural deficit impeding many countries' pathways for development.[240] Two priorities enshrined in the BRI's focus on developing infrastructure and global partnerships are also included in the SDGs 2030.[241] So far there has been no solid evidence to ascertain whether the SDGs can help to reshape the BRI. After all, a rule-orientated international order based on respect for international law is a fundamental prerequisite for securing sustainable development. China has been promoting an idealistic vision of a 'Global Community of Common Destiny' driven in large part by economic interdependence.[242] Unprecedentedly, it represents a milestone on this path in the development of the United Nations Human Rights Council (UNHRC).[243] The UNHRC Resolution of 'Contribution of Development to the Enjoyment of All Human Rights' reflects China's policy of 'Global Community of Common Destiny'. This contributes to the reform of the global governance regime with China's vision included in the UN document. In addition, it was also added to the Chinese Constitution in March 2018.[244] Despite existing political and ideological differences, the UNHRC's adoption of this resolution seems to break the Western monopoly of discourse in human rights development.[245] China may need to be more deeply involved in multilateral organisations.[246]

[237] ibid.

[238] W Hawkins, 'China's Belt and Road Initiative: Globalisation as Imperialism' (Washington DC, Selous Foundation for Public Policy Research, 2 August 2017) sfppr.org/2017/08/chinas-belt-and-road-initiative-globalization-as-imperialism/.

[239] T Shaw and X Li, 'The Political Economy of Chinese State Capitalism' (2013) 1(1) *Journal of China and International Relations* 88, 112.

[240] T Greer, 'One Belt, One Road, One Big Mistake' *Foreign Policy* (6 December 2018).

[241] 'United Nations Poised to Support Alignment of China's Belt and Road Initiative with Sustainable Development Goals' (SG/SM/19556, 26 April 2019) www.un.org/press/en/2019/sgsm19556.doc.htm.

[242] M Cook, 'Three Misunderstandings of China-ASEAN Economic Relations' *Knowledge@Wharton* (10 March 2016).

[243] UNHRC Resolution 35/21 'Contribution of Development to the Enjoyment of All Human Rights'.

[244] The Constitution law of the People's Republic of China, Preamble, §12.

[245] F Godement and M Rudolf, et al., 'The United Nations of China: A Vision of the World Order' (European Council for Foreign Relations, April 2018) www.ecfr.eu/page/-/the_united_nations_of_china_a_vision_of_the_world_order.pdf.

[246] J Ikenberry and D Lim, 'China's Emerging Institutional Statecraft: The Asian Infrastructure Investment Bank and the Prospects for Counter-Hegemony' (Brookings, April 2017) www.brookings.edu/wp-content/uploads/2017/04/chinas-emerging-institutional-statecraft.pdf, 2.

### *ii. The AIIB in the BRI*

There is state financing for Chinese firms seeking to expand their operations overseas.[247] China's financial support of infrastructure projects in many countries could produce positive economic results.[248] The AIIB boasts its core principles to be 'openness, transparency, independence and accountability'.[249] As a multilateral development bank, its mission is to improve social and economic outcomes in Asia and beyond. The establishment of the AIIB constitutes a new mode of interstate cooperation.[250] The AIIB attempts to make fiscal sustainability and transparent procurement processes a condition of financing.[251] In the process, the AIIB has changed the rules of development aid.[252] As Weinland said: 'the China-led bank is prepared to change the basis on which these types of projects have been traditionally financed'.[253] To some extent, it implies that China may have intended to develop its own parallel institutions to the World Bank and the International Monetary Fund (IMF). After all, China's policy banks have US$1 trillion, or four times the assets of the World Bank, IMF and European Bank of Reconstruction combined.[254] One central institution could advance transparency by coordinating China's BRI-oriented decision-making.[255] China's recently created International Development Cooperation Agency will oversee China's foreign aid, and could play such a role.[256]

Indeed, China can use its large amount of foreign reserves as leverage in the BRI-oriented infrastructural development. Ambitious as it is, the BRI should not be overinterpreted. Its stimulus is not large enough to reshape global economic development as well as its growth rates. Given the BRI's economic and geopolitical nature, it all comes down to whether China's strategy is to satisfy its national

[247] J Perkowski, 'China's Financial Institutions Expand Overseas' *Forbes* (25 September 2012).

[248] B Parks, 'Will Chinese Development Projects Pave the Way to Inclusive Growth? (Washington DC, Brookings, 11 September 2018) www.brookings.edu/blog/future-development/2018/09/11/will-chinese-development-projects-pave-the-way-to-inclusive-growth/.

[249] B Gu, 'Chinese Multilateralism in the AIIB' (2017) 20(1) *Journal of International Economic Law* 137, 158.

[250] J Ikenberry and D Lim, 'China's Emerging Institutional Statecraft: The Asian Infrastructure Investment Bank and the Prospects for Counter-Hegemony' (Brookings, April 2017) www.brookings.edu/wp-content/uploads/2017/04/chinas-emerging-institutional-statecraft.pdf.

[251] M Park, 'China-led AIIB as a Gradual Modification of Asian Financial Order: Chinese Strategies to Launch New Financial Institution' (2017) 24(2) *Journal of International and Area Studies* 57, 76.

[252] T Renard, 'The Asian Infrastructure Investment Bank (AIIB): China's New Multilateralism and the Erosion of the West' *Security Policy Brief* (April 2015).

[253] D Weinland, 'Asia's Regional Banks Lend Where Their Western Rivals Dare Not' *Financial Times* (3 May 2017).

[254] M Ferchen, 'China, Economic Development, and Global Security: Bridging the Gaps' (Carnegie–Tsinghua Centre for Global Policy, December 2016) carnegieendowment.org/files/CP_289_Ferchen_China_Final2.pdf.

[255] J Ikenberry and D Lim, 'China's Emerging Institutional Statecraft: The Asian Infrastructure Investment Bank and the Prospects for Counter-Hegemony' *Brookings* (April 2017) www.brookings.edu/wp-content/uploads/2017/04/chinas-emerging-institutional-statecraft.pdf.

[256] J Mardell, 'Foreign Aid with Chinese Characteristics' *The Diplomat* (7 August 2018).

interests, or whether it seeks to achieve a win-win objective through multilateral cooperation.[257] The mercantilist geo-economics framework is backed by remarkably little evidence drawing a direct or even indirect link between China's global economic ties and its geopolitical influence.[258]

## VI. CONCLUSION

Infrastructure investment is part of China's extraordinary ascendancy in the global economy. The BRI is driven by infrastructure overcapacity and the need to deploy China's huge foreign savings and construction capacity. With significant geopolitical and geo-economic implications, the BRI has the potential to redefine the world economy and global governance. This chapter not only identifies challenges posed by the BRI to global governance, but also sorts out the pathways and identifies their implications in the context of development lending and the broader liberal international order. Some strategic measures are highlighted to build mutual trust along with infrastructure, and help improve sustainability. These include, among other things, establishing efficient, open and competitive procurement systems; improving transparency throughout the project life; and establishing effective local engagement policies. More adequate transnational governance improvements would help ensure that the BRI will genuinely contribute to, rather than complicate, China's drive to achieve common development and prosperity. Apart from a potential 'win-win' solution for all, it will also advance China's soft power building. To achieve this ambition, China should operate the BRI on terms consistent with international standards. However, it remains unclear as to whether the BRI could trigger a transition of the international system to a China-centric or multipolar one. It is still too early to judge whether the BRI initiates a new chapter of poverty eradication, backed by China's deep financial pockets, soft power diplomacy and bilateral cooperation.

[257] D Russel, 'Not a Zero-Sum Game: Global Governance Must Adapt to the New US-China Equation' *South China Morning Post* (17 January 2018).

[258] M Ferchen, 'China, Economic Development, and Global Security: Bridging the Gaps' (Carnegie–Tsinghua Center for Global Policy, December 2016) carnegieendowment.org/files/CP_289_Ferchen_China_Final2.pdf.

# 13

# *The Relevance of the Green Swan Risk: Accounting for Climate Change in the Legal Framework of Sovereign Investors*

BIANCA NALBANDIAN*

## I. INTRODUCTION: COLOURED SWANS AND SOVEREIGN INVESTORS

THE NOTION OF human activities generating material and financial risks by polluting the environment, destroying ecosystems and ultimately destabilising the planetary boundaries[1] have been known for quite some time[2] by economists and financial experts.[3] In this regard, the Bank for International Settlements (BIS) has recently enucleated the concept of 'green

* This research has been supported by the Luxembourg National Research Fund (FNR) (PRIDE 17/12251371).

[1] B Sjåfjell and MB Taylor, 'Planetary Boundaries and Company Law: Towards a Regulatory Ecology of Corporate Sustainability' (2015) 11 University of Oslo Faculty of Law Research Paper 32. See also, B Sjåfjell and CM Bruner (eds), *The Cambridge Handbook of Corporate Law, Corporate Governance and Sustainability* (Cambridge, Cambridge University Press, 2019).

[2] Since, at least, the famous 'Stern Review'. See N Stern, *The Economics of Climate Change: The Stern Review* (Cambridge, Cambridge University Press, 2007).

[3] Throughout the past years, the international economic debates have been constellated by considerations on climate change-related financial risks and on how to possibly mitigate them. See, by way of example, the speech given by Mark Carney, former Governor of Bank of England, 'Breaking the Tragedy on the Horizon – climate change and financial stability' (29 September 2015) Speech, Lloyd's of London. www.bankofengland.co.uk/speech/2015/breaking-the-tragedy-of-the-horizon-climate-change-and-financial-stability (accessed 10 July 2021). More recently, Mark Carney directly engaged in the discussion on the impact of climate change on financial markets stating that we 'can't wish away the systemic risk' and that 'in the end, a small investment up front can save a tremendous cost down the road'. He recommended regulatory policies pushing economies towards greener growth, as this opportunity was missed after the 2008 GFC. See, V Gill, 'Mark Carney: 'We can't self-isolate from climate change'' (*BBC News*, 7 May 2020) www.bbc.com/news/science-environment-52582243 (accessed 8 June 2021). See also, P Matos, 'ESG and Responsible Institutional Investing Around the World: A Critical Review' (June 2020).

swan' or 'climate-black swan', which can be preliminarily defined as a highly disruptive event related to climate change. Specifically, in late 2020, the BIS published a report thoroughly assessing the risks[4] posed by green swans to the global financial system and surveying the viable pathways for central banks to address them.[5] Specifically, the study overviews both physical risks (climate-induced unnatural disasters or the spread of diseases) and transitional risks (mass bankruptcies of companies that failed to adapt), as well as the ways banks have traditionally assessed both.

The term green swan draws on the black swan concept. Today the black swan moniker refers to unforeseen and almost unimaginable events bearing a massive socio-economic impact.[6] Indeed, representing a compelling systematisation of the simultaneous crises in banking and housing, the 'black swan' buzzword came into use precisely with the 2008 global financial crisis (GFC), which has been regarded as the black swan textbook case of our times.[7]

Black and green swans are similar yet not identical. Green swans differ from black swans in that there is some certainty they will one day materialise, causing massively negative intergenerational externalities. In addition, green swan risks

[4] See also, CalPERS and Wellington Management, 'Physical Risks of Climate Change (P-ROCC): A new framework for corporate disclosures' (September 2019) 8, www.wellington.com/en/wp-content/uploads/2019/09/physical-risks-of-climate-change_procc_framework.pdf (accessed 10 July 2021).

[5] P Bolton, M Depres, LAP da Silva, F Samama and R Svartzman, 'The Green Swan: Central Banking and Financial Stability in the Age of Climate Change' (January 2020) 115 (hereinafter 'BIS, The Green Swan'). Central banks play a fundamental role in the transition toward sustainable finance. Before the BIS study, already Mark Carney and the current ECB President Christine Lagarde flagged climate change as a major issue for central banks. They also called on the financial sector to follow the recommendations by Network for Greening the Financial System (NGFS), a body established to synchronise the central banking community. See D Uzsoki, 'Sustainable Investing: Shaping the Future of Finance' (February 2020) International Institute for Sustainable Development (IISD), 30, 11, www.iisd.org/sites/default/files/publications/sustainable-investing.pdf (accessed 10 July 2021).

[6] The former trader and financial analyst Nassim Nicholas Taleb defined a black swan event as an outlier posited outside the realm of regular expectations, 'because nothing in the past can convincingly point to its possibility'. Extreme impacts follow this outlier. NN Taleb, '*The Black Swan: The Impact of the Highly Improbable*' (New York, Random House, 2007). In Taleb's view, the problem with black swans is not their occurrence exclusively but also our oblivious attitude toward their potential (re)occurrence. In other words, for this author, humans – and amongst them, social scientists – often act, as such phenomena do and will not materially exist. In the Taleb's words, 'our blindness to randomness' and our inability to focus on, and learn from, the general scenario rather than the precise minutiae creates another layer of problems entirely. Moreover, notwithstanding the black swan's outlier status, human nature tends to normalise the event by making it explainable and depicting it as predictable in hindsight.

[7] The black swan nomenclature has often been used as an all-encompassing label for low probability-high impact events, like in the COVID-19 crisis case. See *contra*, LAP da Silva, 'Green Swan 2 – Climate change and Covid-19: reflections on efficiency versus resilience', Bank of International Settlements, 15, 10.G McGillivray, 'Coronavirus is significant, but is it a true black swan event?' (*The Conversation*, 30 April 2021) theconversation.com/coronavirus-is-significant-but-is-it-a-true-black-swan-event-136675 (accessed 10 July 2021). See J Pethokoukis, 'Is coronavirus really a black swan event?' (*The Week*, 8 March 2021) theweek.com/articles/900400/coronavirus-really-black-swan-event (accessed 20 July 2021).

carry large magnitude and intensity impacts, capable of triggering a systemic financial crisis as well as posing an existential threat to humankind.

Interestingly enough, during the GFC black swan, investments made by some types of sovereign investors, such as sovereign wealth funds (SWFs), came into high demand amongst western countries.[8] Indeed, their long-term investment horizon and high management asset capacity allowed them to play a stabilising role for western economies during the financial and economic global crunch.[9] Consequently, many states increasingly opted to enter into business as investors and buy non-controlling stakes on the equity markets in both foreign and domestic companies instead of owning and operating these businesses as state companies.[10] The GFC 'black swan' has embodied the 'perfect' juncture for such sovereign investors to gain global currency,[11] and, as a result, one may wonder

[8] The sovereign investor category includes a broad range of different types of actors. In this chapter, while mainly keeping the focus on sovereign wealth funds, given their long-term horizon, their public service mission and intergenerational wealth transfer objective, we will also refer to public pension funds, mostly for the part related to fiduciary duty. For the present purposes, SWFs are a category of sovereign investors which can be broadly regarded as government-owned investment funds operating in private markets: public actors carrying out private actions. C Nowacki and A Monk, 'Sovereign Investors: Understanding the Giants of the Financial World' (2017) Global Projects Center Stanford University, 16, 1. As Novacki and Monk describe, contrary to other institutional investors, sovereign investors' shareholders are a State/Country/City rather than a private entity/person.

[9] SWFs may have diverse investment objectives set by their sponsoring countries and display different managerial structures usually having significant intergenerational dimension. However, they differ considerably one from the other in terms of structure, mandate, purpose, stated policy objectives, investment strategy, and asset allocation. That being the case, SWFs are usually set up for a number of purposes, which can include the diversification of foreign exchange reserves or commodity revenues returns, to shield national economies from fluctuations in commodity prices and to invest in foreign assets. D Cumming and others, 'Preface', in D Cumming and others (eds), *The Oxford Handbook of Sovereign Wealth Funds* (Oxford, OUP, 2017). See A Rozanov, 'Who Holds the Wealth of Nations?' (2005) 15 *Central Banking Journal* 1. The socio-economic and political factors driving the increase in numbers and popularity of SWFs are varied. In this regard, see, WPF Schmit Jongbloed, LE Sachs and KP Sauvant, 'Sovereign Investment: An Introduction', in WPF Schmit Jongbloed, L E Sachs and KP Sauvant (eds), *Sovereign Investment: Concerns and Policy Reactions* (Oxford, OUP, 2012) 3. Also see, B Bortolotti, V Fotak and WL Megginson, 'The Rise of Sovereign Wealth Funds: Definition, Organization, and Governance' (2014) Baffi Center Research Paper No 2014-163 ssrn.com/abstract=2538977 (accessed 10 July 2021). See also A Gelb and others, 'Sovereign Wealth Funds and Long-Term Development Finance: Risks and Opportunities' (2014) CGD Policy Paper 041 www.cgdev.org/sites/default/files/sovereign-wealth-funds-risks-opportunities_0.pdf (accessed 10 July 2021).

[10] Also known as 'rainy days funds', some SWFs materially embody pools of cash governments can draw from in times of emergency. The best example of a SWF fulfilling an implicit 'rainy day' mandate is perhaps Singapore's Temasek. In June 2020, Temasek invested US$13 billion into Singapore Airlines and subsequently recapitalised Sembcorp Marine, a domestic shipbuilding and repair conglomerate, for US$1.5 billion. See www.reuters.com/article/us-sovereign-wealthfund-economy-breaking/breakingviews-sovereign-funds-are-having-their-rainy-day-moment-idUSKBN23U0DN (accessed 26 June 2021).

[11] See, Invesco, 'Global Sovereign Asset Management Study' (2020) 74. Many of the best-performing sovereigns of the past ten years are those that ploughed into equity markets after the GFC. Contrariwise, other types of sovereign investors such as PPFs were massively affected as unemployment and lower earnings meant less money flowing into the system. See, B Keeley and P Love, 'Pensions and the Crisis', in OECD (ed), *From Crisis to Recovery: The Causes, Course and Consequences of the Great Recession* (Paris, OECD Publishing, 2010) 146.

whether such actors might play an active role in the context of so-called green swans.[12]

In this last regard, our research aims to investigate if state-backed investors with an intergenerational wealth transfer objective such as SWFs as public pension funds (PFs) might, or even should, invest upon determined scientific findings, such as the ones BIS has underpinned.[13] Indeed, on the one hand, by acting as universal, long-term investors with portfolios diversified across a broad range of sectors and geographies, sovereign investors might be significantly exposed to increased climate change and climate change-related risks, as no industry nor country can self-isolate from them.[14] On the other hand, their sheer magnitude in terms of capital and relevance as patient investors inevitably make them suitable players to build a more sustainable economic model.

While building on concepts familiar to the economic and financial fields, the present inquiry ultimately focuses on the legal instruments available to sovereign investors to scale up their role as participants in addressing climate change and climate change-related risks.[15] To tackle this core issue, the research proceeds

[12] See, B Bortolotti, V Fotak and C Hogg, 'Sovereign Wealth Funds and the COVID-19 shock: Economic and Financial Resilience in Resource-Rich Countries' (August 2020), Baffi Carefin Centre Research Paper No 2020-147, 28, 2. Available at ssrn.com/abstract=3665993 or dx.doi.org/10.2139/ssrn.3665993. See also, TMaret and A Gautier, 'Les fonds souverains, un vaccin pour l'économie en temps de crise?' (*Le Grande Continent*, 17 May 2020) legrandcontinent.eu/fr/2020/05/17/les-fonds-souverain-un-vaccin-pour-leconomie-en-temps-de-crise/ (accessed 10 August 2020). See, State Street, 'Pandemic, No Panic – Evidence from Institutional Investors flows' (March 2020), International Forum of Sovereign Wealth Funds, 11. See, OMFIF, Global Public Investor (GPI 2020), 212 www.gic.com.sg/wp-content/uploads/2019/06/GPI_2019.pdf (accessed 10 July 2021). *cf* on due diligence standards of conduct for sovereign investors, ch 9, in this volume.

[13] The combination of increased climate risk and declining revenues from fossil fuels may significantly affect the sovereign funds of fossil fuel-exporting countries. See OECD, *The Role of Sovereign and Strategic Investment Funds in the Low-carbon Transition* (OECD Development Policy Tools, Paris, OECD Publishing, 2020) 40.

[14] The economic impact of climate change – as of the current pandemic – drove sovereign investors to reconsider major risks and their short-to-medium-term forecast. See, International Forum of Sovereign Wealth Funds (IFSWF) and Invesco, 'The Rise of a Bipolar World – Sovereign Wealth Fund Views on the Global Macro Outlook' (July 2020), 11, 2, www.ifswf.org/sites/default/files/IFSWF_BIPOLAR_WORLD_FINAL.pdf (accessed 20 July 2021). See also, B Caldecott and E Harnett, 'One Planet Sovereign Wealth Funds: Turning Ambition into Action' (2019) Sustainable Finance Program Briefing Paper, No 29. See also, C Feher and I de Bidegain, 'Pension Schemes in the COVID-19 Crisis: Impacts and Policy Considerations' (July 2020), IMF Fiscal Affairs Special Series on COVID-19, 8, 2.

[15] As identified by authoritative institutions, such as the Bank for International Settlement (BIS), Invesco, OECD, World Economic Forum (WEF) and IFSWF. T Maret and A Gautier, 'Les fonds souverains, un vaccin pour l'économie en temps de crise?', (*Le Grande Continent*, 17 May 2020) legrandcontinent.eu/fr/2020/05/17/les-fonds-souverain-un-vaccin-pour-leconomie-en-temps-de-crise/ (accessed 10 July 2021). Governments can make use of their large sovereign investors, for instance, by tipping their rainy day funds to cover budget shortfalls and emergency spending. Sovereign funds can be used to increase domestic investment flows so to inject capital in distressed sectors and businesses or employed for taking advantage of the plummeted stocks' price in distressed industries etc. Oil rich nations from the Arabian Gulf to Kazakhstan seem to have been borrowing from the bond market rather than tapping their funds. See, State Street, 'Pandemic, No Panic – Evidence from Institutional Investors flows' (March 2020), International Forum of Sovereign Wealth Funds, 11. According to the Official Monetary and Financial Institutions Forum (OMFIF) notwithstanding the global shock caused by Covid-19, SWFs and PFs maintain a strong appetite for risk

as follows. Section II cursorily assesses the concept of the green swan as climate change financial risks as developed by the relevant scientific literature and its relevance to financial actors and regulators. In section III, this study addresses specific economic and legal rationales for considering climate change – and climate change-related – risks in the investment choices of sovereign investors. Lastly, a critical analysis of the status of the relevant legal arguments and instruments available to sovereign investors to align to climate change risks will be provided.

## II. THE FINANCIAL RISKS POSED BY GREEN SWANS: THE ASSESSMENT OF THE BIS

The research carried out by BIS describes how, by being both major global risk categories, swans of the black and green type share important common traits. To start with, it is true that they are (generally) unexpected by most agents, who have a retrospective approach (looking at past events as a good proxy of the future). They both propagate in a non-linear way, 'caused by and triggering many destructive forces that feedback on each other, casting their effects onto multiple sectors and countries simultaneously'.[16] Ultimately, they both result in extreme disruption casting damages on the global economy.

Even so, BIS maintains that climate-related risks are not black swans, but as mentioned, green swans. They are indeed a different type of systemic risk[17] involving complex chain reactions between degraded ecological conditions and unpredictable social, economic and political responses, able of triggering tipping points in the climate and social system.[18] Contrary to black swans such as the GFC, which are entirely unexpected events, green swans, such as climate change are, to a certain extent, predictable. Even though their 'when', 'where', and 'how' is not precisely pre-determinable, there is an extremely high likeliness (or quite a certainty) that they will one day occur. Besides, the two types of swan seem to differ in terms of their respective impacts, with green swans of a most likely irreversible character. By contrast, black swans carry long-lasting but reversible damages. Ultimately, their most significant point of departure lies in

assets. Of the sovereign funds surveyed by OMFIF, 63% said they would increase allocations to infrastructure, while 44% are doing the same in equities and 38% in real estate. Among pension funds, 67% said they would increase their equity allocations, and 22% plan to move out of government bonds over the next 12-24 months. Meanwhile, central banks and sovereign funds also plan to add to gold holdings, at 11% and 13% respectively. See, OMFIF, Global Public Investor (GPI 2020), 212, www.gic.com.sg/wp-content/uploads/2019/06/GPI_2019.pdf (accessed 10 July 2021).

[16] da Silva (n 7) 2.

[17] On the notion of climate systemic risks, see M Aglietta and E Espagne, 'Climate and Finance Systemic Risks, More Than Analogy? The Climate Fragility Hypothesis' (CEPII Working Paper, 10 April 2016), 30. See also, European Systemic Risk Board, 'Too late, too sudden: Transition to a low-carbon economy and systemic risk' (6 February 2016) Reports of the Advisory Scientific Committee, 20.

[18] BIS (n 4) 6.

the sort and the degree of threat they pose. Black swans are massively disrupting events whose effects are mainly confined to the realms of finance and the real economy. Conversely, green swans are environmental and ecosystemic changes posing a direct and irreversible threat to humankind. In other terms, climate change disrupts natural and economic resources and opportunities available for present and future generations alike.[19]

Indeed, from an economic policy standpoint, climate-related risks carry devastating impacts on both the real economy and financial sectors, causing 'recessions, unemployment and a large depreciation of value across all asset classes, entailing large negative externalities at a global level'.[20] Hence, climate change may be regarded as a systemic risk, which, if left unmanaged, could have disruptive consequences on the global financial markets and global economic stability.[21]

As the BIS stressed with vigour, the underlying events to a green swan are complex and subject to radical uncertainty. However, they still come with the likelihood of a massive future negative and systemic impact on the global economy, which would call less for improvements in risk modelling and more for decisive and immediate action and coordination.[22]

BIS research focuses on the role of central banks in avoiding disastrous outcomes due to such systemic risk, including through seeking to improve their understanding of climate-related risks by developing forward-looking, scenario-based analysis. However, BIS arrived at the notable conclusion, also confirmed in its recent meeting held in June 2021, that no single actor ultimately has a silver bullet to overcome the climatic threat and that central banks cannot possibly tame climate change risks alone.[23] A new global financial crisis triggered by climate change would indeed 'render central banks and financial supervisors powerless'.[24] That is also why BIS has called on the necessary coordination among governments, the private sector, civil society and the international community to address this complex collective problem. In turn, given this scenario, one may be drawn to think that state-backed investors should be among those called upon.[25]

[19] In this, as in other respects, climate-related risks and epidemics share like structures. More importantly, they should be regarded as reinforcing one another.

[20] da Silva (n 7) 3.

[21] V Ramani, 'Addressing Climate as a Systemic Risk: A Call to Action for U.S. Financial Regulators' (June 2020), Ceres, 68. See also corpgov.law.harvard.edu/2020/06/28/addressing-climate-as-a-systemic-risk-a-call-to-action-for-financial-regulators/ (accessed 10 July 2021).

[22] BIS also analyses other points of divergence between black and green swans such as: (i) professionals engaging in their study (financial analysts, economists and legal experts for the first, and scientists for the second); (ii) the way we derive policy recommendations to prevent their occurrence.

[23] See at www.bis.org/events/green_swan_2021/overview.htm (accessed 23 June 2021).

[24] BIS (n 4) 65.

[25] In a virtual meeting hosted by OMFIF at the beginning of August 2020, Sharil Ridza Ridzuan, managing director of Khazanah Nasional Berhad, said the Malaysian SWF mandate is 'to grow the country's long-term, intergenerational wealth' and that 'it is therefore focused on finding the right mix of assets and risks to ensure sustainable returns'. See OMFIF, 'What's on the sovereign investor's mind?' at www.omfif.org/2020/08/whats-on-the-sovereign-investors-mind/?utm_source=weekendreview (accessed 8 June 2021).

In this vein, before assessing the viable legal tools at their disposal to align to climate change risks, in the next section, we will examine whether sovereign investors may or even should account for climate change and climate change-related risks based on both economic and legal rationales.

## III. RESPONSIBLE SOVEREIGN INVESTORS

Sovereign investors hold a substantial share of global invested capital – US$8.2 trillion worth assets for SWFs[26] and about US$45 trillion for pension funds (PFs)[27] – and few, if any, economic agents have long-term horizon and diversified portfolios like SWFs and PFs.[28] By design, SWFs and PFs act as patient, long-term investors to leave a legacy and safeguard national wealth for future generations and future pensioners. Consequently, it is first and foremost their public service mission combined with the intergenerational objectives that naturally put them at the forefront of the debate on tackling climate change. Indeed, it has been argued that the combination of such factors may create incentives for them to internalise intergenerational externalities by acting as a 'universal shareholder' agent.[29] A universal shareholder is an investor who holds a well-diversified portfolio of securities having a long-term investment horizon. For this type of investor, a negative (or positive) externality produced by one invested corporation becomes a cost (or benefit), ultimately affecting the future cash flow of other corporations whose securities are held by the universal shareholder.[30] Such externalities produced by one individual security affect the sustainability of investment outcomes within the universal shareholder's broadly diversified investment portfolio and reflect societal costs. That is why, in principle, such externalities should be 'internalised' or factored into investment decisions at the level of the universal shareholder's overall portfolio.

Despite climate change generating increasing risks able to significantly affect their portfolios, sovereign investors have historically considered it mainly as an ethical rather than a financial issue.[31] Recent data from a survey run by the

[26] See, J Capapé and M Santiváñez, 'Sovereign Wealth Funds: Sustainable and Active Investors? The case of Norway' (2017) IE Sovereign Wealth Labs – Annual Report, 22 sites.tufts.edu/sovereignet/files/2018/06/SustainableActiveInvestors_Capape.pdf.

[27] WT Watson, *International Pension Plan Survey Report* (2019), 20 www.willistowerswatson.com/en-GB/Insights/2020/01/2019-international-pension-plan.

[28] See OECD, 'Using Extractive Revenues for Sustainable Development: Policy Guidance for Resource-Rich Countries' (Paris, OECD Publishing, 2019) 43.

[29] JP Hawley and AT Williams, *The Rise of Fiduciary Capitalism: How Institutional Investors Can Make Corporate America More Democratic* (Pennsylvania, University of Pennsylvania Press, 2000) 251.

[30] World Economic Forum (WEF), 'Transformational Investment: Converting Global Systemic Risks into Sustainable Returns' (White Paper, 28 May 2020), 39 www3.weforum.org/docs/WEF_Transformational_Investment_2020.pdf (accessed 10 July 2021). See BJ Richardson and M Peihani, 'Universal Investors and Socially Responsible Finance: A Critique of a Premature Theory' (2015) 30 *Banking and Finance Law Review*405–455 ssrn.com/abstract=2726381.

[31] See Matos (n 3) 1.

International Forum of Sovereign Wealth Funds (IFSWFs) reveals a growing concern by SWFs vis-à-vis climate change and an increasing engagement by these investors with the green agenda in their decision-making processes and investment agendas.[32]

Indeed, in 2020, SWFs have invested US$2.3 billion in sectors critical to combating climate change, double the amount they invested in 2019.[33] Overall, the survey showed that SWFs have invested 'more than $5 billion in agritech, forestry and renewable opportunities over the past five years as a part of an increased push toward climate change – aware investing'.[34]

Nonetheless, the survey also showed that only 30 per cent of the 34 responding SWFs had more than 10 per cent of their portfolios invested in climate-related strategies.[35] Indeed, a close connection remains between many sovereign investors, especially SWFs, and their sponsoring country's natural resource wealth. Indeed, 57 per cent of SWFs are capitalised from natural-resource revenues (mainly oil and gas).[36] Hence, one may regard these SWFs as having a 'pivotal yet dichotomous role' trying to maximise investment returns from fossil fuel revenue streams and potentially engaging in climate change mitigation.[37] Yet, one of the significant trends of the current crisis has been the fall in oil demand and the consequent decline in oil prices and related share value. Indeed, during the first part of the pandemic, commodity funds faced one of the most severe

[32] While SWFs seem to be making progress in addressing climate change in their portfolios, the IFSWF recalls that 'around 30% struggle to find reliable data on which to base decisions' highlighting how sustainability reporting by companies remains vital for SWFs to take meaningful action on climate change. See, IFSWF, 'The International Forum of Sovereign Wealth Funds and IE University Team Up to Host 'Carbon & Sustainability Reporting, Tomorrow Is Now' (17 March 2021) www.ifswf.org/general-news/international-forum-sovereign-wealth-funds-and-ie-university-team-host-%E2%80%9Ccarbon (accessed 23 June 2021).

[33] For example, the 2019–2021 business plan for the Italian SWF, Cassa Depositi e Prestiti (CDP) Equity, includes allocating up to 15% of all new mobilised resources to the energy transition and climate change. The increasing (re)allocation of capital in line with climate-specific strategies will be an important measure to track in the coming years as the world looks to SWF to turn ambition into action. Idem, 15.

[34] IFSWFs, 'Mighty oaks from little acorns grow: Sovereign wealth funds' progress on climate change', 8 February 2021, www.ifswf.org/sites/default/files/IFSWF_Climate_Change_Feb2020%20FINAL.pdf (accessed 8 June 2021).

[35] A Marsh, 'Sovereign Wealth Funds Invest in Climate Technology, Renewables', *Bloomberg* (11 May 2021) www.bloomberg.com/news/articles/2021-05-11/sovereign-wealth-funds-invest-in-climate-technology-renewables (accessed 26 July 2021).

[36] The remaining 43% of SWFs are funded from non-commodity sources such as foreign exchange reserves and fiscal savings rules. See OECD (n 13). See RJ Ossowski and H Halland, 'Fiscal management in resource-rich countries: essentials for economists, public finance professionals, and policy makers' (2016) World Bank Studies Washington, 167, documents.worldbank.org/curated/en/311721468011610982/Fiscal-management-in-resource-rich-countries-essentials-for-economists-public-finance-professionals-and-policy-makers (accessed 10 July 2021).

[37] A Perrins, 'Sovereign Wealth Funds: An Evolving Transition' (*Savy Investor*, 28 July 2020) www.savvyinvestor.net/blog/Sovereign-Wealth-Funds-evolving-transition (accessed 10 July 2021).

adverse shocks of their recent history. Even before the pandemic outbreak, prices of fossil fuels were decreasing and, likely, the growth of their global demand will probably decelerate in the following decades.[38] In turn, the experienced high volatility in the oil and gas prices buttresses the case for viewing investments in fossil fuel companies as potentially risky both in the short-term as in the long-term, with demand for fossil fuels possibly gradually falling as the world transition to a low-carbon economy model.

Consequently, one may argue that especially for those sovereign investors financed by fossil and gas revenues, diversifying their portfolio by gradually dropping future 'stranded' assets remains essential for their long term interests and, therefore, also to meet their overall objectives.[39] A prudent approach by such sovereign investors might indeed entail considering the impact of 'green' policies on their future revenues, eg carbon taxes, compulsory offsets or bans on fossil fuels for green buildings and tax breaks for companies providing green solutions.[40] All in all, it is advisable for SWFs to 'professionalise and to strengthen insight that unsustainable investments are a financial risk and could even undermine the foundations which SWFs are based on in the long run'.[41]

In parallel, such a price shock gave an edge to investors who have diversified portfolios away from commodities toward sectors with low exposure to energy stock price volatility.[42] In 2019, some SWFs and PFs have been investing in biotechnology, software and digital services, all industries, which have managed comparatively well during the last period.[43] Those investments have resulted in being shrewd and resilient during, and due to, the pandemic. This seems confirmed by a World Economic Forum's recent research paper on

[38] Bortolotti et al. (n 12).

[39] C Abdallah, D Coady and Nghia-Piotr Le, 'The Time Is Right! Reforming Fuel Product Pricing Under Low Oil Prices' (13 July 2020) IMF Fiscal Affairs, 10. See also B Caldecott, *Stranded Assets and the Environment: Risk, Resilience, and Opportunity*, 1st edn (London, Routledge 2018) 340.

[40] Uzsoki (n 28) 13. M Carney, 'Resolving the climate paradox', (2016) BIS Central Bankers Speeches www.berkshirehathaway.com/letters/letters.html (accessed 10 July 2021). According to recent studies, the effect of policies such as carbon pricing on firm profits and equity value could be material as soon as 2020–2025, see BNP Paribas, 'Wells, Wires and Wheels: Eroci and the Tough Road Ahead for Oil', (2019) BNP Paribas Asset Management, 40.

[41] S Wurster and SJ Schlosser, 'Sovereign Wealth Funds as Sustainability Instruments? Disclosure of Sustainability Criteria in Worldwide Comparison' (2021) 13(10) *Sustainability* 55.

[42] See P Polman, 'It is time to redesign traditional capitalism and put focus on values: The UK is facing its deepest recession since the Great Frost of 1709', *The Telegraph* (18 May 2020) www.telegraph.co.uk/business/2020/05/18/time-redesign-traditional-capitalism-put-focus-values (accessed 10 July 2021).

[43] H Ellyatt, 'Here's why some sovereign wealth funds could outperform despite the coronavirus crisis' (CNBC, 9 June 2020) www.cnbc.com/2020/06/09/sovereign-wealth-funds-investments-helped-by-coronavirus-crisis.html (accessed 10 July 2021). C Wienberg, 'Nordic Pension Funds Invest $700 Million in Renewable Energy', *Bloomberg* (15 May 2019) www.bloomberg.com/news/articles/2019-05-15/nordic-pension-funds-invest-700-million-in-renewable-energy (accessed 19 July 2021).

transformational investment, which explores how large asset owners can support sustainable outcomes in the face of six systemic risks, among which is climate change.[44] By transformative investment, this research identifies those investments with attractive risk-adjusted expected returns that may help mitigate or address one or more long-term risks. The study concludes that by leveraging their size, long-term horizon and collaborative efforts, sovereign investors could invest in infrastructure, venture capital and clean tech, which could positively spill over on climate change, geopolitical stability and technological evolution.

Moreover, being government-owned entities, the overarching investment agenda of sovereign investors should, to the extent possible, align with their sponsoring countries' policies and legal commitments, such as international environmental obligations like, eg, the Paris Agreement. In addition, it has been held that private market actors may follow sovereign investors' investment choices in light of their 'close ties' with governments. Indeed, this connection may be seen as potentially giving SWFs insights on future low carbon transition and fossil fuels regulations.[45] Besides, sovereign investors could drive visibility on climate-related information by requesting their asset managers and portfolio firms to adhere to recommendations of initiatives such as the Task Force on Climate-Related Financial Disclosures.[46]

Another incentive for such investors to engage in responsible and sustainable investing lies in the increasing demand expressed by societal preferences.[47] There is a robust intergenerational argument in their objectives as they are ultimately aimed at overcoming the clash between the present and future generations vis-à-vis the sharing in the economic prosperity that exploiting natural resources creates. As a result, this would reflect in societal demands and needs which, by investing in the sponsoring country interests, sovereign investors would have to respond to.[48]

[44] The WEF defines 'transformational investment' as an investment that is intended to derive an attractive risk-adjusted expected return within the context of a given asset owner's overall portfolio, and at the same time is expected to help mitigate or address one or more long-term risks. The other systemic risks identified in such a study are water security, geopolitics, technological evolution, demographic shifts and low and negative real long-term interest rates. World Economic Forum (n 30).

[45] D Wilde, 'Should Sovereign Wealth Funds Invest to Achieve the Paris Agreement?', *IFSWF*, archive.ifswfreview.org/2019/our-partners/should-sovereign-wealth-funds-invest-achieve-paris-agreement (accessed 26 July 2021). See also, I Ghosh and M Lomas, 'How Sovereign Wealth Funds Can Catalyse Investments into the SDGs', *IFSWF*, ifswfreview.org/2019/our-partners/how-sovereign-wealth-funds-can-catalyse-investments-sdgs (accessed 11 July 2021).

[46] See OECD (n 13).

[47] See, 'Green hypocrisy: Luxembourg's pension fund invests in oil and coal', Greenpeace, www.greenpeace.org/luxembourg/fr/en-press-release/9163/green-hypocrisy-luxembourgs-pension-fund-invests-in-oil-and-coal/ (accessed 9 July 2021).

[48] Ramani (n 21). The pandemic has accelerated our economic and existential vulnerability to future economic shocks of a warming planet. That is why addressing these concerns now is timely and necessary, as this systemic risk will affect all institutions irrespective of industry.

## IV. LEGAL TOOLS FOR SOVEREIGN INVESTORS TO TAKE CLIMATE CHANGE AND RELATED RISKS INTO CONSIDERATION

Given the above, it would be reasonable to expect that sovereign investors take into account the afore-described reflections on systemic risks, such as climate change, subsequent pandemics, floods, droughts, etc – gearing towards responsible firms which have policies aiming at sustainable development, informing their investment decision-making with socially responsible investment principles (SRI) and Environmental Social and Governance (ESG) criteria.[49]

It is interesting to note that the SRI movement originates in the eighteenth-century Quakers' faith-based investment practice by which investors could eschew financial ties to activities contrary to their faith (eg alcohol consumption and gambling).[50] Today, the ethical guidelines directing SRI activities have acquired a more business-oriented nature as their focus has changed to find a balance between environmental concerns, on the one hand, and the promotion of the economic and financial sectors, on the other. The contemporary overarching objective of SRI is to overcome the inherent tension between accounting simultaneously for environmental and societal interests and the capitalistic framework of business.[51]

In turn, this change in focus has affected the methodologies that SRI movements rely on; indeed, it moved away from using only aggressive approaches such as divestment campaigns, eg the anti-apartheid campaign, towards more persuasive and inclusive practices such as corporate engagement, 'best-in-class' asset selection, influencing financial regulations, and promoting voluntary codes of conduct for investors.

This reflects in the way SWFs have been differently handling ESG and socially responsible practices. Indeed, while, for instance, the Norwegian Government Pension Fund-Global (GPFG) has also been exerting a negative influence on invested companies by divesting and exiting companies based on issues related to carbon emissions and human rights violations, other sovereign investors such as the Japanese Government Pension Investment Fund (GPIF) or the Canadian Pension Plan (CPP) have adopted an active engagement by using proxy voting

[49] ESG is a term coined in 2005 to refer to three central factors in measuring sustainability and societal impact of an investment in a company or business, namely environmental, social and governance. Overall, they may be seen as a component of the broader SRI practices which can be defined as 'investments that consider social and environmental criteria alongside conventional financial metrics'. B Sjåfjell, HR Nilsen and BJ Richardson, 'Investing in Sustainability or Feeding on Stranded Assets? The Norwegian Government Pension Fund Global' (2017) 52 *Wake Forest Law Review* 949.

[50] ibid 954. Later on, during apartheid, the focus of the SRI movement shifted onto human rights and included, inter alia, a divestment campaign against South Africa.

[51] In other words, investment in sectors, companies, or projects selected for positive ESG performance relative to industry peers. See Principles for Responsible Investment, 'PRI Reporting Framework: Main Definitions 2018' (2017) 5, www.unpri.org/download?ac=1453 (accessed 20 July 2021).

to push responsible practices from within companies.[52] In this regard, sovereign investors that take into consideration climate change and related risks have been investing in low-carbon assets and technological innovation; exerting negative screenings and excluding or divesting from inefficient high-carbon assets and engaging portfolio companies to reduce their emissions through the adoption of renewable energy, energy efficiency measures, or clean-energy technology.[53]

These investment choices, which would advance sovereign investors in scaling up climate finance, transitioning to low-carbon policy, and mitigating climate change and climate-change-related risks, remain in part in the sphere of the control of the sponsoring governments.[54] Indeed, aligning activities of a sovereign investor with SRI, ESG criteria, and the low-carbon transition is, before being a technical choice, a political decision.[55] Notwithstanding their mandates and governance arrangements, sovereign investors are not stand-alone, insulated institutions.[56]

As considered by Bortolotti, Fotak and Hogg specifically concerning SWFs, their future role in domestic and global economies will strongly depend on each country's economic and financial resilience achieved so far through, among other things, the level of resource diversification.[57] In this respect, a cohesive, clearer guideline and framework from governments may facilitate sovereigns' resource diversification, low-carbon transition, and addressing climate risks in the post-pandemic recovery.[58] Yet, as mentioned, even though on the rise, the numbers among sovereign investors engaged in climate change considerations have been low and shifting their activities would require a concerted effort addressing governance and investment operations, from realigning the mandates of the funds 'through integrating relevant criteria into portfolio processes and allocation decisions'.[59] This means that domestic and international pressure should be increased so that sustainability is seen as necessarily related to the legitimacy of an SWF. From a legal viewpoint, a way to achieve such goals is reframing and strengthening ESG integration and climate risk policies in existing

[52] See Uzsoki (n 28) 10. Today, the GPIF pressures its portfolio companies to manage climate-related risks and to improve ESG performance. Moreover, it is collaborating with the World Bank Group to promote sustainable investments. See K Mullen and P Rose, 'Public Funds Investment Policies: 2017 Survey' (26 February 2018) Ohio State University, 13 ssrn.com/abstract=3130132 (accessed 10 July 2021).

[53] OECD (n 13).

[54] On the other hand, this shift can only be achieved with the direct engagement of the fund (boards and management) and sovereign investors' asset managers, advisers and other providers.

[55] OECD (n 13).

[56] They have been defined as 'fiscal policy tools, fully integrated in the macroeconomic management of the country', Bortolotti et al. (n 12) 6.

[57] As also on each country's present and future conditions. ibid.

[58] Developments such as the EU taxonomy regulation on climate disclosure or the Bank of England's work on climate change are institutional initiatives going in this direction.

[59] J Capapé, 'Financing the SDGs: the Role of Sovereign Wealth Funds for Green Investments' (UN Environment working paper, 2018) 4. sites.tufts.edu/sovereignet/files/2018/02/Policy-brief-Capape%CC%81-SWF-Green-Investments-2018-1.pdf (accessed 10 July 2021).

principles and legal instruments, such as fiduciary duties, investment mandates and self-regulatory frameworks.[60]

## A. Fiduciary Duties

Asset managers who administrate assets in the interests of others must comply with a critical set of standards (usually) called fiduciary duties.[61] Fiduciary duties are traditionally referred to as trust law schemes and PFs.[62] Historically rooted in common law jurisdictions (and equity tradition more accurately), they are usually embedded in legislation and statutes, which varies, among other things, depending on the different jurisdiction and type of fund (public/private; trust/PF/endowment).[63] For the present purposes, it suffices to note that these duties usually encompass a duty of care and a duty of loyalty. The duty of care requires a fund manager (or trustee) to administer the fund with the reasonable care, skill, and caution of a prudent person, given the fund's purposes, terms, and other circumstances.

On the other hand, the duty of loyalty requires the manager to administer the fund in good faith and the interest of the beneficiaries exclusively. This requires fair dealing and full disclosure to the beneficiaries of 'all material facts the trustee [manager] knows or should know' and the responsibility to avoid conflict of interests and self-dealing transactions.[64] In the context of the present study, this description raises two different – yet deeply interconnected – questions.[65] First, to whom are these duties owed and second, does the objective of such duties, that is to maximise returns for the fund beneficiaries, encompass sustainable investment policies?

[60] BJ Richardson, 'Sovereign Wealth Funds and Socially Responsible Investing: An Emerging Public Fiduciary' (2013) 1:2 *Global Journal of Comparative Law*, 125–162, ssrn.com/abstract=2291760 (accessed 10 July 2021).

[61] Asset managers running a fund or a trust.

[62] Conversely, SWFs do not usually operate under a common-law tradition that imposes fiduciary duties on trustees. However, as noted by Paul Rose, 'SWFs generally do report governance structures that require diligence in how investments are selected, accountability for investment outcomes, and restrictions on transactions that have the potential to create a conflict of interest. Whether fiduciary-like obligations are created by the courts, statutes, rules or procedures of the SWF, the governance output may be the same; the differences in governance quality do not depend so much on the type of structure as much as the quality of the institutions that monitor and enforce fund governance'. P Rose, 'What Responsibilities Do Sovereign Funds Have to Other Investors?' (9 June 2017), *Wake Forest Law Review*, Forthcoming, Ohio State Public Law Working Paper No 399, 35, 10 ssrn.com/abstract=2983750.

[63] J Sandberg, 'Pension Funds, Future Generations and Fiduciary Duty', in I González-Ricoy and A Gosseries (eds), *Institutions for Future Generations* (Oxford, Oxford University Press, 2016) 385–389.

[64] Rose (n 62).

[65] Another stance is to set independent obligations on PFs to account for ESGs, see, Sandberg (n 63).

Concerning public PFs, they partially derive their resources from contributions made by employees and their objective is, usually, investing prudently to ensure pension liabilities for their beneficiaries. Vis-à-vis the first above-raised issue, it has been argued that PFs' fiduciary duty is owed to their beneficiaries (contributors, or future pensioners, and 'nothing else').[66] By contrast, another interpretation is for PFs' managers to owe their duties to the public collectively. Rose indeed argued that a shift in the ultimate objective of a public PF's fiduciary duty from a private wealth capitalisation owed to the PF's participants to a public wealth maximisation owed to the public at large (ie the 'true risk-takers', the governments and taxpayers), would entail more attention paid by managers to the externalities produced by the fund's investments. Indeed, the negative externalities that differently would be borne by the public sector would so be adjusted at the source, at the level of the investment policy of the fund.[67]

In more general terms, a strict interpretation of the fiduciary duty to act in the interest of the 'fund' might require a manager to disregard negative externalities so long as they do not affect the investments of the fund. Yet, the recipient – which in this case might be intended either as the fund's future pensioners or even the country's public at large – who will eventually incur in such externalities, should aim at minimising them. To do so necessarily means accounting for climate and environmental factors in the long-term investment horizon. Following this line of thought, fiduciary duty of public PFs should be construed less strictly so to include ESG standards and foster the transition to a more equitable, socially resilient, economic paradigm.[68]

Vis-à-vis SWFs, it has been held that, if they are to develop long-term, trusted investors in international markets, even though such investors may only owe duties stricto sensu to their sponsor governments, they should be bound to many other constituencies.[69] As such, sovereign investors like SWFs might have a fiduciary duty to act upon the final aim to ensure the intergenerational passage of wealth between generations of citizens and pensioners, beyond return maximisation in the short term. Thus, the rationale for a broader interpretation of fiduciary duty is partially based upon the idea that fiduciary duties should be owed to those who will ultimately benefit or suffer from the investment choices of the public fund managers/trustees, namely the current and future citizens and residents.

As far as the second issue is concerned, the classical interpretation of fiduciary duties has not historically comprised considerations other than the return

[66] ibid 388.

[67] P Rose, 'Public Wealth Maximization: A New Framework for Fiduciary Duties in Public Funds' [2018] *University of Illinois Law Review* 3, 34. Available at ssrn.com/abstract=2805427 (accessed 10 July 2021).

[68] Bortolotti et al. (n 12). It is important to note that some authors have expressed their perplexities regarding public wealth maximisation in terms of SRI actual profitability and risks of generating corruption. Rose (n 67) 125 et seq.

[69] Rose (n 62) 10.

of the fund. Hence, including ESGs criteria would have possibly meant straying away from fiduciary responsibilities. This perception seemed to have shifted significantly in light of, among other things, the growing societal demand for considering ESG issues as part of the investment decision-making process by PFs and the increased availability of financial performance evidences on ESG strategies.[70] In 2005, the famous 'Freshfields report' commissioned by the UN Environment Programme Finance Initiative (UNEP-FI) has advanced such debate, holding that integrating ESG considerations into investment analyses was permissible and, under certain circumstances, required. Subsequently, several legal initiatives around the globe have sought to remedy the mismatch between long-term sustainability factors and institutional investors and asset managers' fiduciary duties.[71] In 2015, the UNEP-FI joined with the Principles for Responsible Investment (PRI) and the Generation Foundation in the 'Fiduciary Duty in the 21st Century' project.[72] According to this report, fiduciary duty creates 'positive duties' on investors to integrate ESG issues to mitigate risk and orientate their investment choices. The report highlights that outdated perceptions about fiduciary duty and responsible investment have impaired the use of ESG factors by fiduciaries. It finds that fiduciary duties need to be restructured to reflect the current times and that '[f]ailing to consider long-term investment value drivers, including environmental, social and governance issues, in investment practice is a failure of fiduciary duty'.[73]

In conclusion, a fiduciary must consider financial information as a prudent investor would. This, in turn, means investing based on the information available from research examining financial tools and understandings of today, possibly considering the interests of both current and future beneficiaries.[74] If climate change is indeed a long-term systemic risk posing material and financial threats to investors, then one may regard fiduciaries who disregard material long-term information as violating their duty to be prudent investors.[75]

[70] S Gary, 'Best Interests in the Long Term: Fiduciary Duties and ESG Integrations' (2019) 90(3) *University of Colorado Law Review* 731–801. Courts also play an important role in framing the obligations arising from fiduciary duty. Trends in litigation against pension funds related to their approach to climate-related risks, and brought forward by beneficiaries, should not be ignored.

[71] UNEP FI, 'A legal framework for the integration of environmental, social and governance issues into institutional investment' (2005), produced for the Asset Management Working Group of the UNEP Finance Initiative by Freshfields Bruckhaus Deringer. See also, GW Ziero, 'Fiduciary Duty & ESG Issues: How Are Different Jurisdictions Addressing This?' (*Eco:Fact*, 20 March 2020) www.ecofact.com/blog/fiduciary-duty-esg-issues-how-are-different-jurisdictions-addressing-this/ (accessed 10 July 2021). See also H Wickham, 'Jersey: Sustainable Investment and The Role of The Fiduciary' (*Mondaq*, 16 June 2020) www.mondaq.com/jersey/investment-strategy/953518/sustainable-investment-and-the-role-of-the-fiduciary (accessed 10 July 2021).

[72] UNEP FI, *Fiduciary Duty in the 21st Century*, (2015) 88, www.fiduciaryduty21.org (accessed 8 July 2021).

[73] ibid 2. Finally yet importantly, climate change litigation may have a critical role to play in implementing a broader interpretation of fiduciary duties for pension funds managers. See, inter alia, the case of *McVeigh v Retail Employees Superannuation Trust*, 2 November 2020.

[74] Gary (n 70).

[75] ibid.

## B. Investment Mandates

Like other sovereign investors, SWFs implement the mandate given to them by their owners, namely the sponsoring government.[76] It has been maintained that such mandates should become more audacious in tackling sustainability issues. In this respect, few sovereign investors hold mandates considering ESG and climate change risks. More so, one ought to recall that there is no international legal framework imposing direct legal obligations on them vis-à-vis sustainability. Consequently, tension between non-financial needs necessary to pursue intergenerational objectives and the aim to seek returns maximisation might arise in the context of the activities of such sovereign investors. Governments that would wish to align their sovereign funds could include climate alignment in their mandates while retaining the commercial purpose of maximising returns. In this way, for instance, sovereign funds' boards could request fund managers to define a strategy for climate alignment based on the grounds set by governments,[77] and have a more precise division of responsibilities between the board and the management level and consistent overall governance for engaging with portfolio companies could be structured.

In this respect, some sovereign investors are mandated by law to invest sustainably. Amongst those, the Norwegian GPFG has been the most active in conditioning both international investments and investors in favour of sustainability and, in light of it, we will refer to it as a case study. In its application of the Government Pension Fund Act,[78] the Norwegian Parliament delegated the Ministry of Finance with the overall managerial responsibility for the GPFG and investment strategy. Under the mandate laid down by the Ministry of Finance, the Norwegian Central Bank (Norges Bank) and the Norges Bank's asset management unit, ie the Norges Bank Investment Management (NBIM), retains the operational control of the fund and exerts its ownership rights.[79] Besides, a Council on Ethics, an independent body composed of five members, each appointed by the Ministry of Finance, is entrusted with advising the Norges Bank on the exclusion – or observation – of companies that may be in breach of the GPFG's ethical guidelines.[80]

[76] OECD (n 13).

[77] ibid.

[78] NBIM, 'Government Pension Fund Act' www.nbim.no/en/organisation/governance-model/government-pension-fund-act/ (accessed 10 July 2021).

[79] NBIM, 'Management Mandate for the Government Pension Fund Global' (Management Mandate) www.nbim.no/contentassets/52e589ff7b2d48afb2e2dcd5aa3464f7/gpfg_mandate_23.04.2019.pdf (accessed 11 July 2021).

[80] See Council on Ethics for the Government Pension Fund Global, 'Guidelines for Observation and Exclusion of Companies from the Government Pension Fund Global' etikkradet.no/files/2017/04/Etikkraadet_Guidelines-_eng_2017_web.pdf (accessed 10 August 2020). Originally, the Fund's auxiliary body was the 'Advisory Commission on International Law', which provided assistance on human rights and environmental issues. See S Chesterman, 'The Turn to Ethics: Disinvestment from Multinational Corporations for Human Rights Violations – The Case of Norway's Sovereign Wealth Fund' (2007) 23 *American University International Law Review* 577, 584.

The GPFG management mandate expressly states that the fund 'shall' invest following the ethical guidelines and that the Norges Bank 'shall' integrate its responsible management efforts into the management of the GPFG as 'a good long-term return is considered dependent on sustainable development in economic, environmental and social terms, as well as well-functioning, legitimate and efficient markets'.[81] The ethical guidelines build on the international agreements and conventions regarded 'as sources of ethical precepts' by Norway.[82] Indeed, the committee entrusted with drafting the ethical guidelines (so-called 'Graver Committee') chose to ground them in the international agreements on environmental protection and human rights supported by Norway instead of Norwegian national culture and policy.[83] In this sense, the Graver Committee construed the fund's obligation to ensure financial returns for the future Norwegian generations by conditioning it to the pursuance of a sustainable development rationale and, using the relevant international legal framework, the obligation to respect fundamental rights of those affected by the invested companies.[84]

The Council on Ethics's focus is on divestment from unethical companies, and this, in turn, as Richardson explains, reflects a 'deontological ethical impulse' of the fund. The Norges Bank, on the other hand, leans towards a teleological approach.[85] Indeed, through the NBIM, the Norges Bank exercises the ownership rights of the GPFG and actively engages with those companies deemed to be less seriously involved in unethical behaviour and regarded as capable of improvement. More specifically, Norges Bank engages with targeted companies to pressure them to change their unsustainable practices. While the Council's work is mainly driven by the imperative to avoid complicity in ethical misdeeds and international obligations violations, the Norges Bank focuses on redeeming 'unethical companies'.[86]

By giving 'legal imprimatur' to sustainability interests in the mandate of the fund, and by setting specific guidelines addressing sustainability interests and investment principles, Norway has simultaneously transposed the international soft law sustainability framework into its domestic legal tools and, by investing abroad and extraterritorially pressuring its portfolio companies through

[81] NBIM (n 79).

[82] Sjåfjell, Nilsen and Richardson (n 49). See also BJ Richardson, 'Sovereign Wealth Funds and the Quest for Sustainability: Insights from Norway and New Zealand' (2011) 2 *Nordic Journal of Commercial Law* 1, 1, 13.

[83] BJ Richardson, 'Sovereign Wealth Funds and Socially Responsible Investing: An Emerging Public Fiduciary' (2012) 1 *Global Journal of Comparative Law* 125, 137.

[84] Six years later, after the 2004 ethical guidelines and the Norges Bank's legal mandate had undergone a government review (which was mostly procedural rather than normative), the Norwegian Parliament approved two sets of guidelines; one for the Council and one for the Norges Bank. The first set of guidelines is entitled 'Guidelines for Observation and Exclusion from the Government Pension Fund Global's Investment Universe' while the second is called 'Guidelines for Norges Bank's Work on Responsible Management and Active Ownership'. See Richardson (n 60).

[85] See Richardson (n 83) 138.

[86] ibid.

the GPFG, implemented said framework on the international level. Hence, in addition to entering into international (soft law) agreements and conventions, one way for sovereign investors such as the GPFG to enhance sustainability implementation worldwide and, maybe, to give an edge to the international agreements, which are sometimes perceived as 'toothless', is to use domestic legal instruments such as legal mandates and internal guidelines.

Following the GPFG's example, one could argue that such means may be effective channels to enforce sustainability and climate concerns internationally. In such a way, sovereign investors may better address the intergenerational equity such funds should care for, also being in line with ethical concerns expressed by their final beneficiaries, the population of their sponsoring country. Even though one ought to recall that legal mandates and internal ethical investment guidelines do not per se constitute a *condition sine qua non* for SWFs to address climate change risks and sustainability concerns, depending on their drafting and content, such legal tools may still be a way to enhance their implementation worldwide and condition the legitimacy of the fund to the implementation of sustainable practices. Indeed, if only those SWFs with an overarching sustainability strategy in their mandates covering sustainability criteria were perceived as legitimate, there would be a strong incentive to introduce such a strategy.[87] In this way, other SWFs may be expected to adjust their strategy accordingly. Indeed, while the government of the sponsoring country can set the mandate to include sustainability criteria, investment recipient countries could take protectionist measures against SWFs without sustainability strategies.[88]

### C. Self-Regulatory Principles and Frameworks: The Santiago Principles and the One Planet Summit Initiative

The Santiago Principles are a set of 24 voluntary principles and best practices negotiated in the 2008 International Working Group of Sovereign Wealth Funds (IWG) mandated by the International Monetary Fund (IMF).[89] The negotiations brought together representatives from several SWFs, the OECD, and the World Bank intending to devise a commonly accepted legal benchmark for SWFs to boost SWFs legitimacy worldwide.[90] Due to this initiative, SWFs have

[87] Wurster and Schlosser (n 41).

[88] ibid.

[89] See IFSWF, 'Sovereign Wealth Funds: Generally Accepted Principles and Practices – 'Santiago Principles'' (October 2008) Appendix I, para 2 www.ifswf.org/sites/default/files/santiagoprinciples_0_0.pdf (accessed 20 July 2021).

[90] See IMF, 'International Working Group of Sovereign Wealth Funds is Established to Facilitate Work on Voluntary Principles' (1 May 2008) Press Release No 08/97. These principles are divided into three key areas, relating to their: (i) legal framework, objectives, and coordination with macroeconomic policies (principles 1 to 5); (ii) institutional framework and governance structure

been provided with a standard international regulatory framework to enhance transparency on a global level. As put by the International Forum of Sovereign Wealth Funds (IFSWF), '[t]he essence of the Santiago Principles is that sovereign wealth funds are run for long-term economic purposes, with appropriate governance and investment disciplines'.[91]

Such principles have been criticised for being discretionary and vaguely drafted, carrying little to no persuasive power over their sovereign drafters.[92] Yet, it has to be noted that their vague and broad wording is reflective of their aspirational character to become universally achievable, regardless of the state's level of economic development. Besides, as it is often true in international law, a soft law approach is at times the only feasible option. Indeed, although such principles have not been drafted as detailed rules, they likewise do not amount to a conventional self-regulatory system or code of conduct, preserving their ability to serve as a useful framework that could, with time, evolve into a rule-oriented process.[93] In other words, the Santiago Principles were at least a first attempt to form an international set of agreed principles and guidelines, aiming at building consensus and establishing a discourse around the activities carried out by SWFs.

The Santiago Principles do not directly refer to the concept of sustainable development, SRI objectives, nor climate change risks. They do, however, mention values other than profit insofar that SWFs can exclude investments based on social, environmental, and ethical grounds, so long as such considerations are clearly explained and publicly disclosed.[94] This might be seen as a deficiency of direct protection of non-commercial considerations within the context of SWFs' international main set of general standards. However, this falls squarely in line with their original purpose, Dixon notes, which was to depict SWFs 'as benign pools of capital contributing to the depth and efficiency of

(principles 6 to 17); and (iii) investment and risk management framework (principles 18 to 23). The 24th principle of the Santiago Principles pertains to their implementation.

[91] IFSWF, 'Implementing the Santiago Principles: 12 Case Studies from Demonstrating Commitment to Creating Value' (IFSWF Eighth Annual Meeting, Auckland, 10 November 2016) www.ifswf.org/sites/default/files/IFSWF_CaseStudies_Nov2016_0.pdf (accessed 20 September 2019). See X Karametaxas, 'Funding the Future: Sovereign Wealth Funds as Promoters of Intergenerational Equity', in T Cottier, S Lalani and C Siziba (eds), *Intergenerational Equity: Environmental and Cultural Concerns* (Leiden, Boston Brill Nijhoff, 2019) 178–191, 188.

[92] J Wang, 'State Capitalism and Sovereign Wealth Funds: Finding a 'Soft' Location in International Economic Law', in CL Lim (ed), *Alternative Visions of the International Law on Foreign Investment: Essays in Honour of Muthucumaraswamy Sornarajah* (Cambridge, CUP, 2016) 403.

[93] This is exactly why such a framework has been rightly described as 'a sui generis, ad hoc, multi-level, rule-oriented governance network process', see JJ Norton, 'The 'Santiago Principles' for Sovereign Wealth Funds: A Case Study on International Financial Standard-Setting Processes' (2010) 13 *Journal of International Economic Law* 645, 645.

[94] See Principle 19. Though SWFs priority remains the maximisation of risk-adjusted financial returns in a manner consistent with their investment policy, and based on economic and financial grounds.

global financial markets' rather than as creatures of mercantilist *Realpolitik*.[95] In this same regard, Monk recently stated:[96]

> The problem [he] had with the IMF process that delivered the Santiago Principles is that we pushed sovereign funds to be western, which the west said they needed to keep markets open. But the western form of institutional investment, with its strict interpretation of fiduciary duty, has led to increasing short-termism and unchecked externalities. So while the Santiago Principles may have succeeded in keeping markets open, they also represent to [him] a lost chance to re-make our system of capital allocation to be more long-term and sustainable. Because SWFs are the ultimate long term investor – they could have led the world in ESG integration, which is something we're still struggling with today.

Yet, as mentioned, these principles seem structured in such a way as to be open for further development, almost resembling a starting point for discussion rather than a final version of SWFs' self-regulation. This, in turn, may beg the question as to whether sustainability interests might still be envisaged as an ongoing dialogue in the context of SWFs' role in the international financial and economic systems. Hence, following Monk's statement, amending the principles requiring a credible sustainability strategy to be disclosed and abided by is possible to obtain higher sustainability commitment by SWFs. As some commentators recall, if a substantial share of the IFSWF members requested introducing a mandatory overarching sustainability framework, there would be an intense pressure for the other funds to follow this development, ie, since leaving the IFSWF would be a substantial disadvantage.[97]

As it has been pointed out, further developments in this direction are not to be categorically excluded.[98] This is inferable from recent activities by SWFs showing increased attention to climate change and sustainability issues. Since adopting the 17 Sustainable Development Goals (SDGs) in the context of the 2030 United Nations Agenda for Sustainable Development, SWFs seem to have started to duly consider sustainability as a relevant factor for their investment agenda. Indeed, during the eight IFSWF annual meetings held in November 2016, SWFs have openly reconsidered their commitment to curb greenhouse gas emissions.[99] In July 2018, the 'One Planet Sovereign Wealth Fund Working

[95] On the academic discourse surrounding the concept of transparency with relation to SWFs and the Santiago Principles, see A Dixon, 'Enhancing Transparency Dialogue in the 'Santiago Principles' for Sovereign Wealth Funds' (2014) 7 *Seattle University Law Review* 581, 583.

[96] C Jones, 'Will geopolitical tensions reshape sovereign wealth funds?', *Financial Times* (17 July 2020) ftalphaville.ft.com/2020/07/17/1594975065000/Will-geopolitical-tensions-reshape-sovereign-wealth-funds--/1/5 (accessed 10 July 2021).

[97] Wurster and Schlosser (n 41).

[98] See Norton (n 93).

[99] IFSWF, 'Sovereign Wealth Funds Focus on Governance and Investment Risk in a Climate of Uncertainty' (IFSWF Eighth Annual Meeting, Auckland, 10 November 2016) www.ifswf.org/general-news/sovereign-wealth-funds-focus-governance-and-investment-risk-climate-uncertainty (accessed 10 August 2020). See also IFSWF, 'Joint Communiqué: One Planet Sovereign Wealth Fund Working Group' www.ifswf.org/general-news/joint-communiqu%C3%A9-one-planet-sovereign-wealth-fund-working-group (accessed 10 July 2021).

Group' was established within the context of the 'One Planet Summit' initiative. The Working Group and, more specifically, the consultations held between the six founding members,[100] institutional stakeholders, and those investors interested in factoring in climate change risks into their asset management resulted in the 'Framework on Climate Change'.[101] The latter general aim is to spur the transition to a low greenhouse gas emissions economy by addressing climate change in managing the SWFs assets.[102] It focuses on developing an ESG framework to address climate change issues, 'including the development of methods and indicators that can inform investors' priorities as shareholders and participants in financial markets'.[103] Clearly, as a spill over effect, such an initiative is also aimed at spreading awareness among financial stakeholders on climate change and the green economy.[104] This initiative suggests that sustainability concerns, such as environmental and climate issues, have started to gain a substantial degree of attention in the international investment framework and from sovereign investors such as SWFs, which have begun to reflect on sustainability collectively.[105] On the other hand, being a voluntary set of principles adopted by only a few SWFs, the question remains as to the extent to which climate change and sustainability considerations will be implemented through them.

[100] The six founding members are as follows: the Abu Dhabi Investment Authority (ADIA), the Kuwait Investment Authority, the Norges Bank Investment Management of Norway, the New Zealand Superannuation Fund, the Public Investment Fund of the Kingdom of Saudi Arabia, and the Qatar Investment Authority (QIA).

[101] The One Planet Summit press release expressly states that '[…] having both size and long-term investment horizons, sovereign wealth funds are in a unique position to promote long-term value creation and sustainable market outcomes. Climate action is a shared responsibility and we aim to identify climate-related risks and opportunities in our investments to achieve this objective within our mandates. With more accurate and standardized data on climate issues, the global financial markets can more smoothly adjust in the transition to a global low-emissions economy that is more resilient to climate change and hence more stable'. See IFSWF, 'One Planet SWF Working Group Publish Framework on Climate Change' (6 July 2018) www.ifswf.org/general-news/one-planet-swf-working-group-publish-framework-climate-change (accessed 10 August 2020). See also One Planet Summit, 'The One Planet Sovereign Wealth Fund Framework' (6 July 2018) www.ifswf.org/sites/default/files/One_Planet_Sovereign_Wealth_Fund_Framework.pdf (accessed 10 July 2021).

[102] In other terms, such a framework aims at promoting the integration of climate change analysis in the management of large, long-term and diversified asset pools. See AP Newcombe, 'Sustainable Development and Investment Treaty Law' (2007) 8 *World Investment & Trade* 357.

[103] See 'One Planet SWFs', oneplanetswfs.org/ (accessed 10 July 2021).

[104] Voluntary codes of conduct providing performance or process standards for investors are on the rise. See United Nations Global Compact www.unglobalcompact.org/ (accessed 10 August 2020). See www.unpri.org/ (accessed 10 August 2020). On the incorporation of ESG issues into practice, see Equator Principles, 'The Equator Principles' (June 2013) equator-principles.com/wp-content/uploads/2017/03/equator_principles_III.pdf (accessed 20 September 2019); Rainforest Action Network, 'The Principle Matter: Banks, Climate and the Carbon Principles' (20 January 2011) issuu.com/tobend/docs/the_principle_matter (accessed 10 August 2020). See also CDP, 'Carbon Disclosure Project'www.cdp.net/en (accessed 10 July 2021).

[105] J Owens, H Halland and M Noel, 'The Role of Sovereign Wealth Funds (SWFs) and Strategic Investment Funds (SIFs) in Green Finance' in OECD, *Progress Report on Approaches to Mobilising Institutional Investment for Green Infrastructure* (Paris, OECD Publishing, 2016).

## V. CONCLUSION

Green swan events, an expression of systemic risk related to ecosystemic disruption and climate change posing a threat for the global economy and human lives, are regarded as being the next trigger of a financial crisis. That is why financial institutions, academics and society at large have been expressing growing concerns vis-à-vis the urgency to account for climate change and climate change-related risks in the investment decision-making process of both public and private actors.

In the light of their long-term horizon, public service mission and intergenerational passage of wealth objective, sovereign investors might be required to align to climate change considerations, especially given of their design and final aim.

Fiduciary duty theories, investment mandates and international frameworks may help build a general model of sovereign investors as fiduciaries of existing and future citizens. While their traditional interpretation does not include ESG criteria and sustainability concerns, today fiduciary duties seem to be regarded as a crucial legal instrument to advance responsible and sustainable investment policies. With social, economic and political change shifting the expectations and requirements of beneficiaries, the role of fiduciaries seems to have been perceived as evolving accordingly.[106] Nonetheless, we still lack a general theory of fiduciary duty for sovereign investors to act upon one of their final and most relevant goal, notably benefiting future generations. More generally, if there is a perceived collision between a sovereign investor's fiduciary duty and climate considerations, priority will most likely be given to the so interpreted fiduciary. That is why, on the one hand, in the design of future investment strategies, sovereign investors should broaden the interpretation of fiduciary duty and fully embrace ESG standards. Conversely, sovereign investor's climate strategies should then foster the transition to a more equitable, socially resilient, economic paradigm consistently to their fiduciary duties.[107]

Management mandates may also serve as a 'fuel' to foster climate change risk consideration by SWFs and other sovereign investors. Long-term investment mandates and strategies may better address systemic risks and improve the long-term value of a fund, as in the case of the GPFG. When incorporating sustainability and climate concerns, these legal instruments may effectively address the core intergenerational equity objective many of such funds should aim at ensuring. Besides, when referencing international environmental principles and guidelines, they might also enforce climate concerns while giving an edge to soft law instruments. This also connects to SWFs self-regulatory frameworks

[106] See also Wickham (n 71).

[107] EJ Waitzer, 'Defeating Short-Termism: Why Pension Funds Must Lead' (2009) (2)2 *Rotman International Journal of Pension Management* 6. Available at ssrn.com/abstract=1493307 (accessed 20 July 2021).

such as the Santiago Principles or the One Planet Summit Initiatives. While the former initiative does not contain any reference to environmental, sustainability or climate change concerns, these are factors which could, if the signatories agreed to, be incorporated. The latter initiative, on the other hand, even though still amounting to soft law principles devoid of any implementation mechanism, is still a clear expression of a shift in the perception by part of sovereign investors of climate change and akin risks and a step towards increasing commitment vis-à-vis climate change.

To conclude, sovereign investors and their sponsoring governments clearly already possess legal tools for integrating climate change risks within their overall investment agenda. Such instruments may have to be amended or re-interpreted to envision climate change risks and connected threats better, yet they still amount to a solid starting point. Whether, however, sovereign investors will become climate-aligned or remain passive is another question entirely. It can be inferred that either way, their actions will bear significant implications for current and future generations of citizens. In the context of the COVID-19 pandemic and the massive public debts that young generations will have to face, the first abovementioned scenario would probably be the best way for sovereign investors not to let 'a good crisis' go to waste by preparing against potential future green swans. In a way, this 'pandemic swan' might be the venue for re-discussing the theoretical foundations and ambitions of sovereign investors.

# *Index*

**Introductory Note**

References such as '178–79' indicate (not necessarily continuous) discussion of a topic across a range of pages. Wherever possible in the case of topics with many references, these have either been divided into sub-topics or only the most significant discussions of the topic are listed. Because the entire work is about 'state capitalism' and 'investment law', the use of these terms (and certain others which occur constantly throughout the book) as entry points has been restricted. Information will be found under the corresponding detailed topics.

www.ingramcontent.com/pod-product-compliance
Ingram Content Group UK Ltd.
Pitfield, Milton Keynes, MK11 3LW, UK
UKHW020235290926
15470UKWH00002B/565

9 781509 962976